More praise for
TEACHING TEENS WITH ADD AND ADHD . . .

"Chris Dendy's first book, *TEENAGERS WITH ADD,* demonstrated her uncommon ability to provide useful information about teenagers, ADD/ADHD, and family life with empathy and good common sense. In her new book, *TEACHING TEENS WITH ADD AND ADHD*, this experienced mental health counselor, parent of two sons with ADD/ADHD, and former teacher writes with the same sensitivity and skill about teenagers with ADD/ADHD as they encounter challenges of learning in classrooms and homework. Written in brief summaries covering 75 important topics, this book offers strategies and detailed, practical information useful to all educators and parents striving to help teenagers with ADD/ADHD make good use of junior high and high school."

—Thomas E. Brown, Ph.D., Associate Director,
Yale Clinic for Attention and Related Disorders,
Yale University School of Medicine

"Chris Dendy has succeeded once again in providing excellent information about teenagers with attention deficit disorders. This work promises to be one of the most complete guides available for secondary school teachers. It is filled with practical strategies that teachers can implement quickly and easily in classrooms. Dendy provides a storehouse of additional information for teachers who are interested in knowing more about the causes of ADD/ADHD, methods of diagnosis, medical treatments, legal rights, and more. I have no doubt that this book will be a treasured resource in schools throughout the country."

— Harvey C. Parker, Ph.D., Clinical psychologist and author of
PROBLEM SOLVER GUIDE FOR STUDENTS WITH **ADHD**

TEACHING TEENS
with ADD and ADHD

A

Quick

Reference

Guide

for

Teachers

and

Parents

Woodbine House
2000

Library of Congress Cataloging-in-Publication Data

Zeigler Dendy, Chris A.
   Teaching teens with ADD and ADHD : a quick reference guide for teachers and parents / by Chris A. Zeigler Dendy.—1st ed.
      p. cm.
   Includes bibliographical references and index.
   ISBN 1-890627-20-8 (paper)
      1.Attention-deficit-disordered youth—Education (Secondary) Handbooks, manuals, etc. 2. Attention-deficit hyperactivity disorder—Handbooks, manuals, etc. I. Title.

LC4713.2 .Z45 2000
371.92'63—dc21   00-063433

Manufactured in the United States of America

First edition

10   9   8   7   6   5

DEDICATION

This book is dedicated to several special people:

My parents and community loved me unconditionally, and gave me roots and opportunities for success, as well as a belief that we have a responsibility to help others.

- Lillian Jennings Abney, my mother, a gifted woman who was ahead of her time
- Judge W.L. Abney, Jr., my father (1917-1997)

My best teachers about ADD and ADHD:

- my sons, Alex and Steven
- my grandson, Nathan
- the teenagers with ADD or ADHD who contributed to this book:

Jerry	Aaron	Zack
Julie	Darren	Ryan
David	Billy	Adrian
Ashley	Evan	Davey
Michelle	Amelia	Kristin
Eric	Kevin	

I greatly admire these teenagers who strive to be the best they can be in spite of their ADD/ADHD!

A WORD ABOUT TERMINOLOGY

In this book, the abbreviation **ADD/ADHD** and the term **attention deficit disorder** are used when referring to both the hyperactive and inattentive types of attention-deficit/ hyperactivity disorder. The abbreviation **ADHD** is used when information is specific to the hyperactive form of the disorder alone, and **ADD** is used for information specific to the inattentive form. (This is consistent with federal IDEA regulations, which contain the abbreviations ADD/ADHD, ADD, and ADHD. This is perhaps because they seem to more accurately convey the difference between the two conditions than AD/HD, the term used by the American Psychiatric Association for both forms of attention deficit disorder.)

I also chose to use the masculine pronoun "he" in some sections of the book and the feminine pronoun "she" in other sections so as not to imply that all teenagers with ADD or ADHD are either male or female.

Table of Contents

SECTION 4: FEDERAL LAWS GOVERNING ADD/ADHD
IDEA (EDUCATION LAW) AND SECTION 504 & ADA (CIVIL RIGHTS LAWS) 153

SECTION 5: MEDICATION ISSUES 205

SECTION 6: CLASSROOM MANAGEMENT AND CHALLENGING BEHAVIORS 225

Acknowledgements

Special thanks go to my editor and three incredible friends, my partners who have given unselfishly of their time and wisdom to help make this book better. I think one of the things that made my first book, *Teenagers with ADD*, so successful is that I was smart enough to know that I didn't know all the answers. So, I called upon some very wise and talented colleagues to help make certain this book was the absolute best we could make it.

Susan Stokes, my extraordinary editor, has taught me the beauty of writing with simplicity and clarity. My writing is greatly enriched by her gifted editorial touch.

Claudia Dickerson, Ph.D., veteran Gwinnett County, Georgia, School Psychologist, read every word in this book, just as she did with my first book. But most importantly, I thank her for her knowledge and alertness when she diagnosed my son's ADD in 1986.

Kathy Hubbard Weeks, ADD/504 Consultant, Kenosha, Wisconsin Schools, Southeast Wisconsin CHADD, private therapist, and mother of a teenage son with ADHD, was a creative pioneer in helping our students succeed in school. Her knowledge has enriched this book.

Pam Esser, Executive Director, ADDA-SR, Houston, Texas, educator, and mother of a teenage son with ADHD. Pam's optimism, common sense, and vast teaching experience were helpful in making this a very practical guide for teachers. She and her staff were excellent sounding boards for so many of my ideas.

A Special Thank You to Contributors

I am deeply indebted to so many wonderful, dedicated educators, mental health professionals, physicians, and parents who helped me greatly enrich the quality of this book. Many people went above and beyond the call of duty, spending significant time talking with me and sending me great materials. Special thanks to everyone who contributed.

Section 1: The Basics & Section 5: Medication

- William Buzogany, M.D., Medical Director of Lad Lakes Residential and Community Treatment Program, Consulting Psychiatrist, Ethan Allen School, a juvenile correction facility, Associate Professor of Psychiatry, University of Wisconsin, Madison, WI.

- Edward Gotlieb, M.D., Director, Pediatric Center, Stone Mountain, GA.

- Peter Jensen, M.D., Department of Child Psychiatry, The Center for the Advancement of Children's Mental Health, Columbia University/New York State Psychiatric Institute; lead investigator, NIMH Multimodal Treatment Study of Children with ADHD (MTA).

- Theodore Mandlekorn, M.D., Director, ADHD Clinic, Virginia Mason Clinic, Mercer Island, WA, and formerly member of CHADD National Professional Advisory Board.

Girls with ADD/ADHD (S-9)

- Joan Helbing, EEN Diagnostician/Trainer (ADD Consultant), Appleton Area School District, Appleton, WI.

- Rose-Marie P. Hippler, former Vice President of Federal Relations, Florida Hospital Association, Orlando, FL.

- Sharon Hodge, Ph.D., M.B.A., Assistant Professor, Florida Mental Health Institute, U. of South Florida, Tampa, FL.

- Susan Bible Jessup, math teacher, Gainesville Middle School, Gainesville, GA.

- Carol Jordan, former teacher and reading coordinator, Lawrenceville, GA.

- Trish Mann, University of South Florida Consultant to the Florida Department of Health, Tallahassee, FL.

Section 2: Academic Issues

- Kathleen Allen, Licensed Counselor, Pediatric Center, Stone Mountain, GA; Clinical Advisor, DeKalb County CHADD

- Janice Bond, CHADD National Board of Directors, Coordinator, CHADD of Greater Chattanooga, Chattanooga, TN.

- Virginia Brickman, Director of Support Services, DeKalb County Schools, Decatur, GA.

- Arleene Brunn, Office Manager, ADDA-SR, Houston, TX.

- Carla Crutsinger, Director, Brainworks, Carrollton, TX.

- Helen Frick, past Coordinator, Gwinnett CHADD, Lilburn, GA.

- Norma Garza, CPA, Director, St. Joseph Academy Learning Center, Brownsville, TX.

- Michelle Gill, special education teacher, Brookwood High School, Lilburn, GA.

- Evelyn Green, President Elect, National CHADD, CHADD of Chicago, pre-kindergarten teacher, Chicago Public Schools, Chicago, IL.

- Opal Harris, teacher, Mesquite Independent School District (ISD); Past President ADDA-SR, Houston, TX.

- Joan Maril, MSED, Educational Consultant-ADHD, Austin, TX.

- Debra Moore, Counselor, Brainworks, Carrollton, TX.

- Becky Mosby, RN, Parent Liaison for Special Education, Robinson ISD, Waco, TX.

- Susan Paul, reading teacher-trainer, Southwest District of Houston Independent School District, Houston, TX.

- Cindy Payne, media specialist, Chattooga County High School, Summerville, GA.

- Sherry Pruitt, Clinical Director, Parkaire Consultants, Alpharetta, GA.

- Carol Robertson, instructor, ACT Program for Special Education, Woodinville High School, Woodinville, WA; Branch Coordinator, Snohomish County CHADD

- Lodus Schreiner, Metro East Georgia Learning Resource Services (GLRS), Decatur, GA.

- Adele Steele, special education teacher, Brookwood High School, Snellville, GA.

- Sue Suppes, Coordinator, Learning Disabilities Association of Gwinnett County, Lawrenceville, GA.

- Joan Teach, Ph.D., Director Lullwater School (a special private school), Decatur, GA; DeKalb County CHADD Clinical Advisor; also, an adult with ADHD.

- Ivan Vance, Senior Consultant, Special Education Department, Region 10 ESC, Richardson, TX.

- Mary Kay Wells, Chairman, Math Department, Lincoln High School, Tallahassee, FL.

Written Expression

- Coyle Dykes Bryan, high school language arts teacher, North West Whitfield High School, Tunnel Hill, GA.

- Claudia Jordan, remedial and developmental language arts teacher, including English as a second language (ESOL), Central Gwinnett High School, Lawrenceville, GA.

- Susie Smith, middle school language arts teacher, Lullwater School, Decatur, GA.

- Marcy Winograd, Chairman, English Department, Paul Revere Middle School, Los Angeles, CA.

Mastering Math

- Erin Davis, math teacher, Lullwater School, Decatur, GA.

- Susan Bible Jessup, math teacher, Gainesville Middle School, Gainesville, GA.

- Susan Putman, math teacher, Coppell Middle School North, Coppell, TX.

- Carol Robinson, Ph.D. candidate in Math Education, FSU, Tallahassee, FL.

- Carol Strickland, interpreter and sign language instruction, Lincoln High School, Tallahassee, FL.

- Denise Vogelesang, Chairman, Exceptional Student Education (ESE) Department, Testing Coordinator, Lincoln High School, Tallahassee, FL.

- Mary Kay Wells, Chairman, Math Department, Lincoln High School, Tallahassee, FL.

Time Management and ADD (S-31-38)

- Don and Penny Dieckman, Gwinnett CHADD officers, Lilburn, GA.

- Joan Helbing, EEN Diagnostician/Trainer (ADD Consultant), Appleton Area School District, Appleton, WI.

- Joan Teach, Ph.D., Director Lullwater School (a special private school), Decatur, GA; DeKalb County CHADD Clinical Advisor; also, an adult with ADHD.

Section 4: IDEA and Section 504

- Virginia Brickman, Director of Support Services, DeKalb County Schools, Decatur, GA.

- Dick Downey, Ph.D., Director Special Education, Gwinnett County Public Schools, Lawrenceville, GA.

- Dixie Jordan, Coordinator, Project for Parents of Children with Emotional or Behavioral Disorders, PACER Center, Minneapolis, MN.

- Sara Mauk, legal assistant, specializing in special education law, Chicago, IL.

- Michael O'Connor, attorney, specializing in special education law, Chicago, IL.

Transition Planning (S-48)

- Melanie Eick, Disabilities Services Specialist, Oklahoma Department of Career and Technology Education, Oklahoma City, OK.

- Debbie Wilkes, Transition Specialist, Richardson Independent School District, Richardson, TX.

Behavioral Strategies (S-60)

- Ann Abramowitz, Ph.D., Director, ADD/ADHD Clinic, Emory University, Decatur, GA.

Coaching (S-65)

- Janet Ardoyno, Executive Director, Big Brother Big Sister Program, ADD Coach, Abilene, TX.
- Dee Doochin, Professional Certified Coach, and Holly Hamilton, Master Certified ADHD coaches, ADD-UP, Nashville,TN.
- Nancy McDougall and Janet Roper, guidance counselors, Oakmeadow Elementary School, San Antonio, TX; co-authors of *Creative Coaching*.
- Melissa Petty, MSW, President ADDA-SR, Houston, TX.

Conflict Resolution and Peer Mediation (S-66-67)

- Ottie Manis, Guidance Counselor, Ridgeland High School, Ft. Oglethorpe, GA.
- Jane Moser, Vice Principal, Meadowcreek High School, Norcross, GA

Violence Prevention (S-68)

- Janet Ardoyno, Executive Director, Big Brothers Big Sisters of Abilene, TX.
- Hill Walker, Ph.D., Associate Dean, Division of Special Education and Rehabilitation, Institute on Violence and Destructive Behavior, University of Oregon, Eugene, OR.

Valuing the Student with ADD/ADHD (S-70)

- Michael Epstein, Ph.D., William Barkley Professor of Special Education, University of Nebraska, Lincoln.

Introduction

"I've come to the frightening conclusion that I am the decisive element in the classroom. It's my personal approach that creates the climate. It's my daily mood that makes the weather. As a teacher, I possess a tremendous power to make a child's life miserable or joyous. I can be a tool of torture or an instrument of inspiration. I can humiliate or humor, hurt, or heal. In all situations, it is my response that decides whether a crisis will be escalated or deescalated and a child humanized or dehumanized."

—Haim G. Ginott
From *Teacher and Child: A Book for Parents and Teachers*

This book offers concise summaries of seventy-five key issues related to helping teenagers with ADD/ADHD succeed in school. Each of these summaries was written specifically with teachers and parents of middle and high school students in mind. The summaries address characteristics of ADD/ADHD and their impact on a teenager's school performance and behavior. Specific intervention strategies are provided for common behaviors and ADD/ADHD symptoms that interfere with success.

As a former teacher, I understand the time-consuming extra demands that often interfere with the teacher's primary job of teaching students. Consequently, I have made this material as easy to use as possible. Teachers may wish to use these summaries as a quick reference when dealing with a specific aspect of ADD or ADHD. If needed, more detailed information is available in my first book, *Teenagers with ADD: A Parents' Guide* (Woodbine House, 1995).

Teachers, guidance counselors, school psychologists and social workers, administrators, and parents should find this material helpful. Educators may use these summaries to educate themselves, or they may elect to give them to parents who need more information on ADD/ADHD. Parents may also find the information helpful for their own teenager or extended family members, or they may decide to share selected summaries with interested teachers.

A Personal Message
to Teachers from the Author

*D*espite having spent most of the last thirty years of my professional career working in the children's mental health field, I have come to believe that….

Succeeding in school is one of the most therapeutic things that can happen to a teenager. In fact, school successes may often be more helpful for students struggling with ADD or ADHD than an hour of counseling a week. In my opinion, teachers are often the critical factor determining the success or failure for students with this condition!

Attention deficit disorder *can* be a baffling and frustrating disorder even for someone like me, a former teacher, school psychologist, and mental health counselor. Although some might consider me a parenting "expert," I must tell you that raising a teenager with an attention deficit was the most difficult and humbling challenge of my life.

Having ADD/ADHD puts students at risk for problems in school. Researchers tell us that ***90 percent of these children will experience serious difficulties in school.*** Plus, according to the recent landmark National Institute of Mental Health study on ADHD, ***two-thirds of children with ADHD have at least one other coexisting problem.*** The more complex the attention deficit disorder, the greater the risk for a multitude of problems:

- learning disabilities,
- failing a grade,
- skipping school,
- suspension,
- expulsion, and, ultimately,
- dropping out of school and not going to college.

Consequently, the school years for these students are often the most difficult and challenging of their whole lives. The very characteristics of ADD/ADHD—inattention, difficulty sitting still, impulsivity, forgetfulness, disorganization, and learning problems— mitigate against success in school. On top of their difficulties completing school work, many of these students also get into trouble by speaking or acting impulsively.

Teachers play a pivotal role in the ultimate success or failure of these teenagers in adulthood. When adults were asked how they coped successfully with an attention deficit disorder, they said, *"Someone believed in me."* ***Teachers,*** next to parents, ***were named as the most influential person*** who had helped them succeed. Clearly, teachers have a powerful impact on shaping each student's life! Remember, a teenager's self-esteem is often built upon the messages that adults give him.

Teachers are the mirrors by which students measure their self-worth and ability. When a teacher conveys the message that a teenager is capable and worthwhile, the teen believes the message. Unfortunately, the converse is also true: negative messages can quickly cause serious harm. Researchers tell us that a struggling child's self-esteem can be damaged as early as second grade. Successful adults who did poorly in school still recall painful memories and self-doubts about their school failures.

Sadly enough, both of our sons struggled in school even though they were very bright. During their early school years, it was obvious to me that both sons wanted to do well but couldn't sustain their good intentions. As a former teacher, it was painful to watch them struggle in school and yet not know the best way to help them.

Today, both our sons are doing well: one is a senior in college and the other is a college graduate, married, a father, and, every parent's dream, "gainfully employed" in a job he loves. However, looking back, we were not so optimistic during our sons' high school years. My husband and I worried a lot and, at times, were very frightened for our teenagers.

Across the nation, thousands of families of teenagers with ADD/ADHD are wrestling with the same concerns that my husband and I faced: What does the future hold? Will our child be able to graduate from high school, much less go to college, or even hold down a job? The answer to these questions is an enthusiastic "yes"—**if *informed educators and parents intervene by providing extra supports and accommodations to help students succeed in school.*** My family has been lucky. Many extraordinary teachers, counselors, school psychologists, and administrators believed in our teenagers and helped them succeed.

I firmly believe that ***teachers want these students to succeed,*** but may not always fully understand the complexities of ADD/ADHD and the problems often accompanying this disorder, or know the most effective intervention strategies. My purpose in writing this book is to give teachers this information and make their jobs a little easier, in the process making school a more positive experience for students with attention deficits.

I believe that each teenager should have the opportunity to love learning and school, just as I did. So, as the humble parent of sons with ADD and ADHD, I want to share with you what I have learned about helping these teenagers succeed in school. Hopefully, these materials, developed during my thirty-year professional career as a teacher, school psychologist, and mental health counselor, will help *you* be the inspirational teacher who makes a positive difference in the lives of teenagers with attention deficit disorders!

Sincere best wishes,

Chris Abney Zeigler Dendy

P.S. Please send me an e-mail and tell me which strategies in the book were particularly helpful, as well as those that did not work very well. I also welcome suggestions of new ideas or ways of improving these strategies. I look forward to hearing from you at chris@chrisdendy.com. To find out more about me and my family, you may visit our website at **www.chrisdendy.com***.*

SECTION 1

The Basics

By understanding the basics about ADD and ADHD, teachers will be able to teach teenagers more effectively. Most teachers already know that attention deficit disorders are much more than just a case of simple hyperactivity. What often makes an attention deficit so complex is that two-thirds of students with the disorder have at least one other coexisting condition such as learning disabilities, anxiety, or depression.

Because of the potential negative impact of untreated ADD and ADHD, the national focus on these disorders has expanded tremendously within the past two years. A brief overview of these initiatives will explain the profound impact these studies will have on how we teach and treat these students. Hopefully, this section will answer an important question for any remaining doubting educators: *"Does ADD really exist or is it an excuse for a lazy student"?* Hopefully, this section will make it clear that for some students ***an attention deficit disorder is truly a disability***.

KEY STRATEGY: Be aware of the complexities of attention deficit disorders, especially coexisting conditions that can affect school performance:

1. Talk with parents to determine whether coexisting conditions are being treated.
2. Anticipate common ADD and ADHD behaviors and don't be surprised when they occur.

What Every Teacher Must Know about ADD and ADHD

1. **ADD/ADHD occurs in approximately 5 percent of all children worldwide.** However, rates of attention deficit disorder vary around the globe and in the United States. Within the U.S., reported rates vary from 3 percent in Salt Lake City to above 10 percent in several states, including parts of Arizona and upstate New York. Internationally, rates of 8.9 percent were reported in China, 9.5 percent in Puerto Rico, and 29 percent in India. Boys diagnosed with ADD or ADHD outnumber girls approximately three or four to one. The primary difference between girls and boys with attention deficits is that the boys are usually more aggressive and oppositional.

2. **ADD/ADHD is a complex neurobiological disorder.** Researchers believe that people with ADD/ADHD have a few structures within the brain that are smaller and that their *neurotransmitters,* the chemical messengers of the brain, do not work properly. The neurotransmitters norepinephrine, dopamine, and serotonin are thought to work inefficiently. See Summary 2.

3. **There are two distinctly different types of attention deficit disorders.** Federal education law refers to those with hyperactivity and impulsivity as having ADHD (attention deficit hyperactivity disorder) and those who are predominately inattentive as having ADD (attention deficit disorder). However, AD/HD (attention-deficit/hyperactivity disorder) is the technically correct diagnostic label established by the American Psychiatric Association. See Summary 5.

4. **All children with ADD/ADHD are not alike.** Symptoms of attention deficits may be mild, moderate, or severe, *or* combined with other conditions. This means adults will see variability in skills and maturity levels in these students.

5. **ADD/ADHD often occurs with other conditions.** According to information from a major study at the National Institute of Mental Health (NIMH), two-thirds of children with ADHD have at least one other coexisting condition. See Figure 1.

Figure 1. Conditions That Occur with ADD/ADHD		
	NIMH or Others	**Mis. Studies on ADHD Teens**
Learning Disabilities	25%	--
Tourette Syndrome (TS)	11%	--
Anxiety	34%	37%
Depression	(16%)	28%
Bipolar Disorder (BPD)	4%	12%
Substance Abuse	(5%)	40% (ADHD/CD only)
Oppositional Defiant Disorder (ODD)	(40%)	59%
Conduct Disorder (CD)	14%	43%

(Percentages given above in parenthesis are from studies by Joseph Biederman, M.D., and Tim Wilens, M.D. Percentages in the second column are found in Dr. Russell Barkley's book, ATTENTION-DEFICIT HYPERACTIVITY DISORDER, second edition.)

Most research has been done on *children* with ADHD. However, when information is gathered on teenagers, the occurrence of these conditions tends to be higher. When symptoms are severe and co-occurring conditions are present, both ADD and ADHD are much more challenging to the child, family, and school to diagnose and treat effectively.

6. **A two to four year lag in age-appropriate developmental skills (adaptive functioning) may be present.** Developmental delays are often observed in motor skills, self-help abilities, personal responsibility, independence, and peer relationships. Consequently, these students may seem less mature and responsible than their peers. Typically, a sixteen-year-old with ADD or ADHD acts more like a twelve-year-old.

7. **Several behaviors linked to deficits in neurotransmitters often accompany ADD/ADHD,** causing problems at home and school. Students with ADD or ADHD may experience problems with some, but usually not all, of these behaviors:

   - **Executive functioning difficulties:** These skills are critical for success in school, yet are often lacking in students with attention deficits. (See Summary 28.) Deficits in key executive function skills that interfere with the ability to do well academically may include:
     - **working memory and recall:** briefly holding facts in your head and manipulating them;
     - **activation, arousal, and effort:** getting started, staying alert, and finishing work;
     - **impulsivity:** saying or doing things impulsively before thinking;
     - **control of emotions:** low frustration tolerance, emotional blow-ups;
     - **internalizing language:** using "self-talk" to guide behavior;
     - **complex problem solving:** taking the whole apart, analyzing it, and putting it back together.

   - **Forgetfulness and disorganization:** These problems interfere with completion of school work (forgetting to do or turn in homework and tests, forgetting due dates for projects, forgetting to stay after school or for detention). See Summaries 29 and 30.

   - **Variability in school work** from day to day and class to class: This is often baffling to teachers and parents. Some days a student can do the work completely and accurately but most days he can't. Without medication, the student's ability to force himself to continually refocus on school work is impaired.

   - **Not learning from punishment and rewards** as easily as other children: This characteristic makes teaching and disciplining them more difficult. Misbehavior may be repeated. They "don't seem to learn from their mistakes," prompting observations that they "know what to do but don't always do what they know."

   - **An impaired sense of time:** Students with attention deficits may be tardy, not allow adequate time for homework and school projects, and have difficulty planning ahead, especially for assignments and long-term projects. See Summaries 31-35.

- **Sleep disturbances:** Approximately 50 percent of these students may have trouble falling asleep and waking up. Furthermore, half are not getting restful sleep and are still tired even after eight hours of sleep. Consequently, students may be sleep deprived and sleep in class.

- **Levels of alertness.** These students not only have trouble regulating levels of waking and sleeping, but also levels of alertness. They may have difficulty staying alert enough to listen and take class notes. They may sleep in class.

- **Difficulties with transitions and changes in routine:** Changing classes, lunch, recess, having a substitute teacher, or riding the bus home after school are often high-risk times for misbehavior.

8. **ADD/ADHD runs in families.** Forty to fifty percent of all children with attention deficits have at least one parent and thirty percent have a sibling with the condition.

9. **Medication works effectively for most children (75-90 percent).** When medication works properly, schoolwork and behavior will improve significantly. Unfortunately, stimulant medication often wears off during two key transition times: lunchtime and the bus ride home after school. Plus, medication doesn't seem to significantly correct problems related to disorganization, forgetfulness, and impaired sense of time. See Summaries 51-55.

10. **Teenagers don't outgrow ADD/ADHD.** Symptoms of attention deficits often present lifelong challenges. The primary observable difference in teenagers is that they may become less hyperactive than they were as children. However, the hyperactivity is often replaced by restlessness. For 50 percent, the symptoms of attention deficits do not cause major problems in adulthood. Adults often find a career that is compatible with their personality so symptoms don't present problems in the workplace, symptoms become less severe with age, or the adult learns to compensate. For some adults, continuing to take medication will be a necessity.

ADD and ADHD Are Neurobiological Disorders

Scientists have made great progress in research on attention deficit disorders. However, research is still in its infancy. Although researchers still do not know exactly what causes this condition, they do know that it is often inherited. A couple of tests—the PET Scan (positron emission tomography) and the MRI (magnetic resonance imaging)—have provided evidence that ADHD is a neurobiological disorder. (Most research has been conducted on ADHD, rather than ADD.) During the next few years, researchers should discover even more information about this challenging condition. Here is what researchers have learned so far:

- **Cerebral blood flow is reduced** in some parts near the front of the brain. These areas of the brain control several functions: 1) attention, 2) impulsivity—the ability to "stop and think" before acting, 3) sensitivity to rewards and punishment, 4) emotions, and 5) memory.

- **Several genes have been identified that are linked to ADD/ADHD.** Out of thirteen or so genes that have been linked to attention deficits, there are three that are of primary interest to researchers: two dopamine receptor genes—DRD2 and DRD4—and a dopamine transporter gene—DAT1. The receptors and transporters control the level of dopamine in each neuron. A Harvard researcher has found that people with attention deficits have 70 percent higher levels of dopamine transporters in the synaptic space. Because these receptors and transporters are not working properly, the right levels of dopamine are not available in the neurons. Researchers have shown that inefficient levels of dopamine interfere with attention, learning, and proper behavior.

- **There is underactivity in the brain.** Problems with neurotransmitters such as dopamine and norepinephrine may cause underactivity in the brain, according to studies performed in the early 1990s at the National Institute of Mental Health (NIMH). (Neurotransmitters are chemicals in the brain that help messages travel from one brain cell to the next. See Summary 3.) NIMH researcher Dr. Alan Zametkin used a PET scan to study adults and teenaged girls with ADHD while they were involved in thinking tasks. He found reduced blood flow and lower metabolism, or absorption, of glucose in the frontal areas of the central nervous system of the brain. Figure 2 shows the reduced brain

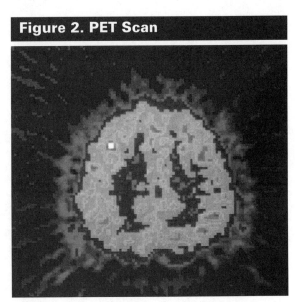

Figure 2. PET Scan

activity in an adult with ADHD. The one small white area was the only active area in the brain during a thinking task. In contrast, people without ADHD had several white areas, indicating higher levels of brain activity. When people with ADHD take stimulant medications such as Ritalin or Dexedrine, PET scans show an increase of activity in these areas of the brain.

■ **Three sections of the brain are smaller** in people with ADHD, according to results of recent magnetic resonance imaging (MRI) studies: the cerebellum, caudate nucleus, and corpus callosum. No brain damage was found to these sections; they were simply smaller. The reduced volume was primarily attributed to smaller areas of white matter, which contain the connections between the nerve cell bodies located in the brain's gray matter. Researchers report that these sections of the brain affect 1) alertness, 2) executive function, 3) the ability to control shifts from one task to another, and 4) the ability to assist with the transfer of information between neurons.

Resources

Prince, Jefferson B. "An Update on the Neurobiology of Attention Deficit Hyperactivity Disorders." ADDA-SR Conference presentation, Irving, TX, 2000.

Ratey, John. "A User's Guide to the Brain: Through the Lens of Attention," ADDA Conference presentation, Atlanta, Georgia, 2000.

Swanson, James, et al. "Cognitive Neuroscience of Attention Deficit Hyperactivity Disorder and Hyperkinetic Disorder." *Current Opinion-in–neurobiology*, April 1998, V. 8(2), 263-71.

Zametkin, Alan J., et al. "Cerebral Glucose Metabolism in Adults with Hyperactivity of Childhood Onset. *The New England Journal of Medicine*, November 15, 1990, V. 323, N. 20, 1361.

SUMMARY 3 — Neurotransmitters Can Make or Break a Good School Day!

For better or worse, why do teenagers behave as they do? Do students with attention deficits get up each morning and maliciously say, "Today my goal is to ruin Mrs. Smith's day"? Of course not, but after a tough day at school, teachers may sometimes wonder.

Although you probably haven't thought much about neurotransmitters, they play a key role in determining whether you, the teacher, have a good day at school. Researchers have found that neurotransmitters have a profound impact on shaping our day-to-day behavior, including our mood, ability to pay attention, memory, sociability, and sleep habits.

When brain neurotransmitters are working properly, students:
- pay attention,
- complete work,
- comply with teacher requests, and
- are well behaved.

When neurotransmitters are too low or inefficient and don't work properly (as in students with attention deficits), teachers may observe several unpleasant behaviors:
- students don't listen,
- don't complete class work,
- are irritable and argumentative. ,
- sleep in class due to lack of restful sleep at night.

Academically, students:
- have difficulty comprehending what they read,
- can't memorize isolated facts,
- have trouble organizing their thoughts to write an essay,
- have difficulty holding facts in their heads while working a math problem, or quickly retrieving information from stored memory.

How Do Neurotransmitters Work?

Since deficits in neurotransmitters are thought to contribute to symptoms of ADD and ADHD, let's look at how neurotransmitters are *supposed* to work.

The human nervous system has billions of nerve cells or *neurons* that carry messages throughout the body. These messages may tell a teenager to listen, pay attention when the teacher is talking, remember the assignment, and stick with the task until it is finished.

Technically speaking, the nerve cells carry *impulses* (nerve signals) from one end of the cell to the other—from the dendrite to the axon. There is a space between neurons, known as a *synaptic cleft*. Since the axon and dendrites of adjacent neurons do not touch, messages must cross this synaptic space. Neurotransmitters, the chemical messengers of the brain, are released at the synapse to help the message move across to the *receptor sites* on the neighboring neuron.

When an attention deficit is present, researchers believe that messages move down the neuron, but stop and don't always cross the synapse to the next one. This disruption is most likely caused by a **chemical inefficiency in neurotransmitters,** which interrupts the normal flow of messages throughout the body.

Neurotransmitters That Affect ADD and ADHD

Three neurotransmitters are thought to have a strong impact on behaviors considered typical of attention deficit disorder: norepinephrine, dopamine, and serotonin.

Figure 3. Diagram of a Neuron

From Know Your Brain, *NIH Publication No. 92-3440-a.*

- **Dopamine:** Research has shown that when the neurotransmitter dopamine is *too low,* a teenager is inattentive, distractible, has difficulty completing a job, thinking ahead, and delaying a response, or may be cognitively impulsive. But there can also be problems when dopamine is *too high:* a teenager with *Obsessive Compulsive Disorder (OCD)* attends to and repeats behavior too often. (Researchers suspect that supersensitivity to dopamine may be an underlying cause of both OCD and Tourette syndrome, discussed in Summary 72).

- **Norepinephrine:** When norepinephrine is *too low,* a teenager may be indifferent, depressed, or aggressive. If it is *too high,* the teenager may tend to be a thrill seeker or be aggressive impulsively.

- **Serotonin:** Serotonin gives us a sense of well being. When serotonin is *too low,* a person is more irritable and aggressive. In fact, when serotonin was lowered intentionally in a research study, normally tranquil people became more aggressive.

The Impact of Stimulant Medications on Neurotransmitters

Stimulant medications such as Ritalin, Dexedrine, and Adderall are so called because they stimulate activity in the central nervous system, often increasing the level of neurotransmitter activity and blood flow in the brain. These medications are known to promote the efficient use of dopamine and norepinephrine—the very neurotransmitters that appear to be involved in attention deficits.

The ADD/ADHD Iceberg

The characteristics of ADD and ADHD may be compared with an iceberg: *only the tip of the problem is visible!* Typically, teachers and parents see the obvious "tip" first: the behavior problems, such as failing to complete homework, talking back, arguing, and other impulsive misbehavior. Yet for so many teenagers, an attention deficit is much more complex than just these obvious behaviors. School is often incredibly challenging because of their inattention, disorganization, executive function deficits, and other serious learning problems. Remember, *two-thirds of students with an attention deficit disorder have a least one other diagnosable condition* that often has a significant impact on school performance.

Conditions that commonly accompany ADD or ADHD, including specific learning disabilities, depression, anxiety, bipolar disorder, and sleep disturbances, often are overlooked by treatment professionals and may *never* be treated. These coexisting conditions are discussed in detail in Summary 72, "When Teens Continue to Struggle."

When you think of attention deficit disorder, visualize this iceberg with only one-eighth of its mass visible above the water line. As is true of icebergs, often the most challenging aspects of ADD and ADHD are hidden beneath the surface.

Teachers may find the blank ADD/ADHD Iceberg (Appendix A1) helpful in identifying areas of concern for the student. In preparing for teacher-parent staff meetings, one school in Texas asks teachers and parents to fill in the blanks in this form.

Figure 4. The ADD/ADHD Iceberg

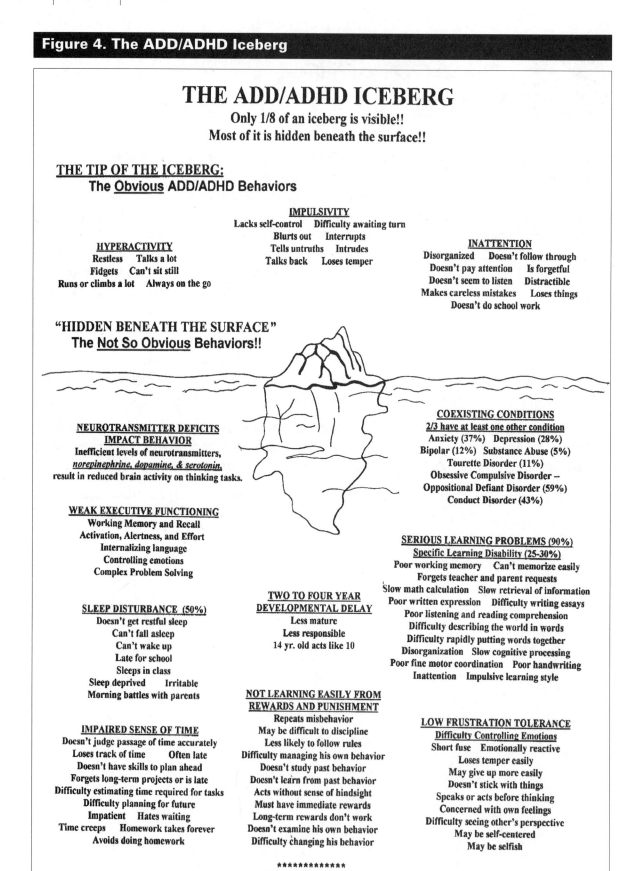

THE ADD/ADHD ICEBERG
Only 1/8 of an iceberg is visible!!
Most of it is hidden beneath the surface!!

THE TIP OF THE ICEBERG:
The Obvious ADD/ADHD Behaviors

IMPULSIVITY
Lacks self-control   Difficulty awaiting turn
Blurts out   Interrupts
Tells untruths   Intrudes
Talks back   Loses temper

HYPERACTIVITY
Restless   Talks a lot
Fidgets   Can't sit still
Runs or climbs a lot   Always on the go

INATTENTION
Disorganized   Doesn't follow through
Doesn't pay attention   Is forgetful
Doesn't seem to listen   Distractible
Makes careless mistakes   Loses things
Doesn't do school work

"HIDDEN BENEATH THE SURFACE"
The Not So Obvious Behaviors!!

NEUROTRANSMITTER DEFICITS
IMPACT BEHAVIOR
Inefficient levels of neurotransmitters,
norepinephrine, dopamine, & serotonin,
result in reduced brain activity on thinking tasks.

WEAK EXECUTIVE FUNCTIONING
Working Memory and Recall
Activation, Alertness, and Effort
Internalizing language
Controlling emotions
Complex Problem Solving

SLEEP DISTURBANCE (50%)
Doesn't get restful sleep
Can't fall asleep
Can't wake up
Late for school
Sleeps in class
Sleep deprived   Irritable
Morning battles with parents

IMPAIRED SENSE OF TIME
Doesn't judge passage of time accurately
Loses track of time   Often late
Doesn't have skills to plan ahead
Forgets long-term projects or is late
Difficulty estimating time required for tasks
Difficulty planning for future
Impatient   Hates waiting
Time creeps   Homework takes forever
Avoids doing homework

TWO TO FOUR YEAR
DEVELOPMENTAL DELAY
Less mature
Less responsible
14 yr. old acts like 10

NOT LEARNING EASILY FROM
REWARDS AND PUNISHMENT
Repeats misbehavior
May be difficult to discipline
Less likely to follow rules
Difficulty managing his own behavior
Doesn't study past behavior
Doesn't learn from past behavior
Acts without sense of hindsight
Must have immediate rewards
Long-term rewards don't work
Doesn't examine his own behavior
Difficulty changing his behavior

COEXISTING CONDITIONS
2/3 have at least one other condition
Anxiety (37%)   Depression (28%)
Bipolar (12%)   Substance Abuse (5%)
Tourette Disorder (11%)
Obsessive Compulsive Disorder --
Oppositional Defiant Disorder (59%)
Conduct Disorder (43%)

SERIOUS LEARNING PROBLEMS (90%)
Specific Learning Disability (25-30%)
Poor working memory   Can't memorize easily
Forgets teacher and parent requests
Slow math calculation   Slow retrieval of information
Poor written expression   Difficulty writing essays
Poor listening and reading comprehension
Difficulty describing the world in words
Difficulty rapidly putting words together
Disorganization   Slow cognitive processing
Poor fine motor coordination   Poor handwriting
Inattention   Impulsive learning style

LOW FRUSTRATION TOLERANCE
Difficulty Controlling Emotions
Short fuse   Emotionally reactive
Loses temper easily
May give up more easily
Doesn't stick with things
Speaks or acts before thinking
Concerned with own feelings
Difficulty seeing other's perspective
May be self-centered
May be selfish

****
ADD/ADHD is often more complex than most people realize!
Like icebergs, many problems related to ADD/ADHD are not visible. ADD/ADHD may be mild, moderate, or severe,
is likely to coexist with other conditions, and may be a disability for some students.

Official Diagnostic Criteria for AD/HD: The DSM-IV

The official criteria for diagnosing attention deficit disorders are contained in the DSM-IV (*The Diagnostic and Statistical Manual of Mental Disorders* of the American Psychiatric Association, fourth edition). These are the same criteria that all physicians and licensed treatment professionals use to diagnose ADD and ADHD. To be technically correct, **four official diagnoses for AD/HD were established** in 1994:

1. Attention-Deficit/Hyperactivity Disorder, Predominately **Inattentive** Type
2. Attention-Deficit/Hyperactivity Disorder, Predominately **Hyperactive-Impulsive** Type
3. Attention-Deficit/Hyperactivity Disorder, **Combined Type** (1 & 2)
4. Attention-Deficit/Hyperactivity Disorder **Not Otherwise Specified** (NOS)

To be diagnosed as having AD/HD, a student must have six of nine characteristics in either section *(1)* **Inattentive** or *(2)* **Hyperactive-Impulsive** (see below). If he has six (or more) characteristics in the Inattentive section, he is diagnosed with **AD/HD, Predominately Inattentive Type.** If he has six (or more) characteristics in the Hyperactive-Impulsive section, he is diagnosed with **AD/HD, Predominately Hyperactive-Impulsive Type. AD/HD, Combined Type,** is diagnosed if an individual has at least six characteristics under *both* ADD/inattentive *and* ADHD/hyperactive-impulsive, for a total of twelve or more characteristics.

For these diagnoses to be given, the symptoms need to have been present before the age of seven and also cause some impairment in two or more settings (such as at school and at home).

Obviously, many of the characteristics under hyperactive-impulsive may no longer be present in teenagers. However, the characteristics may have been observed during elementary school and perhaps recorded in school records.

Blanks have been added in front of each of the DSM-IV criteria so teachers may place a checkmark by those behaviors exhibited by the student:

Implications for Teachers

■ **ADD/ADHD is more difficult to diagnose in teenagers.**

The hyperactive/impulsive characteristics are more common in younger children and may no longer be present in teenagers. If in doubt about the presence of hyperactivity, ask parents to describe the teenager's behavior as a young child or review the cumulative folder for information about elementary school years. Hyperactivity is often replaced by restlessness in adolescence. See Summary 6.

Diagnostic Criteria for Attention-Deficit/Hyperactivity Disorder

1. Inattention

__ often fails to give close attention to details or makes careless mistakes in schoolwork, work, or other activities

__ often has difficulty sustaining attention in tasks or play activities

__ often does not seem to listen when spoken to directly

__ often does not follow through on instructions and fails to finish school-work, chores, or duties in the work place (not due to oppositional behavior or failure to understand directions)

__ often has difficulty organizing tasks and activities

__ often avoids, dislikes, or is reluctant to engage in tasks that require sustained mental effort (such as schoolwork, or homework)

__ often loses things necessary for tasks or activities at school, home, or the work place, (e.g., toys, school assignments, pencils, books, or tools)

__ is often easily distracted by extraneous stimuli

__ is often forgetful in daily activities

2. Hyperactivity [Did the teenager exhibit these behaviors in elementary school?]

__ often fidgets with hands or feet or squirms in seat

__ often leaves seat in classroom or in other situations in which remaining seated is expected

__ often runs about or climbs excessively in situations where it is inappropriate (in adolescents or adults, may be limited to subjective feelings of restlessness)

__ often has difficulty playing or engaging in leisure activities quietly

__ is often "on the go" or often acts as if "driven by motor"

__ often talks excessively

Impulsivity

__ often blurts out answers before questions have been completed

__ often has difficulty awaiting turn

__ often interrupts or intrudes on others (e.g., butts into conversations or games)

(Reprinted with permission from the Diagnostic and Statistical Manual of Mental Disorders, *Fourth Edition. Washington, DC: American Psychiatric Association, 1994.)*

■ **Several groups of students who have ADD/ADHD may be overlooked.**

1. **Students with the Inattentive Type:** Some people still believe the myth that a child must be hyperactive to be diagnosed as having an attention deficit disorder. So, some middle and high school students who have the inattentive type may not have been diagnosed in elementary school.

2. **Girls:** Since girls with ADD or ADHD typically are not as aggressive as boys, they may not meet all the criteria to be diagnosed. Some experts argue that girls with attention deficit disorders may meet fewer than six criteria. See Summary 9 for more information on girls.

3. **Gifted Students:** Gifted students are often able to compensate for difficulties with attention, hyperactivity, or impulsivity until middle or high school, when they have more classes and more teachers to handle. Demands for school work and organizational skills increase significantly and less supervision is provided during these years. Teachers may have unrealistic expectations that the student will work independently and take greater responsibility for completion of his school work.

4. **Minority Students:** For a variety of reasons, students who are members of minority groups may be less likely to be treated for ADD or ADHD. For example, one researcher, Julie M. Zito, found that white students were given stimulant medications for ADHD twice as often as African American students.

5. **Students in Special Education:** Some children diagnosed in earlier years as having a specific learning disability (SLD) or emotional and behavioral disorder (EBD) may also have ADD or ADHD. So, take another look at students in special education classes to see if they have symptoms of inattention or hyperactivity. If they do, effective treatment may help them be more successful in school.

Resources

Zito, J.M., Safer, D., dos Reis, S., Riddle, M. (1998). "Radical Disparity in psychotropic medication prescribed for youths with Medicaid insurance in Maryland." *Journal of the American Academy of Child and Adolescent Psychiatry*, 37: 179-184.

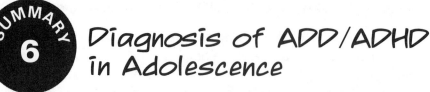

Diagnosis of ADD/ADHD in Adolescence

At school, ***classroom teachers are the people most likely to first suspect that a student has an attention deficit disorder.*** Even if the attention deficit isn't obvious, teachers recognize when students are struggling in class. If a teenager is suspected of having ADD or ADHD, a school psychologist, social worker, or counselor may then confirm the teacher's suspicions or determine that another problem exists. A medical doctor will probably also be involved in making the diagnosis, especially if medication is being considered.

Most experienced teachers are already pretty good at recognizing students with ADD and ADHD. This overview of procedures for diagnosing an attention deficit may help teachers correctly identify teenagers with this condition and refer them for formal evaluation. Recognizing an attention deficit can be confusing at times because ***all of us may have some symptoms of ADD/ADHD.*** However, what sets these teens apart is the number and severity of the symptoms. Unlike pregnancy, attention deficit is not an "either you are or you aren't" diagnosis. Symptoms of the disorder may be mild, moderate, or severe. To be diagnosed as having an attention deficit, a student must exhibit six of nine official criteria to a degree that interferes with his ability to function successfully at school and at home. Official diagnostic criteria from DSM-IV are listed in Summary 5.

Many children with ADD or ADHD, particularly those who are hyperactive, are diagnosed in early childhood or elementary school. By the time they reach adolescence, they have usually been receiving treatment for several years. However, ***it is not unusual for some teenagers to reach adolescence or even adulthood without having the disorder diagnosed!***

There are a variety of reasons that the diagnosis of attention deficit may be delayed until adolescence or later. Very bright students with an attention deficit often compensate in elementary school and can get by without being detected. Sometimes problems don't surface until students enter middle and high school when they must cope with more classes and teachers, as well as increased academic demands. Girls with ADD or ADHD are often overlooked, because they are not aggressive nor do they typically have behavior problems. See Summary 9.

Important Points to Know about Diagnosing ADD/ADHD

- There is **no test for ADD/ADHD.**

- **Underachievement** in school should be a red flag signaling teachers and parents to evaluate for ADD or ADHD or other learning problems.

- **The best indicators** of an attention deficit are the diagnostic criteria contained in the DSM IV (Summary 5). How many characteristics does the student exhibit? If he has six of nine characteristics, chances are good that he has an attention deficit.

How a Diagnosis Is Confirmed

The treatment professional, school social worker, or school psychologist might collect information from the following sources to confirm a diagnosis of ADD or ADHD:

- **DSM-IV diagnostic criteria** (meets 6 of 9 criteria in Summary 5)

- A **childhood/family history** from the parents (history of ADD or ADHD or ADD/ADHD behaviors in the family; hyperactivity may or may not be observed)

- **Description of school performance** by parents and the student (bright but underachieving; gets by in elementary school, but struggles in middle and high school)

- **School report cards.** Grades may be low. Teacher comments on report cards may include: "Not working up to potential. Doesn't listen. Fails to use time wisely. Doesn't complete work. Doesn't turn work in on time. Makes too many zeros." For hyperactive students, teachers may find: "Talks too much. Can't stay in seat. Fidgets. Has difficulty sitting still." Or for students with the inattentive type: "Daydreams or stares into space."

- **Classroom observations** (may not listen, may be off-task, doesn't complete work)

- **Official school records,** including standardized academic achievement tests such as the *IOWA* Test of Basic Skills; Individualized Education Programs (IEP); school psychological evaluations. Group tests such as the IOWA are reviewed looking for patterns that are indicative of learning problems.
  - **Group tests:** Certain subtests of the *IOWA*, such as math computation, spelling, or capitalization, may be low.
  - **Psychological evaluations:** Scale scores on the Weschler Intelligence Scale for Children (*WISC-III*) may be low on what is known as the *Freedom from Distractibility Scale* [Arithmetic and Digit Span]. Another analysis of WISC-III scores, the *ACID test*, often shows low scores on those same three subtests, plus the Information subtest. However, students with ADD/ADHD do not *always* make low scores on these subtests.

Other Helpful Indicators of ADD/ADHD

Student support staff, such as a school counselor, social worker, or psychologist, may ask teachers to complete a behavior rating scale or the school psychologist may administer other formal tests:

1. **Intellectual Assessment:** Typically, a school psychologist administers an intelligence test such as the Weschler Intelligence Scale for Children-III (WISC-III). (Group test score results may be acceptable in some states for a Section 504 evaluation.)

2. **Academic Achievement Tests:** These tests help identify academic strengths and learning problems.
   - Iowa Test of Basic Skills (*IOWA)*
   - Curriculum based assessment; in other words, review of class/homework.
   - Woodcock Johnson Psychoeducational Battery—Revised
   - Weschler Individual Achievement Test (WIAT)

- Stanford Achievement Test
- Kaufman Test of Educational Achievement
- Peabody Individual Achievement Test (PIAT)
- Test of Written Language (TOWL)

3. **Behavior Rating Scales:** Several checklists include typical behaviors common in ADD and ADHD and may be helpful:
   - Behavioral Assessment System for Children (BASC)
   - Conners Rating Scale – Revised: Long Version (*CTRS-R:L and CPRS-R:L*)
   - *CBCL*-Child Behavior Checklists/Auchenbach, parent, teacher and youth versions
   - Brown Attention Deficit Disorder Scales

4. **Other tests** such as the Developmental Test of Visual Motor Integration (VMI) may be given to identify related problems.

5. **A thorough physical examination** should be conducted to rule out other disorders.

Coexisting problems such as *learning problems, sleep disturbances, anxiety, depression, defiance, or aggression* are found in two-thirds of students with ADD or ADHD and must be identified and treated. Typically, treatment of attention deficit disorder in isolation is not enough to ensure that a teenager will be successful in school and life. See Summary 72 for a discussion of coexisting conditions.

For more detailed information about diagnosing ADD and ADHD, refer to Chapter 2 in *Teenagers with ADD* (Woodbine House, 1995).

Words of Caution and Concern

Obviously, teachers cannot officially diagnose ADD or ADHD, nor is it appropriate for teachers to tell parents that they think a teenager has an attention deficit. Educators don't want to unnecessarily alarm parents. It may be wise to **talk about the behaviors of concern** rather than giving a diagnostic label:

> *"Your son has trouble completing his homework and turning it in on time. I know you are also concerned about his school work. I would like to ask the school psychologist to observe him and review his records. Perhaps he will have some suggestions about appropriate next steps to help him succeed in school."*

The problem the teenager is experiencing may not be an attention deficit, but may be another disorder such as a specific learning disability, depression, or anxiety.

School administrators sometimes face a moral dilemma related to identifying students with attention deficits as being eligible for special education services. On one hand, they may worry that if parents are told that a teen may have ADD or ADHD, then the school system will be responsible for providing or paying for an evaluation, classroom accommodations, "related" supportive services, or, in rare instances, educational services in a residential setting. On the other hand, administrators have an ethical and legal responsibility to see that all students get the help they need. **The primary goal should be to help each student succeed in school and realize his ultimate potential!**

Common Myths about ADD/ADHD: Fact vs. Fiction

Several common myths may interfere with diagnosis and treatment of teenagers with ADD or ADHD:

Myth I: All children/teenagers with ADD or ADHD are hyperactive.

Some teachers and parents still mistakenly believe that a child or teenager with ADD or ADHD must be hyperactive. They may be unaware that by the teenage years, hyperactivity is usually no longer present and has been replaced by restlessness. In addition, children with milder cases of ADHD may not seem excessively hyperactive. Students who have ADD may actually seem more like couch potatoes who lack energy. Consequently, teenagers with ADHD who are restless, but not hyperactive, or who have ADD may be overlooked.

> *"When I have called some teachers and mentioned that 'John' had ADD/ADHD, frequently the teacher will say that can't be true. John isn't hyperactive."*
> —Pediatric Center Staff, Decatur, GA

> *"Very few ADHD children are hyperactive in the true sense. I see maybe one or two a year, referred in by kindergarten or first grade teachers. Most ADHD children and teenagers are fidgety, playing with something in their hand, standing by their desk, but not overtly hyperactive or antisocial."*
> —Dr. Theodore Mandlekorn, M.D., Director, ADHD Clinic,
> Virginia Mason Clinic, Mercer Island, WA

Myth II: Hyperactive children/teenagers with ADHD can't sit still for ten minutes.

By the teenage years, students *can* sit still in class, although sometimes they may daydream or sleep. They can also maintain a conversation with the school psychologist or other school administrator during a half-hour interview. Most teenagers with ADHD concentrate and focus better in one-to-one and novel situations.

Myth III: ADD/ADHD disappears in adolescence and adulthood.

One of the reasons it was originally believed that youngsters outgrew ADHD was because their hyperactivity decreases as they reach adolescence. The attention problems often persist, however, and manifest themselves in a different way in teenagers. Instead of hyperactivity, restlessness, inattentiveness, or sleeping in class may be observed. Sometimes teachers will see physical signs of restlessness such as tapping a pencil, swinging a foot, or doodling. The teenager with ADHD who feels "hyper" knows it isn't acceptable to get up and walk around in class, so instead he may tune out mentally or sleep. Some teenagers say they feel as if their brain is still hyperactive, jumping from one topic to another.

Myth IV: Stimulant medications such as Ritalin no longer work in adolescents.

Research has shown that stimulant medications are effective for children, teenagers, and even adults with attention deficits. When medication is working properly, students will show a decrease in hyperactivity, impulsivity, negative behaviors, and verbal hostility, while attention, concentration, compliance, and completion of school work will improve significantly. See Summaries 51-55.

Myth V: ADD/ADHD will always be diagnosed in early childhood.

The age of diagnosis may vary depending on the severity and type of ADD/ADHD. Children who are extremely hyperactive are usually diagnosed early. Children with milder cases of ADHD or those who have ADD may not be diagnosed until middle or high school or later. Some teenagers with an attention deficit may even continue into adulthood without detection. Unfortunately, some parents and high school personnel may not have considered an attention deficit as a potential culprit underlying student underachievement! They incorrectly assume that if ADD or ADHD were present, it would have been diagnosed in elementary school.

Myth VI: ADD/ADHD is over-diagnosed.

Researchers tell us that attention deficit disorders occur in roughly 5 percent of children. Unfortunately, no one knows for certain whether ADD and ADHD are being over-diagnosed or not. Currently, no research is available nationally regarding the actual number of children who are taking medication for attention deficits. Media headlines touting over-diagnosis of attention deficit disorders often are not based upon hard facts.

Some local school systems report high levels of ADD and ADHD and some don't. A 1995 survey of the number of children on medication for attention deficits in my local school system does not indicate over-diagnosis. Roughly 4 percent, still less than the anticipated 5 percent prevalence rate, were taking medication. In 1999, a study in Salt Lake City found the rate of children on medication for ADHD at 3+ percent. Yet, other cities have reported higher rates ranging from 7 to 14 percent. Other countries around the world have also reported higher rates of attention deficits: Japan—7.7 percent; Puerto Rico—9.5 percent; Germany—10.9-17.8 percent; and India—29 percent.

Obviously, now that more students are being treated, the number of students on medication has increased. Let's look at some possible reasons why:

- ***ADD/ADHD has been under-diagnosed for years.*** Some researchers speculate that we "are finally playing catch-up" to the predicted 5 percent prevalence rate. Many researchers believe this is the primary reason for increases in the number of students being diagnosed.

- ***ADD/ADHD may be increasing because of environmental trauma.*** Although ADD and ADHD are often inherited, trauma or toxins in the environment may also cause attention deficits. For example, exposure to lead, or having a mother who drinks or smokes during pregnancy, may cause children to exhibit symptoms of this condition.

- ***The criteria for the inattentive type of ADD were not included in the DSM IV until 1994.*** This means that some teenagers with the inattentive type of ADD may not have been diagnosed with ADD if they were evaluated in elementary school.

- ***Children and teenagers with borderline ADD/ADHD may be receiving treatment now.*** Perhaps children and teenagers who have a borderline attention deficit (with 5 but not 6 characteristics of the DSM IV criteria) are being identified and referred for treatment by parents who are desperate to find help for their struggling child.

Differences between Students with ADHD and ADD

Although students with ADHD and ADD share some basic characteristics, they are different in several areas.

Teenagers who have ADHD tend to be:

- hyperactive,
- energetic,
- talkative, and
- outgoing.

In contrast, **teenagers with ADD,** previously called ADD without hyperactivity, tend to be:

- low energy,
- introverted,
- less likely to talk in class, and
- daydreamers.

The charts below give a quick summary of the similarities and differences between these two major types of attention deficit disorders. Remember, any given student with ADD/ADHD will have some, but probably not all, of the characteristics in any given column.

Similarities: Students with ADD and ADHD share these characteristics:

impulsivity
inattention
trouble getting started on homework or schoolwork
poor sustained attention (persistence on tasks)
problems with written expression and math
poor handwriting (fine motor skills)
positive response to stimulant medications
short-term memory problems
working memory problems

Differences: Students with ADHD and ADD also have very distinct differences. However, students with combined type ADHD will have symptoms from both columns.

ADHD (hyperactive-impulsive type) *(Behaviors more likely in elementary students)*	ADD (inattentive type)
hyperactive	has low energy, not hyperactive
out of seat	sits in seat daydreaming
talkative	quiet, less talkative
blurts out answers	slow to respond in class
talks and acts before thinking	slow processing speed (seems confused at times); slow retreival of information; slow perceptual-motor speed; slow writing
class clown	quiet, socially distant
difficulty making and keeping friends; misses social cues	gets along better with peers

Less Common Characteristics: The following behaviors are not present in all students with ADD or ADHD, but when present, they are more likely to be associated with the type of attention deficit noted.

ADHD (hyperactive-impulsive type)	ADD (inattentive type)
aggression	anxiety; may reduce impulsivity
oppositional behavior	less oppositional behavior
defiance; conduct disorder	less defiance

Girls with ADD/ADHD

A national debate is growing over whether or not girls with ADD or ADHD should be judged by slightly different criteria than boys. The official criteria used to diagnose attention deficits were based primarily on research into the behavior of boys. Since boys are more hyperactive, aggressive, and defiant, teachers are more likely to notice their problems. Consequently, boys and girls can have the same level of cognitive problems caused by attention deficits, yet girls may not be diagnosed. Girls who actually have attention deficit disorders may meet fewer than the six symptoms required for a diagnosis by DSM IV. See Summary 5.

Differences Reported by Parents

Unfortunately, very little research is available on girls with ADD or ADHD, so I sought information from women who have attention deficit disorders or who have daughters with this condition. The ADHD and ADD behaviors both girls and boys exhibit are similar. However, mothers noted these major differences:

- **Societal expectations for girls and boys are distinctly different.** Society expects "boys to be boys," but those same behaviors from girls are viewed as much worse. Even mothers treat their sons and daughters with attention deficits differently. One interesting study found that mothers give more praise and direction to their sons, even though the boys are less compliant than girls. Treatment professionals are not immune to this bias either. In another study, clinicians missed the diagnosis of attention deficit disorder in girls 50 percent of the time.

- **Girls with ADD or ADHD feel the sting of social rejection** much more intensely than boys do, according to their mothers. Both girls and boys with attention deficits may miss social cues, alienate classmates, and have few friends, but girls seem to be more bothered by their social delays. One clinician has observed that girls with ADD or ADHD who have trouble with social relationships are more likely to make low scores on the Picture Arrangement subtest of the *WISC-III* (Wechsler Intelligence Scale for Children). This subtest requires the student to pay attention to detail, pick up social cues from the pictures, and then sequence the pictures in the order that the event occurred.

- **Anxiety may be a major problem.** One mother talked about her daughter's anxiety. "She worries about things I haven't even thought up yet. When she worries, she just can't let it go. School is a major source of anxiety for her. She wants to do so well, often thinks she's doing well, and then is completely shocked to find out otherwise. In addition, she sets unrealistically high standards for herself. She'd like to be perfect, and anything less than that sets her up for anxiety."

- **Girls may compensate for their anxiety with compulsive behavior.** Informally, parents tell us that some girls resort to compulsive list making because they are so anxious about forgetting their school work. For example, one mother reported that when her older daughter with ADD turned 17 or 18 she started making lists because she was involved in so many activities that she was afraid she would forget something. This daughter can also lose track of time, or hyperfocus for three hours or more on a project she really loves. Her younger daughter, who also has ADD, is more laid back and doesn't seem to be particularly anxious.

Differences Reported by Teachers

- **Boys with ADD or ADHD tend to be more oppositional and aggressive than girls** and thus are more of a discipline problem. While 67 percent of boys with ADHD are diagnosed as having Oppositional Defiant Disorder (ODD), only 33 percent of girls qualify. Twenty-five percent of boys with ADHD have Conduct Disorders, while only 10 percent of girls meet the same criteria. So, girls who are struggling more quietly may not come to the teacher's attention as having any major problems.

Differences Reported by Researchers

Research regarding the differences between boys and girls with ADD or ADHD is limited. However, research that has been done seems to indicate that both girls and boys experience many of the same challenges. More research is needed to know the answers with some certainty, especially among teenagers.

- **Girls are less likely than boys to have ADD with hyperactivity** (girls—63 percent and boys—78 percent). To state this statistic in reverse, 37 percent of girls have the inattentive form of ADD compared with 22 percent of boys.

- **Girls have fewer intellectual problems and less severe deficits in executive functioning,** according to some research studies. Researchers found that only 16 percent of girls with ADHD qualify as having a specific learning disability (SLD), while 25 percent of boys do. Although girls in this study did not have learning deficits as severe as those of boys with ADD or ADHD, girls still have more learning problems than students who don't have an attention deficit. For example, 65 percent of girls in the study sought tutoring compared to only 10 percent of students without ADHD.

- **Information on the presence of coexisting conditions among girls with ADD/ADHD, especially teenagers, is lacking.** During childhood, girls with attention deficits have about the same rates of depression, anxiety, and bipolar disorder as boys. However, one study noted that during the teenage years, depression was twice as high in girls with ADHD (in 50 percent of girls and 24 percent of boys). When anxiety is high, a student is less likely to act or speak impulsively. Students who are anxious may also be more likely to follow school rules and complete school work on time.

Resources

Nadeau, Kathleen & Patricia Quinn. *Understanding Girls with AD/HD.* Silver Spring, MD: Advantage Books, 1999.

Solden, Sari. *Women with Attention Deficit Disorder.* Grass Valley, CA: Underwood Books, 1995.

SUMMARY 10 — Increased National Attention Focused on ADD/ADHD

When I was just starting out as a teacher, I thought that students with attention deficit disorders were simply not trying hard enough or were not disciplined enough to do well in school. Other teachers have undoubtedly felt the same way. Eventually, most teachers realize that it is not just laziness. However, very few realize just how complex and devastating attention deficit disorder can be in a student's life, especially if it is untreated.

Fortunately, in recent years many of the leading organizations in the country have begun to recognize what a profound impact this condition may have on a student's life. Recent breakthroughs in research on the brain have riveted national attention on this important condition, and there are several important ongoing studies. Key activities that have occurred within the last two years are briefly listed below. A more detailed summary of these activities is provided in Appendix B1.

NIMH ADD/ADHD Study

The National Institute of Mental Health (NIMH) has launched a new study involving almost 600 students with attention deficits aged seven to ten at six sites around the country. The fact that this research, known as the MTA study, is the largest ever instituted by NIMH on any topic for any age group makes a strong statement regarding the profound influence of ADD/ADHD in the lives of children and their families. This study will have a significant impact on educational and health care policies regarding these young people. Preliminary results were released in December 1999.

Key findings so far include:
- Two-thirds of these children had at least one other disorder such as depression, anxiety, or learning disabilities.
- Medication alone was much more effective than behavioral interventions alone.
- Medication alone was almost as effective as the combined treatment of medication plus behavioral interventions.
- Many students may be receiving medication doses that are too low for maximum improvement in school work and behavior.

The implications for teachers to consider are:
- Students with ADD or ADHD who continue to struggle after receiving treatment and classroom accommodations may have a coexisting condition that is not being treated.
- Behavioral strategies alone will not significantly change the school work or behavior of students with an attention deficit.
- Medication is a key part of treatment.

- Reports from teachers on how well medication is working are critical in helping doctors know when medication doses should be adjusted. (See Summary 55.)

American Academy of Pediatrics (AAP) Clinical Guidelines on Assessment of ADHD

On May 1, 2000, the AAP released new recommendations for primary care physicians, including pediatricians, to use when assessing school-age children for ADHD. Treatment guidelines are also currently being developed.

Surgeon General's Report on Mental Health

The first ever Surgeon General's Report on Mental Health was released in 1999. Attention deficit disorder was one of the few conditions that was discussed in some detail. Over the years, the Surgeon General's Reports have had a profound impact on shaping public policy and the health of the nation.

CDC/DOE Sponsored Conference on ADHD

The Atlanta-based Center for Disease Control and Prevention and the U.S. Department of Education, Office of Special Education Programs, jointly sponsored a conference in September 1999 on *"ADHD: A Public Health Perspective."* The CDC and DOE are concerned about the public health implications of ADD and ADHD on the behavior of our young people, including their increased risk for school failure, dropping out of school, risk-taking behavior, and, for some, substance abuse or involvement with the juvenile justice system.

NIH/NIMH Consensus Conference on ADD/ADHD

A Consensus Conference on Attention Deficit Disorders was held in November 1998 by the National Institutes of Health and National Institute of Mental Health. National experts were invited to meet and reach consensus on the disorder, its diagnosis, assessment, and best treatment practices.

1997 Revisions to the Individuals with Disabilities Education Act (IDEA)

After hearings were held around the country regarding needed revisions to IDEA, the federal education law, ADD and ADHD were added to the list of specific disabilities that could potentially qualify a student for special education services. A more detailed discussion of the impact of these revisions and the related regulations that were released in 1999 are provided in Section Four, Summaries 39-44.

Resources

AAP: *www.aap.org*—at website click "Search"; "guidelines for diagnosing ADHD."

CDC: *www.cdc.gov*—at website click "Search"; "ADHD home page" and "ADHD conference homepage," September 23-24, 1999; numerous articles on ADHD, some in Spanish.

DOE-IDEA: *www.ed.gov/offices/osers/idea*—at the website click "The Law." *www.lrp.com/ed/*—at the website click "IDEA Full Text." *www.pacer.org*—reader-friendly commentary on impact of IDEA on students with disabilities, including ADD/ADHD.

NIMH: *http://archpsyc.ama-assn.org*—at website click "Past Issues," December 1999.

Jensen, Peter, M.D. "Implications of the Multimodal Treatment Study (MTA) for Parents and Professionals," CHADD Conference presentation, Washington, DC, 1999.

Surgeon General: *www.surgeongeneral.gov*—at website click "Mental Health Report."

SECTION 2

Academic and Learning Issues

Three major problems often interfere with school success for students with ADD/ADHD:

1. **hidden learning problems,**
2. **executive function deficits,** and
3. **problems with medication.**

If these learning problems are untreated, students with an attention deficit disorder are more likely than their peers to fail a subject, be retained, be suspended, drop out of high school, or never graduate from college. Ninety percent will experience some difficulty during their school years. Several issues that cause major problems for students with attention deficits are discussed in detail in this section:

- Written Expression,
- Math,
- Memory,
- Homework,
- Major projects,
- Weekly reports.

Because of these problems, as well as the challenges presented by the attention deficit itself, most students with attention deficit disorders need *accommodations* to succeed in class. Under federal law, schools are mandated to make changes in the classroom, or accommodations, to help the teenager with a disability compensate for academic problems. For example, students who can't memorize multiplication tables may use a calculator, or students who have slow processing skills may be given extended time on tests. This section of the book provides an overview of accommodations that are helpful for teenagers with and without coexisting conditions. Specific suggestions are given to help teachers modify instruction in several key areas:

- Teaching methods and resources,
- Assignments,
- Testing and grading,
- Level of supervision,
- Technology.

Key Strategy: If the student is struggling, ***look for the learning problems discussed in this section and make accommodations in the classroom***.

Learning Problems Commonly Associated with ADD/ADHD

Several learning problems are common among teenagers with ADD/ADHD. Some learning problems are the result of: 1) the actual symptoms of ADD or ADHD, and others occur because a student also has 2) a Specific Learning Disability (SLD). Most studies of students with attention deficits have found that 25 to 30 percent have learning disabilities. However, when *written expression* was also evaluated in a recent study published in *ADHD Reports*, higher rates of learning disabilities were found. These problems, as well as practical implications for a student's school performance, are described below. However, keep in mind that each teenager with ADD or ADHD is *unique* and may have *some*, but not all of these learning difficulties.

Under the Individuals with Disabilities Education Act (IDEA), **students with attention deficits are clearly eligible for classroom accommodations** if their learning is adversely affected by their disorder. (See Summary 40.) However, all too often it is the behavior problems related to the ADD or ADHD that become the primary focus of school interventions. Unfortunately, learning problems are often overlooked as a result. Most students with attention deficits are experiencing serious academic problems that may be at the root of much of their misbehavior. Special efforts must be made to identify these academic problems and to implement appropriate adaptations in the regular classroom. Adaptations should be individualized and designed to accommodate each student's specific learning problems.

Symptoms of ADD/ADHD That Interfere with Learning

Several characteristics that are a direct result of having an attention deficit cause serious learning problems. Most teens with ADD/ADHD have problems in these areas:

1. Inattention/Poor Concentration

- Difficulty listening in class: may daydream; space out and miss lecture content or homework assignments.
- Lack of attention to detail: makes careless mistakes in work; doesn't notice errors in grammar, punctuation, capitalization, spelling, or changes in signs (+,-, x) or exponents in math.
- Difficulty staying on task and finishing school work; distractible: moves from one uncompleted task to another; when distracted, has difficulty refocusing on work.
- Lack of awareness of grades: may not know if passing or failing a class.

2. Impulsivity

- Rushes through work: doesn't read directions; takes short cuts in written work (such as doing math in his head); may not read the whole question before giving an answer; doesn't double check work.

- Difficulty delaying gratification: gives up working for rewards occurring in too distant future (two weeks to six months or more). (Working for grades requires delaying gratification for six weeks or more.)

3. Poor Organizational Skills

- Disorganized: loses homework, assignments, books, pencils, gym clothes, and supplies.
- Difficulty organizing thoughts: problems with sequencing ideas and writing essays.
- Difficulty getting started on tasks.
- Difficulty breaking tasks into manageable segments.
- Difficulty knowing what steps should be taken first.
- Difficulty planning ahead for completion of long-term projects.

4. Impaired Sense of Time

- Doesn't accurately judge the passage of time: loses track of time and is often late; when waiting, feels as if time creeps, and becomes impatient.
- Doesn't manage time well: doesn't anticipate how long tasks will take.
- Procrastinates: puts homework and projects off until the last minute.
- Weak time management skills.
- Difficulty developing timelines for completion of school work.

Learning Problems Often Accompanying ADD/ADHD

Several learning problems, although not directly related to ADD or ADHD, often occur along with it. If these problems are severe enough, the student will be diagnosed with a Specific Learning Disability (SLD). Deficits marked with an asterisk (*) may qualify as a Specific Learning Disability. The ADD/SLD connection is discussed in more detail in Summary 43.

1. **Language Deficits:** Several language-processing problems are common among teenagers with ADD/ADHD.

   1.1. Spoken Language* (Oral Expression)
   - Talks a lot spontaneously (ADHD) if she can choose the topic.
   - Has difficulty responding to questions where she must think and give organized, concise answers; may talk less or give rambling answers.
   - Reluctant to speak in class (ADD) because of slow processing speed and difficulty organizing ideas; may even be willing to accept failing grade rather than speak in front of the class.

   1.2. Written Language* (Verbal Expression; Input and Output)
   - Slow reading and writing; takes longer to complete work, produces less written work.
   - Difficulty writing essays; difficulty organizing ideas and putting them in proper sequence.
   - Difficulty getting ideas out of head and on paper; written test answers, discussion questions, or essays may be brief.

1.3. Processing Speed: Low scores on the Coding and Symbol Search subtests of the Weschler Intelligence Scale for Children (WISC-III) may be indicative of problems with ***hand eye coordination*** or ***slow processing speed.*** Slow processing may be caused by a combination of handwriting problems and cognitive processing problems. One way to rule out handwriting problems is to look at scores on the Symbol Search. Low scores on the Symbol Search alone may be indicative of problems with slow speed in processing of information since handwriting is not required on the subtest.

- Slow processing of information: reads, writes, and responds slowly; may take twice as long to do homework, class work, and complete tests; doesn't have time to double check answers;
- Recalls facts slowly;
- Can't quickly retrieve information stored in memory such as math facts, algebra formulas, foreign languages, history dates or facts, or grammar rules.

1.4. Math Computation*

- Difficulty automatizing basic math facts/slow math computation: cannot rapidly retrieve and use basic math facts such as multiplication tables, division, addition, or subtraction facts (Summaries 18-21).

1.5. Listening Comprehension

- Difficulty following directions: becomes confused with lengthy verbal directions, may not "hear" or pick out homework assignments from a teacher's lecture;
- Loses main point; difficulty identifying key points to write while taking notes.

1.6. Reading Comprehension*

- Can't remember what is read, then has to read it again; difficulty understanding and remembering what is read; difficulty with long reading passages.
- Makes errors when reading silently; may skip words, phrases, or lines; may lose place when reading.
- Difficulty identifying and remembering key facts from reading; linked to executive functioning deficits (holding key information in working memory).

2. **Poor Memory:** Students with ADD/ADHD may have difficulties with short-term, long-term, and/or working memory. Often these memory skills are interrelated. For example, if the student's working memory is limited, not as much information gets into storage or is easily retrieved from long-term memory.

2.1. Short-Term Memory Problems

- Difficulty remembering information in the here and now, for roughly 20 seconds: may not remember teacher requests, instructions, multi-step directions, or verbally presented math problems.

2.2. Working Memory Problems

- Difficulty holding information in mind while actively processing it; for example, may have difficulty holding a math problem in short-term memory while reaching into long-term memory to retrieve needed formulas and math facts to solve the problem.
- Difficulty retrieving information from long-term memory that is needed in working memory to solve a problem.
- May take longer on tests because of poor access to memory.

2.3. Long-Term Memory Problems

- Difficulty placing information into, and retrieving it from, long-term storage.
- Difficulty memorizing material such as multiplication tables, math facts, or formulas; spelling words; foreign languages; and/ or history dates.
- Difficulty quickly retrieving information stored in long-term memory.
- May not recall information memorized the night before, such as math facts, spelling words, or history facts.
- May not do well on tests requiring recall of information from long-term memory, even though the student studies.

2.4. Forgetfulness Related to Short- and Long-Term Memory Problems

- May forget homework assignments.
- May forget to take books home.
- May forget to turn in completed assignments to the teacher.
- May forget special assignments or make-up work or tests.
- May forget to stay after school for teacher conferences or detention.

3. Poor Fine-Motor Coordination

- Handwriting is poor; sometimes, small and difficult to read.
- May write slowly; may avoid writing and homework because it is difficult.
- May prefer to print rather than write cursive, even as an adult.
- Produces less written work.
- May be artistic; motor coordination required for art may be quite good.

Difficulties in school may be caused by a combination of several learning problems. One student may not take good notes in class because she can't pay attention, can't pick out main points, and has poor fine-motor coordination. Another student may not do well on a test because she reads, thinks, and writes slowly, has difficulty organizing her thoughts, and has difficulty memorizing and quickly retrieving the information from memory.

An example of how teachers and parents may use information about a student's specific learning problems is provided in Summary 46. This summary contains an outline of one student's learning problems in high school and appropriate classroom accommodations.

Learning Styles

SUMMARY 12

Most teachers today are well aware that students have different learning styles. Consequently, teachers know they can be more effective if they vary their teaching strategies. Although the issue of learning styles is a complex concept that obviously cannot be addressed in detail in this book, a brief overview may be helpful. Students with ADD or ADHD are often visual learners and do not learn as easily in traditional lectures where they passively listen to teachers.

Gardner's Theory of Multiple Intelligences

Although it would be impossible for teachers to read everything that educators and psychologists have written about learning styles, most teachers are familiar with Howard Gardner's seven different learning styles. Gardner believes that each of us is 100 percent smart, and that our total intelligence is made up of at least seven different types of "smartness." This is in contrast to traditional IQ tests, which measure only language and math intelligence.

Here is how Sandra Rief, author of several best-selling books on ADD/ADHD, summarizes Gardner's types of intelligence:

1. **Linguistic Learner**—*Word smart*: "learns best through oral and written language and by hearing, saying, and seeing words."
2. **Logical Mathematical Learner**—*Number smart*: "learns best by categorizing, making their own discoveries, classifying and working with abstract patterns and relationships."
3. **Spatial Learner**—*Art smart*: "learns best through visual presentations and by visualizing, using his mind's eye, and working with colors/pictures."
4. **Body-Kinesthetic Learner**—*Body smart*: "learns best through hands-on activities and by doing, touching, moving, and interacting with space."
5. **Musical Learner**—*Music smart:* "learns best through rhythm, music, and melody."
6. **Interpersonal Learner**—*People smart*: "learns best by sharing, relating, interacting, and cooperating with others."
7. **Intrapersonal Learner**—*Self smart*: "learns best by working alone, having self-paced instruction, and individualized projects."

Although students with attention deficits are not all alike in their learning styles, many of them may learn *spatially* (by seeing) and *kinesthetically* (by doing). They seem to have greater difficulty with linguistic and logical mathematical learning.

Dr. Edna Copeland, author *of Attention, Please!* and one of the early pioneers in this field, reports that she has observed a shift in student learning styles from auditory to visual during the last twenty years or so. She estimates that ***60 percent of all students prefer and perform better with visual learning strategies!*** Furthermore, 30 percent do not learn well auditorily, in other words from just listening to the teacher. At least 50 percent of all students are frustrated with traditional left-brain, sequential type assignments. In other words, school work that requires logical, linear sequencing and memorization of facts is difficult and students prefer work that involves creative exploration. So, learning by listening to teachers lecture and by reading their textbooks (*linguistic learning*) often will be more challenging for students with attention deficits. Sometimes because these students learn differently from others, they may come to believe that they are not very smart.

Impact of Teacher Learning Style on Teaching

Since my own learning style is more *auditory, logical mathematical, linear, sequential, and convergent*, as a young teacher, I tended to teach that way. In other words, I gave lectures to my students and expected them to memorize the right answers. I wanted students to go step by step, in a logical order, and quickly narrow things down to one right answer. Since it comes naturally to teach using one's personal learning style, ***teachers should be aware of their personal style and make an effort to use a greater variety of teaching strategies***.

Students with attention deficits may have a more innovative, intuitive, and divergent learning style. So, being creative and finding their own way of solving a problem may be more appealing to them. Although these students must learn to produce school work that is logical, linear, and sequential, it is often very difficult for them. Consequently, ***students with ADD or ADHD often need more hands-on activities that incorporate visual cues*** to master skills such as math or writing essays or book reports!

Numerous strategies that rely on visual cues and hands-on and interactive activities are included in Summaries 13A – 13E. In addition, these learning and thinking differences, also referred to as ***left and right brain thinking***, are discussed in Summary 33 with regard to their impact on time management.

Resources

Copeland, Edna. "We Have Treated the ADD: Now We Shall Begin." ADDA National Conference workshop, Atlanta, GA, May 2000.

Gardner, Howard. *Multiple Intelligences: The Theory in Practice*. New York: Basic Books, 1993.

Rief, Sandra F. *How to Reach and Teach ADD/ADHD Children*. West Nyack, NY: The Center for Applied Research in Education, 1993. (Additional helpful information is available at *www.sandrarief.com*)

General Teaching Tips

Teaching today is such a demanding job, especially when individualized instruction is required to meet each student's needs. It's incredibly difficult for a teacher to single-handedly tailor his or her teaching to meet everyone's needs. So, tapping other resources is critical. Remember that **you don't have to be the only teacher** in your class! Seek assistance from students, computer technology, classroom aides, or parents.

If you've done everything you can and the student with ADD or ADHD continues to struggle, ask for help. Talk with veteran teachers or the guidance counselor to come up with some new ideas. Some states have opted to establish teams of educators who meet to brainstorm ideas to help struggling students. In Georgia, they are called "Student Support Teams" but these groups may go by different names in different states. Typically, a team of educators is available to help any student who is struggling academically, whether or not she needs special education services. However, if problems are serious, this team may refer the student to the IEP team for an evaluation for special education services. The IEP Team, comprised of a group of teachers and administrators, meets to discuss the strengths and needs of students receiving special education and to develop educational plans for them. For more information, see Summary 50, "So the Student Is Failing: What Should the Teacher Do Now?"

A summary of teaching strategies that I have culled from local colleagues, nationally recognized educators, and my own experiences as a teacher and school psychologist is provided below. These tips may be helpful in teaching all students, not just those with attention deficits.

Although it goes without saying, these strategies will *not* work with *all* students with ADD/ADHD. Pick and choose strategies from this section that you think are most likely to work with a specific student and that fit comfortably with your teaching philosophy. Modify the plan or try a different strategy until you find the ones that work best for each student.

If you want to know if an accommodation is working, look at a few key barometers:

1. Is the student completing more school work?
2. Are grades improving?
3. Does the student seem less tense, happier, and in fact seem to enjoy class?
4. Don't overlook the value of asking the real experts—the teenagers themselves—whether it's working.

Some General Advice

1. **Simple interventions are usually best!** Don't make more modifications than are necessary.

2. **Seek student input and approval.** As accommodations are developed for each student, remember to involve them in making decisions. Student buy-in is a critical part of this process. You may develop the most extraordinary plan, but if the student is too embarrassed or overwhelmed to use it, the plan won't work. So, give the student some choices. For example, you might say something like this:

> *"Students with ADD often have difficulty with math. I think there are a few things we could do to help you in class. Here are two or three choices....Would you like to try one of these options?"* If you want to be more direct, *"Which one would you like to try?"* If you feel strongly that one particular accommodation would be helpful, then say just that: *"Many students with ADD find it helpful to . . . do every third problem. Would you like to try that?"*

3. **Remember the most common problem areas.** Although each student's problem areas will vary, often the greatest challenges occur in written expression, math, memorization, spelling, punctuation, or foreign languages.

4. **Teacher assignments are critical.** Teenagers with attention deficits tend to do well in those classes where the teacher likes them and may fail the same subject with a teacher who doesn't like them Students and teachers do better when students are matched with teachers who:

   - tend to use a variety of learning strategies,
   - have a hands-on, active classroom learning environment,
   - can channel their students' energy and cope with their learning challenges, and
   - enjoy working with them.

The strategies mentioned below are explained in greater detail in Summaries 13-A through 13-E (on classroom accommodations) and Summaries 57-61 (on general classroom management and behavioral strategies).

Use these Strategies:	to make these needed changes in class
Modify Teaching *Methods* (13-A)	to match the teaching style to students' learning strengths.
Modify *Resources* for students (13-A)	to give more individualized help.
Modify *Assignments* (13-B)	to reduce written work.
Modify *Testing and Grading* (13-C)	to give adequate time to complete work and tests.
Modify *Level of Supervision* (13-D)	to increase student monitoring with help from others.
Use *Technology* (13-E)	to maximize learning and to take advantage of the student's strengths.
Modify *Classroom Management Strategies* (58)	to provide needed structure and prevent behavior problems.
Modify *Classroom Set-up* (58)	to provide the best seating assignment.
Modify *Class Schedule* (58)	to ensure that medication "peak work" time occurs during difficult classes.
Monitor *Medication Effectiveness* (52-57)	to ensure that medication is providing maximum benefit.

Resources for Section 2

Bromley, Karen, Linda I. DeVitis & Marcia Modlo. *50 Graphic Organizers for Reading, Writing, & More: Grades 4-8.* New York: Scholastic Professional Books, 1999. These organizers can be helpful for middle and high school students.

Crutsinger, Carla. *Thinking Smarter: Skills for Academic Success.* Carrollton, TX: Brainworks, 1992. This book offers strategies and reproducible worksheets for teaching memory techniques, time management, note taking, test taking, and homework skills.

Dendy, Chris A. Zeigler. *Teenagers with ADD.* Bethesda, MD: Woodbine House, 1995.

Deschler, Donald, Edwin S. Ellis & B. Keith Lenz. *Teaching Adolescents with Learning Disabilities: Strategies and Methods.* Denver, CO: Love Publishing Co., 1996. (Available from mastrmnds@aol.com or www.lovepublishing.com)

Dornbush, Marilyn P. & Sheryl K. Pruitt. *Teaching the Tiger.* Duarte, CA: Hope Press, 1995.

Elliott, Raymond & Lou Anne Worthington. *ADHD Project Facilitate: An Inservice Education Program for Educators and Parents.* Tusculoosa, AL: University of Alabama, Programs in Special Education, 1995. (Information available from mastrmnds@aol.com)

Ellis, Ed. *Using Graphic Organizers to Make Sense of the Curriculum.* Tusculoosa, AL: MasterMinds, 1998. (mastrmnds@aol.com)

Eisenberg, Nancy L. & Pamela H. Esser. *Teach and Reach Students with Attention Deficit Disorders.* Houston: MultiGrowth Resources, 1997.

Flynn, Chris. *Graphic Organizers . . . Helping Children Think Visually.* Cypress, CA: Creative Teaching Press, Inc., 1995. These organizers may be helpful even though the book's listed age range is Grades 3-6.

Greene, Jane Fell. *Language!* Longmont, CO: Sopris West, 1996. (1-800-547-6747; www.sopriswest.com) Dr. Greene developed the program for incarcerated middle and high school age youths. The students gained three years in reading in only 22 weeks. See www.ldonline.org for more information and an interview with Dr. Greene.

Irwin-DeVitis, L. & D. Pease. "Using Graphic Organizers for Learning and Assessment in Middle Level Classrooms." *Middle School Journal*, 1995, 26 (5), 57-64.

Jones, Clare. *Attention Deficit Disorders: Strategies for School-Age Children.* San Antonio, TX: Communication Skills Builders, 1994.

Jones, Clare. "Strategies for School Success: Middle School through High School." CHADD National Conference workshop, New York, NY, 1998.

Levine, Mel. *Educational Care.* Educators Publishing Service, Cambridge, MA, 1994.

Rief, Sandra F. *How to Reach and Teach ADD/ADHD Children.* West Nyack, NY: The Center for Applied Research in Education, 1993. Although this book is for elementary-age children, many of the suggestions may be modified for middle and high school students. Rief has developed numerous materials, including videotapes, that educators will find helpful. (See www.sandrarief.com)

Rief, Sandra F. & Julie A. Heimburge. *How to Reach and Teach All Students in the Inclusive Classroom.* West Nyack, NY: The Center for Applied Research in Education, 1996.

Rose, Mary. *10 Easy Writing Lessons that Get Kids Ready for Writing Assessments.* New York: Scholastic Professional Books, 1999. My daughter, Audrey, found this book for her elementary age son at a local school supply store. It contains some great, creative ideas. For example, for one writing assignment, students are asked to take three things that tell something about themselves and put them into a lunch bag. Next they talk about it in class, the teacher asks leading questions, and then they write about it.

University of Kansas Center for Research on Learning. Dr. Don Deschler and others at UK have developed an intensive teacher-training curriculum known as *SIMS, the Strategic Instruction Model.* See their website for information: www.ku-crol.org

Welch, Ann. "Increasing Academic Engagement of Students with ADHD." *ADHD Reports,* V.7, N.3, June 1999.

Judy Wood Publishing Company, 12411 Southbridge Dr., Midlothian VA 23113. The Judy Wood Catalog contains a wealth of resources to help teach challenging students, for example, guided outlines for writing, understanding literature, or research reports; spelling sprints; 7 ways to easy A's in writing literature, math, or foreign languages. 877-583-9966, www.judywood.com.

Zentall, Sydney. "Growing Pains in Education: Blame/Shame, Rename, and Responsibility." National CHADD Conference presentation, San Antonio, TX, 1997.

Modify Teaching Methods and Resources

1. **Provide More Visual Cues and Reminders:** Since students with ADD or ADHD frequently have multiple learning problems, they may benefit from teaching styles that use a multisensory approach. In other words, they remember more if they *hear* the teacher say something while *seeing* them demonstrate the skill. Later they may see pictures of the skill or words in their minds. Obviously, students are more likely to remember material that is related to their personal experience.

   1.1. Model skills for students. Since students with attention deficits are often visual learners, modeling by the teacher can be extremely effective. Overhead projectors are especially helpful for this purpose. In addition, teachers can face the class when they write on the overhead rather than having their backs to students while writing on the board. One teacher writes in different colors to denote important information.

   1.1.1. In Language Arts class, *teach students how to write an essay by actually writing one* in class. See Summaries 15 and 16.

   1.2. Leave *key points* being taught on the overhead or on the board for the whole class. For example, leave rules for grammar or conjugation of foreign language verbs. Preferably leave information in the same location on the board so students know where to look for it. Number steps rather than use letters of the alphabet.

   1.3. Place *key words* from the lecture around the room and point to them when discussed. Dr. Ron Walker, educational consultant, developed this creative strategy, known as *visual posting*. The teacher writes key words on strips of poster board and places them around the room in easy sight, for example on the wall, board, or filing cabinet. The strips may also be placed in areas where students tend to focus when they tune out, such as near the window. Then as the teacher lectures, she points to each key fact as she discusses it.

   1.3.1. *Pretest* before instruction. The students are tested on key information before the lesson is presented. The teacher states in advance what the key facts are that she wants students to learn.

   1.3.2. *Quiz* briefly after the lecture. After the lecture is completed, the teacher does a brief oral quiz. "Who sailed across the ocean and discovered America?" Point to the correct card and the whole class repeats the answer.

   1.3.3. Test with cards in place. The students are given the test with all the information still on the wall in plain sight.

   1.3.4. Give the final test. Take all the material down from the walls and give the final test on the material.

1.3.5. Post important information near the pencil sharpener. The teacher may post spelling words or a reminder for a test near the pencil sharpener, the classroom door, or other areas where students may stand for a short period of time.

1.4. Use *color* to highlight important facts. If a student continually makes the same spelling or grammar error, highlight the corrected word or letters within the word that she usually misses. Color helps students remember things better. Red (or hot pink) may be the most memorable of colors.

1.5. Give *guided lecture* notes daily to all students. Give students copies of the teacher's daily lecture notes in outline form with key points marked. Use skeletal outlines that allow space between sentences for the student to write notes.

1.6. Make a wallet size *laminated copy* of key facts for reference (basic math facts, formulas, verb conjugation for Spanish). Allow the student to keep a copy of the card for use in class.

1.7. Use informative *posters* in the classroom. Posters may provide visual reminders of important historical events, grammar rules, or math concepts. "Wild and wacky" illustrations will help students commit these facts to memory more easily. Students may be able to picture the poster in their mind during the test. An example of a memorable poster that helps in teaching multiplication tables is available in Summary 20. See Summary 22 for memory tips.

1.8. Use *graphic organizers*. Numerous books of graphic organizers are commercially available at school supply stores. Graphic organizers are often helpful because they: 1) make abstract concepts concrete, 2) help students visually organize material, and 3) assist with memory recall. These preprinted reproducible blank forms provide great visual cues for these students, increasing the likelihood of their remembering the information. A few examples of graphic organizers are listed at the end of this section under Resources, plus two blank organizers (Appendices A2 and A3) are provided for writing essays. One form includes drawings that help a student visually organize her thoughts and the other provides an outline for writing the essay. For example:

- The student practices *sequencing skills* for describing a novel or historical event by filling words or pictures in sections of movie film frames or railroad tracks.
- She develops essay ideas by brainstorming and *writing the ideas in clusters*. This process is sometimes referred to as mind mapping or webbing.
- She may use *guides for comparison* or persuasive writing.
- She uses a *summary organizer* to prepare to write a book summary.
- She learns to make choices by *listing pros and cons* on a form and deciding which option is best.

- She identifies *the five Ws of report or essay writing* on the drawings ("who" is written on a face, "when" on a clock, and "where" on a state outline).
- She can use a *double Venn diagram* (two overlapping circles) to show how two issues are alike and how they are different.
- She uses a *content organizer* to learn terms and definitions in a new chapter. Terms and definitions are listed in columns and the student is asked to match them.
- She uses a *content diagram* to place key information in columns such as type of rock, how formed, and examples of each.
- She classifies and describes triangles by angles and sides.

Dr. Ed Ellis, Chairman of the Special Education Department at the University of Alabama, has done extensive work in the development of graphic organizers. Teachers may find his books, *Using Graphic Organizers to Make Sense of the Curriculum* and *Strategic Graphic Organizer Instruction,* especially helpful. (More information on these and other teaching strategies is available at www.mastrmnds.com or mastrmnds@aol.com).

1.9. Review for exams in class. Review materials in class that will be on tests.

1.9.1. Give review summaries for exams. Outline a summary of material being reviewed. Write each fact on an overhead projector. By writing the outline in class, teachers slow the pace of their lecture, which makes it easier for students to keep up with taking notes.

1.9.2. Identify key points as such. State the obvious: "This is a key point. Mark it. This will be on the test."

1.9.3. Teach review skills. Show students how to review material—for example, look for bold or *italicized* print, capitalized headings for each section, captions under pictures, and summaries at the end of the chapter.

2. **Give additional individualized help:** If you are too busy, ask others to help. You can make your teaching even more effective by seeking other "teachers" to help you.

   2.1. Use paired learning. Provide class time for students to pair off and discuss (teach each other) the new concepts in an assignment. This method of instruction is also referred to as classwide peer tutoring. See discussion in Summary 19 as it relates to math and peer tutors.

   2.2. Use peer tutors. Ask the student with ADD or ADHD to tutor a younger student or a classmate who is learning similar concepts. Tutors usually learn more than the person receiving the tutoring does.

   2.3. Use classroom aides. Classroom aides may help give the student more individualized attention when working on academics or monitoring homework assignments and completion. Typically, this accommodation is available only to those students who qualify for special education under federal law. Inclusion of a classroom aide must be written into the student's individualized educational program (IEP) or Section 504 Plan.

3. Increase active class participation of all students:

3.1. Use group response. Some teachers increase student participation by asking a question, then having all the students respond with a card or hand signal system. Students raise their thumbs or hold up a card to indicate their answer. The teacher calls on a student who has the correct answer. Then the teacher may use choral response, asking everyone to repeat the correct answer. These active teaching techniques involve more students, plus give the teacher a sense of which students don't understand the material. They may work better for students with an attention deficit since there are fewer opportunities to daydream or space-out.

3.1.1. *Hand signals* **may include:**
- thumbs up, if the answer to the question is yes, thumbs down (no), or palm out flat (uncertain or don't know).

3.1.2. *Response cards* **may include:**
- three colored *plastic cards*: red (no), green (yes), and yellow (don't know).
- *Yes* and *no* cards with the same answer printed on both sides of the card so the student can see which word she is holding up and not get confused about her answer.
- Other cards may include the words: *True/false, noun/verb, or add/subtract.*

3.1.3. *Card fans* **may be made by fastening cards together with a ring or fastener.** Categories may be listed on the card and the students hold up the correct card in response to the teacher's question. For example, list categories such as *parts of speech (noun, verb, adjective); states of matter (solid, liquid, or gas), or A/B/C/D for multiple choice questions.*

3.1.4. *Dry erase boards* **are better for subjects like math or spelling that require specific, brief answers.**

3.1.5. Use *Choral response.* **Students answer questions in unison. See Summary 22 on memory.**

3.2. Provide active, hands-on learning experiences.

3.2.1. Develop a play to act out major historical events or the story line of a book.

3.2.2. Make a pop-up book. Create a book with pictures and drawings that explain a story or event. Directions for making a pop-up book are provided in Summary 22.

3.2.3. Use videotape. Allow the student to videotape herself giving a book report or research on a specific event or topic.

3.2.4. Use physical movement. Try the teaching strategy referred to as *total physical response (TPR).* As the term implies, the student is physically involved in the learning. For example, students might arm wrestle to demonstrate the importance of creating equally powerful protagonists and antagonists. See Summary 16 for examples of using TPR in language arts class.

4. **Allow students to use manipulatives to increase alertness and attention:** Manipulatives and seemingly purposeless fidgeting or doodling may actually help students learn, according to Dr. Sydney Zentall, a leading educational researcher on attention deficits and co-author of *Seven Steps to Homework Success.* This ***physical activity seems to help the student maintain a higher level of mental alertness*** so that she can listen to the teacher or work on an assignment. Otherwise the student's attention and alertness may begin to fade.

One school psychologist explained that when students with attention deficits were being tested, they seemed to concentrate better if they were allowed to handle a Koosh Ball while they were thinking. Sometimes when my son studies for a test, he holds and rubs a strand of worry beads. Pipe cleaners or paper clips are other good manipulatives for students to use.

5. **Use supplies that are helpful to students:**

   5.1. Use mechanical pencils. Many students with an attention deficit like to write with mechanical pencils. Some students even have included use of these pencils in their IEP as an accommodation. Although the reasons for this preference aren't totally clear, the students believe it helps them with their handwriting difficulties. Perhaps the pencils provide better writing control, greater accuracy in writing, tactile sensitivity, and novelty.
   Pentel has a "quicker clicker" and a new "thicker clicker" that are popular. Students like the textured grip plus the location of the finger-tip "clicker." The student can extend the lead without having to mash a button on the top. Number 9 lead is preferable since it is the strongest.

   5.2. Use a textured pencil grip. Some students like to put textured grips on their regular number two pencils to improve their writing grip.

   5.3. Use a clipboard. Some students find they can work more efficiently if they put their paper on a clipboard. This seems to give them more working desk space and keeps their paper from sliding away.

6. **Teach learning strategies for specific academic skills:** Students with ADD/ADHD may lack basic academic skills such as reading, comprehension, and written expression. Teachers may have to backtrack and teach basic skills such as the learning strategies taught at the University of Kansas.

   6.1. Provide teacher training. With special education students increasingly being included in regular classes, demands on teachers' skills have increased significantly. Teachers may need specialized training for teaching students with learning problems. Examples of training curricula include:
   • ***The Strategic Instruction Model for Teaching Learning Strategies.*** The University of Kansas Center for Research on

Learning is one of the national leaders in studying learning issues. They have developed an intensive teacher training curriculum known as SIMS, the Strategic Instruction Model. This curriculum breaks down skills such as sentence and paragraph writing and shows teachers how to teach these skills more effectively. Training sessions are scheduled at several sites around the country. The 26 learning strategies included in their curriculum include skills such as paraphrasing strategy, four strategies to help with memory, test taking strategies, cooperative thinking strategies, self advocacy, and basic math strategies. Additional information is available from *www.ku-crl.org.* Local school systems and education agencies also sponsor numerous training opportunities that may be helpful.

- *Language!* **for Teaching Reading and Comprehension.** Dr. Jane Fell Greene developed *Language!*, a special program to help improve the reading skills of students who were significantly below grade level. Dr. Greene created this program for incarcerated middle and high school age youths. The students who participated in the program gained three years in reading in twenty-two weeks. This could be a great resource for middle and high students who are having trouble reading and comprehending material. See *www.ldonline.org* for more information and an interview with Dr. Greene. (Program available from Sopris West 1-800-547-6747; *www.sopriswest.com).*

- **Inservice Training Program for Teachers.** In 1995, the U.S. DOE/OSEP and the University of Alabama jointly funded *ADHD Project Facilitate* to develop "An Inservice Education Program for Educators and Parents." This comprehensive program included some very helpful materials on a range of topics: ADHD General Knowledge Base, Assessment of Children with ADHD, ADHD Interventions, Legal issues and ADHD, and a Facilitator's Manual. The materials in ADHD Interventions were very practical and especially welldone, including topics such as behavioral intervention strategies, setting up point and token economies, graphic organizers, teaching study skills, and self-monitoring. (See Summary 60 for more information on *Project Facilitate.*)

Modify Assignments

As discussed in Summary 11, students with ADD or ADHD may have difficulties with verbal expression, slow processing speed, fine motor coordination, or other problems that make written work more challenging. As a result, these teenagers often take much longer to complete class- and homework, sometimes twice as long as their peers. This may explain why students with attention deficits so studiously avoid homework. It takes a lot more effort for them to complete written work than their peers. This is not to suggest that teachers should never give written class- and homework to students. Rather, the length of assignments should be modified so that these students are not spending significantly more time than their peers on the same assignments. Typically, *teachers can reduce the amount of written work pretty easily without compromising the amount of academic material mastered.*

1. **Reduce written work:** Since completing written work—especially homework—is often the biggest academic challenge that these teenagers face, reducing written work is very important. Suggestions for the best ways to reduce written work are given below.

   1.1. **Reduce the amount of homework.** Estimate how long homework should take, and then ask the student to report how long it actually takes her to complete homework. If it is taking too much time, reduce the amount of homework. To help determine how much homework is too much, see Summary 24. For example, a National NEA/PTA policy suggests that a sixth grade student should spend up to a total of about one hour on homework (ten minutes per grade).

      1.1.1. **Assign fewer problems or questions.** Where feasible, assign fewer problems, sentences, or questions, if that still covers the necessary skills and mastery of major concepts. For some students with ADD or ADHD, math homework may be the biggest problem and should be reduced. For example, the student may be asked to complete every second or third problem.

      1.1.2. **Write the correct answers only.** Have the student write only the correct answers, rather than the whole sentence or question. The goal is to see whether the student knows the answer to the question, not to see if she can copy the question.

      1.1.3. **Fill in the blanks.** Allow students to photocopy math problems or scan in science or history questions from the book and fill in the blanks instead of writing the whole problem or sentences.

      1.1.4. **Allow students to dictate school work.** Sometimes the student may dictate a report to a parent or friend (scribe) who types up the information. Researchers have found that the quality and length of reports and essays were better when students with learning problems dictated their work.

1.1.5. Substitute creative activities for written assignments. Develop an *Assignment Menu* that offers students the choice of creative, active assignments as a substitute for written assignments. For example, one Language Arts teacher allowed her students to give book reports accompanied by a videotape of two or three favorite scenes from a book, a cake as described in a book, and an oil painting of a famous poet. Other examples include writing a play, building a model, writing about imaginary travels, and contacting a space center and getting their reaction to the topic. See Summary 16 for more details.

1.2. Teach tips to improve notetaking.

1.2.1. Teach shorthand. For common words, help the student create her own shorthand to speed up taking notes. Don't use this strategy if this becomes too complicated, distracting, or difficult.

Examples: wrds tht R commly u'd 2 cre8 y'r own short/hd.

T = the	sp = spelling
rd = read	hw = homework
wr = write	w/i = within
w/o = without	< = less than
> = more than	$ = money
? = question	bks = books
EZ = easy	mtg = meeting
cap = capital	wr/u = write up
p. = page	wrk = work
ex = example	B4 = before
wkly = weekly	@ = at
impt = important	& = and
asign = assignment	% = percent
y = why	c = with
gov = government	whn = when
- = negative or subtract	+ = plus or positive
# = number	

1.2.2. Take notes in two columns. Show the student how to take notes in two columns, one for the main idea and the second column for more details about the main idea. The student may fold her notebook paper in half lengthwise or simply draw a vertical line to divide the paper in half.

1.2.3. Identify key points. Tell the student, "This is important, write it down."

1.3. Reduce *notetaking*. Students with ADD or ADHD can have trouble focusing on what is being said in class because they are distracted by the writing process. Try these strategies to enable them to listen better:

1.3.1. Identify a notetaker for the whole class. Ask another student who is good in the subject to take notes and star the important issues of the lesson. The designated student takes notes, makes ten copies, and places them in a box in the room available to any student in need.

1.3.2. Jointly identify a notetaker. Sometimes a student with an attention deficit does better with a personal notetaker. Try to involve her in the selection process. Perhaps give a choice of two or three students. Sometimes, the notetaker and student don't even know each other since the notetaker may be in another class. The notetaker in one class takes notes and leaves them in a designated spot for pickup later. The big question is, "Will the student with ADD/ADHD remember to pick it up?" If she consistently forgets, develop a way to help her remember.

1.3.3. Use NCR (carbonless) paper, or even carbon paper, to make notetaking easier. For example, duplicate checks are made from this special paper. You simply tear off the bottom copy of notes and give it to the student. Unfortunately, the paper is not easy to find and many school systems have to print their own. Try asking the director of special education where to get the paper.

1.3.4. Provide guided lecture notes. The need for notetaking is reduced when a student has guided lecture notes to follow, as described in Summary 13-A.

1.4. Shorten keyboarding assignments. Although working on a computer is often a lifesaving skill for students with attention deficits, initially their keyboarding skills are often terrible. Their combined learning problems related to memorization, slow retrieval and processing, and fine motor skills are horrendous obstacles to mastering keyboarding skills. Teachers may consider using the *Type to Learn* program discussed in Summary 13-E, which uses memory tricks to help student learn. Some teachers are reluctant to reduce keyboarding assignments but it is a *critical accommodation* for most of these students!

1.5. Accept unfinished class work, sometimes. Occasionally, if the student seems to understand the concepts or is in crisis, accept unfinished class work without piling it on in addition to homework assignments. These students may reach a point where the amount of overdue school work is overwhelming. They may give up because they feel they can never catch up.

1.6. Don't assign sentences to be written as punishment. Years ago, it was common to have a student write a "hundred sentences" for punishment for failing to pay attention in class, running in the hall, not turning in homework, or chewing gum. Obviously, this old-fashioned punishment does not help these students pay attention or complete homework.

2. **Break assignments and long-term projects into segments:** When assignments or projects seem long or complicated, students withattention deficit disorders may feel overwhelmed and struggle to get started. Breaking the task into segments can be extremely helpful and help break the logjam. In addition, long-term projects often cause problems because students forget them, lack the organizational skills and awareness of time to plan ahead, or fail to budget enough time to complete the project. See Summaries 35-38.

2.1. Read to the clip. For reading assignments, Dr. Clare Jones suggests dividing the material into three or four manageable sections and marking the sections with colorful paper clips. The student tells herself to "read to the clip." Now she can "see" how close she is to being finished.

2.2. Divide assignments into sections. Divide math or other homework into manageable sections. The student may take a break when she finishes a section. Worksheets may actually be cut or folded in half so the student can "see" how much she has left to complete.

2.3. Assign separate due dates for different parts of a long-term project.

2.4. Grade each section of the project independently.

3. **Give a job or cue card for difficult tasks:** One reason students with attention deficits often procrastinate is that they feel overwhelmed by large multi-step projects. They lack the skills necessary to break the assignment down into the required action steps. Sometimes they truly don't know what to do or where to begin. Providing a job card with a brief outline of the steps necessary to complete the project can help. Working on these skills provides the opportunity to teach or *shape* the new skill. (For a discussion of shaping behavior see Summary 61.) For example, the teacher may initially:

- Discuss the steps required to complete the assignment with the whole class.
- Then write the steps on the board.
- Ask the class to copy the steps down on paper.
- If the student seems to have trouble getting started on the assignment, discuss the steps required and help her write them down on the job card.

4. **Seek quality, not quantity:** Ann Welch, a veteran special education teacher, says, "Fewer high quality responses are preferable to more poor quality responses." She explains that when teachers give assignments they are often looking for three things: 1) speed, 2) completeness (number of problems done), and 3) accuracy. Teachers want

students to finish 30 problems (number), before the end of class or by tomorrow (speed), and have the right answers (accuracy). Since students with attention deficits often work very slowly, typically they will complete fewer problems. Unfortunately, grading criteria "that focus only on speed or completeness, encourage many students to do poor quality work." Welch suggests that modified assignments of reasonable length and difficulty are more likely to produce quality work. For example: "'Write three complete, interesting sentences with no more than two spelling or punctuation errors.'"

SUMMARY 13-C Modify Testing and Grading

Let's assume that the primary goal of testing is to measure what a student knows, *not* how well the student takes a particular type of test. Since students with ADD/ADHD have learning problems that make some types of tests much more difficult for them, it makes sense to modify the style of testing. Test modifications have been a lifesaver for many students with attention deficits. In fact, many students with attention deficits say that receiving extended time on tests, special projects, and homework has been their most helpful classroom accommodation.

Giving **extended test time** is a great idea, but it may be difficult to provide easily in middle and high school:

- Finding uncommitted class time to finish the test is difficult. Students may change classes every hour. Or, under the block scheduling system, they may be expected to finish the test the first forty-five minutes and then start a new lecture the second half of the period. If students continue working on the test, they will miss their next class or lecture material from the second half of the block class. They will also have difficulty concentrating on the test if the rest of the class is listening to a lecture.
- Maintaining the integrity of the test, also known as preventing cheating, is a primary concern in giving extended time on tests. Teachers and administrators are concerned that if test times are broken up, some students might look up correct answers before they return to finish the test. Most teachers prefer that students finish the test the same day they start work on it.

Test integrity is very difficult to maintain even under normal circumstances. For example, if a teacher has four sections of the same class and gives the same test to each, students in earlier classes can share test information with students in later classes.

However, most students with ADD or ADHD are hoping simply to pass the test, not make an A. These students often don't remember or plan ahead to get answers or ask friends for help. I don't think it ever occurred to my son to ask other students or look up answers to the remainder of the test questions. Of course, if a student with an attention deficit were in the running for class valedictorian, maintaining test integrity would take on more urgency.

1. Give extended test time while preserving test integrity:

    1.1. Find *alternative times* for test completion.

        1.1.1. Include a special education supervision period or study hall in the student's schedule. This period may be used for several purposes such as finishing tests, doing make-up work, receiving assistance, or collecting the right books and homework assignments to take home.

1.1.2. Give the test before or after school or during a portion of lunch. The student could stay after school or come early in the morning to start the test or complete any unfinished questions. Or the test could be tied into a lunch period. Perhaps, the student may bring lunch from home or another student may bring her something from the lunchroom. For students with sleep disturbances, tests before school may not be a good choice.

1.1.3. Complete the test during the second half of a block scheduled class. Some students can learn the new information that is missed with notes from a note-taker.

1.1.4. Allow a tutor to monitor test completion. Some students with attention deficits receive tutoring after school as required in the IEP/504 Plan or because the parents have paid for private tutoring. If there is a comfortable working relationship between the school and tutor, the tutor could monitor all or a portion of the test.

2. **Select a good test location:** Students need a quiet place without traffic or others talking. In block classes, students with ADD or ADHD may be too distracted to continue working on the test in the same classroom while the teacher gives instruction for the remainder of class.

    2.1. Send the student to the library or guidance office to finish the test, especially during the last half of a two-hour block class.

    2.2. Select a test location without distractions even if a student doesn't need extended time.

3. **Implement honor system testing:** Depending on the student, this may or may not be a good choice. Because of their impulsivity, students with attention deficits are more likely to speak before they think. So if another student either asks them or tells them about the test, the student may talk before she remembers that she has signed an honor code pledge. Don't institute a system that you know won't work because it just sets the student up for failure. Discuss the difficulty of this system with the student and ask her if she thinks she can do it. If so, ask her to sign an honor system form indicating that she has not given or received information from other students about this test.

4. **Modify the format of the exam to test for a student's true knowledge:** Even when these students know the material, they may not do well on tests because of slow processing speed and information retrieval, weak verbal expression skills, and poor memory. Some methods of testing are more difficult for all students, not just those with attention deficits. For example, tests requiring recognition rather than cold recall of information are usually easier. Typically, students with ADD/ADHD do better with a test format that provides word cues to jog their memory.

    4.1. Use multiple choice or true-false questions. Since slow processing speed and slow information retrieval may be a problem, consider giving multiple choice tests or true-false questions. This may not work for younger students who are too impulsive and mark their answers without reading all the options.

4.2. Use "word banks." Consider using word banks that include a list of words from which to choose the correct answer or two columns that require matching answers. Since these students often have trouble quickly retrieving stored information, word banks can be a better way to accurately measure their knowledge. The words provide a visual prompt for the student so that she does not have to rely on her deficient retrieval skills.

4.3. Allow the student to carry a small laminated card. This is another way to make accommodations for the student's memory problems. The card may contain secondary facts such as formulas, acronyms, rules for verb conjugation in foreign languages, or grammar rules to help trigger memory of key information during tests.

4.4. Avoid lengthy essay exams, especially if the student has deficits in verbal expression. The student may know the material but be unable to express her thoughts in a clear, organized manner.

> **4.4.1. Give a word bank for essay exams.** Supply the student with a word bank of key issues that must be discussed on the test.

4.5. Shorten the test. Develop a shortened version of the test for students with special needs. One drawback is that with fewer questions, each one missed counts off more points, which may increase the likelihood of failure.

4.6. Consider oral exams. A few students have such severe written expression problems they can't pass written tests. Typically, these students do better on oral exams. Sometimes the teacher will read the questions and have the student respond orally. Another alternative is for the student to read the questions and dictate her answers into a tape recorder or to a scribe. Occasionally, teachers may give an oral test to a student who obviously knows the material but has failed a written test.

4.7 Consider giving open book tests.

5. **Adjust grading techniques:** Try adjusting grading techniques so that they don't punish a student's learning deficits, an "off day," or lapse in memory:

5.1. Drop the student's lowest daily or test grade.

5.2. Don't count off for spelling on written assignments, unless spelling is the subject being tested. Allow the use of a spell checker if spelling is an important part of the assignment. At a minimum, allow the student to earn full credit by correcting misspelled words. Or ask the student to record the correct spelling of the word five times into a tape recorder.

5.3. Allow the student to earn extra credit, especially in classes she is in danger of failing. If possible, identify creative projects related to the subject that may be completed for extra credit:

- Videotape an interview of a war veteran for a history class.
- Audio- or videotape an interview with someone who speaks Spanish for a foreign language class.
- Create a scrapbook on a related topic.
- Cut articles or pictures from newspapers or magazines on issues related to class.

Or the student may earn extra credit by correcting errors on tests or completing additional work or projects.

5.4. Award bonuses to students for good work. In their book, *Teach and Reach Students with ADD*, Dr. Nancy Eisenberg and Pam Esser, Executive Director of ADDA-SR, give samples of blank forms roughly 4"x6" for teachers to award *bonus points or a homework pass*.

- Give coupons for ***bonus points*** to be added to a grade. For example, if a student turns in her book report on time, three bonus points may be added to her final grade. Five bonus points may be awarded for 1) correcting spelling and grammar errors on an essay or 2) writing in the correct answers to missed questions or problems on a test.
- Give coupons as a ***homework pass*** to reward good work, effort, or a positive attitude. "This student is awarded a homework pass for any daily homework assignment other than studying for a test." Students may save the coupon and use it one day to skip a homework assignment. Discuss the possibility of saving it for a day when they have forgotten or lost an assignment.

5.5. Grade completed material. Base the grade only upon the amount of work the student turns in or allow extended time to complete the test.

6. **Allow the student to *make up work*:** Weak organizational skills and an impaired sense of time often interfere with prompt completion of school work, unless accommodations are put in place. So, allow the student to make up work but develop a plan to correct the problem. Since this is such a major problem for students, expect occasional backsliding and failure of the plan. ***Nothing works all the time with these students!*** Make adjustments and try again.

7. **Special Testing Situations:** Several special testing situations may arise for students with either ADD or ADHD, including:

   1. the mandatory state tests that measure the student's academic achievement,
   2. benchmark tests to determine whether a student passes to the next grade,
   3. competency exams for high school graduation, and
   4. college entrance tests such as the ACT or SAT.

Some schools assume that students cannot have accommodations for these special tests. However, ***federal law mandates that students with ADD or ADHD whose learning is adversely affected are eligible for accommodations***.

Typically, to be eligible for accommodations on these special tests, students must currently be receiving those accommodations as part of an IEP or Section 504 Plan. (See Summaries 44 and 47.) There must be a notation in the IEP (or 504 Plan) indicating which accommodations and/or modifications are required for testing situations. Eligibility for extended time for these students may be determined by test scores or classroom performance indicating related problems such as slow information processing speed.

Information on accommodations available for the SAT is available from the Educational Testing Service (609-921-9000; www.ets.org); on accommodations for the ACT, from ACT, Inc. (319-337-1000; www.act.org).

Examples of Accommodations Used During Achievement or Graduation Tests

Most states have compiled a list of accommodations for statewide achievement tests that are available to eligible students. The examples below are taken from the lists of Arizona and Georgia. Each state may have different requirements, so check with your state department of education for a copy of their guidelines.

Extended time	Reread directions
Administer test in shorter sessions, perhaps over several days	Simplify language in the directions
Allow frequent breaks	Highlight verbs in the directions
Mark answers in the test booklet	Provide a calculator
Increase size of answer bubbles	Provide a word processor
Change the time of day for giving the test	Provide a dictionary or spell checker
Test in small groups in a separate location	

Modify Level of Supervision

Teenagers with ADD/ADHD mature at a slower rate. This means that a fourteen-year-old student with an attention deficit may have the organizational skills and planning abilities of a ten-year-old. In addition, working memory deficits often impair the ability to remember things. Young people with an attention deficit *will* act more responsibly in the future, but at a later age than their peers. In the meantime, students with attention deficits need more supervision and need to have their work monitored more closely.

For teachers, it is a good idea to recruit others to help with routine monitoring. It doesn't matter who provides the supervision as long as the job is done.

1. **Ask other students to help with monitoring:**

   1.1. Designate "row captains." Select captains in each row to assist you by checking that work is complete and homework assignments are written down, and by collecting homework.

   1.2. Pair off all students. Students can check each other's work to see that it is completed and assignments are written down. Devote the last 3-5 minutes of class to this task.

   1.3. Monitor the assignment book. Give paired students five minutes at the end of class and ask them to initial that assignments are written down.

   1.4. Recruit a friend or other student to be a "coach." Typically, this close level of monitoring is necessary only when the student is in danger of failing a class. One "coach" may be selected for all classes or a coach may be assigned in those classes where the student is struggling. The coach checks to see that assignments are written down or reminds the student to turn in homework. The coach may even meet her after school to review which books and assignments should be taken home. Sometimes, girlfriends or boyfriends help with this task. For some students, being monitored this closely can be embarrassing. So, if the student is passing, a "coach" could be offered as one option that might result in more success at school. See Summary 65 on coaching.

   1.5 Hire a coach. Parents might pay a "coach" to meet their freshman daughter at her locker at the end of the school day. The coach could double check to see that all assignments and books are taken home.

2. **Ask parents to monitor:** Since these students are developmentally two to four years behind their peers, don't hesitate to give parents permission to be more involved in monitoring school work. Parents of students with attention deficits must be involved longer and to a greater degree in monitoring school work than either the teacher or they want to be! In essence, most parents who are still involved in their middle or high

school student's school work are providing "developmentally appropriate supervision." Please don't make them feel guilty for doing this.

Remember, too, that a fair number of parents of these students may also have an attention deficit and have their own difficulties with memory and organization. So, if parents forget to check that assignments are completed, you might tactfully ask them to develop a reminder system or whether someone else (non-ADD/ADHD) parent or sibling (non-ADD/ADHD) might be available to help with monitoring. Obviously, teachers would not talk about the parent's attention deficit unless the parent brings the issue up first. However, some parents are fully aware of their own personal challenges and are very open to discussing them.

2.1. Advise parents when monitoring may be necessary. Let them know if a particular assignment requires greater organizational skills and if they may need to provide more guidance than usual to the student.

2.2. Involve parents as partners in completion of homework. Assignment books and weekly reports are excellent tools for ensuring homework completion. See Summary 25 for suggestions for helping parents coach students through homework.

2.3. When the student is in danger of failing, communicate with parents by phone, e-mail, or telephone answering machine.

2.4. Ask parents to check assignments. When a student with an attention deficit is struggling academically, take time to talk with parents about assignments. Explain that they should ask to see and sign the student's assignment book each night. They can also help make certain it is returned to school each day. In addition, the parent's role also may be spelled out in the IEP or Section 504 Plan.

3. Involve other adults in monitoring:

3.1. Ask a classroom aide to monitor class work, homework, or assignments as described in 1.3 in this summary. When the classroom aide is provided as part of special education services, the aide may provide support to several students, not just the one with ADD or ADHD. This avoids embarrassing the student by singling her out as being different.

3.2. Ask a special education teacher to monitor. Some students meet with a special education teacher near the end of the day and review which assignments and books must be taken home.

3.3. Ask a case manager to monitor. A few schools have additional staff designated as "case managers" to monitor the progress of students who are at risk of failure.

4. Decide how you, the teacher, can help with monitoring:

4.1. Use an assignment book that the student takes home each day. Assignment books have become one of the primary ways teachers monitor school work and communicate with parents. To use these books effectively, students with ADD/ADHD will require more supervision. They often have trouble using assignment books due to their memory deficits. For example, they have to remember to write down assignments, get their book signed by six teachers, take it home, get it signed, and return it to school.

4.2. Check the book daily. Typically teachers check the assignment book themselves to ensure that assignments are written down and then initial it. When the book is sent home, parents review, initial and return the book to school. It is critically important that a plan be implemented to ensure that the assignment book is carried successfully back and forth between home and school. If the plan doesn't work, modify it. Avoid punishing the student for forgetting the book.

4.3. Develop a plan to make the assignment book process work. Teachers may get some helpful ideas from Summary 61 to help the student remember her assignment book. For example, a *row captain* may remind the student to write down assignments, her best friend may remind her to take it home, or she may set her wrist alarm to remind her to take it home. If the student goes home without her book, her parents should take her or send her back to school to get it. Although obviously there may be consequences for forgetting the book, avoid punishing the student for this ADD/ADHD behavior. Punishment teaches the student what *not* to do. It doesn't help her learn what she *should* do. Teach the student to compensate for her challenging ADD/ADHD behaviors.

4.4. Use a weekly report. Weekly reports may be sent home to let parents know how the student has been doing on assignments and tests. Teachers may write a note listing any uncompleted assignments, plus grades for the week. Reports are very helpful for getting students back on track academically if they are not doing their school work. When the student brings her grades up, she is rewarded by no longer having to do weekly reports. Remembering to get any papers signed is very difficult for these students, so try to keep document signing to a minimum. For tips on effective use of weekly reports, see Summary 26.

Use Technology

Computers, word processors, and other electronic devices can sometimes be the answer to memory, organization, or handwriting problems that students with ADD/ADHD face at school. The decision as to which technology to use, however, must be made with some caution. Sometimes technology may complicate an issue rather than simplify it. For example, it may take a student longer to accomplish a task with technology than without, or she may become so involved in playing with a gadget that she may not use it for its intended purpose. It is best to try a specific technology and see if it is really practical and helpful before committing to use it.

1. **Encourage use of a computer or word processor:** Working on a computer solves several problems for students with attention deficits. They are not slowed down by their problems with handwriting. They can get their ideas down on paper more quickly before they lose them from their working memory. Plus, their grades may actually improve since teachers who cannot read their messy handwriting can easily read typed work. Because students with ADD/ADHD are often forgetful and lose assignments, having a backup copy of work done on a computer is a major advantage for them. Allow students to use computers for as much of their work as possible.

   1.1. **Teach keyboarding skills.** Many students with attention deficits have a terrible time learning keyboarding skills because of their deficits in working memory and visual memory, and their slow access to stored information in long-term memory. Their keyboarding skills are usually extremely slow and they have difficulty completing assignments in regular keyboarding classes. Many instructional programs are rather traditional and rely on rote memorization, which is difficult for students with ADD/ADHD. Obviously, ***classroom assignments in keyboarding must be shortened***. Students may do better with keyboarding software, if carefully chosen as discussed in 1.3. Once these students master keyboarding they will do extremely well working on the computer.

   1.2. **Consider AlphaSmart.** *AlphaSmart* is a simple, portable, affordable computer companion that allows students to type, edit, and electronically store written work. A student may write a report or essay, compose e-mail messages, or take notes and then transfer them to any computer for formatting or directly to a printer. Some school systems are using AlphaSmart in conjunction with their regular computers. AlphaSmart features include:
      - a full-size keyboard,
      - a four-line display,
      - eight memory storage areas for daily schedule, assignments, or questions,

- battery power (runs on three AA batteries for 200-500 hours),
- a relatively low price (roughly $200).

Assignments completed on AlphaSmart are easy to read, so take less time to grade. Teachers can send vocabulary lists, questions, or assignments electronically to the student's AlphaSmart. At this cost, if the machine is lost, as students with ADD/ADHD are prone to do, it's not as bad as losing a $2,000 laptop computer. Check out the AlphaSmart and see if it is practical for everyday use at school. The small display area of only four lines may be a drawback for some students. More information is available at www.alphasmart.com.

1.3. Find effective computer software programs. Find computer programs that will assist the student with difficult subjects. Ask the school media specialist for suggestions or call the school district office and talk with the person in charge of assistive technology. Some parents can afford to buy computer programs for use at home. Below are some software packages recommended by several educators as well as reviewers in a CHADD newsletter:

- **Keyboarding software:** One keyboarding program, *Type to Learn* by Sunburst Communications, Syracuse, New York, incorporates memory tricks to help students ages 8 to 14 memorize the keyboard. The program has received good reviews from users. See reviews at www.superkids.com. Available from www.smartkidssoftware.com for approximately $100, or sometimes on sale for $40. 888-881-6001.

- **Concept mapping software:** *Inspiration Software* (http://www.inspiration.com; 800-877-4294) is a type of concept mapping software. The software allows you to manipulate information to organize it in various written and graphic formats. For example, students can develop ideas for papers using a web organizer and then convert them automatically to an outline prior to writing. Teachers can also create blank webs for students to use. The reviewers felt it helped students learn about linear and non-linear organization. For a review of the software, see "Using Inspiration to Organize Reading and Writing", at http://www.ldonline.org.

- **Academic subject software:** Teens with ADD/ADHD often find computer games highly motivating and can sustain their attention longer than while listening to lectures. Examples of software programs that may be useful include:
  - *Writer's Helper*—which prompts a student through the writing process by asking a series of questions or presenting reminders. Several functions such as brainstorming, freewriting, categorizing, and structured questions are included. Teachers may also lock in test questions and then have the student type in the answers between the questions. 800-887-9998.

- *Skills Bank 4* and *Corner Stone*—two self-paced, comprehensive programs from the Learning Company that address reading, math, vocabulary, and language. Students can work at their own skill level (www.learningcompanyschool.com).
- *Math Companion V.2*—which allows teachers to create worksheets, posters, games, and game cards to help students learn math concepts such as fractions, percents, and geometry. 800-877-0858.
- *MathStar*—a compact, hand-held teaching tool that quizzes math skills in seven fundamental areas with eight levels of difficulty. Students who enjoy Nintendo will like using MathStar. 800-381-0381.

■ **Web Page Development software:** *Microsoft Front page 2000* is a user-friendly software program for creating a webpage. You can also view the page as you have written it, as it looks in code and a browser. To really do a web page right, a student should also know HTML code. Occasionally, web-authoring software will have an error that can only be corrected by using HTML code. *First Page 2000* was designed by Evrsoft to help people learn to use HTML very easily. Best of all, it is free. *First Page 2000* is in the process of being updated (www.evrsoft.com).

■ **Desktop Publishing software:** *Microsoft Publisher, Adobe, and Corel* are all good desktop publishing software programs that are available at local book, computer, or office supply stores.

■ **Software for earning make-up credits:** Teachers participating in the Kenosha Schools model ADD Program use self-paced instructional software from the Plato Company for students who want to earn make-up credits toward graduation. Plato offers a wide range of courses including Algebra, Science, Chemistry, Social Studies, and a writing series. Although the program is expensive, probably close to $2,000, the long-range benefits far outweigh the initial cost.

Since most students who use the program have already failed the course once, they already have mastered some of the knowledge taught in the class. Plato courses allow the student to quickly review a chapter and then take a test to indicate mastery. Typically, the student may move fairly rapidly until she reaches the later chapters where she does not know the material. Once the student reaches this point, then she will have to read all the material, answer any questions, or work all the problems, before she is ready to take the next test. For students who are poor readers, Plato also has an audio component. More information is available on the Internet at www.plato.com and at 800-447-5286 (800-44-PLATO). See Summary 49 for information on Kenosha Schools.

- **Other technology:** More sophisticated technology is available and may be helpful for students with more severe learning problems. For example, a speech synthesizer can read what a student has written aloud so that she can listen for errors or ways to strengthen the essay. Or *Phonic Ear,* typically used for hearing impaired students, can be used to amplify the teacher's voice to help the student pay attention. (www.phonicear.com).

1.4. Use computer spell check. Allow students with serious spelling deficits to use spell check when writing an essay or taking an essay test at school. Obviously, most students will use spell check at home, if they have computers.

2. Use a tape recorder: Tape recorders offer a low-tech way to reduce the amount of written work for students with ADD/ADHD.

2.1. Assign reports on the tape recorder. For subjects such as Language Arts, History, or Government, a student with ADD or ADHD could sometimes dictate a brief report, summary of a newspaper article, or interview with a war veteran on the tape recorder and give the teacher the tape as a substitute for a written report. Or the student may dictate the information to a scribe (another student or a parent), who writes the information down.

2.2. Allow students with attention deficits to tape class lectures instead of taking notes. This is helpful for some students, but for other students, it is a waste of time because they will not listen to the same material a second time.

2.3. Consider buying an inexpensive handheld memo or tape recorder. The student could dictate homework assignments to a small tape recorder rather than writing them down. Such recorders are usually available at K-Mart, WalMart, or Radio Shack.

3. Use a video camera: As another alternative to written reports, students with ADD/ADHD can videotape themselves or others. Making a video may help them remember more about the subject than they would from writing a traditional report, and allowing them to use their creative instincts may enrich the learning experience.

4. Use Books on Tape: These audiotapes provide an alternative resource for students who are slow readers or have reading comprehension problems. The multisensory approach enables the student to see the book while at the same time hearing it. Fiction, nonfiction, and textbooks on audiotape, plus the equipment on which to play it, are available in each community. Check with your local school or regional library, or contact either of these two organizations:

National Library Service for the Blind and Physically Handicapped (NLS)
Library of Congress
Washington, DC 20542
Phone: (800) 424-8567
E-mail: nls@loc.gov
www.loc.gov/nls

Recording for the Blind and Dyslexic (RFB&D)
20 Roszel Road
Princeton, NJ 08540
Phone: (800) 221-4792
E-mail: custserv@rfbd.org
www.rfbd.org

5. **Allow use of a calculator for class work and homework:** Some students may *never* master multiplication tables. In the real world, most adults use a calculator for doing everyday math calculations. Even the SAT now allows use of a calculator during testing. See Summaries 19-20 for more information on math accommodations.

6. **Use electronic tools to help students with reminders and organization:**

   6.1. Consider using electronic organizers such as a Wizard or Palm Pilot. These may be helpful for some students, but the Palm Pilot may actually be too sophisticated and a distraction for some students with ADD/ADHD. They may be tempted to play chess or send e-mail messages rather than just write down homework assignments.

   6.2. Try prompting devices. Several tools are available to remind students with attention deficits of things they need to do. Examples include:

   - *WatchMinder*™: This wrist alarm may be programmed as a reminder to take medication, stay after school, or go by the locker and pick up books.
     (1-800-961-0023; www.watchminder.com)
   - *Ticklebox:* This prompting device is more like a pager. It sends message reminders to students. However, because some schools prohibit use of pagers, check to be certain the school will allow use of the device before buying one. Of course, if it is written into the IEP, a school policy exception may be allowed.
     (888-4TICKLE; www.ticklebox.com)

Resources

Assistive Technology in Special Education Policy and Practice and *Has Technology Been Considered? A Guide for the IEP Team"* are available from the Technology and Media Division of the Council for Exceptional Children (CEC), developed in conjunction with the Council of Administrators of Special Education. (505-243-7622; www.cec.sped.org or www.tamcec.org)

Learning Disabilities and Assistive Technology: An Emerging Way to Touch the Future. A publication from the Georgia Tools for Life Program (404-657-3081; www.gatfl.org). Includes numerous resources such as software for writing or math difficulties plus a list of Internet resources. Check in your home state to see if similar resources are available.

MacArthur, Charles A. "Using Technology to Enhance the Writing Processes of Students with Learning Disabilities," *Journal of Learning Disabilities*, V.29, N.4, pp. 344-354.

Common Problems with Written Expression

Teenagers with ADD/ADHD often have very creative ideas for writing essays, but often have great difficulty getting their ideas down on paper. In fact, in a study published in *ADHD Reports*, 65 percent of students with ADD/ADHD were found to have problems with written expression, making it the most common learning problem they experienced (see Summary 11). This is not surprising, considering that written expression involves many complex steps requiring organization, sequencing, memory, and other skills that are often challenging for students with attention deficit disorders. The suggestions in this summary and the next one on writing an essay may help address these problems.

Five Common Writing Problems

Dr. Mel Levine, the author of numerous books on teaching students with learning problems, has identified five common problems that interfere with written expression for many middle and high school students:

1. **Organizational Problems**—Often students don't have a good organizational plan for where and how to begin writing or what the next step should be. Sequencing of key information is also difficult. Students must think about what they are writing, figure out what comes next, and organize the essay or report.

2. **Poor Retrieval Memory or "Exceeded Memory Capacity"**—Students, especially those with attention deficits, often lack sufficient memory capacity to write well. Students must access their long-term memory for correct spelling and to find rules of grammar, punctuation, and capitalization. At the same time, students have to use their active working memory to remember what they are writing about and decide which thought they want to express next. Simply holding that thought or a chunk of information in short-term memory long enough to get it written down on paper is often difficult.

3. **Graphomotor Dysfunction**—For students with fine motor problems, writing may be very slow and laborious. Some students with ADD/ADHD, even as adults, prefer printing instead of cursive writing for good reasons. Cursive writing places greater demands on fine motor and memory skills than printing does.

4. **Unsophisticated Ideation**—*Ideation,* or generation of thoughts, includes selection of a topic, analysis of the topic, development of related ideas for the topic, elaboration on the ideas, and incorporation of information learned previously.

5. Written Language Problems—Students who have weak language production, or difficulty putting thoughts into words, may write very simple essays using brief sentences. Problems in the first four areas listed may contribute to written language problems.

Resources

Levine, Mel. *Educational Care*. Cambridge, MA: Educators Publishing Service, 1994.

Mayes, Susan D. & Susan Calhoun. "Prevalence and Degree of Attention and Learning Problems in ADHD and LD." *ADHD Reports*, V.8, N.2, April 2000.

Improving Written Expression

1. **Create a safe writing environment:** Most students with ADD/ADHD are extremely anxious about writing assignments. This is such a difficult task for them, they avoid writing as much as possible. When they do finally write something, the words may not flow easily and they dread criticism from the teacher. Strategies for building skills and reducing anxiety include:

   1.1 Work on fluency first. Claudia Jordan, a veteran high school Language Arts teacher, recommends building student confidence by establishing writing fluency first. She does not grade early writing. Instead she gives students credit for giving their best effort.

   - **Sentences first.** Start with two- to three-sentence assignments. Jordan starts out by asking students to write two to three sentences every day about an interesting paragraph or short story she reads them or a picture or cartoon shown on an overhead. Masterpiece Sentences, a part of the ***Language!*** program developed by Dr. Jane Fell Greene, offers another way to give students guided practice writing creative sentences. See the discussion in Summary 13-A and the resources listed in Summary 13 for more information.

   - **Paragraphs next.** Marcy Winograd, an experienced middle school Language Arts teacher, says, "Students need lots of practice with this type of writing (paragraphs) before putting pen to paper on a five paragraph essay." Winograd asks students to write daily paragraphs "in the air." She writes a topic sentence on the overhead—for example, "Students should wear uniforms at school." She then throws a beach ball to select a student to write a sentence. Students who voluntarily catch the ball must use a transition word before giving a supporting statement. (Transition words are written on posters on the wall: For example; In addition; First; Second; Third; Finally; Consequently.) Each student's statement is written on the posters or the overhead. For the conclusion, she may ask, "What difference will it make if students wear uniforms? What is the bottom line?" Again, students respond with sentences beginning with transition words such as "then" or "as a result".... "Consequently, students who wear uniforms to school will learn more."

   - **Lengthen assignments.** Increase the length of writing assignments gradually. Next, students may begin writing at least one brief paragraph four or five days a week.

   - **Finally, polish.** After writing fluency is achieved, *then* polish grammar, spelling, and punctuation.

1.2. Encourage journal writing. Set aside time in class and ask students to write two sentences about what they are feeling or thinking at that exact moment. Since the work may be personal, teachers may tell the students they will not read any journal unless a student asks them to do so. Don't grade the content but simply give credit when the student shows you a completed paragraph.

- Read from inspirational books. One teacher reads from the "Chicken Soup" books each Friday and gives her students ten minutes to free write in their journal.
- Show pictures or cartoons on the overhead to trigger ideas. For example, you might show a picture of a smiling, happy person, then briefly discuss examples of happy times given by students and ask them to write their memories of a happy time.

1.3. Be sensitive and caring about students' writing anxieties. Many students with ADD/ADHD feel inadequate because of problems expressing themselves in writing and poor handwriting. Do not embarrass students about their messy written work or put it on display without their permission. If the student has written a good essay, the teacher may read it in class. However, if the student is embarrassed about her writing or is a poor reader, don't ask her to read it in class.

2. **Model skills for students:** Show, don't just tell, students how to do specific types of writing assignments. Claudia Jordan *"writes with her students."* She actually writes essays or poetry in class and walks students through the process step by step while using an overhead projector. Students contribute to her essay by brainstorming and giving suggestions for topics to address, identifying four to five paragraph topics, developing supportive sentences for each topic, and writing an opening and closing paragraph. After the teacher models these steps in class, the students complete the same step for their own personal essay. This process is completed over a period of weeks.

3. **Modify assignments:** See Summary 13-B for more details on modifying assignments.

   3.1. Give extended time. Allow more time for written assignments and essay questions on tests.

   3.2. Reduce written work. Shorten reports or assignments. Expect that answers to essay questions will be brief, comprised of only a few short sentences.

   3.3. By-pass writing. For students who are overwhelmed by the writing process, periodically substitute other means of communication such as a recorded or oral report, a project instead of a written report, or multiple-choice or true-false tests.

   3.4. Allow students to print their work. Do not require cursive writing if students are more comfortable and write more rapidly with printing.

   3.5. Allow students to write in pencil. Some students are more comfortable writing with a pencil because of frequent errors and erasures.

3.6. Give cooperative writing projects.

- Group projects: Allow a group of students to write a report cooperatively. Students may be assigned different roles: researcher, brainstormer, proofreader, and illustrator.
- Joint projects: Sometimes students may alternate working on the computer as they jointly compose an essay. This process encourages scaffolding or building upon the other student's work and improving the final product. Researchers have found that the quality of student writing improves as one student learns from another.
- Telecommunication network collaboration: A few schools have tried teleconferencing with local and distant school systems as they share writing products.

3.7. Select topics related to personal growth.
Coyle Bryan teaches an Applied Communication class to high school seniors in Whitfield County, Georgia. The content is related to real-world work experience, as well as personal growth. Students talk and then write about important topics such as self-esteem, values, self-awareness of personality characteristics, recognizing these personality traits in others with whom they may work, and getting along with peers and co-workers.

4. Modify testing and grading: See Summary 13-C for more details.

4.1. Don't grade early work.
Do not grade the content but simply give the student credit (e.g., 25 points) for completing the assignment. Too much criticism early on is terribly discouraging and may result in the student giving up.

4.2. Prioritize key elements of the assignment.
Next, focus on the content but don't count off for spelling or grammar errors the first time around. Mark errors and have students revise and make corrections. Or consider giving the student a word bank with the correct spelling of key words to be incorporated into the essay.

4.3. Grade only one aspect of the essay.
For example, sometimes Coyle Bryan grades the students only on their use of verbs, nouns, spelling, or capitalization. She tells the students in advance so they will know which element to review most carefully.

4.4. Assign each essay two grades and average.
If grammar, spelling, and punctuation are being graded, give the student two grades, one for creative content and one for grammar, spelling, and punctuation. Then average the two grades. Clare Jones, Ph.D., author of *Attention Deficit Disorder: Strategies for School-Age Children*, suggests including this as an accommodation in the student's IEP or Section 504 Plan.

4.5. Give tests that measure recognition rather than recall.

- Provide word banks on tests. Give the student a list of words from which to choose the correct answer.

- Give prompts for essay tests by providing a bank of words that should be included in the paper.
- Provide "starter sentences." "Starter sentences" will help them organize their thoughts. For example, "Both the North and South are to 'blame' for the start of the Civil War. In the years preceding the war, both sides took actions that angered the other side. For example, the North...."

5. **Use Technology:** For more information on electronic resources, refer to Summary 13-E.

  5.1. Allow use of a computer. Students with ADD/ADHD should be encouraged to use computers for written work as early as possible. Keyboarding is often extremely difficult, so see Summaries 13-B and 13-E for software for teaching this critical skill.

  5.2. Use a spell and grammar check. Allow students with ADD/ADHD to use spell check as part of a computer program or use a hand-held spell check.

  5.3. Make students and parents aware of helpful websites:
  - *www.ldonline.com,* then click on "LD In Depth," then click on "Writing." This informative site includes copies of several helpful articles about teaching writing, suggested software for math and writing instruction, a review of Inspiration software, plus suggestions for helping with organizational skills. This site is a definite must to visit.
  - *www.iss.stthomas.edu/studyguides/*—This interesting website has a list of over twenty-five websites with tips on writing.
  - *www.west.cherryhill.k12.nj.us*—This website was developed by the English Department at Cherry Hill High School West. It includes information regarding common errors in English, grammar and spelling tips, and tips on writing five-paragraph essays and organizing term papers.
  - *www.sdcoe.k12.ca.us*—This website, developed by the San Diego County Office of Education, includes suggestions for journaling, literature, and sample graphic organizers that may be duplicated.

Writing an Essay

Most teachers divide essay-writing assignments into segments such as brainstorming, outlining, first draft, revisions, second draft, revisions, and final version. Students with ADD/ADHD may need to have these segments broken down into even smaller parts or be guided through them step by step if they are going to succeed in writing an essay.

1. **"Think it"/Brainstorm:** Brainstorming for ideas to include in the essay is often the most difficult step for students with ADD/ADHD. Sometimes students almost panic because they have such difficulty quickly retrieving ideas or information from their brain. It's as though their brain is frozen or stuck. Teachers can help them break ideas loose and get started in several ways.

   1.1. **Provide guidance on topic selection.** As discussed in Summary 39, students with attention deficits have a terrible time narrowing down and selecting a writing topic. Limit the number of topics from which they may select. Since it is easier to write about what the student knows, tell her to select the topic she feels strongest about or knows the most about.

   - **Topic ideas may include:** something you believed was true; the most beautiful place you've ever been; an enemy who isn't a person; foods you love; something that got you in trouble; secrets you had; a time you were scared or sick; things you did with a brother or sister; or a favorite book, TV show, or movie. Then, to stimulate thinking, briefly talk through one idea with the students.

   1.2. **Break the idea log jam.** Encourage students to write down their ideas in whatever form they occur—for example, global ideas, phrases, or specific details. Don't do anything to stop or slow the flow of the student's ideas.

   1.3. **Use Post-It notes.** Encourage the student to freely throw out ideas that she or someone else writes on Post-It notes. Write down all ideas. Don't make judgments of what is good or bad or what to keep or eliminate.

   1.4. **Provide prompts to stimulate thinking.**
   - Give visual prompts. Show students pictures, cartoons, newspaper headlines.
   - Have a class discussion; or read them a short story. Help students bring a picture to mind of their topics.
   - Use manipulatives. One teacher gave each student a pipe cleaner or clay and told them to form it into something that was of interest to them or that stood as a symbol for themselves and then write about the topic.

- Act out plays. Read and act out a classic play such as *Romeo and Juliet.* Then later have the students write an essay on a related topic.

1.5. Answer key questions. Have students answer who, what, when, where, and why regarding their topic.

1.6. Reinforce with physical activity. Teacher Marcy Winograd uses a physical activity to reinforce the elements of a conclusion:
- "Touch back" – she has the students bring their pinky to their thumb to illustrate touching back on the thesis of the essay.
- "Go to the heart" – students touch their hearts to show you have to explain the bottom line—what difference the thesis makes—otherwise who cares?
- "Look to the future" — hand on forehead, looking outward.
- "End strong" — flex the biceps to emphasize the need to express a strong opinion.

Students usually think these activities are fun and are learning at the same time.

Asking students to write a "How to do something" narrative also helps them become physically involved in writing. For example, explain step by step how to change the oil in your car.

1.7. Use graphic organizers. Several graphic organizers are available to help students brainstorm by using *clusters, webs, or mind maps* to develop and expand upon ideas. Summary 13-A lists resources that contain graphic organizers.
- Draw your own graphic organizer. (See Appendix A2.) Have the student draw a circle in the center of the page, draw six lines radiating out from the center, add small circles, and draw additional lines away from the small circles.
- Use the student's hand as a graphic organizer. At Paul Revere Middle school in Los Angeles, students:
  - trace their hand,
  - label the thumb with the thesis statement,
  - label the index finger with the topic sentence of the first supporting paragraph,
  - label the middle finger with the topic sentence for the second supporting paragraph,
  - label the ring finger with the topic sentence of the third supporting paragraph, and
  - label the pinky with the conclusion.

2. "Write it":

2.1. Begin organizing thoughts.
- Regroup Post-It notes. If students recorded ideas on Post-It notes as described in 1.3, move Post-It notes into clusters. Perhaps

group by who, what, when, and where or other logical categories (such as by pros and cons about the issue).

- Cut and paste. Type ideas into a computer and print them out. Either physically cut up the words on paper or cut and paste on the computer to move ideas around, group them together, and begin thinking of a logical writing sequence.
- Dictate to a "scribe" or parent.

2.2. Provide writing prompts.

- Use an Essay Organizer. Refer to information on the graphic organizer for essays as the student begins writing (Appendix A2). Usually the information listed under "who, what, when and where" sections is included in the first paragraph of the essay. Information under "why and how" is expanded to provide the body paragraphs of the essay. The small circles by each of these six sections may be numbered to indicate the order in which they are included in the essay.
- Develop guided writing tips. When students are just beginning and believe that they cannot write a good essay, guided writing tips will help them succeed and gain confidence. Here is an example from one class:
- Picture in your mind a pleasant place from your childhood, a special time when you felt really happy. Try to see it in your mind's eye. Where are you? Draw a picture of the place where you are. Who is there? What time of year and time of day is it?
- Ask questions regarding the five senses to help enrich the essay.
  - *Sight*. What do you see? Picture yourself as a little kid. Who else is there? Describe yourself and them. What are you wearing?
  - *Smell*. What do you smell? (food, granddad's after shave)
  - *Taste*. What do you taste? (cake, salty tears)
  - *Hearing*. What do you hear? What does it sound like? (AC, fan, buzz of talking)
  - *Touch*. What does it feel like? (scratchy, smooth, cold, soft)
  - After the student has written this material, ask her to go back and add two adjectives to each sentence.

2.3. Share tips with parents.
Since parents are often involved in helping students write essays and reports for numerous subjects, teachers may want to share with them the information in Appendix B2 on writing a three-part essay. This information should help teenagers and parents cope successfully with this challenging problem.

3. "Fix It":

3.1. Allow students to use computer editing and proofreading functions to polish their first draft.

3.2. Use peer review.
Ask students to swap papers with each other. Each student tells: 1) one thing the writer did well, and 2) one thing the writer could improve. The students may go through two or three rounds of peer

review. Students are much more likely to remember writing tips that they learn by "teaching" or sharing corrections with another student.

3.3. Provide teacher review. While students are doing peer review, the teacher can begin reading each student's paper and asking questions. Sometimes the teacher may say, "Do you think something is wrong here? Read it to me. Does it sound right to you?"

3.4. Provide editing practice. Give students material that someone else has written or that the teacher has created for practice editing and have them act as an editor, making needed changes and corrections.

3.5. Do not correct all errors. Don't correct all the errors that are found in a student's early writings. Correct major errors such as sentence fragments or run-on sentences. Otherwise, they may be so discouraged, they will be afraid to even attempt to write anything.

4. **Evaluate and polish it:** Many teachers are developing rubrics or checklists of questions a student may ask herself after she has written an essay. For example, here are some questions to answer yes or no about the essay.

- I begin with a topic or thesis sentence.
- I provide details to support the topic sentence.
- All my sentences have a subject and a verb, begin with a capital letter, and end with a punctuation mark.

Winograd asks her students these questions when they write a mystery story:
- Did your mystery have a beginning, middle, and end?
- Did it include a crime, clues, suspects, and alibis?
- Did it include some element of conflict?
- Was your detective character believable?
- Did you create a detailed setting that intrigued the reader?
- Did you create a climax where all the action came to a head?

5. **"Share it":**

5.1. Have students hand in final papers.

5.2. Ask students to read their essays in class. The student with ADD/ADHD may read her essay in class or ask the teacher or another student to read it.

5.3. Publish it in a school or class newspaper or magazine. In Georgia, *Foxfire* is an excellent, well-known publication of student writings. Graduating students from Winograd's classes have work published in their very own *Story Walk*, a literary arts magazine. You could also find a good desktop publishing program (Summary 13-E) and publish student writings. Researchers have found that the quality of written work improves when writing is published.

5.4. Display student papers on the class or school bulletin board. Sometimes private businesses display student art; why not display student writing in private businesses or the school administrative offices?

Other Written Assignments

1. Book Reports: Some Language Arts teachers are shying away from traditional written book reports. Written reports don't provide assurance the book has actually been read; reports are easily available from the Internet and other students. Instead, students may be asked to do a project, then give an oral report on the book. There are also a variety of other options that may work better for students with ADD/ADHD than the written book report.

1.1. Use "Books on Tape." If a student has problems with reading, allow her to listen to books on audiotape. See Summary 13-E for details on Books on Tape.

1.2. Assign book projects. For example, one student baked a cake like Mrs. Haversham's from *Great Expectations*. Fake spider webs and roaches were added to make it look fifty years old. Another student did an oil painting of Emily Dickinson and told about her life.

1.3. Give verbal book reports. Students are asked to report on their book, show their project, and then answer questions from the class. Students are not asked to stand up to speak unless they wish to do so.

1.4. Read classic books in class. The teacher may read two chapters to the class and then ask students to read one chapter at home on their own.

1.5. Assign creative alternatives to book reports. Sometimes students have to do book reports for other classes such as Social Studies, History, or Government. Make these books memorable by assigning creative projects. Susie Smith, a Language Arts teacher at Lullwater School in Decatur, Georgia, has her students make pop-up books to accompany their oral book reports. (See Summary 22.) A secondary benefit for students with attention deficits is that these projects frequently call for little or no writing. For example,

- videotape interviews of war veterans,
- draw a poster of how a bill becomes a law,
- design a movie poster to sell the book,
- do videos of key scenes in the book,
- create a three-dimensional sculpture depicting at least three of the major characters.

1.6. Use a graphic organizer. Allow students to fill in the blanks in a "who, what, when, where, why, and how" graphic organizer.

2. Creative Writing:

2.1 Provide prompts for creative writing assignments. Teacher Marcy Winograd explains that she gives her students prompts to help them write more interesting creative stories. For example, when writing to create suspense, she "slows down the moment" by asking students to *go slow and raise doubt.*

"She thought she heard someone in the house."
- Describe the sound.
- What is she thinking?
- Have her smell something different; connect the smell to a memory.
- Bring the feeling back to the present.

"It reminded him of the time he got lost in the woods and was dying for a drink of water. Now his throat felt parched, too. He was so scared he couldn't swallow."
- Have the character notice something visually different about the scene.
- What is she thinking now?
- Have her do something; keep moving closer until she makes a discovery.

3. Poetry: With poetry, students are learning to use imagery and paint pictures with words.

3.1. Act out narrative poems. Marcy Winograd assigns students roles in *Casey at the Bat* or *Paul Revere's Ride* and has them dress accordingly for their part. The students act out the poems as a class. They have a batter, people on bases, a pitcher, and fans in the audience. People in the stands may yell at the umpire.

3.2. Provide prompts for inspiration. For example, give students a theme for their poetry. Winograd taught a "Fruit Poetry Lesson." She brought a bowl of fruit including mangos, apples, strawberries, limes, and others. She picked a fruit and then talked about what it was like on the outside and on the inside. Then the class as a group wrote a poem about fruit. Students looked for outside/inside parallels between fruit and key events in their lives such as a girlfriend who makes them happy or their parents' divorce. Here is a "Strawberry Poem" the class wrote as a group:

> *On the outside*
> *The strawberry is rough*
> *Like the hands of the farmworker who toils*
> *Back bent in the fields*
> *On the inside*
> *The strawberry is a ruby*
> *A heart*
> *A tunnel to a new beginning*
> *Taste the Strawberry*
> *And savor the sweetness of summer.*

3.3. Use the five senses to help enrich the description, as explained earlier about writing an essay.

3.4. Provide written prompts. Winograd gives her students a graphic organizer to write either a poem or essay on "Where you're from."

Each student is given a map of a town complete with roads and descriptive words to help her write a poem on the topic, "I'm from...." In addition to "you" in the center of the map, other words on the map include town and street names, parent's work, relatives near you, central events, smells, tastes, church experience, hiding place, what grew in your yard, and a wild card.

3.5. Write poetry that is imitative of famous poems.

3.6. Publish student poetry. Winograd has helped her students get their poetry published in *Story Walk,* a literary magazine. Kevin Cooper, a student with ADHD, wrote this lovely poem in class. He takes his medication just before her class begins.

> **First Interest ...**
> *By Kevin Cooper*
>
> *When I started I only knew one thing*
> *About the amber-brown violin.*
> *I was the greatest, the best violinist in the world.*
> *My dad tells me to practice*
> *Everybody knows*
> *That the best violinist needs no practice.*
> *My posture was like celery*
> *That had been left out for three months:*
> *Limp, slouching, bad, and worse;*
> *My hand was flat as if it had been steam rolled*
> *And my bow hand clutched my bow*
> *Like a crab clutches a stick.*
> *How was I to know good posture from bad*
> *And I was the best in the world.*
>
> *After that year I took private lessons*
> *The bird-like screech of before*
> *Was now a cricket's chirp.*
> *My posture slowly improved.*
> *Old celery was replaced with new.*
> *Flat sharps and sharp flats went away*
> *I saw and heard those who were far ahead of me*
> *As if I were racing the fastest men in the world.*
> *The one thing I wonder is*
> *If I have improved since I began*
> *How is it that then I was the best*
> *And now I am not.*

4. **Reports or long-term projects:** Major semester projects and reports are discussed in two sections: 1) Summary 23 provides general tips on long-term projects and 2) Summaries 29 and 35-37 suggest organizational and time management strategies for long-term projects.

Common Math Difficulties

Poor math performance, especially weak math computation, is one of the most challenging problems facing students with ADD/ADHD. Interestingly enough, even those students who don't qualify as having a learning disability can still have terrible problems with math. Typically, most students with attention deficits don't *automatize* basic math facts. In other words, they are unable to quickly retrieve addition, subtraction, multiplication, and division facts. Unfortunately, this gaping hole in their "math foundation" interferes with their ability to complete math problems quickly. In spite of this serious deficit, however, these students may learn complex math concepts as easily as other students.

It is critical for teachers to allow the students to move on to more advanced math concepts and give them accommodations to compensate for their learning deficits!

Common sense tells us that time spent struggling to retrieve multiplication facts is wasteful and could be spent more wisely mastering advanced math concepts. This makes it vital to provide appropriate classroom accommodations, such as use of a calculator or a chart of math facts, or shortened assignments. These accommodations enable students to focus on mastering concepts rather than having to agonize over their faulty rote memorization skills. Although students may use calculators for figuring basic math facts, it is critical that they also know how it is done—for example "how to" multiply fractions. Periodic review of these basic procedures may be necessary as students move through more advanced math topics.

Factors Contributing to Difficulties in Math

1. Deficits in working memory (difficulty holding information in mind while performing math functions),
2. Slow processing speed and long-term memory (slow retrieval of stored math information),
3. Poor fine motor skills (poor handwriting),
4. Weak visual perceptual skills (difficulty judging placement on paper, aligning columns, carrying numbers from one column to the next).

Without extensive testing, one of the easiest ways to spot their math deficits is to look for lower than average scores on standardized tests such as the IOWA, especially the Math Computation section, or the Arithmetic subtest of the WISC-III.

How These Factors Affect School Performance

1. Students with ADD/ADHD usually work math problems more slowly than their peers and may not finish assignments or tests during the time allotted in class.

2. They may take an hour or more to finish homework that other students do in thirty minutes. See Summaries 24 & 25 for suggestions to help with homework.

3. They cannot quickly retrieve basic addition, subtraction, multiplication, or division facts.

4. They may learn multiplication tables one night and seem to forget them by the next evening. Even intellectually gifted students with ADD/ADHD may never master their multiplication tables.

5. Organizational and sequencing skills are often deficient, making multi-step math problems extremely difficult.

6. Students may attempt to "do the work in their heads" and write down the answer only. However, when they do work in their heads, they may skip steps and make "careless" errors.

7. They may write their numbers very small, too close together, and all on one line rather than spacing the problem properly so that it is more easily read and errors more easily detected.

8. Forgetting to write down homework assignments and to take assignments and the appropriate books home are also major challenges.

With all these challenges to overcome, doing math homework becomes overwhelming. Students may avoid homework by saying they don't have any or that they completed it at school.

SUMMARY 19 ## General Tips for Mastering Math

Students will learn many complex math concepts, especially in Algebra, Geometry, and advanced math courses. Obviously, this summary cannot provide tips for every single math concept to be taught. Instead, it offers tips that can be generalized for teaching other math concepts. Teachers will find it helpful to use this summary in conjunction with Summaries 18 and 20 as well as Summaries 13-A to 13-E on providing modifications.

Words of Wisdom from Math Teachers

Several middle, high school, and college math teachers, a few of whom have children with ADD/ADHD, contributed excellent ideas for this summary. Their suggestions for accommodating math deficits are below:

1. Modify assignments:

> **1.1. Modify/shorten homework assignments.** Assign every second, third, or fourth math problem that still covers the necessary skills and mastery of major math concepts.

> **1.2. Reduce writing.** Photocopy pages for students so they do not have to rewrite the math problems. Enlarging the original copy may give the student more room to show her work and write answers.

> **1.3. Reduce notetaking.** Jointly identify a notetaker. Ask another student who is good in math to take notes and underline the important issues of the lesson. NCR (carbonless) paper makes notetaking easier. See the suggestions for notetaking in Summaries 13-B and 23.

2. Modify teaching *methods*:

> **2.1. List steps for completion of math problems on the board.** As examples are written on the board, especially multi-step math problems, Denise Vogelesang, chairman of a high school special education department, suggests listing the steps taken for solving the problem on the board. She always puts the problem in the same spot on the board and leaves it there throughout class. Number (don't use letters) the steps in the order they are to be completed.

> **2.2. Keep sample math problems on the board.** Keep a step-by-step model of the problem on the board for the student to refer to while the concept is being taught.
> > - If students have working memory problems and can't hold the problem in mind as they look back and forth from the board, ask them to copy the problem on a colored card and put it by their

paper as they work. If they are unable to remember to do this, ask another student to write the problem down and give them a copy.

2.3. Use a "paired-learning" teaching strategy. Paired learning, also known as *class-wide peer tutoring,* is a very effective interactive learning strategy. After the teacher demonstrates a problem, students are paired off and each student within the pairs is asked to make up her own problem, work it, and write the answer down. Next the student gives her partner the blank problem to work. Then they compare answers to the problem. If their answers are not the same, the students discuss their differences and make corrections.

Dr. Ed Thomas, a Cobb County, GA, Curriculum Coordinator for Math and instructor at Kennesaw State University, recommends this strategy for teaching middle, high school, and college math classes. This technique was extremely effective with my college-age son who had always struggled and barely passed his math classes. He earned his first ever "A" in a math course with a 100 average in Dr. Thomas's Calculus course.

2.4. Pair with another student. If the teacher is unable to use a full blown paired-learning teaching strategy with the whole class, jointly identify a nearby student who is: 1) willing and capable of answering questions the student may ask, and 2) can double check to see if homework assignments are written down.

2.5. Use an overhead. Write sample problems on an overhead projector. Since the teacher is facing the class, students can hear and see the work, plus the teacher can see them. Mary Kay Wells, chairman of a high school math department, uses different color markers for each new step of a problem and for different lines on a graph.

2.6. Use group response. As explained in Summary 13-A, increase student involvement in class by using a group response. All students are asked to work a math problem. When they know the answer, students write the answer on a 3x5 card and hold it up for the teacher to see. Some schools provide notebook-size dry erase boards on which students may write answers. A teacher can quickly see which students don't understand the material.

2.7. Give review summaries for exams. Review summaries are very helpful for students with attention deficits. Summaries are even more critical for parents who may help their teenager study for the test.

3. **Modify Teaching *Resources.*** Use more visual cues and allow students to use prompts to compensate for their memory and retrieval deficits. See Summary 13-A for more details.

3.1. Allow use of a calculator for class- and homework. However, as explained in Summary 18, students may become "calculator dependent." They punch the numbers in the calculator to multiply fractions but may not remember "how to do" the basic problem. Students must understand these basic math skills for use in higher math courses such as Algebra I, II, and Trigonometry. So, periodic review of "how to" perform basic math skills may be necessary.

3.2. Laminate a copy of important math facts. Shrink multiplication tables to a size that will fit in a student's wallet and allow her to use it when a calculator is not permitted or is unavailable. Allow the student to keep a small card with formulas or acronyms. These cards will help trigger her memory of important math facts.

- Or print divisibility rules on a small wallet-size card and laminate. Understanding divisibility is important because it helps the student reduce fractions or factor problems more quickly. A student who understands divisibility rules won't have to do long division on a problem to find the factors.

  Divisibility Rules: You'll know if a number is divisible by
  - 2 ...... if the number is even (ends in 0, 2, 4, 6, or 8);
  - 3 ...... if the sum of the digits is divisible by 3;
  - 4 ...... if the number in the last two digits is divisible by 4;
  - 5 ...... if the number ends in 0 or 5;
  - 6 ...... if the number meets the rules for 2 & 3 above;
  - 8 ...... if the number in the last three digits is divisible by 8 (less often used);
  - 9 ...... if the sum of the digits is divisible by 9;
  - 10 .... if the number ends in 0

3.3. Use graph paper for place value instruction. Graph paper helps separate the places and decimal (ones, tens, hundreds, thousands; one-tenth, one-hundredth, one-thousandth). This keeps columns straight, reducing the likelihood of making errors.

3.4. Model appropriate spacing of math problems.
- Use graph paper to demonstrate proper spacing of a problem. Show the student how to write a few math problems correctly. See the examples written on graph paper in Summary 20.
- Turn notebook paper 90 degrees to help students organize math problems and line up their numbers. When the paper is turned sideways, the student writes numbers between the vertical lines.

3.5. Use graphic organizers. Graphic organizers usually work better for classes such as Language Arts, History, or Social Studies. An example of a graphic organizer that helps with classification of triangles by angles and sides is shown in Summary 20.

3.6. Use informative posters in the classroom. Posters provide visual reminders of important mathematical facts or concepts. The more interesting and novel the illustrations are, the more likely the student will remember them. For example, the information contained in Summary 19 on multiplying and dividing numbers with decimals could be drawn up as a poster.

3.7. Use color to highlight key facts. *Before* beginning work on math problems, ask students to highlight key "math operations" or issues. For example, students with ADD/ADHD often don't notice when the sign changes from + to -. Highlight each time the sign changes. In Geometry, highlight perimeter, area, or volume and the name of the shape you're working with (triangle, square, trapezoid). Use different colored highlighters to help differentiate what is being emphasized.

If your school won't allow students to mark their books, have the student highlight worksheets or scanned or photocopied pages from the textbook.

3.8. Provide an extra textbook at home. Having a math book at home is often helpful for a couple of reasons: 1) Students with ADD/ADHD are so forgetful and disorganized they often forget their books. 2) Since math is one of their most challenging subjects, forgetting a book and not doing homework may make the difference between passing and failing the class.

4. **Modify testing and grading:** More detailed suggestions are provided in Summary 13-C.

4.1. Give extended time on tests.

4.2. Use "word banks" for tests. Provide the student with a list of the formulas required for the math test. The student must understand the information to know which formula to use in each problem. Also allow the student to use these word banks, perhaps on laminated cards, as she works on class and homework.

4.3. Allow use of a laminated card with key math facts, as described in 3.2 above.

4.4. Adjust grading techniques by allowing the student to drop her lowest grade, earn extra credit, or do make-up work. Some teachers prefer not to make adjustments to grades after the fact, but have found other ways to adjust grading. For example, one teacher only gives four tests in a grading period. She doesn't drop the lowest grade but allows students to replace it with the final exam score, if they earn at least a C on the final exam. For example, if a student made test grades of 51, 71, 77, and 75, plus 72 on her final exam, she could substitute the 72 for the failing grade of 51.

5. **Modify the *level of supervision:*** As explained in Summary 13-D, these students will need more supervision than their peers. Also see Summary 26 on weekly reports.

6. **Modify *class schedules:*** A more detailed discussion is given in Summary 57 on Classroom Management.

6.1. Schedule math class during peak medication times. Work with school officials to schedule math approximately 1 to 1½ hours (regular tablets) or 1 to 3 or 4 hours (sustained release medication) after medication is taken. See Summaries 52-55 for information on peak medication times.

6.2. Reschedule with math teachers with whom the student has been successful. Suggest to parents that they talk with or write the administration—for example, the assistant principal for curriculum—requesting the same teacher and explaining why it is so important. Schools often will honor this type of request.

7. Modify classroom set-up:

7.1. Consider whether assigning a seat is important for this student. If so, see the discussion in Summary 57.

Challenging Middle and High School Math Skills

SUMMARY 20

Teachers and parents alike have identified the following math skills as being especially challenging for middle and high school students with ADD/ADHD.

Multiplication Tables

- **Use assistive technology.** By the middle school years, if students are still struggling with multiplication tables, allow them to use a *calculator* or *laminated chart* of these tables during class and for homework.

- **Provide visual cues.** Use resources that provide more visual cues, such as *Times Tables the Fun Way!* by Judy Liautaud and Dave Rodriguez (see illustration below). Included in the *Times Tables the Fun Way!* kits are multiplication books, cards, workbooks, and posters that utilize mnemonic tips. (Available from 800-585-6059; www.citycreek.com)

Remember: When it's 4 x 4, the fours become a 4 by 4 (4 x 4) and you have to be 16 to drive it.

From *Times Tables the Fun Way!*

- **Use songs or chants.** A couple of helpful resources are available from Remedia Publications:

  - *Multiplication Rap,* available on both audio and videotapes.
  - *Multiplication Songs,* available on worksheets and lyrics.

Section 2 | Academic and Learning Issues

■ **Teach multiplication short cuts.** For problems remembering the nines multiplication tables, try this finger counting technique. Hold your hands out in front of you and spread your fingers. For 9 x 7, count from left to right until you reach the seventh finger. Hold that finger down and then count the remaining fingers on either side to obtain the correct answer. There are six fingers to the left and three fingers to the right. The correct answer is 63.

9 x 7 = 63

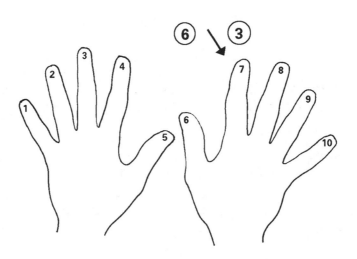

■ **Give simple, easily understood rules** when possible. For example:

If multiplying by 10, add one zero. (10 x 5 = 50)

If multiplying by 100, add two zeros. (100 x 5 = 500)

If multiplying by 1000, add three zeros. (1000 x 5 = 5000)

Long Division

■ **Develop mnemonics** to help students remember math concepts or facts. Here's an example of an acronym to help students remember the steps of long division. (Teachers or students are encouraged to make up their own mnemonics.)

Dumb **M**onkeys **S**ell **B**ananas

Divide	[39 by 22]	
Multiply	[1 times 22]	
Subtract	[39-22=17]	
Bring down	[6]	
[repeat the process with 176]		

```
           1 8
    2 2 3 9 6
        2 2
        1 7 6
        1 7 6
              0
```

Fractions and Decimals

- **Use concrete visual examples.** Susan Jessup, a middle school math teacher, uses money when she begins teaching students how to change fractions to decimals and then percentages. Many students find it easier to learn abstract concepts when using a concrete example with which they are already familiar.

  ½ of one dollar = $.50 = 50%

  ¼ of one dollar = $.25 = 25%

  ¾ of one dollar = $.75 = 75%

  1/10 of one dollar = $.10 = 10%

Multiplying and Dividing Numbers with Decimals

- **Give a mnemonic.** Jessup gives students these rules of thumb for multiplying and dividing numbers with decimals.

$$\begin{array}{r} .25 \\ \times\ .33 \\ \hline 75 \\ 75 \\ \hline .0825 \end{array}$$

When ***multiplying*** numbers with decimals the new number is always smaller and the decimal moves to the left.

$$.25\ \overline{)\ .300\ }\ \ \ \ \ \begin{array}{c}1.2\end{array}$$

$$\begin{array}{r} 25 \\ \hline 50 \\ 50 \\ \hline 0 \end{array}$$

When ***dividing*** numbers with decimals the new number is always larger and the decimal moves to the right.

- **Draw a poster of this information** and post it in the room.

Problem Solving (Word Problems)

Problem solving typically involves completing word problems. Many students with ADD/ADHD have difficulty setting up the equation correctly for these problems.

- **Make the process more concrete and visual.** Jessup asks her students to *label* parts of the problem to make it easier to solve. Circles and X's are drawn on the key words in the math problem.

    1. **CIRCLE** needed facts in the problem.

        Example: Mr. Fuller paid his son Brian $10 each time he mowed the lawn. If Brian mowed the lawn 12 times, how much did he earn?

    2. **MARK OUT** any unnecessary facts.

        Example: Ten members of a drama club each bought a $4.75 ticket to see a play on Tuesday night. The play ran for 3 nights. How much did it cost for the group to see the play?

    3. **UNDERLINE** the strategy word or phrase.

        Example: Mary spent $9.95 on a tape and $12.95 on a CD. How much did she spend?

    4. **FOR A 2-STEP PROBLEM**, place 1 LINE under the first step and 2 LINES under the second step.

        Example: Stacy has 1 yard of ribbon. She needs 5/6 of a foot, 1 1/3 feet, and 3/4 of a foot. Does she have enough of the ribbon?

- **Give students a list of strategy or action words** and the appropriate math procedures they translate into. Sometimes the terms in word problems such as "combined,"

Addition	Subtraction	Multiplication	Division
how many?	the difference	product	quotient
altogether	how much less?	times	how many groups?
total*	how many more?	times as much	divided into
sum	more than	multiple of	divided by
combined	less than	twice	one-half of
in all*	subtracted from	(a number) times	one-third of
perimeter	less	multiplied by	one-fourth of
total cost*	increase	times as much	what part?
surface area*	decrease	times as many	make equal parts
	fewer	area	factor
	minus	volume	per unit
	how much change	surface area*	unit cost
	have enough?	squared	
		total*	
		in all*	
		total cost*	

These words may mean to either add or multiply, so read problems carefully.

"what amount," or "how much less" can confuse students so they are unsure which math procedure to use. This list should help students avoid confusion when these terms are found in word problems. Obviously, the student must understand the problem to be able to find the answer and to interpret it. Teachers may want to reduce or expand the list based upon the grade level being taught.

- **Use association** with something familiar in setting up the problem. Try using a student's name in sample word problems. Or use metaphors, analogies, or examples from the student's daily life. For example, if there are eight slices of pizza and your brother eats three of them, how much is left? Express in a fraction (5/8), percent (62.5%), or decimal (.625).

Using Math Ratios in Problem Solving

Math ratios are used to set up a proportion in a math equation. A ratio compares two numbers and can be shown as a "fraction" (3/4), "colon" (3:4) and "to" (3 to 4).

- **Use a mnemonic.** When setting up an equation using a math proportion or ratio as a fraction, this mnemonic may be helpful:

  When there are two numbers in a problem before a comma (,) or period (.), set up the ratio between the first two numbers.

  Then the second two numbers must be set up in the same order—in other words, comparing apples to apples and money to money.

  If 10 apples cost $2.50, how much will 20 apples cost?

$$\frac{\# \text{ apples}}{\text{cost}} = \frac{\# \text{ apples}}{X} \qquad\qquad \frac{10}{2.50} = \frac{20}{X}$$

$$10X = 50.00$$

$$X = 5$$

  The cost of 20 apples is $5.00

Classifying Shapes

- **Create a Mind Map** (graphic organizer) to classify geometric shapes. To help students understand and remember the difference between shapes, teachers may classify them in more than one way. As shown here, triangles may be classified by naming angles and by describing their sides.

  See the illustration on the next page for an example of this.

Classify Triangles

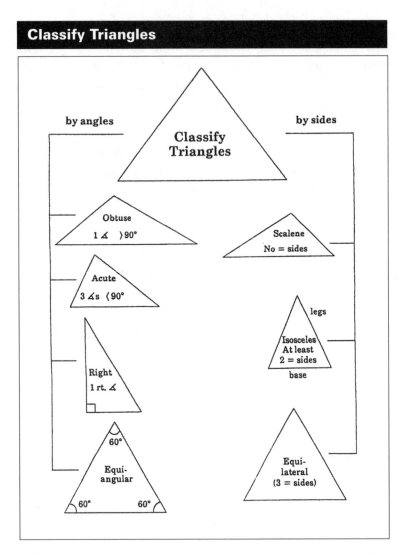

- ■ **Use color and visual cues** to teach students to distinguish between similar and congruent figures. Cut out shapes from color-coordinated construction paper (or clear colored sheets for use on an overhead) to illustrate various shapes and concepts.

  Similar figures have the same shapes but one may be larger or smaller.

  Congruent figures are exactly alike and will match identically if laid on top of each other.

  - 2 congruent squares

  - 2 similar triangles

    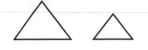

  - 2 similar rectangles

The Order of Operations

Math teachers Vogelesang and Wells both use **mnemonics** (acronyms) frequently. When addition, subtraction, multiplication, or division may be mixed into a problem, they suggest using this acrostic to help students remember the order to follow in solving the problem. PEMDAS is one of the most frequently used mnemonics in math. However, many math problems involve only MDAS, My Dear Aunt Sally, and may not include exponents or parenthesis.

Please **E**xcuse **M**y **D**ear **A**unt **S**ally **(PEMDAS)**:

EXAMPLE #1

Parenthesis: Do the operations in parenthesis first.	$50 \div (3-8)^2 \cdot 4 + 3$	
Exponents: Do numbers with exponents next.	$50 \div (-5)^2 \cdot 4 + 3$	
Multiply or **D**ivide: Do whichever comes first, left to right	$50 \div 25 \cdot 4 + 3$	
	$2 \cdot 4 + 3$	
Add or **S**uubtract: Do whichever comes first, left to right	$8 + 3$	
	11	

EXAMPLE #2

$6 - 2\,(3+5)$

$6 - 2\,(8)$

$6 - 16$

-10

EXAMPLE #3

$7 - 4 + 6 \cdot 5 \div 5$

$7 - 4 + 30 \div 5$

$7 - 4 + 6$

$3 + 6$

9

Multiplying Binomials

Vogelesang and Wells also use this **mnemonic** to help when students are multiplying binomials.

FOIL. Perform multiplication of terms in the following order:

EXAMPLE #1

$(x + 2)(3X - 5) = ?$

First: Multiply the first terms in each set of parenthesis.	$x \cdot (3X)$	$= 3X^2$
Outside: Multiply outside terms.	$x \cdot (-5)$	$= -5X$
Inside: Multiply inside terms.	$2 \cdot (3X)$	$= 6X$
Last: Multiply the last terms.	$2 \cdot (-5)$	$= -10$
	$3X^2 - 5X + 6X - 10$	
Combine like terms.	$3X^2 + X - 10$	

Properties of Whole Numbers

- **Use a mnemonic.** There are five common properties of whole numbers, but typically two of them are especially confusing for students. The challenge here is to differentiate between Commutative and Associative property: CO and AP.

COmmutative Property: applies

- to addition and multiplication
- even though the order changes,
- the sum or product is still the same

CO allows a **C**hange in **O**rder of numbers:

$5 + 7 = 7 + 5;$

$a + b = b + a;$

$3 \times 7 = 7 \times 3$

Associative **P**roperty of Addition:

- even though the parentheses move
- (the grouping of numbers changes) the sum is still the same

AP **A**rranges **P**arenthesis:

$(12 + 8) + 5 = 12 + (8 + 5)$

$(3X + 2) + 2X = 3X + (2 + 2X)$

Algebraic Equations

It can help to explain to students that an equation is like a balance scale. If you subtract the same number from each side, the equation stays balanced. So, "To solve the problem, whatever you do to one side of an equation, you need to do to the other side (add, subtract, multiply, divide)."

$$27 + x = 93$$
$$-27 \qquad -27$$
$$\overline{}$$
$$0 + x = 66$$

Linear Equations

Linear functions are described by both a formula and a line drawing on a graph. Typically, students have problems in two special cases, one where the line has no slope (a vertical line) and the other has a 0 slope (horizontal line)

- **Ask the student to make up her own mnemonic for a problem concept.** Liteena, a high school senior, was struggling with linear equations and made up this acronym that her teacher now uses for other students.

Slope of a Horizontal Line: **HOY**—**H**orizontal, **0** slope, **Y**=?

Example: A **H**orizontal line has a slope of **0** and is represented by an equation, **Y**= a constant.

(If you know HOY, then it is easier to remember that a vertical line has no slope and is represented by an equation x= a constant.)

Metric System Graphic Organizer

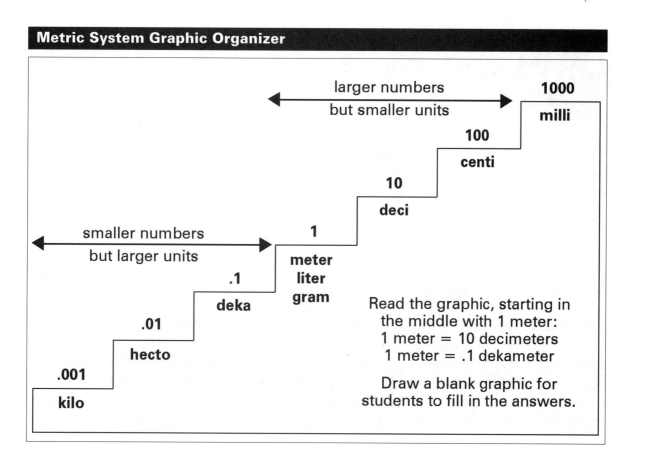

larger numbers
but smaller units

1000
milli
100
centi
10
deci
1
meter
liter
gram

smaller numbers
but larger units

.1
deka
.01
hecto
.001
kilo

Read the graphic, starting in
the middle with 1 meter:
1 meter = 10 decimeters
1 meter = .1 dekameter

Draw a blank graphic for
students to fill in the answers.

Metric System Prefixes

Use the staircase (shown on the next page) to remember the relationship of the prefixes for the metric system. This **graphic organizer** helps students "see" the relationship between the numbers.

Resources

Liautaud, Judy & Dave Rodriguez. *Times Tables the Fun Way!* Sandy, UT: City Creek Press, 1999. A picture method of learning multiplication tables. (800-585-6059; www.citycreek.com)

Remedia Publications, Scottsdale, AZ (800-826-4740; www.rempub.com). This company, founded by special education teachers specializes in educational materials for students who have trouble learning in traditional ways. Request a publications catalog.

Thomas, Ed, Ph.D. *Styles and Strategies for Teaching Middle Grades Mathematics.* Woodbridge, NJ: Thoughtful Education Press, 1999.

Thomas, Ed, Ph.D. *Dr. Thomas' P3CR Paired Learner Math Activities for General Math, Pre-Algebra, Algebra, and Geometry.* Woodbridge, NJ: Dimension 2000, 1999.

The World Book of Math Power. Chicago: World Book Encyclopedia, 1996. This informative book includes math rules listed within a block that clearly and simply explains key math concepts.

Math Games

Some middle and high school teachers occasionally allow their students to play math games, especially on the day before a holiday or as part of a review for a test. Students with ADD/ADHD especially enjoy math games because they are fun and involve activity and novelty. To find additional math games that may appeal to your students, check the local library for books on math games.

Math Competition

Susan Jessup, a middle school math teacher, organizes math competitions to motivate her students to review for tests. She selects the game problems from a math review sheet that was assigned for homework the night before. Students may even use their homework paper to copy the problem onto the board. The first student to finish the problem with the right answer is awarded a point. Up to four students can work simultaneously at the board, which actively involves more students than most other math games.

Teams, Games, and Tournaments

Dr. Ed Thomas uses math games as a form of cooperative learning. In his book *Styles and Strategies for Teaching Middle Grades Mathematics*, Dr. Thomas describes a game in which he ranks his students by grade average or performance levels and spreads them across four home teams. Team members practice and review key concepts before the game. Members of each team may then rank order their team members based upon their skill level. Four competitive tables are set up in the room. The number one ranked members of each team go to table number one for their game. Number two players go to table number two and so on. There are cards with questions on each table. One student draws an index card containing a math problem from the center of the table. After she gives her answer to the problem, the next student may challenge her answer. The student who has the correct answer gets to keep the card. At the end of the competition, the top four winners at each table are declared; points are awarded and then added together for their home team members.

Math Baseball or Kickball

In math baseball or kickball, the class is divided into teams. The first student comes to the board, is given a problem, then works the problem. If she works the problem correctly, she advances to first base (a designated desk or other landmark in the classroom). Each time a student gets a problem correct, players move forward to the next base. Students keep walking around the bases until they score or their team gets three outs. Dr. Thomas makes the game more interesting by creating questions of varying difficulty that may earn a single, double, triple, or home run.

The Multiplication Facts WAR game

Dr. Thomas describes a game to help with a review of multiplication facts. A deck of cards is shuffled and divided evenly between two players. On command, each player turns a card up. The first player to give the correct answer of the two numbers multiplied together wins the cards. Face cards are worth ten points and Aces one point. One team member tells players when to start and another may act as the calculator judge.

The game may be modified to review other math facts such as squares and integers, positive and negative numbers. In *Integer War*, black cards are negative and red cards are positive numbers. Each of the two players turns up a card. The student who has the highest positive number wins the cards.

Math war games are also available commercially for addition, subtraction, multiplication, and division facts.

Math Bingo

Students are given bingo cards with numbers written on them. Math problems are read aloud, students solve the problem, and look for the answer on their card. The math problems can be tailored to the unit the class is studying, or be used to review basic concepts. In his book, Dr. Thomas explains how teachers may make their own cards and gives samples of Bingo questions.

Who Wants to Be a Millionaire?

A math game using a format similar to the popular television program *Who Wants To Be a Millionaire?* would likely pique the interest of many students, with and without ADD/ADHD. Divide the class into two teams. Then, rather than letting one student answer a series of questions, have each student on a team take turns answering one question posed by the teacher. As they are given increasingly difficult questions, students have the opportunity to stop, giving up their turn, and keep the points they have won for their team. To add challenge, students may risk losing the points they have won if they continue on to harder questions and give an incorrect answer. A total of three "lifelines" are allowed for the whole team and may include 1) polling teammates for the correct answer, 2) eliminating two wrong answers, and 3) asking another student for help with one question.

Math Snowball Fights

Susan Putman, a middle school math teacher, uses one math game her students love. Students make up three math problems, work the answers, copy each blank problem onto a separate piece of paper, and write their names on their papers. They then wad up each paper separately. For two to three minutes, the students throw the wads of paper at each other. Then they stop and collect three wads of paper (math problems) and solve them. Next they compare answers with the person who made up the problem and correct any errors.

Settling Down after the Game

Anytime students are active, getting them to settle down afterwards often presents problems. So, teach the students what they should do as they stop playing the game. Explain the rules for the math game, then how to change from being active to sitting down. For example:

"When it's time to stop, I'll say, 'The snowball fight is over. Get your three problems and sit down in your desk.'"

"I'll count to five. If anyone is still standing when I say 6, then we won't be able to play the math game tomorrow."

Strategies for Improving Memory

On the surface, memorizing information seems like such a simple task that it is often taken for granted. However, this complex skill is a major problem for many students with ADD/ADHD. (See Summaries 11 and 22.) The major problems appear to be:

1. limited **working memory** capacity,
2. getting information into **long-term memory** (to remember facts any longer than twenty seconds, information must be transferred from short-term into long-term memory),
3. quickly retrieving information from **long-term memory** when needed.

Practically speaking, students with attention deficits often have difficulty remembering information such as assignments, chores, multiplication tables, or foreign languages. They may learn multiplication tables or vocabulary words one night, only to forget them by the next day. Rote memorization of isolated facts, dates, numbers, or "boring" information is especially difficult.

Actually, it may be wise to *minimize requirements for memorization* as much as possible. Ask yourself: "Is it critical to this student's life to stress her limited skills to memorize this material?" If the answer is no, allow the student to refer to basic facts on a small card. When memorization is necessary, consider the following strategies:

1. Use mnemonics: Mnemonics are devices or techniques consciously used as aids in remembering. They are among the most effective memory tools for all students, not just those with ADD/ADHD. Students may use mnemonics created by others, or make up ones that are more meaningful to them—and therefore easier to remember.

    1.1. Make an acronym. Use the first letters of the information to make a word. One of the best known acronyms is **HOMES,** an acronym for the Great Lakes: **H**uron, **O**ntario, **M**ichigan, **E**rie, and **S**uperior.

    1.2. Make an acrostic. Use the first letters of key words to make a new word or sentence. For example, the order of planets can be remembered as: "**M**y **v**ery **e**ducated **m**other **j**ust **s**ent **u**s **n**ine **p**izzas" (**Mer**cury, **V**enus, **E**arth, **M**ars, **J**upiter, **S**aturn, **U**ranus, **N**eptune, **P**luto).

    1.3. Categorize and chunk. Divide information into smaller categories. If twenty vocabulary or spelling words are given, group them by three or four common categories: 1) people, places, events; 2) verbs, nouns, adjectives; 3) words related to science or history; or 4) words starting with the same letters. Then study them.

    1.4. Chant, or use rhymes or choral response. Use rhyme or a beat to help remember information. Younger middle school students may find "math rap tapes" or "singing multiplication tables" helpful. See Summary 20 for math resources.

2. Use concept imagery: Help students create a mental picture or draw a picture of the object to be remembered. Exaggerating features or adding absurdities will make it easier to remember. For example, Dr. Claire Jones, a learning disabilities and ADD consultant, suggests picturing a bay with pigs each wearing a T-shirt with 1961 on it to remember details about the Bay of Pigs. My embellishment would be to picture these pigs in a boat and the names, Kennedy, Castro, etc. written on the shirts. For political science, draw a picture of how a bill becomes law: the idea (a light bulb), first draft (a curtain blowing in a drafty window), or the bill is introduced ("Hi, Bill"). Ideally, when students hear the key word on the test, the mental picture pops into their heads to help them remember the correct answer.

2.1. Try visual posting. As explained in Summary 13-A, some teachers write key information or put pictures on the wall in the classroom. As the teacher talks, she points to the material to be learned. Later, she asks questions on this material, points to the correct card, and the students answer in unison. Students are much more likely to remember information presented in this manner.

2.2. Use mental visualization. In another example, Dr. Claire Jones asked three students independently what they saw in the word "opulent." Then they were asked to make a mental picture of what they saw in order to remember the meaning of opulent. Responses included: "if wealthy, *lent* money," "buy *opals*," "buy *OP*—Ocean Pacific clothes)." The key was allowing the student to pick the association that was meaningful to her, rather than make up one for her.

2.3. Create a "pop-up" book. Susie Smith, a middle school teacher at Lullwater School (Decatur, GA), teaches her students to make pop-up books. Students create four or five scenes that capture the essence of the novel they are reading and put them in a "pop-up" book. They make the book by folding construction paper in half to make pages 4x5½", cutting the fold in two or three places (1" wide x 1" deep), and folding the cut strip outward so that it stands up when the book is opened to a 45 degree angle. Then pictures are glued on the standup parts.

3. Use color cues: Dr. Sydney Zentall, special education professor at Purdue University, has found that using color helps students with ADD/ADHD remember information.

3.1. Use color to highlight the correct response. For example, if the student transposes letters within a word, highlight the letters where the error occurs but not the whole word. Highlight the correct response, not the error. For example, if a student consistently spells "girl" as "gril," then highlight the "ir" in "girl." Dr. Jones suggests a possible rank order for use of colors for highlighting. Red is a memorable choice since researchers indicate that the color most quickly recognized by recovering stroke victims is red, then green, blue, and yellow.

3.2. Use color to highlight key facts or unique aspects of spelling or vocabulary words. Highlight who, what, when, where, or why in an essay or the three sets of double letters in Mississippi.

3.3. Color code materials. Students may use color-coded items to denote each subject: for math, red book covers and assignment folder, or circle or write assignments in red ink.

3.4. Color code test review information. Teachers may divide study material for tests and print it on different color paper: key facts on a blue sheet; important names on yellow; themes/issues on pink. Or, in Language Arts or foreign language class, put nouns on blue cards, verbs on pink, adjectives on yellow.

4. **Use contextual cues:** Students are more likely to recall vocabulary words and facts that are used in a sentence, especially if the example is funny or unusual. Here are a few examples: "This honey is too *viscous,*" she said in a syrupy voice. OR: The *supercilious* cheerleader looked super silly with her nose in the air. OR: The long-distance runners raced along the line of *longitude* from the North Pole to the South Pole.

5. **Try the Loci Method:** Using this method, you label familiar local settings as a frame of reference for learning. You use visual cues to help make the topic three-dimensional and bring it to life. For example, when teaching about World War II, arrange large hand-drawn maps of the key countries involved around the room to portray their relationships to each other. Put the map of the U.S. on the file cabinet at the front left side of the classroom, England on the left side of the board, France and Germany on the right, and Africa hanging off the front of the teacher's desk. Have students cut out pictures of people, label them to represent the key leaders, and place them in their countries. Cut out pictures of buildings and label them to represent key cities in each country. In another lesson, start with clean maps and add major battles. As Germany advances, use clear red plastic wrap to cover the countries that fell under its control.

6. **Rehearse information (the right way):** Frequently, when new vocabulary words are introduced, students are asked to "rehearse," or write each of them five or more times. This strategy is not especially effective with students with ADD/ADHD. Adding a verbal element to the rehearsal makes it more helpful. Ask students to say the word aloud, repeat it to themselves, record it on a tape recorder using unusual speech (vary timing or pitch), and then listen to it for review.

7. **Use a multisensory approach:** As Summary 12 on Learning Styles discusses, students with ADD/ADHD often benefit from a multisensory approach to learning. They may learn better by watching *and* listening, for instance.

7.1. Use popular videotapes. Allow students to watch videotapes of classic novels or war portrayals at home or school.

7.2. Use "Books on Tape." Books on audiotape can be helpful for students who have trouble concentrating and remembering the content of material they read. This multisensory approach involves both auditory and visual cues. See Summary 13-E.

8. **Remember the keys to learning for students with ADD/ADHD:** Two educators I admire, Dr. Sydney Zentall and Dr. Claire Jones, have identified what they feel are the key elements for improving memory. As I mentioned earlier, Dr. Zentall emphasizes the ***use of color***. Dr. Jones stresses:

- ***the use of association*** to help link isolated information to things we already know. In addition, allowing the student to identify her own "personal association" for information is also critical.
- ***the use of exaggeration,*** since it is easier to remember the "wild and wacky" than the "same and similar."

Remember, too, that information that is presented with both *auditory and visual cues* is usually easier to remember.

Evaluation of Memory and Learning

Since retrieving information from long-term memory can be so difficult for students with ADD/ADHD, teachers may want to consider alternative ways of evaluation:

- Rather than requiring students to find an answer for a test question in their long-term memory, ask them to select the correct answer from among several incorrect answers.
- Allow the student to use memory aids such as a word bank or a laminated card with math formulas, rules for conjugating verbs, or the correct spelling of key words to be included in an essay.

For students with a memory impairment, tests of recognition, rather than cold recall, provide a more accurate assessment of what they have learned. See Section 13-C for more on testing alternatives.

Five Common Reasons for School Failure: Eliminating Academic Agony

Teachers and educators with whom I have worked identified these five areas as primary reasons for school failure among students with ADD/ADHD. These issues, as well as intervention strategies to help eliminate academic agony, are discussed below. References to other related summaries are noted by (S-#).

PROBLEMS	GENERAL STRATEGIES
1. NOT DOING HOMEWORK/GETTING ZEROS	S 13-D
(Due to disorganization, forgetfulness, executive function deficits)	**Use an assignment notebook.** 1. Have the student write down assignments. 2. Have a classmate double check assignments. 3. Teacher double checks assignment and initials it.
(Forgets assignments)	**Provide a variety of ways for student to get assignments.** 1. Provide a couple of classmates' phone numbers so the student can phone them at home for the assignment. 2. Fax or e-mail a copy of assignments to parents, perhaps daily or weekly. 3. Ask a student or teacher's aide to write down assignments to send home. 4. Give assignments and test dates in writing (every week or month). 5. Record homework assignments on a classroom answering machine or teacher voice mail. 6. Have a "homework hotline," a school operated phone line that students can call to get homework assignments. 7. Post homework assignments on the school or teacher web page. 8. Post homework assignments on an outside window so students can return to check it after school hours. 9. Make homework assignments available at the local library. 10. Write assignments on the board before class; remind student to write down assignment. **Tell parents the homework pattern** *(i.e., Algebra: homework four nights weekly; test every two weeks or at the end of a chapter)*
(Forgets books)	**Have student borrow a book from a classmate.** **Allow student to keep an extra book (or set) at home.** **Be flexible: allow work to be turned in late.** Develop a plan to turn it in on time. **Use a weekly report to reinforce completion of work.** See Summary 26 on weekly reports.

PROBLEMS	GENERAL STRATEGIES
(Forgets to turn in assignments.)	**Enlist other students' help. (S 13-D)** 1. Ask "row captains" to check that assignments are written down and to collect homework. 2. Pair all students. Ask them to spend the last five minutes checking to see that assignments are written down and homework turned in.
(No medication when doing work)	**Start homework during the time when medication is still effective.**
(Too much homework)	**Determine whether too much homework is being assigned.** If appropriate, reduce the amount of homework (S 24).
2. FAILING TESTS	(S 13-C)
(Does not do homework or study)	*Ensure homework completion, using strategies listed above.* **Provide a study review sheet of key facts.** **Modify testing format. (S 13-C)** 1. Use word banks. 2. Avoid essay exams. **Allow the student to earn extra credit.**
(Does not have time to finish tests)	**Give extended time on tests.** **Give tests in an area without distractions or interruptions.**
3. FORGETTING KEY ASSIGNMENTS, TESTS, AND LONG-TERM PROJECTS	**The teacher or row captain reminds the student of due dates.** **Send a notice home to parents regarding special projects or tests.** **Break projects into three or four segments.** Grade each segment separately. (S 13) **Teach time management. (S 34-37)** 1. Complete a weekly/monthly schedule. 2. Divide task into required steps. 3. Schedule each step. 4. Work backward to complete the timeline.
4. NOT TAKING NOTES/DIFFICULTY COPYING FROM THE BOARD	**Teach the student to take notes. (S 13B)** Teach students to make up their own shorthand. **Designate a notetaker for the whole class.** 1. Make photocopies of a student's notes and leave them in a designated spot for any student who needs them. 2. Have the notetaker use NCR (non-carbon replica) paper and tear off the bottom copy to give to the student with ADD/ADHD. **Give guided lecture notes.** Outline the key points, leaving spaces for students to write additional notes. **Allow the student to tape record the class lecture.** *(This strategy may be ineffective for students who are unwilling to listen to the same material twice.)* **Minimize copying from the board.** When copying is necessary, allow the student to copy from the book or a handout.

PROBLEMS	GENERAL STRATEGIES
5. DIFFICULTIES MAKING THE TRANSITION FROM ELEMENTARY TO MIDDLE TO HIGH SCHOOL	**Encourage parents to notify a new school about ADD/ADHD.** 1. Notify in May-June, or check with the guidance counselor at the new school to find out when student schedules are developed. 2. Provide input on the Fall schedule. (S 57) **Develop an IEP for special education students before they transition to the next school.** **Schedule a student support team meeting (SST).*** **Assign an upper class mentor to help with the transition.** **Give parents an update on grades after 2-3 weeks in the new school.**

* *Although not mandated by federal law, many states have developed teams of educators that meet to discuss ways of helping students who are struggling. These teams may have different names in different states such as student support team (SST) or child study team (CST). The SST is not the same thing as an IEP team. IEP teams are mandated by federal law to screen students for special education eligibility. The SST team is available to help any student regardless of whether or not she is eligible for special education services. Team members may include veteran teachers and ideally also a guidance counselor, school psychologist, or social worker.*

What Is "Good Homework" for Students with ADD/ADHD?

Teenagers with ADD/ADHD are notorious for getting lots of "zeros" because they don't complete their homework. In addition, their school performance is often erratic: one day they do well and the next day they do poorly. For example, my son once made an 87 on a final exam but failed a class because he didn't complete all his homework and a make-up test. The seemingly simple task of completing and handing in assignments often erupts into a major battle between teenagers and their parents and teachers.

Since homework, by definition, is done at home, **a partnership between teachers, parents, and the teen is critical** to ensure that students with attention deficits successfully complete their work. So, suggestions are given on two levels: 1) for teachers (this summary), and 2) for parents (the next summary).

National Interest in Homework

Homework for all children has been a controversial issue raised recently in the national press. Headlines in both *Time* and *Newsweek* have questioned whether our children are being given too much homework.

Let's talk briefly about what we know is **best practice for giving homework**. First, the National PTA and National Education Association (NEA) offer general guidance for time spent on homework. They suggest that roughly ten minutes per grade be spent on homework each night. So, a ninth grader could spend a total of an hour and a half (90 minutes) on his homework for all his subjects. Drs. Sydney Zentall and Sam Goldstein, in *Seven Steps to Homework Success*, suggest a general homework time range for middle school of one to two hours and for high school, up to two and a half hours. Remember, researchers advise that homework doesn't have to be lengthy to be effective! *Newsweek* gave an example of a seventh grader who was given 15 minutes of math homework every school night through eleventh grade winding up one full grade ahead in achievement.

How Much Homework Is Too Much?

When homework is a problem, two key issues must be considered:

1. How do teachers, especially in middle and high school, know how much homework students are getting from other teachers?
2. How much longer does the student take to complete the work than the teacher expects it to take?

A conference can be scheduled to answer the first question. As for the second question, Zentall and Goldstein have a suggestion that may be helpful. If there are problems with homework completion:

1. The teacher writes on the student's paper how long she thinks homework should take.
2. Parents and the teenager write on the homework paper how long it actually takes to complete and then return it to school.

Zentall and Goldstein point out that many teachers underestimate how long students with learning problems actually take to complete homework! When assigning homework, also keep in mind the general homework guidelines given by the NEA and PTA.

Negative Consequences of Too Much Homework

National researchers have found that there is a tipping point where too much homework can have negative consequences by turning students off to school and a love of learning.

School is an especially stressful environment for students with ADD/ADHD, according to Dr. Robert Reid, who is affiliated with the special education department at the University of Nebraska. A vicious cycle may develop if the student returns to school upset because she did not complete her homework, fails to complete class work, and is assigned even more homework. During this cycle, the student's behavior usually deteriorates rapidly. "Therefore homework should be kept to the absolute minimum and the teacher should not assign uncompleted class work as homework," recommends Dr. Reid. Although Dr. Reid's advice is directed at students in special education, it is also good advice for many students with ADD/ADHD who are struggling in regular education classes.

When students struggle with an overwhelming amount of homework, grades aren't the only thing to suffer. Fighting between parents and their children over homework completion may seriously damage the crucial parent-teen relationship. When parents press too hard, teenagers may withdraw, avoid interactions with them, and become defiant. In addition, too much homework keeps students from sports and community or religious activities that build self-esteem and teach important values. According to a Columbia University education professor, *when homework turns kids off to school, it becomes a part of the problem rather than the solution.*

What Is Homework in Middle and High School Typically Like?

Dr. Zentall and Dr. Goldstein found in their research that, typically, most teachers assign two types of homework:

1. questions or problems from textbooks, and
2. worksheets.

Students say these types of assignments are often boring. Boredom may lead to:

1. decreased attention to assignments,
2. reduced student motivation, completion of less school work (half of all students don't finish these assignments),

3. reduced accuracy on completed work (only 40 percent of students complete work with 80-100 percent accuracy),
4. negative evaluation of school by students,
5. disinterest in school, which may result in a student dropping out of school.

What Is Good Homework for Students with ADD/ADHD Like?

Good homework can help reduce boredom. It should:

1. Promote a love of learning.
2. Be meaningful, not too hard, not too long or repetitive.
3. Be brief: completed in a reasonable time.
4. Review material taught in class, not introduce new material.
5. Be critical for the next day's work.
6. Be broken into smaller chunks (20-30 minutes at a time).
7. Develop understanding through experience and discovery.
8. Provide a novel or creative learning experience. For example, have the student interview her grandfather about his Viet Nam or World War II experiences rather than write a boring essay on the war.
9. Help students in application of knowledge, in discovery thinking, and transfer of learning to new settings.
10. Use a variety of ways to demonstrate competency, rather than just writing. For example, the student could:
    - Dictate the learned information on audiotape.
    - Dictate the information to a scribe (another student or adult), who types the information for her.
    - Produce a videotape of the information to be learned—for example, her interpretation of the way a bill becomes law.
11. Give students some choices, such as a choice of two or three topics for writing an essay or report. When students are given limited choices, they:
    - complete more assignments,
    - are more compliant,
    - are less aggressive.
12. Give math and reading homework on alternate days.
13. Allow students with learning problems to begin assignments in class to see if they understand the material.

It is important for teachers to keep these tips in mind when they assign homework! Remember, homework doesn't have to be extremely long to help students learn the information.

Barriers to Homework Completion

The most common barriers for students getting full credit for doing homework are listed below. Summaries that discuss each issue are noted as follows (S-#):

1. Forgetting books and assignments (S-23 & 30),
2. Failing to complete assignments (S-23 & 30),
3. Failing to turn in completed assignments (S-23 & 30),
4. Avoiding homework assignments because they are too long and thus overwhelming,
5. Attempting homework when medication has completely worn off; the student can't easily pay attention and has difficulty getting started and completing work (S-24, 51-55),
6. Parents don't know how to monitor homework and provide guidance to the student (S-24, 25, 64).

Families may need help correcting each of these problems. Sharing copies of the summaries noted in parentheses will be helpful for parents who want to be involved.

Closing Thoughts on Homework

Teachers and parents must work to ensure that homework is a helpful learning experience. If a student continues to struggle completing homework, teachers should determine how long homework is taking. Although giving extended time on assignments is helpful, that accommodation alone is often not enough. Ultimately, if assignments are taking students with ADD/ADHD longer to complete than their classmates, the ***amount of homework must be reduced!***

Resources

Dendy, Chris A. Zeigler. *Teenagers with ADD: A Parents' Guide.* Bethesda, MD: Woodbine House, 1995.

Helbing, Joan. "Handling the Homework Hurdle." *Focus on ADD,* the Wisconsin Consortium Newsletter, February 1998.

NEA & PTA Policy Paper on homework. Available from www.nea.org.

Reid, Robert. "Attention Deficit Hyperactivity Disorder: Effective Methods for the Classroom." *Focus on Exceptional Children*, V.32, N.4, December 1999.

Zentall, Sydney & Sam Goldstein. *Seven Steps to Homework Success*. Plantation, FL: Specialty Press, 1999.

Helping Parents Cope with Homework

Parents often say that the greatest challenge in parenting a teenager with ADD/ADHD is getting them to complete homework! Parents are often frustrated by their teen's failure to do homework and sometimes also feel guilty for having to be so involved. Nightly emotional blow-ups are common, leaving many parents and teenagers feeling angry and overwhelmed. The teacher is often the key to helping families solve the homework problem. Typically, part of the teacher's job is to help parents learn how to provide the right level of support for their teenager.

Appropriate Parental Involvement

The level of parental involvement in homework supervision will vary for each student depending on the severity of ADD/ADHD symptoms, presence of learning problems, and level of maturity. Because of the teen's learning problems and her two- to four-year developmental delay, parents are involved far longer and to a greater degree in monitoring school work than they would like to be! It is critical for teachers to convey the message that it is okay for parents to guide and monitor their teenager's schoolwork. Keep in mind that these parents are simply providing developmentally appropriate supervision.

A strong bond between parents and the teenager is critical for coping successfully. One way to help solidify this bond is to treat the teenager as a respected partner in the problem-solving process. Remember, attention deficit disorder is not a picnic for teenagers. They did not ask to be born with this challenging biochemical condition. If supervision becomes too intense and begins to damage the parent-teen relationship, parents may have to back off and develop a new monitoring plan. Ultimately, parents will be able to reduce their level of supervision over time, but some degree of supervision may be needed into college and young adulthood.

Suggestions for Teachers to Share with Parents

If the student is passing, less teacher and parental monitoring will be necessary. If she is failing a class, many of the following steps may be necessary. (See Summary 26 on Weekly Reports and Summary 61 on "shaping" behavior for more suggestions on homework. Suggestions for dealing with homework issues are also discussed in more detail in Chapter 9 of *Teenagers with ADD*.)

1. **Review basic strategies for knowing homework assignments** in Summary 23: using daily planners, monitoring assignments, and keeping extra textbooks at home.

2. **Schedule the timing of the last medication dose** between 4:00-6:00 p.m. so that the student can focus on her homework. Parents may use a trial and error ap-

proach to determine how late the student can take medication without it interfering with her sleep.

3. **Give students some choices;** it will usually make them more cooperative. Ask the teen to complete the homework survey in Appendix A4: "What Helps Me Study Best at Home?" Then find out the answers to any remaining questions. *"Where do you want to study, the kitchen table or in your bedroom?" "Do you want to start at 7:00 or 7:30?" "Do you want to set a timer or do you want somebody to remind you when to start?" "Do you want to take a break in half an hour or would you rather finish your whole Language Arts assignment first?"* Use the survey with the student to help her determine the homework routine that works best for her.

4. **Have an established study area and set time for doing homework.**

   - Assume that homework will be assigned most school nights for at least one or two subjects.
   - Ask teachers about their homework routine for problem subjects. For example, *"How many nights a week do you give Algebra homework? Are tests given at the end of each chapter?"*
   - Keep extra poster board, report covers, and magic markers on hand for forgotten projects.

5. **Encourage use of a computer** for work. Having a back-up copy of completed work is helpful when the original is lost on the way to school or simply never turned in to the teacher.

6. **Set a timer or alarm** or personally prompt the teenager to get started on school work.

7. **Allow the teenager to take brief "joy" breaks** at twenty- to thirty-minute intervals: snack, stretch, walk, or listen to music. Or allow her to take breaks after completion of work by subject or segments thereof (15 of 30 math problems).

8. **Check in** on the teenager periodically to see if she is working.

9. **Monitor closely** if the teenager is in danger of failing. Consider having her do school work at the kitchen table. While parents are cleaning up the kitchen, they can gently nudge her back on task when her attention wanders. Or take the laundry to her room and fold it while she works. But if the teen is adamantly opposed, don't insist. This is not one of the major issues worth fighting over.

10. **When she is completing homework regularly, reward her** by allowing her to study where she chooses, without close supervision, or without requiring a weekly report. Weekly reports are discussed in more detail in Summary 26.

11. **Review completed work** for accuracy and completion. Have the student correct any errors. Some students with ADD/ADHD will be able to double check their work; others won't.

12. **Praise** the teen's effort and willingness to tackle this challenging task.

13. **Allow the student to invite a friend over** to do homework together, especially if the other student is a good role model.

14. **Help the student use some of the memory techniques** discussed in Summary 22 to learn and remember material.

15. **If the student is failing, a weekly or daily report may be needed.** (Summary 26)

16. **Take a break on days when no homework is assigned.** Some students have been required to study at home even when no homework has been assigned. Personally, I fail to see any value in this practice. This time could be spent more productively with the parents and teen participating in a fun event together. These joint activities can achieve the more important goals of deepening family relationships and building the teenager's self-esteem so as to withstand future challenges that may lie ahead.

Helping Families Avoid Homework Battles

We all know that students with ADD/ADHD are more likely to have *emotional blow-ups* than their peers. Obviously, tense homework sessions are high-risk times for these flare-ups. It is important to remember that these students are attempting homework under less than optimal conditions.

- The effects of medication have usually worn off completely by evening.
- Attention and learning problems, plus lack of medication in the evening, all interfere with the teenager's ability to complete homework successfully.
- Furthermore, the student is probably tired and may have trouble getting started and paying attention long enough to complete the assignment.

Teachers may want to give parents some or all of the following suggestions to help them lessen homework conflicts:

1. If tempers flare, *take a brief break* to allow things to cool down. Both parents and the student may need a brief break from homework and from arguing with each other.
2. If the teenager blows up, *stay calm and lower your voice.* A loud emotional response from parents tends to escalate the problem, generating an even louder emotional response from the teen.
3. If homework becomes a constant battlefield, parents, teachers, and the teenager should *develop a joint plan to resolve the problems.* (See "Changes to Consider," below.)

Teachers should ask parents to advise them if problems continue. If parents report that terrible nightly battles are still raging, encourage them to back off some, change strategies, or ask someone else to monitor homework (the other parent, an older sibling, an upperclassman or adult tutor). Changes should be made if screaming battles are the rule, if teens are so upset they cry frequently, or if they have to stay up too late to complete work.

Changes to Consider

Teachers who know a family is struggling with homework battles may want to advise parents that these options are available to them:

1. One of the first changes to consider is **reducing the amount of homework** (S-24). If the total time spent on all homework is more than one to two hours, reducing the amount of work assigned may be necessary, depending on the student's grade level. Ask parents to time how long each subject takes to complete. Identify which subject is taking an inordinate amount of time and reduce the length of the assignments.

2. During occasional emotional crises, it may also be necessary to let the teenager go to bed, **request a time extension, and complete the assigned work at a later time** when both the teen and parents are less frazzled.

3. Or parents can be empowered to **determine when "enough" homework has been completed:**

> Ivan Vance, a special educator/parent of a teenager with an attention deficit, included this accommodation in his child's IEP: "The parents will determine when "enough" homework has been completed at night." Parents are in the best position to judge the emotional climate at home and know whether or not the student is capable of finishing the assignment. The parent's signature on homework returned to school should be sufficient justification for not penalizing the student with a failing grade.
>
> The teacher must decide on a case-by-case basis whether or not to accept the work completed "as is" or to ask for some additional work. However, if make-up work is simply piled on a lengthy assignment for the next night, the student may well become depressed and overwhelmed. In my experience, the majority of parents and students will not take advantage of this accommodation. Obviously, if the accommodation does not work, and the student is not learning the basic material, the educational plan must be revised.

Using Weekly Reports to Ensure Completion of Schoolwork

Sometimes when students are not completing work consistently, parent-teacher conferences are scheduled. Typically, the purpose of the meeting is to identify problem areas and to develop an intervention plan. A first step is often to check whether the student is writing her homework down in her planner or assignment book each day. Next, teachers may try some of the strategies listed in Summaries 13-D and 23, such as asking row captains to check that assignments are written down or getting phone numbers for a classmate who usually knows the assignment. Often as the next step, teachers begin sending home a weekly report to keep families posted on a student's progress.

A weekly report usually indicates whether class work and homework were completed and may give grades for school work or tests. These reports are often used for short periods to help students get back on track academically. Sometimes when students are struggling terribly, a "daily report" may be used. However, "weekly reports" work well for most teenagers.

Weekly reports are one of the most effective tools teachers can use, but asking teenagers with attention deficits to use them is often complicated. Because of their ADD/ADHD symptoms and learning problems, teenagers often forget to get reports signed or to take them home. In middle school, homeroom teachers may still give the student the form and remind her to get it signed by other teachers. By high school, however, the student must remember to pick up a blank form, take it to each class, and get it signed by the teacher.

Purpose of Weekly Reports

Let's consider what most teachers and parents say is the purpose of these reports.

1. To **help students:**
   - complete their class work and homework,
   - learn the academic material, and
   - succeed in school,
   - rather than to simply punish them for failure to complete work!

2. To **help parents:**
   - stay informed of their teenager's progress so they may monitor homework when needed,
   - know when work is not done so they can make sure make-up work is completed.

Weekly Reports and Students with ADD/ADHD

If asked the purpose of weekly reports, *students* would probably say they are for punishment. Since this process can be so aversive, look for a way to minimize the negative aspects of the weekly report. After all, ADD/ADHD is a serious disability for some students. The very skills (attention, memory, organization, and executive function) that are deficient in students with ADD/ADHD are often the underlying reasons that homework is often incomplete and weekly reports are forgotten. So do not be surprised when these students have problems with weekly reports. Use weekly reports sparingly and in as few classes as possible. Expect to make adjustments to ensure that the weekly report works.

Developing the Weekly Report

Weekly report forms should be simple and contain basic information. They should include:

1. **comments on the student's good work,** not just her failures;
2. **a statement of missing assignments** that must be done—for example, math, p. 89, 1-30, odd problems.

As a teacher I preferred weekly reports that were "teacher friendly":

1. easy to read,
2. quick to complete,
3. required little writing,
4. used in as few classes as necessary.

A weekly report might look something like this one:

DAILY/WEEKLY REPORT

Name: _____ Date: _____

Class: _____

homework turned in this week   ☐ Yes   ☐ No

grades for the week: _____

Comments: _____

_____

_____

(Write something positive—for example, note improvement)

Unfinished assignments: _____

_____

_____

Teacher : (in ink) _____

Secrets for Making Weekly Reports Work

First and foremost, good communication between teachers and parents is essential. It is best if teachers and parents discuss how to implement the report, as well as rewards or consequences that might be used. Remember to keep the above goals in mind, involve the teenager in some decision making, and don't let the weekly report simply become a form of punishment for the teen.

Rewards

Depending on the student, rewards may or may not be necessary. If a student is totally overwhelmed and depressed, a reward may give her the boost she needs to finish her work. Privileges and money are two of the most common rewards used. Parents may say, "If you get a good report this week, I'll pay for a movie and gas and let you drive my car." Eventually, when the student gets hooked on success and her grades improve, completion of homework without nagging from parents and teachers may be a reward in itself.

Negative Consequences

Restrictions and logical consequences are two of the most common strategies that parents use. However, be careful, because sometimes negative consequences can give the student the wrong unspoken message or can actually be a reward for the teen.

Restrictions. Typically, harsh restrictions cause resentment and angry feelings between parents and teens and make the weekend miserable for the whole family. If students are placed on restrictions for a weekend or longer, they probably hear this unspoken message: "If you would just try harder, you could do your work. You're lazy. You don't care."

Logical Consequences. I prefer using logical consequences because they give the correct unspoken message and also meet our goals: "Do your class work/homework now or you'll still have to do it eventually, possibly Friday night or Saturday before you go out with friends." So, when the student comes home with the weekly report, parents may say, "When your homework is completed, you may go out." If the student finishes at 8:30 Friday night, then she may go to a movie.

If the student has a lot of homework, parents may divide it into reasonable segments: half due Friday and half Saturday. Thus, the student is rewarded for completing her school work, even though it is late, plus she learns the academic material. Parents create a win-win situation where both the parent and the teenager get something positive from this approach.

Logical consequences are not always easy to use effectively. See the discussion of this strategy in *Teenagers with ADD*.

A Word of Caution. Requiring completion of homework before the weekend may *not* be the best strategy if the amount of unfinished work is overwhelming. In this situation, go back to the drawing board and revise the plan. Help the student get caught up with her work and then continue the plan. If a lot of homework must be "made-up," one way to help the student is to:

1. ***Reduce the assignments to a manageable level*** that will still teach the concepts the student may not have mastered.
2. Sometimes teachers may ***forgive some assignments*** when make-up work is too overwhelming, so the student can catch up with the rest of the class.
3. It may be necessary to ***do daily monitoring of school work*** for awhile.

The Wrong Sort of Rewards.   For a student who hates doing homework, the *best* reward adults can give is to say, "You didn't do your work, so you get an F. We will not let you turn it in late." The unspoken message a depressed teenager hears is "If you don't do your math assignment today, you'll *never* have to do it."

The next step in "shaping" the student's behavior is to have her complete the school work when it is due. See Summary 61. (Homework and weekly reports are also discussed in more detail in Chapter 9 of *Teenagers with ADD*.)

Ensuring Parents Receive the Weekly Report

Although weekly reports help adults monitor and ensure completion of school work, the secondary task, remembering to get the report signed and to bring it home, often becomes as great a challenge as homework completion. Remembering the report relies on a skill that is often deficient as a result of the student's ADD/ADHD. After all, forgetfulness and disorganization are major characteristics of this condition.

So, the bad news is, if parents and teachers are unreasonable, a student could complete all her school work, forget the report, and still be punished, even though her work was done. Teach the student to master this skill or compensate rather than just punish her for her disability! Or, as suggested below, find an innovative way to send the report home until she has mastered the most important skill, completion of school work! Some students with attention deficits can remember the report; others cannot and will need extra help.

If students are failing a class, master one step at a time!

> **FIRST,**
>
>> Address completion of school work:
>>
>> Get students hooked on academic success!
>
> **NEXT,**
>
>> Work on the secondary skill: Remembering the note.

If students cannot remember the note...

Find Alternate Ways to Send the Weekly Report Home

1. **Another student,** girlfriend, or boyfriend may remind the teenager to get the weekly report signed and returned home.

2. **Have the student use a wrist alarm** to help her remember to bring the note home. When the alarm rings, if the student has forgotten to get the note signed during each period, she can still get teacher signatures after school, providing she does not ride the school bus.

3. **Ask each teacher** to remember to give the student a signed note to take home.

4. **The guidance counselor may send a note around to teachers** asking for the weekly report information.

5. **Teachers may call home** and leave a message on the answering machine.

6. **Teachers may fax or e-mail** the report home or to the parent's office.

SECTION 3

Executive Function and Organizational Skills

Teachers and parents are often puzzled when bright students with attention deficits don't do very well in school. Recently, leading researchers on attention deficit disorders have determined that these academic struggles can be traced, at least in part, to difficulties with *executive function.* Executive function may be described as the brain's ability to manage learning activities and behavior. We have learned that an average or above average IQ alone is *not* enough to do well in school. Students must also have strong executive function skills. These key elements of executive function and their impact on school performance are reviewed in Summary 28:

- Working memory and recall,
- Activation, arousal, and effort,
- Impulsivity,
- Controlling emotions,
- Internalizing language,
- Complex problem solving (analysis and synthesis).

In addition, teachers and parents have identified three other ADD/ADHD behaviors linked to executive function deficits that are extremely challenging in school:

- Forgetfulness,
- Disorganization,
- Impaired sense of time.

These three deficits also contribute to problems with traditional **time management skills.** Unlike most ADD/ADHD behaviors, these skills do not improve that much with medication. Although some modest improvement may be observed during the short period of time medication is working, these changes are lost immediately when the medication wears off. **Forgetfulness, disorganization, an impaired sense of time, and weak time management skills are often lifelong problems!** Because these skills are linked to differences in brain chemistry, behavioral programs alone are *not* especially effective in making lasting changes in these skills.

Dr. Russell Barkley, one of the leading international researchers on attention deficit disorder, uses this metaphor to describe how attention and executive function deficits profoundly affect a student's life:

> When a student has an attention deficit disorder, it's as if he is walking down the railroad tracks (of life) with an opaque curtain hanging in front of him that obscures his view of the track ahead (the future). His view is limited to the nails or smashed pennies on the tracks right in front of him (the here and now). He does not look ahead to see or plan for the future. Further down the tracks, he cannot see the upcoming railroad crossing (the due date for the Chemistry semester project) nor the train coming from the other direction (major crisis).

As Dr. Barkley explains, teachers and parents help the student by *bringing the future into the here and now*. In other words, teachers and parents:

1. provide prompts to remind the student of key events that lie ahead, and
2. provide support needed to cope with and plan for the future.

Although classroom adjustments are often made for academic issues, accommodations are seldom given for executive function deficits! Instead, the student may be punished for "ADHD behaviors" which are related to the disability. So, if the teenager has problems with executive function deficits that interfere with his ability to learn:

1. The specific deficits should be listed in the IEP or Section 504 Plan as issues of concern, and
2. appropriate accommodations should be included in the IEP/504 Plan. See Summaries 44 and 47 for more on IEPs and 504 Plans.

Key Strategy: Use a comprehensive approach:

1. Model necessary skills.
2. Teach the student to compensate for executive function deficits.
3. Involve an "organizational or academic coach."
4. Work with the family and doctor to ensure medications are effective.
5. Provide classroom accommodations for executive function deficits.

Impact of Executive Function on School Work

Researchers have not yet agreed on the exact elements of executive function, as research is still in the very early stages. Two researchers who specialize in attention deficit disorders, however, have written good working descriptions.

Dr. Russell Barkley describes "executive function" as it relates to students with ADD or ADHD this way: ***"actions we perform to ourselves and direct at ourselves so as to accomplish self-control, goal-directed behavior, and the maximization of future outcomes."*** Most of these actions are cognitive—in other words, "done in our heads," and thus not observable.

Dr. Tom Brown gives us a metaphor that compares executive function of the brain to the function of a conductor in an orchestra. The conductor organizes various instruments to begin playing singularly or in combination, integrates the music by bringing in and fading certain actions, and controls their pace and level of intensity.

Students with attention deficits may have difficulties with some, but not all of these characteristics, of executive function:

1. **Working memory and recall** (actively processing information; holding facts in mind while manipulating the information; accessing facts)
2. **Activation, arousal, and effort** (getting started, staying alert, paying attention, finishing work)
3. **Impulsivity** (inhibiting speech and actions; thinking before acting or speaking)
4. **Controlling emotions** (low frustration tolerance; emotional blow-ups; sensitivity to criticism)
5. **Internalizing language** (using "self-talk" to control one's behavior and direct future actions)
6. **Taking an issue apart, analyzing the pieces, reconstituting and organizing it into new ideas** (complex problem solving; writing an essay or report).

Working Memory and Recall

1. Affects the here and now:

- limited working memory capacity
- weak short-term memory
- forgetfulness, can't keep several things in mind

As a result, students:

- have difficulty performing mental analyses such as math computation in one's head

- have difficulty remembering a "to do" list
- have difficulty remembering multiple requests; forget assignments, books, chores

2. Affects their sense of past events:

- difficulty recalling the past

As a result, students:

- do not study past actions
- do not learn easily from past behavior
- act without a sense of hindsight
- repeat misbehavior

3. Affects their sense of time:

- difficulty holding events in mind (This skill is needed to develop a sense of time and passage of time)
- difficulty using their sense of time to prepare for upcoming events and the future
- difficulty holding events in mind in the order they occurred (This ability is needed as a building block for a sense of time)

As a result, students:

- have difficulty judging the passage of time accurately
- cannot accurately estimate how much time it will take to finish a task (homework)
- perceive time as passing slowly when tasks are rote, boring, or low interest
- are impatient when asked to wait; time drags by
- occasionally hyperfocus on high-interest tasks and lose all track of time
- have a sense of time like younger children who do not have ADD or ADHD

4. Affects their sense of self-awareness

- diminished sense of self-awareness (This awareness is needed to feel a sense of self-control)

As a result, students:

- do not easily examine their own behavior
- do not easily change their own behavior
- do not see how their behavior affects others

5. Affects their sense of the future:

- limited foresight: students live in the present, focus on the here and now, rather than the future
- less likely to talk about time or the future

As a result, students:

- have difficulty projecting lessons learned in the past, forward into the future (foresight)
- have difficulty preparing for the future
- are less likely to prepare for the future

Activation, Arousal, and Effort

1. Affects their *ability to start and complete a task*

- appear unmotivated
- difficulty getting started
- difficulty maintaining their effort

As a result, students:

- procrastinate
- do not follow through
- fail to finish school work

2. Affects their *level of alertness and ability to pay attention*

- difficulty becoming alert enough to pay attention
- difficulty maintaining attention
- serious sleep problems
- low energy levels (in students with ADD)

As a result, students:

- are easily distracted
- do not pay attention consistently
- don't seem to have enough energy to get started or complete tasks (ADD)
- are irritable, perhaps because of sleep deprivation
- sleep in class

Impulsivity

1. Affects their *ability to inhibit their speech and behavior*

- difficulty stopping and thinking before they act or speak
- difficulty stopping their behavior, even when it isn't working, and changing to an effective behavior

As a result, students:

- blurt out in class
- talk back to teachers before they think
- get into yelling matches or fights with other students
- act impulsively and get into trouble, maybe even suspended

Controlling Their Emotions

1. Affects the *ability to control their emotions*

- difficulty putting emotions on hold
- difficulty separating emotions and actions; they are one
- difficulty splitting facts from feelings (This skill is needed to be objective)

As a result, students:

- are more emotionally reactive
- are more sensitive to criticism
- are mainly concerned with their own feelings
- have difficulty seeing another person's perspective
- may seem self-centered or immature
- may be selfish

2. Affects their *ability to direct behavior toward goals*

- difficulty delaying gratification
- difficulty regulating emotions to achieve goals
- difficulty putting up with boring or tedious activities
- difficulty focusing on future goals; immediate feelings (here and now) are most important
- difficulty motivating oneself; rewards in school (grades) are too far in the future to be effective

As a result, students:

- want to quit if they become bored with homework, a job, or college
- don't stick with things; give up more easily than their peers
- must receive rewards immediately
- have difficulty generating their own intrinsic rewards (feeling good simply because the work is done)

Internalizing Language

1. Affects *internalization of speech or self-talk (It is delayed.)*

- difficulty using language to control oneself
- difficulty directing one's behavior with one's own voice

As a result, students:

- have difficulty with reflection
- have difficulty thinking through their actions beforehand
- are less likely to use their past experiences
- are less likely to follow rules
- have difficulty managing their own behavior

Taking an Issue Apart, Analyzing the Pieces, Reconstituting, and Organizing Into a New Entity

1. Affects their ability to do *complex problem solving*

As a result, students:

- have difficulty analyzing and breaking down a problem
- have difficulty determining what caused a problem and developing a plan to correct it
- have difficulty knowing how and where to start to solve the problem

2. Affects their *spoken and written communication*

- weak verbal fluency, especially when responding to a question or giving a concise answer
- difficulty communicating with others

As a result, students:

- have difficulty writing essays or reports, sequencing and organizing ideas
- have difficulty rapidly stringing words together
- have difficulty describing an issue in words
- have difficulty expressing themselves rapidly and effectively

Resources

Barkley, Russell A. *ADHD and the Nature of Self-Control.* New York: The Guilford Press, 1997.

Barkley, Russell A. *Attention Deficit Hyperactivity Disorder*. New York: The Guilford Press, 1998.

Brown, Thomas E. *Attention Deficit Disorders and Comorbidities in Children, Adolescents, and Adults.* Washington, DC: American Psychiatric Press, 2000.

3

Section 3 | Executive Function and Organization Skills

Disorganization

Most teenagers with ADD or ADHD appear to be extremely disorganized! Ask any teacher or parent who has worked with these students and they will tell you that losing books, homework, written assignments, reports, backpacks, clothes, shoes, jewelry, tools, or keys is often a daily occurrence. Messy desks, backpacks, school lockers, and rooms are also common. Problems with disorganization are often compounded by poor memory. Consequently, it is often difficult to identify which skill deficit is causing a problem. Most likely, many of the difficulties these students face at school result from a combination of several problems.

On the surface, disorganization may look like simple laziness. In reality, however, it is a much more complicated issue. Problems with organization spill over into academics, where students with attention deficits may have difficulty with several basic tasks:

- having basic school supplies for class participation,
- bringing homework to class and remembering to turn it in,
- knowing how and where to get started on a school project,
- organizing a plan of action to complete a project,
- organizing information into a logical, flowing written essay or report.

They also lack another prerequisite for being organized: the ability to sustain interest on "boring" tasks such as organizing a backpack, locker, or room.

To help these students learn organizational skills, **"maintenance time"** must be set aside both at school and home to master these skills. For example, a teacher, aide, or classmate may meet the student near the end of the school day to review assignments and books needed for homework. At home, parents should periodically go through their teenager's notebook with him to sort, file, and throw away papers.

Give accommodations for executive function deficits: If any of the following behaviors occur on a regular basis and interfere with the student's ability to learn, they should be

1. described in Section 1, "present performance," of the IEP/Section 504 Plan, and
2. included in the IEP/504 Plan to teach the student
    a. the needed skill or
    b. methods for compensating for the problem. (Summaries 44-45.)

The following table charting strategies may be helpful.

Strategies to Combat Disorganization

Problem	My favorite strategies
1. Loses school supplies (comes to class without pencils, books, papers, or folders).	1.1 Keep extra pencils, paper, and books in the classroom. Ask parents to donate supplies. 1.2 Suggest that parents keep extra school supplies on hand at home.
2. Loses gym uniform or musical instruments.	2.1 Put the student's name on all school supplies, band uniform, instruments, or other items. 2.2 Put belongings in the gym or band room first thing in the morning. 2.3 Reduce the number of times the student must transport uniforms or instruments back and forth to school.
3. Loses class work and homework.	3.1 Put all school work in one colorful pocket folder; place work to be completed on the left side and finished work on the right side.
4. Does not turn in homework to teacher; forgets to turn in homework. (Does not hear the request to turn in homework before leaving class; homework may be completed but at home, in the locker, backpack, book, or car.)	4.1 Establish routine that homework is always turned in to the teacher's same "red" box or folder at the end of class. 4.2 Ask "row captains" to collect homework or to check to see that homework is turned in at the end of class.
5. Loses or forgets, but never makes it home with homework assignments or the right books.	5.1 Establish an "organizational homeroom;" the student returns at the end of each day; teacher or an aide reviews assignments, needed books, due dates, and projected timelines. 5.2 Use an "organizational coach" (classmate, teacher, or parent) to help with organization and memory. 5.3 Use an assignment notebook. 5.4 Ask "row captains" to remind the student. 5.5 Post all assignments in writing. Consider listing materials needed to do a task. 5.6 Have student call a classmate for assignments. 5.7 E-mail or fax assignments home. 5.8 See Summary 23 for more detailed suggestions for remembering assignments.

6. Has a messy notebook, backpack, desk, or locker.	6.1 Use an organizational notebook that contains a sealed plastic pouch for pencils or calculators; a colorful folder (with pockets for uncompleted class work and finished homework)
	
	6.2 Arrange the locker for maximum organization:
	    top shelf/put the books for morning classes;
	    middle shelf/books for afternoon classes;
	    after each class put books on the **bottom shelf**; at the end of day put the books back in order;
	    If only **one shelf** is available, put a divider, small box, or stand-up magazine holder in the bottom to create a third compartment;
	    Have the student create his own unique system of organization for the locker.
	
	6.3 Have someone meet the student after school to practice this routine until he does it automatically.
	
	6.4 Ask parents to regularly schedule time to clean out backpacks, desks, or lockers. Notebook should be cleaned out every few weeks. Save all completed work until after the end of the grading period just in case the student forgot to turn it in to the teacher.

7. Has great difficulty keeping a detailed log of daily assignments, grades, and test scores written in sequential order. (Some advanced classes require this to practice organizational skills; however, it requires extra instruction, support, or an adaptation for students with attention deficits.)	7.1 If this task is mandatory, provide daily assistance from an "organizational coach." Generally speaking, avoid requiring this level of detail from students with ADD or ADHD. 7.2 Do not deduct points from student's grade for failure to keep these records. Grade the student on the subject (English), rather than organization.

Problem	My favorite strategies
8. Does not know grades and whether passing or failing. (Some students will be able to keep up with grades and others will not.)	8.1 If the student wants to and is capable of keeping up with his grades, staple a sheet in the front of the student planner; the teacher or another student checks to see that grades for homework and tests for each class are written on that sheet. 8.2 The teacher or aide may e-mail his grades for the week to the family.
9. Has difficulty writing an essay or reports.	9.1 Summaries 14-17 contain a discussion of written expression and essay writing.
10. Poor time management/organizational skills; has difficulty developing a plan of action and following through.	10.1 Getting organized and developing a plan of action are also discussed in Summaries 34-37.

Forgetfulness/Impaired Memory

Forgetfulness is one of the primary characteristics of teenagers with attention deficits! Forgetfulness is one of those ADD/ADHD behaviors that may look like laziness or a bad attitude but in reality is a classic characteristic of the disability. In fact, remembering is a more complex task than we often realize. A student must:

1. pay attention,
2. store information,
3. find information,
4. quickly retrieve it, and then
5. act upon the information.

Getting information into ***long-term memory*** is especially difficult for students with ADD/ADHD. Even when information is stored properly, they still have trouble accessing information when they need it. In addition, students with attention deficits have problems with ***working memory,*** an executive function that enables a student to manipulate information in his head. (See Summary 22.) Typically, students know they have a terrible memory. As a result, they are often chronically anxious that they are going to forget something important! Over time, they may learn to hide their anxiety by acting as though they really don't care.

Rather than punishing the teen for having a poor memory, teachers and parents must help him learn skills. A two-pronged approach may help:

1. Teach students ***how to compensate*** for their memory problems.
2. Simultaneously, teach them the ***memory strategies*** discussed in Summary 22.

In this summary, the discussion will focus primarily on learning to *compensate* for memory problems.

Since memory deficits are often a lifelong problem, ask another student to be a backup memory or "coach" who reminds these students of important tasks. Remember to give the student with an attention deficit some control in deciding which student is involved and how and when assistance is provided. Obviously, the student doesn't want to be embarrassed or made to feel stupid for having a poor memory.

Give accommodations for executive function deficits: If any of the following behaviors occur on a regular basis and interfere with the student's ability to learn, they should be

1. described in Section 1, "present performance," of the IEP/Section 504 Plan, and
2. included in the IEP/504 Plan to teach the student
   a. the needed skill or
   b. methods for compensating for the problem. Summaries 44-45.

Strategies to Combat Forgetfulness/Impaired Memory

Problem	My favorite strategies
1. Forgets to write down homework assignments (also may not hear the assignment; may be too rushed at the end of period; puts books away early to sprint to the next class or visit with friends at the locker).	1.1 Use an assignment notebook/student planner. 1.2 Allow students to dictate assignments into a "Memo Minder" ($20), a small three-minute tape recorder. 1.3 Schedule adequate time for students to write down assignments and put papers and folders away (perhaps earlier in the period when students aren't rushed). 1.4 Ask another student or "row captain" to double check to see that assignments are written down for the student with an attention deficit or the whole class. 1.5 E-mail or fax assignments home. 1.6 See Summaries 13-D and 23.
2. Forgets to bring home the correct assignments and books.	2.1 Ask the student to check "Homework Hotlines," school websites, teacher voice mail, the library, or teacher assignment board for homework. 2.2 Give parents a class syllabus with general timelines for assignments & tests. 2.3 Staple the teacher's weekly lesson plan in the student's planner. 2.4 Ask someone to be an "organizational coach" and meet with the student after school to ensure that homework assignments and appropriate books make it home. 2.5 Keep an extra set of books at home. 2.6 See Summaries 23 & 61 for more detailed suggestions: "Five Common Reasons for School Failure" and "Shaping" Behavior."
3. Forgets to return things to school, especially if they must be signed (Homework, reports, papers; Tests; Weekly reports; Assignments initialed in a student planner; Money for school photos; Sign-up for sports or field trips).	3.1 Notify parents that papers will be sent home regularly, if this is true. 3.2 Establish a routine: papers or weekly reports are sent home on Fridays. 3.3 Suggest that parents ask the student to place the completed paper in the same folder or book each day, perhaps near the door. 3.4 Reduce the number of papers sent home to be signed.
4. Forgets to stay after school for a teacher conference or detention. (Medication has usually worn off, so memory is even less efficient.)	4.1 Ask a friend to remind him. 4.2 Put a Post-It note on a notebook for the last class or in his locker. 4.3 Set a wrist-alarm (WatchMinder™) with a message reminder. (It vibrates and gives a message, S-13-E.) 4.4 Identify the problem (antecedent behavior) resulting in detentions (tardy to school caused by sleep disturbances); implement a behavior intervention plan to correct the problem.
5. Forgets to put his name on his paper.	5.1 Tape a 3x5 cue card on his desk that states what to do: 1) "Write name on paper." 2) "Turn in homework." 5.2 Give the student a name stamp or stick-on name labels. 5.3 Give him pre-stamped or pre-labeled papers. 5.4 Ask another student to remind him to write his name. 5.5 Don't take off points for failing to put a name on the paper. Help the student master the skill. 5.6 "Row captains" check for names on papers.

Problem	My favorite strategies
6. Forgets to bring pencils, papers, books to class.	6.1 Keep an extra supply of pencils and paper for forgetful students. Parents may volunteer to pay for this or buy these supplies for their teen to keep at school. 6.2 Ask a classmate to remind the student to return the pencil. 6.3 Keep one or two extra loaner textbooks in the classroom. 6.4 Remind student to write down in the assignment book any extra or unusual materials that are needed for class the next day.
7. Forgets to complete long-term projects.	7.1 Break projects into segments, each with a separate due date. 7.2 Send a reminder to parents of projects and due dates. 7.3 See Summaries 23, 36, and 37 for more detailed suggestions regarding completion of long-term projects.

SUMMARY 31 Impaired Sense of Time

Many teens with ADD or ADHD *don't accurately judge the passage of time.* These students are often described as "living in the here and now." They have great difficulty estimating how much time a job will take. So, they may feel overwhelmed by a homework assignment because they have no sense of how long it will take to complete. In addition, time seems to creep, especially if they have to do "boring," repetitious work or wait for someone.

This impaired sense of time is another lifelong problem that does not improve significantly even with medication. Again, helping the student learn to compensate is essential. An accurate sense of time is an executive function that is essential for succeeding in school or planning ahead for the future.

Their impaired sense of time contributes to several problems:

- tardiness,
- avoidance of homework assignments since they "will take forever,"
- late completion of class assignments,
- not planning ahead for homework completion or major class projects,
- not allowing enough time to complete work.

If a student is often late to class, don't automatically assume that his tardiness is intentional. Instead, review his routine between each class and develop a plan to adjust his trips to the locker (Summary 29) so he isn't late. If he can't find the right books, help him organize his locker.

Dr. Russell Barkley believes that teachers and parents need to help bring the future into the moment to help teenagers cope successfully with their attention deficit. For example, adults must use strategies to assist students in remembering homework assignments or planning ahead and completing applications for college or vocational schools. In other words, teachers and parents may have to provide more guidance and support for a longer period than usual.

Continually punishing ADD/ADHD behaviors by sending students to detention or penalizing grades is not especially effective in changing their behavior. In fact, punishment may create even more anxiety and even poorer school work. When their forgetfulness and disorganization are combined with their impaired sense of time, these students often find themselves rushed and overwhelmed as they confront major long-term projects that are due "tomorrow."

Give accommodations for executive function deficits: If any of the following behaviors occur on a regular basis and interfere with the student's ability to learn, they should be

1. described in Section 1, "present performance," of the IEP/Section 504 Plan, and
2. included in the IEP/504 Plan to teach the student: a) the needed skill or b) methods for compensating for the problem. (Summaries 44-45.)

The following strategies may be helpful.

Strategies to Combat Impaired Sense of Time

Problem	My favorite strategies
1. Tardiness: late to class	1.1 Review routes taken between each class and change routes that contribute to tardiness. 1.2 Advise student not to go by the locker between each class, but to take 2-3 books at a time from the locker. 1.3 Advise student to pick up books when there is more time, such as before school or during lunch. 1.4 Keep a couple of extra textbooks in the classroom. When the student must borrow a book, ask someone to remind him to leave it in the room. 1.5 Let the student leave a couple of minutes early for his next class. 1.6 Help the student find books more quickly by organizing his locker more efficiently. (See Summary 29, suggestion 6.2)

2. Late to school (often related to a sleep disturbance, lack of awareness of the passage of time, and problems getting organized to leave home on time)	2.1 Ask the student to set a wristwatch alarm with a five-minute reminder that school is starting. (WatchMinder™ S-13E)
	
	2.2 If parents ask for help, suggest they involve the student and pick one of these options:
	    2.1.1 Have the student get up earlier if necessary.
	    2.2.2 Set his own alarm clock to wake up. Connect a timer to the radio, TV, and lights.
	    2.2.3 Tape a wake-up message from him or a friend.
	    2.2.4 Ask a friend or girlfriend to call.
	    2.2.5 Advise of the passage of time. "You need to leave for school in 30 (10) minutes (now)."
	    2.2.6 Lay clothes out and put books together in one place the night before.
	    2.2.7 Ask the family to consider an evaluation for a sleep disturbance, which is common in attention deficit (50%).
	    2.2.8 Medication may help. See discussion of sleep problems in Teenagers with ADD.

3. Late turning in homework	3.1 Establish a homework collection routine: 3.1.1 Ask an aide, "row captain," or an "organizational coach" to remind the student of assignments or to turn in completed work. 3.2 Allow flexibility in turning in late assignments while working to develop a plan to correct the problem. 3.3 See more detailed suggestions regarding homework in Summaries 23 and 24.
4. Does not plan ahead for long-term projects	4.1 See the discussion on long-term projects in Summary 23. 4.2 Teach the time management skills discussed in Summaries 33-37.

5. Impatient. Hates waiting.	5.1 Give the student something to do while he is waiting for the teacher to help him or answer his question. "Go on to the next problem while I finish this."
	
	5.2 Allow students to help each other.
	
	5.3 Make time concrete and visual.
	    5.3.1 Place a clock in sight in the room.
	    5.3.2 Set an alarm or use a timer to announce a homework "joy break" at home.
	
	5.4 Practice time awareness and time estimation.
	    5.4.1 Advise of the passage of time. "It has been twenty minutes since you started. You have ten minutes to go before break."
	    5.4.2 Ask the student to estimate how long the homework assignment will take to complete. Write his answer down. Compare it to actual time spent
	
	5.5 Reduce waiting time.

The ADD/ADHD "Window on Time"

Dr. Russell Barkley explains that ***acquiring a sense of time is a developmental skill that is significantly delayed in students with attention deficit disorder.*** For the average person without ADD or ADHD, a mature sense of time is not completely developed until the *early thirties,* when the prefrontal cortex reaches full maturity. He describes this maturational process as a ***"window on time"*** that opens more slowly for students with attention deficits. The drawing below shows how time should develop for the average student who does *not* have ADD or ADHD.

When students are in preschool, their window on time is closed and everything is "now." As they reach the teenage years, the typical student can plan ahead up to two days. However, the student with an attention deficit is more likely to have a window on time that is closer to 12 hours. So as you can guess, without any prompts, their semester chemistry project doesn't enter their narrow window of time until the night before it is due (roughly 12 hours). So, teachers and parents often hear a familiar refrain, "I forgot my project."

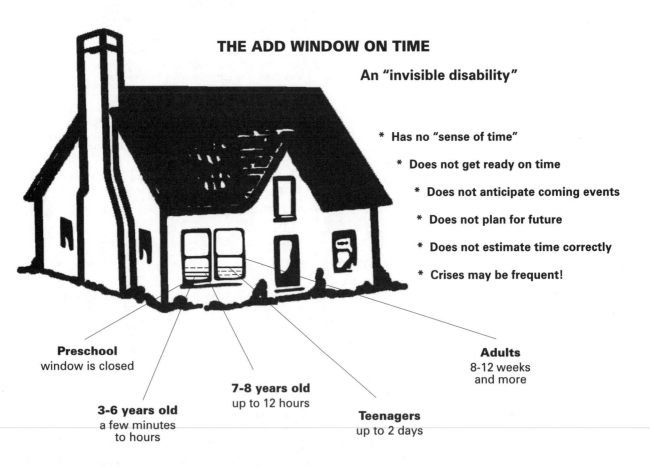

THE ADD WINDOW ON TIME

An "invisible disability"

* Has no "sense of time"
* Does not get ready on time
* Does not anticipate coming events
* Does not plan for future
* Does not estimate time correctly
* Crises may be frequent!

Preschool
window is closed

3-6 years old
a few minutes
to hours

7-8 years old
up to 12 hours

Teenagers
up to 2 days

Adults
8-12 weeks
and more

Nagging will not change this behavior!
> **An event must enter the student's window on time before he will take action!**

Time Management and ADD/ADHD
(A brief discussion of the issues)

Traditional time management strategies typically rely on a four-step process:

1. planning,
2. prioritizing,
3. scheduling, and
4. following a plan.

Using this strategy is essential for success in school. Unfortunately, without some modifications, this system doesn't work very well for students who have an attention deficit. This should come as no surprise, since we know these students are forgetful and disorganized and often have trouble judging the passage of time. Even adults with attention deficits still have problems with time management; so don't expect miracles from teenagers. According to Dr. Joan Teach, principal of a school specializing in educating students with ADD and ADHD, the best strategy is to **expose students to a variety of organizational and time management strategies and hope that something sticks.** In other words, they will ideally adapt the strategies that you teach to their own unique organizational style.

Why Is Time Management a Challenge?

Left Brain vs. Right Brain Thinking

Traditional time management systems are often designed by people who are: **left brain dominant, logical, convergent, linear, and sequential thinkers.** Unfortunately, many people with attention deficits may be described as the exact opposite: **right brain dominant, divergent, innovative, and intuitive thinkers.** This style of thinking is not just limited to people with attention deficits. One time management consultant explains that nearly half the population is right brain dominant. Actually, most people use both sides of their brains, but typically one side is dominant.

Traditional time management is usually introduced to enhance productivity and efficiency in contrast to the right-brain organizing style that is creative, spontaneous, and flexible. Right brain organizing styles are not bad, just different! Although this style of organizing may not be a major problem in adulthood, it causes significant problems while a teenager is still in school. The chart on the next page looks at a few of the differences between left-brain and right-brain approaches to time management.

Visual vs. Abstract Organization

Students who have difficulty with traditional organizational strategies may in fact be **visual processors**. They remember and locate things visually, not abstractly. In other words, these students find their Algebra homework by seeing a picture in their mind of where they left it, rather than remembering the name of a specific folder or location in a drawer.

Perhaps the key to good organization for students with attention deficits is to help them *maximize their skills as visual organizers* rather than try to convert them to an abstract system that may never work for them. I have found that within their apparent disorganization, they often have their own unique organizational system. Amazingly, they often do find things within the "chaos." So, if a student's system works, don't make any changes. One time management consultant offers an easy test of whether or not a system is effective: "If you can find most things in three minutes or less, your system is working. Don't change it." If a student's system *doesn't work,* see the next summary for suggestions on teaching time management.

Time Management Strategies	Left Brain Thinkers	Right Brain Thinkers
1. Plan	1. Asks, "What should be done?"; develops a manageable list.	1. Asks, "What could be done?"; brainstorming occurs; "to do" list expands greatly.
2. Prioritize	2. Lists items in order of priority: important, next in importance; 1, 2, 3 or A, B, C.	2. Everything is important or it wouldn't be on the list; can't pick just one; priorities change quickly.
3. Schedule	3. Writes dates and times on a calendar.	3. Can't decide which calendar to buy; must research all options; writes notes and misplaces them; then loses the calendar.
4. Follow plan	4. Follow through is fun and is a reward in itself.	4. Once steps 1-3 are completed, the student becomes bored and weary; craves fresh ideas and new challenges. Joy and rewards come from producing new ideas and finding new challenges, not follow-up.

Resources

Covey, Stephen R. *Seven Habits of Highly Effective People*. New York: Simon and Schuster, 1989.

Lehmkuhl, Dorothy & Dolores Cotter Lamping. *Organizing for the Creative Person.* New York: Crown Publishing, 1993.

McGee-Cooper, Anne with Duane Trammell. *Time Management for Unmanageable People.* New York: Bantam Books, 1994.

Teaching Time Management

Frequently students with attention deficits must be taught skills most of us do quite naturally. Since organizational and time management skills are often major deficits, an IEP/504 objective should be written to help improve these skills. Even if a teacher has time to teach the skills, parents should also be given a copy of these summaries. To help parents teach and reinforce use of these skills at home, perhaps the guidance counselor or special education teacher could provide a training session on time management for parents of all students in special education. Obviously, having similar time management systems in place at school and home is helpful.

The four traditional steps in time management are listed below, along with suggestions for helping students with attention deficits improve these skills. Some of these suggestions may sound great, but in reality, the student may be unable or unwilling to do them. For example, it's a great idea to do homework while waiting for a ride or for basketball practice to start. In reality, I don't know too many students with either ADD or ADHD who will actually do that. However, it is still worth the effort to teach students these skills. Even if they aren't developmentally ready now, they may be able to use these strategies in later life. Don't get discouraged and give up, but rather try a different strategy.

I. Plan

1. **Develop a "to do" list (master list):** An *organizational coach*—usually parents or a girlfriend—may help students develop a list of things they have to do each day. For example, turn in picture money, sign up for the basketball team, audition for the school play, check a book out of the library for next week's report, or do chores.

2. **Keep a student planner or assignment notebook:** To help students be better organized, many P.T.A. groups pay for school-mandated student planners. If the school does not have a standard planner for everyone, suggest that parents help the student find a planner he likes. Then show him how to use it. Someone at school or the parents should spend time with the student each day checking or writing in the planner until it becomes part of his routine.

   Help the student decide exactly what kinds of things to write down each day—for example, assignments, sports practice, a teacher conference, and tests. Consider color coding or using stars or something to make test dates stand out.

   Students with attention deficits often need assistance to ensure that they arrive home with assignments written in their planner. If the student continues to forget to write down assignments, see Summary 23 for suggestions to ensure that assignments make it home.

3. **Review the list each day:** Ask parents to review the "to do list" the night before, then remind him about urgent things as he leaves the next morning. Handing him a written reminder, such as a Post-It note, or asking him to set his wrist alarm may be helpful.

II. Prioritize

1.Practice setting priorities: Teachers and parents must guide students in setting priorities. Many students with attention deficits have trouble ranking things to do by priority. They often get sidetracked and spend too much time considering all the options for ranking items. The options below may help streamline this process.

> **1.1. Divide items into two groups.** Have the student write items on Post-It notes or cards and move the important ones to the top of the table, others to the bottom. In this system, items are considered either *1) important (do it now)* or *2) unimportant (do it any time)*. Students may need a third stack for undetermined or semi-important items. Those items may be pushed to the side, out of the way.

> **1.2. Pick the top three items.** Ask the student to look over the cards at the top of the table and select the three most important topics. If he can pick the top three items, proceed to scheduling tasks. However, if he has problems, a parent or teacher should select cards for four to six of the most important tasks. Ask the student to pick the three of these he thinks are most important to do. If he can't make a quick decision, briefly discus why the top four are the most important. For example, items with time deadlines may be urgent and have to be done immediately.

> **1.3. Or divide the list into four groups.** Time management a la Stephen Covey and other time management trainers typically involves dividing a "to do list" into the four groups shown below. But one of the major problems here is the age-old conflict between parents and teens regarding what is important! A teen's definition of important and urgent most likely will not be the same as an adult's. Their priorities tend to become crises, deadlines, and fun activities. Planning ahead to avoid a crisis is often not particularly important. More importantly, most students with attention deficits are not developmentally ready for this level of organizational planning. For example, below is how one teenager with ADHD ranked a number of events on a "to do" list.

I. Urgent & Important	II. Important but Not Urgent
• forgot money for school field trip; must go to teacher's house tonight and turn it in • practice clarinet for marching band tryouts tomorrow • spend time with girlfriend • read a car magazine or comic book	• read a book/begin work on the book report • visit library, get material for semester project due in 2 weeks • develop a web page for Mom • watch a good movie on TV • set up a tent in the woods near home • play Nintendo

III. Urgent but Not Important	**IV. Not Important or Urgent**
• start reading book for book report due tomorrow • install a friend's stereo in the car today	• do homework for tomorrow • develop a weekly schedule • spend time with family • copy homework over • correct errors on an essay for extra credit • clean room • mow yard • answer phone calls during dinner or homework

Ideally, students should spend most of their time on "Important but not Urgent" items, planning to avoid crises. But in reality, even adults with attention deficits put things off until they become "Urgent and Important" and spend far too much time on items in Group I, as well as fun things that seem "Urgent but not Important." In other words, time management for teens with attention deficits is incredibly difficult! To successfully manage their time, teens must tailor-make a system that is interesting and meaningful to them.

1.4. Put items on a stand-up clipboard. Place small Post-It notes in priority order on a clear acrylic clipboard or a frame that will stand up. This way you don't have the dreaded task of recopying "to do lists." Simply move Post-It notes from one column to another as priorities change or throw them away when they're finished. Columns on the clipboard might be selected to help the student arrange notes by priority or by activity: "Today, Soon, Do Anytime" vs. "Family, School, Sports, or Religious Activities." He could use different colored notes: hot pink to denote an urgent deadline; sports events on yellow. If the student needs a copy at school, place the Post-It notes on a piece of paper and photocopy it. Or simply place the stand face down on a copy machine to make a copy.

III. Schedule

1. **Transfer the "To Do List" onto a daily planner or calendar.**

2. **Teach the student to allow enough time for activities:** Major activities to be scheduled may include school work, extracurricular activities, chores, community or religious events, and activities with friends. Students need to learn to allow adequate

time to complete chores or special projects for school before they go out with friends. *Schedule backwards*. Show the student that if he has a ball game at 7:00, then he should schedule time to work on homework at 3:00 or 4:00. The steps necessary to complete a long-term project must be scheduled well in advance of the final due date. See the sample schedule in Summary 37.

3. **Practice time estimation:** If the student has an impaired sense of time, practice may or may not help. At Brainworks, an educational consulting program specializing in ADD and ADHD in Carrollton, TX, Carla Crutsinger and Debra Moore recommend having students practice time estimation for tasks. Ask the student to write his estimate down. Then record how long it actually took to complete the job. If nothing else, the student may learn that he consistently tends to over- or underestimate the time required for certain jobs.

4. **Try a Palm Pilot:** Some older teenagers may benefit from using a handheld computerized planner, such as a Palm Pilot, Wizard, or perhaps a less sophisticated, cheaper version. Students with attention deficits love gadgets and might actually enjoy keeping a computerized schedule of homework and appointments. However, the down side is that the Palm Pilot costs $400 and forgetful teens may lose it. Plus, the Pilot has e-mail capacity and so many options and games that it may be too much of a distraction in class. See Summary 13-E for other electronic devices.

5. **Look ahead in the planner or calendar:** Remind the student to check the upcoming week in his planner or calendar on a regular basis. One parent explains that the next week does not exist in her daughter's mind until she turns the page. So the student does not know that something is due on Monday until she turns the page in her planner late Sunday night or on Monday morning.

6. **Block time for homework:** Suggest to the teen and parents that they establish an evening routine by blocking off time four nights a week for homework. For example, the student will choose the time to start homework, perhaps after dinner at around 7:00 each evening, lasting approximately until 8:00 or 9:00. No other commitments are made for that time unless the student has no homework or does it earlier so that he can attend a school or religious event. Or the student may do half the homework before the event and half afterward. Obviously, if the student has no homework, there is no need for him to sit down and study something simply to be studying.

7. **Use a weekly or monthly schedule for long-term projects:** When planning for a long-term project, have the student use a planner/calendar with the hours and days marked. The calendar makes an abstract concept (time) concrete because the student can see the hours and days.

   7.1. **Break the task into segments** and spread over a one- or two-week period.

   7.2. **Show the teenager how to schedule backward** to include each step.

   7.3. **Build in extra time for "unexpected emergencies"** that always come up to keep a student from working on the project.

   See Summary 35-37 for more information. Blank forms are available in Appendices A5 and A6.

8. **Put a master calendar (monthly) in the teen's room and/or at school:** Suggest that the student hang a large monthly calendar in his room that includes all events (school, family, religious, sports), as well as long-term projects. Chances are that the student will need prompting from teachers and/or parents to start early enough to finish long-term projects. Parents will also need to work with the student to keep the calendar up-to-date.

Teachers may want to post a large monthly calendar on the classroom wall and refer to it regularly. This may help make time more concrete and make students more aware of due dates.

9. **Make the planner or calendar interesting:** Consider adding an element of color and design to the planner/calendar. Use colored pens to write down assignments for different classes. Use colored dots, such as red for due dates. If the student seems to enjoy it, use colorful stickers when an assignment is finished. Of course, these teens will need ongoing help to make this system work. Help them monitor time and develop a fairly simple system. Teachers/parents may need to nudge them along because they could spend hours picking calendars, colors, stickers, or a system.

10. **Use procrastination wisely:** Sometimes procrastination, otherwise called *idea incubation*, really can make a contribution to a project. Allowing some time to think about a project or sleep on it may give the brain time to subconsciously come up with solutions or creative ideas.

11. **Allow some things to die a natural death:** Parents or teachers may need to explain that everything on a "to do list" does not have to be finished. If the project is a low priority, the student should not feel guilty. Sometimes the best thing is to let a task die, especially if it keeps ending up on the bottom of the priority list.

IV. Follow the Plan

1. **Keep the "to do" list in sight:** *Think visual!* Students may find it helpful to have the "to do" list stand above everything on the desk. Write the to do's on Post-It notes and put them on the clear acrylic standup frame/clipboard. Or for variety, write them on 3x5 cards and put them on a corkboard. Use push pins so you can move them around when needed.

2. **Use a Palm Pilot or a WatchMinder™:** These computerized gadgets have the capacity to provide a prompt (beep) or written reminder to start projects. See Summary 13-E.

3. **"Jump start" reluctant students:** Sometimes when a student is having trouble getting started, he may get stuck and then cover up his frustration by becoming defiant. Getting started on tasks is extremely difficult and remains a lifelong problem for many people with ADD or ADHD. The student may be willing to work but need prompting to get started, or he may feel totally overwhelmed by the assignment and have no clue where to start.

   Teachers and parents can help jump start the student a number of ways:
   - Review the instructions.
   - Have him call a friend for clarification.
   - Help the student break the assignment into manageable segments.

- Sometimes if the student will simply begin working, the assignment becomes clearer.
- Draw a mind map or brainstorm using similar graphic organizers to get creative ideas flowing. See Summary 15 for a discussion of graphic organizers plus names of websites that offer examples.
- Have the student play a game with himself: "I'll just read for 15 minutes and then I'll stop whenever I want to." Once students get started, they usually continue.
- Suggest the student watch a TV program and read material during the *muted* commercials (for short reading assignments).
- Sometimes if a student starts with physical activities, it may increase his alertness enough to allow him to begin mental activities such as reading. He could:
  - walk around, reading aloud from a book, until he can settle down and read while sitting in a chair.
  - walk on a treadmill while reading; put the book on the stand attached to the treadmill; be careful, this is not for the uncoordinated.
- A subtle reminder of consequences for not completing the work may be helpful. "I know you want to finish this project tonight or Ms. Smith will count off a whole letter grade (or you'll be embarrassed in class, or you'll fail the test). Let's work together on this." (However, don't use this tactic if the student is already terribly discouraged or it raises anxiety too much.)

4. **Skip missing information:** Not surprisingly, these students are often looking for excuses to stop doing their homework. So, if needed information is missing, have the student work around it, leaving a blank that can be filled in later that night or the next day.

5. **Teach "quick and dirty" short cuts:** Some students with attention deficits have a ***compulsive need to do things perfectly*** so the work takes forever to complete. Perfection-seeking behavior combined with executive function deficits may mean that an essay takes three hours to draft rather than the expected hour. So the student looks at the assignment, knows it will take three hours, and groans a silent "Oh, no!" Sometimes he may avoid the assignment completely.

  Teach students how to use "quick and dirty" short cuts or adaptations. For example, a crisis arises when the student suddenly remembers at 9:30 p.m. that an essay is due tomorrow. The student may dictate ideas to a parent, who types the first draft. Then the student can cut and paste the paragraphs, either on the computer or the paper itself, and arrange the paragraphs in order. See Summaries 15 and 16 on written expression for other ways to help a student get ideas down on paper.

6. **Discuss the concept that there is never enough time to do everything:** Help students understand that there is never enough time to complete every task to perfection. Help them learn to tell the difference between projects that require their "best work" and those they can complete by doing them just well enough to "get by." The example in the preceding section is one of those occasions when the student cannot

expect to achieve perfection and must accept lower standards. Even though the work may not earn an A, a grade of C or D is better than an F for not turning in anything.

7. **Work during peak energy times:** Recommend scheduling homework during times when the student's energy is more likely to be at a peak. Each day there are times when our brains seem to think more clearly and working is easier. In addition, medication affects the times of peak attention for students with ADD/ADHD. This peak study time occurs during a narrow window before the medication begins to wear off. (See Summary 53 to determine peak times.)

8. **If a task is boring, add something to spice things up:** Play music or TV (no story plot) at low volume. When reading, break assignments into segments marked by colored paper clips. When the student "reads to the clip," he can take a break or have free reading.

9. **Avoid interruptions:** Once the student begins homework, hold any telephone calls until break time or homework is completed.

10. **Schedule a "joy break":** Suggest that the student renew energy and at the same time reward completion of work by taking a walk, exercising, calling a friend, or playing Nintendo for a brief period. Some students may actually do better with breaks at the end of an assignment rather than the middle. Figure out what works best for each student.

SUMMARY 35 Putting Time Management to Work

Failing to complete a major long-term project is one of the primary reasons students with ADD/ADHD fail a class. The typical student with an attention deficit immediately feels overwhelmed when he is given a major project. He sees this huge project and has no idea how to break it down into smaller segments or where to begin working on it. Since the due date is usually a few weeks away, students often procrastinate or forget the project until the night before it is due.

Sometimes the greatest challenges the student faces are simply getting organized, knowing exactly what the project requirements are, figuring out where to begin, and getting started. Often, once the student gets started, he really doesn't mind doing the work.

Depending on the skill level of each student, teachers will find that specific steps for helping students use organizational and time management strategies will vary. The first time a student has a fairly complicated semester project, the teacher will probably walk the student through the project, step-by-step. Using an overhead, the teacher may show the student how to do a sample project.

The tools in this summary will give teachers and parents ideas of how to help the student break down and organize his project. An example of a semester project for Jerry, a high school junior, is described here. The forms contained in the next two summaries will help the teenager and parents organize their thoughts and develop a plan for timely completion of a project. Although blank forms are available in Appendices A5 and A6, teachers and parents should feel free to create their own forms to help organize this process.

A Sample Project

Let's put organizational skills and time management tips to work on Jerry's semester project.

Jerry has been given a major project in history. Each student must develop a portfolio of his best work on World War II. From a list of twenty-two activities related to the war, the student must complete six mandatory and four optional activities.

The Organizational Plan

An organizational plan using the time management strategies discussed in Summary 34 includes these four steps:

1. plan,
2. prioritize,
3. schedule,
4. follow the plan.

A teacher, or perhaps a coach, will need to go through all these steps with the student to *shape behavior,* or, in other words, to teach him how to complete a major project. With enough supervised practice, students with ADD/ADHD will eventually learn to do a major project on their own.

1. Plan

■ *Complete a graphic organizer.* Don, Jerry's father, used this amusing example to help his son understand how to tackle a big project. *"How do you eat an elephant? One bite at a time."* He then helped Jerry complete a graphic organizer to visually present all the project requirements. He knew that giving a student with ADD/ADHD a graphic organizer may help him "eat the project one bite at a time"—in other words, break the project into manageable sections.

Teachers may help students complete the graphic organizer in Summary 36 to visually present all the project requirements on one page. First, write all the important information regarding the assignment on this page so the student can tell at a glance what the requirements are. Later, check off each task as it is done. A blank form is available in Appendix A5.

■ *Post a class calendar for the project.* Joan Helbing, the ADD Consultant for Appleton Area Schools in Wisconsin, explains that teachers have found it helpful to post a monthly calendar as shown here for the whole class. Note major dates and information and remind students as those dates draw near. This concrete, visual reminder is more likely to help them "see" and remember the due dates.

Monday	Tuesday	Wednesday	Thursday	Friday
		project assigned		turn in topic
choice		turn in list of 4 sources		
	turn in note cards (outline)			rough draft due
project	charts and graphs due		final copy check	due

■ *Display a completed project.* According to Helbing, teachers have found that the quality of student projects improves when completed projects are displayed for them to review. Students are able to visualize what the final project should look like and create their project accordingly.

2. Prioritize

■ *Decide which of the ten steps should be done first.* First review the requirements and decide if any of them require special time considerations. For example, allow adequate time in case a book must be requested from another library or the book has been checked out by someone else. Or, for instance, does the family need to schedule a visit to grandfather's house for an interview about the war?

- **Then rank order the steps.** List the steps in the order in which they should be done. However, after the first two or three steps the order may not be important.

3. Schedule

- **Schedule activities on a weekly calendar** as shown in Summary 37. Once the material is written out on the graphic organizer and the student knows all his assignments, he can begin scheduling each step by writing it on his calendar. As explained in Summary 35, schedule each step backward from the due date. A blank form is available in Appendix A6.

4. Follow the plan

- **Help the student get started and monitor regularly.** First the student will collect all the information needed for one or several segments of the project. Jerry visited the library, completed all his research during several visits to the library, photocopied important material, and was then ready to start writing the report.

  As explained in Summary 34, sometimes parents have to jump-start students to get them working on the project. More than likely they'll need prompting to simply pick which topic to start researching or writing on first. Summary 38 gives some tips for limiting choices to help students make decisions more quickly. If the student is struggling, the parent may arbitrarily narrow the choices to two and say, "Would you rather do '1' or '2'?"

- **Set up folders or binders for collected material.** Help the student organize a storage system using either folders or binders with separators. Put all the various pieces of the project into these folders—for example, label a folder for the cover, the table of contents, the written content, photocopies of reading materials, pictures/ graphs/charts, bibliography, and resources.

- **Keep an up-to-date list of references.** Nothing is more frustrating than finishing up the report late the night before it is due and discovering that you don't have the author's full name, the publisher's name, publication date, and city in which a reference book was published. Photocopy the front and back of the title page of each book consulted. Most of the needed information is typically found on those two pages.

- **Set up pocket folders.** Any work that is done at school should be collected in one folder for each student.

Advice for Coaches

Anyone who is helping coach a student through a major project may appreciate this humorous advice from Penny, Jerry's mother.

"My son is totally overwhelmed by most projects. He doesn't know where to begin." Somewhat tongue in cheek, she explains the best strategy: *"Lie!*

Don't ever tell your teenager everything at once. Even though he has the papers, he doesn't understand what it all means. Keep things simple. Break the project into sections and start working on them. Feed the material to him one "bite" or section at a time."

"You can't write on the schedule to do two of ten sections of the project each visit to the library. You have to be flexible. Because it all depends on how he feels or the mood he's in or whether or not his medicine has worn off. Today he may do work on four of them but on the next visit to the library, he may just barely be able to finish one."

SUMMARY 36 · Project Graphic Organizer

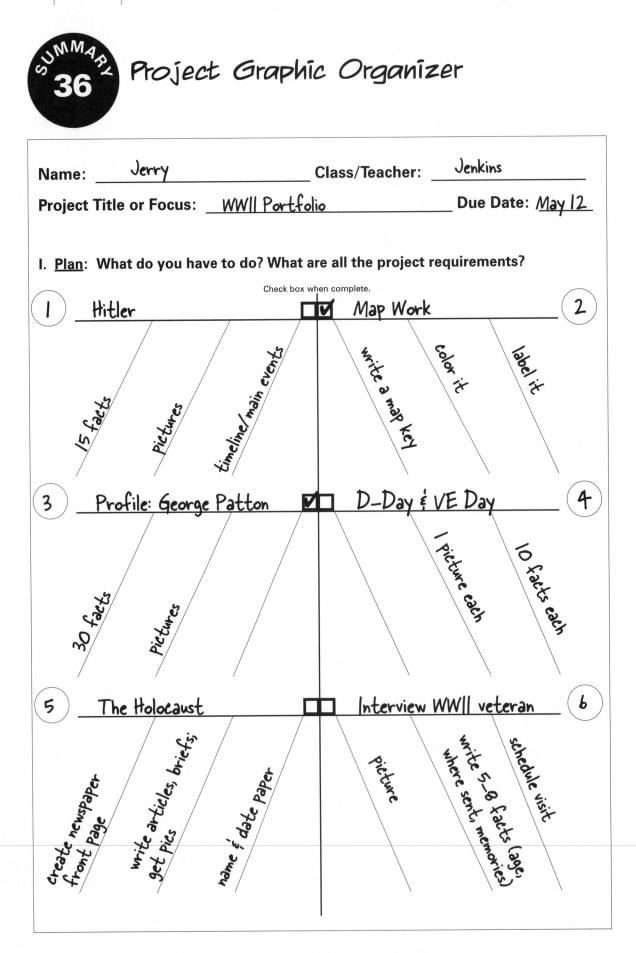

Name: Jerry   **Class/Teacher:** Jenkins

Project Title or Focus: WWII Portfolio   **Due Date:** May 12

I. Plan: What do you have to do? What are all the project requirements?

Check box when complete.

1. Hitler
   - 15 facts
   - Pictures
   - timeline/main events

2. ☑ Map Work
   - write a map key
   - color it
   - label it

3. Profile: George Patton ☑
   - 30 facts
   - Pictures

4. D-Day & VE Day
   - 1 picture each
   - 10 facts each

5. The Holocaust
   - create newspaper front page
   - write articles, briefs; get pics
   - name & date paper

6. Interview WWII veteran
   - picture
   - write 5–8 facts (age, where sent, memories)
   - schedule visit

Project Graphic Organizer

Projects may be complex and involve multiple steps. Sometimes in the rush of completing the project some key information may be overlooked. Record all requirements on this page so that no steps will be forgotten. Good luck!

I. Plan: What are all the project requirements? What do I need?

- Complete the Project Graphic Organizer on the other side.

Check resources needed:

- **X** library visit
- ____ books
- ____ magazine articles
- **X** Internet
- **X** interviews
- _____
- _____

Check products needed:

- **X** written report
- **X** report cover
- ____ poster
- **X** pictures
- **X** bibliography
- **X** timelines with dates

- ____ build a model
- **X** maps
- create newspaper
- _____
- _____

II. Prioritize: Do I need to set priorities? **X** yes _____ no

- Which one do I need to do first? #5 & 6
- Which one is most complicated and will take the most time? #5-- newspaper
- Do I need to allow time to order a book from the library or schedule a visit for an interview? yes--schedule to visit veteran
- Number the remaining parts of the project on the organizer in the order you will do them. do 5 & 6 first; no special order after that

III. Schedule: How long will the project take? 2 weeks (estimate)

- Put steps on the Weekly Project Calendar in Appendix A6. (Summary 37)

IV. Do it: Complete all the steps on the Weekly Project Calendar.

- Check each step off in color marker on the Project Graphic Organizer when it is completed.

Weekly Project Planner

Week 1　　　　　　　　　　　　　　　　　　　　(month) <u>May</u>

During the first week, the student completed all the research for this project, photocopied it and put it in a folder.

Part of the work was completed at school during class and visits to the school library; the rest was done via the Internet at the local library and his computer at home.

Interviewing the WWII veteran was completed while on spring break.

	Monday	Tuesday	Wednesday	Thursday	Friday	Saturday
7:00						
7:30						
8:00						
8:30						
9:00						
9:30						
10:00						
10:30						
11:00						
11:30						
12:00						
12:30						
1:00	Holocaust	Holocaust	Holocaust	Holocaust	Holocaust	Sunday
1:30	Group	newspaper	newspaper	newspaper	newspaper	
2:00	Work					
2:30						
3:00						
3:30						
4:00						
4:30						
5:00						
5:30						
6:00	Library	Library	Library	Library		write 2
Evening	Hitler	"D" Day	Battles	Patton		sections

Week 2   (month) <u>May</u>

The student began working on the project one section at a time.

Activities were scheduled at regular intervals to provide ballpark guidance. Of course, flexible scheduling is required for these students. Some nights the student may do four activities and only one the next night.

Teachers will check student progress at regular intervals, answer questions, problem-solve, plan, advise if on track, and give encouragement.

	Monday	Tuesday	Wednesday	Thursday	Friday	Saturday
7:00						
7:30						
8:00						
8:30						
9:00						
9:30						
10:00						
10:30						
11:00						
11:30						
12:00						
12:30						
1:00	Map	Map	Map	put report	*	Sunday
1:30	work	work	work	together	REPORT	
2:00					DUE	
2:30						
3:00						
3:30						
4:00						
4:30						
5:00						
5:30						
6:00	write 2	write 2	write 2	Final		
Evening	sections	sections	sections	Polish		

Coping with Executive Function Deficits

So Why Are the "Big Four" So Important?

I hope that the preceding summaries in Section 3 have clarified just how critical *organization, memory, awareness of time,* and *time management* are for making good grades in school.

At school, teachers provide structure so that school time is highly scheduled. This means that most of the problems with the "big four" occur after school (remembering books and assignments) or at home (getting started, doing homework, and taking it back to school). One solution is to involve an "organizational coach," typically the parents or another student. Some schools have a teacher or aide who meets with the students at the end of the day to review assignments and books for the evening. One parent even went so far as to hire a senior to meet her freshman daughter after school to decide which books and assignments to take home. In other schools, the teachers or counselors may be too busy to spend class time teaching these skills. If so, then give appropriate summaries from this section to parents. It is critical that someone help teenagers with attention deficits master these basic skills. Tips for coaching are provided in Summary 65.

General Suggestions for Handling Executive Function Deficits

When students with attention deficits are struggling with memory, organization, or time management, keep these four key pieces of advice in mind:

- *Keep it simple!*
- *Keep it brief!*
- *Keep it visual!*
- *Keep it novel!*

Provide Additional Guidance

As they learn to become more organized, students with ADD/ADHD need more hands-on guidance than their peers. Remember, adults will have to be involved in this teaching process longer for these students primarily because of their two- to four-year developmental delay and executive function deficits. If parents are interested and want help, give them copies of the summaries in Section 3.

Help Teens Understand and Cope with Executive Function Deficits

Review relevant summaries in this section with teens. Ask them, "Does any of this sound like you? Which part?" Help them understand their own organizational system better and select ways to make it more effective.

Model Time Management and Organizational Strategies

A teacher, parent, or tutor may need to help the student develop an organizational system from the strategies listed in Summary 34. Someone may have to show him how to write a "to do" list, pick priorities, make a schedule, and implement the plan. Remember, it is much harder for these students to get information into long-term memory, so they will need visual cues and tricks to help them remember these strategies. Frequent repetition will be required until the skill is mastered.

Limit Choices

Many students with attention deficits get bogged down if they have too many choices: they may spend enormous amounts of time considering all their options. By the time they have selected a topic, they are worn out and ready to move on to something else. Perhaps teachers and parents can help them find short cuts around this time-consuming and exhausting process.

- Give only two choices of essay or report topics.
- If a teacher gives an open-ended choice ("write an essay on a topic of interest to you"), someone should help narrow the topics down to two choices.
- Even then, it may be necessary for teachers or parents to briefly discuss the topics, help the student make a decision, and sometimes, arbitrarily select a topic.

Expect Students to Change Their Organizational Systems Periodically

These creative students become bored with sameness! So, most organizational systems lose their effectiveness after awhile. Change is essential to hold their interest. Add something new and interesting to the system.

Federal Laws Governing ADD/ADHD

IDEA (Education Law) and Section 504 & ADA (Civil Rights Laws)

Three important federal laws impact the education of students with ADD or ADHD:

1. **IDEA:** a federal **education** law guaranteeing a free appropriate public education to all students with disabilities. This law applies primarily to students served by public schools, ages birth through high school, and in some cases through age 21.

2. **Section 504:** A federal **civil rights** law prohibiting discrimination against people with disabilities in programs that receive *any* financial aid from the federal government, including schools, public and private, as well as colleges and technical schools.

3. **ADA:** a federal **civil rights** law, broader than 504, that prevents discrimination against people with disabilities in many settings, including public schools, private non-religious schools, and the workplace.

Researchers tell us that of all students with ADD or ADHD, approximately 50 percent qualify for services under IDEA and almost all qualify under Section 504. So, if a student with ADD or ADHD is struggling in school but is not eligible for services under IDEA, hopefully the school will consider eligibility under Section 504. Regardless of eligibility category, most students with attention deficits will spend the majority of their time in regular classrooms, rather than special education classes.

Writing about these laws is very difficult, because explanation of any law requires interpretation. If you ask two lawyers, you may get two different interpretations, just as you would if you asked a school official and a parent, or two different judges. In addition, the interpretations of the law may change overnight on the basis of a court ruling. Furthermore, states may pass laws and regulations that provide more detail than the federal law does. For example, states may specify the number of days during which an evaluation and special education placement must occur, or add to the list of objects qualifying as weapons. So, please be aware that **the information given in this section is stated in general terms and is not intended as legal advice.**

Overview of IDEA: A Federal Education Law

The Individuals with Disabilities Education Act (IDEA), a federal education law, **provides for a free appropriate public education to all children, regardless of their disability.** Approximately 50 percent of students with attention deficit disorder are eligible for services under IDEA, either in special classes or within a regular classroom setting. Many other students with this condition can be adequately served in their regular classroom with supports provided under Section 504. (See Summary 47.) Only a few students with attention deficits may *not* need or qualify for any extra classroom supports. Typically, qualifying for services under IDEA is more difficult than qualifying under Section 504.

If students need IDEA services, they usually receive services under a category called **Other Health Impairment.** (See Summary 42.) However, in the past most of these students received services under other categories, such as Emotional and Behavioral Disorders (EBD) or Specific Learning Disabilities (SLD). Sometimes, if students need services that are more costly, the school prefers to provide assistance under IDEA instead of Section 504. Under current funding guidelines, local school systems are reimbursed by the state for services provided under IDEA but *not* Section 504.

Key Provisions of IDEA

1. **A free appropriate public education (FAPE):** Schools must provide a free education for all students, even those with disabilities. Most school systems develop a range of services, including classroom accommodations and modifications so that the student can be served in a local public school. Otherwise, if they can't serve the student, the school system may have to pay a larger public school system, a private school, or a residential school to provide an education. "Appropriate" means a program designed to provide some "educational benefit."

2. **An Individualized Education Program (IEP):** An IEP is a written plan jointly developed by teachers, parents, and the student that identifies strengths, problems, goals, needed services, and expected benefits. Reasonable accommodations and/or modifications, supplemental aides, and services are provided based upon information from the evaluation. See Summaries 44 and 45.

3. **Parental involvement:** Parents are considered **"equal participants"** in making educational decisions as members of the IEP Team that determines eligibility and placement and develops the IEP.

4. **Right to remedy (due process):** If teachers and parents disagree about the evaluation, IEP, reasonable accommodations and/or modifications, or placement, then parents have the right to appeal decisions at an impartial hearing.

5. **Education in the least restrictive environment (LRE):** Schools must first provide services to the student in the regular classroom, with the help of reasonable accommodations and/or modifications, if necessary. In addition, supplementary aides and services such as a one-on-one behavioral aide or tutor may be provided as part of a Behavioral Intervention Plan (Summary 41). For some students, the LRE may be part-time or full-time placement in a special class, a separate school, a therapeutic day program, or other alternative.

6. **Nondiscriminatory evaluation:** Schools must do a comprehensive evaluation to determine whether a child qualifies for services. For ADD and ADHD, that may mean paying careful attention to test results in areas that are related to this condition, such as attention, working memory, cognitive processing, or organizational skills. (See Summary 6 for examples of diagnostic tests.)

Other Important IDEA Provisions

- **Accommodations and/or modifications in either a regular or special education classroom:** Materials, instructional methods, testing methods, etc. may be adapted so that a student with disabilities can still receive the majority of instruction in a regular classroom. A list of reasonable classroom accommodations and modifications, such as tutors or one-on-one behavioral aides, is available in Summary 41.

- **Related services:** Students may receive any "related services" recommended in the IEP—e.g., counseling groups, occupational therapy, study skills, organizational skill instruction, time management instruction, problem solving, anger management. (See Summaries 32-34 and 64-69 for tips on teaching these skills.)

- **Individualized Transition Plan (TP):** By age 16, a detailed TP must be developed to help students prepare for life after graduation (transition into a job, vocational training, or higher education). TPs are discussed in more detail in Summary 48.

- **Limits on the length of suspensions:** Except for drug/alcohol or weapon offenses, or physical aggression, there are limits to how long a student may be suspended. See discussion in Summary 40.

- **Opportunities to participate in extracurricular activities:** To be eligible to participate, the student must meet the same grading criteria as other students—for example, maintain a C average. However, if the student qualifies under IDEA or Section 504, the student may receive accommodations and/or modifications in the classroom to help prevent future failure. In addition, students placed in classrooms outside of their neighborhood school may return to attend their home high school prom, participate in after school clubs, or go to their graduation ceremony.

- **Change in placement:** An IEP meeting must be called whenever the school considers any change in placement, including most suspensions of more than 10 days (since a suspension or expulsion is considered a change in placement). The team must:

  - review the behavior,
  - determine if the behavior is related to the disability, and

- determine the punishment. In some school systems, punishment is pre-determined for certain drug, alcohol, or physical violence offense. See Summaries 59-63 on behavioral strategies.

- **Mediation:** A dispute resolution proceeding conducted by an impartial third party must be offered if parents and school officials reach an impasse and cannot agree upon the evaluation, placement, or IEP.

- **Education at another school or tutoring in the home:** This must be provided if the student is suspended for more than ten days or expelled (*if the misbehavior is related to the disability*).

- **Involvement of a team of educators plus the parents and student:** All decisions regarding the student's educational placement, eligibility for classroom accommodations and/or modifications, or other supportive services must be made by the IEP team. See Summary 40 for a listing of the IEP Team Membership.

Resources for Section 4

Helpful publications with a variety of viewpoints are available regarding IDEA and Section 504. With regard to any law, interpretation varies with the viewpoint of the person reading the law. Some of these resources speak from the perspective of the best interests of the parents, local schools, or state or federal education agency involved. However, in the end, the interpretation should be based upon the best interests of the student involved.

Batemen, Barbara D. & Mary Anne Linden. *Better IEPs: How to Develop Legally Correct and Educationally Useful Programs.* 3rd ed. Longmont, CO: Sopris West, 1999.

Cohen, Mathew. "Individuals with Disabilities Education Act 1999: What You Need to Know about AD/HD under the Individuals with Disabilities Education Act." *Inside CHADD*, June/July 1999.

Dendy, Chris A. Zeigler. *Teenagers with ADD: A Parents' Guide.* Bethesda, MD: Woodbine House, 1995. Includes an in-depth discussion of IDEA, IEPs, and Section 504, plus several completed sample forms. Keep in mind that *Teens* must be used in conjunction with this book, which addresses key 1997 revisions.

Dwyer, Kevin P. "Disciplining Students with Disabilities." *Communiqué*, the official newsletter of the National Association of School Psychologists, October 1997. (www.naspweb.org)

Gregg, Soleil. "IDEA, the Final Regulations, and Children with ADHD." *Inside CHADD*, June/July 1999.

"IEPs and Parents: What the IDEA 1997 Amendments Offer." *Claiming Children*, the Federation of Families for Children's Mental Health, November 1997.

Jordan, Dixie. *Honorable Intentions: A Guide to Educational Planning.* 2nd ed. Minneapolis, MN: Pacer Center, 2000.

Reed Martin's Web Site. Offers information on IDEA and Section 504. Martin is a well-known attorney who specializes in special education law. (www.reedmartin.com)

PACER Center. "Individualized Education Programs: A Tool for Parents Engaged in their Children's Learning. *Inside CHADD*, June/July 1999.

PACER Center Web Site. Includes the full text of IDEA and its amendments and articles by PACER staff about various aspects of the law, including "PACER Center Looks at IDEA '97." (www.pacer.org)

Procedural Due Process Rights in Student Discipline. Washington, DC: Center for Law and Education, 1999. (202-462-7688)

"Section 504 Celebrates Its 25th Year: Top 15 Tips for Writing IEPS and Section 504 Plans." *Attention: The Magazine of Children and Adults with Attention-Deficit/ Hyperactivity Disorder.* V. 5, N. 3, Winter 1999.

Summary of the Individuals with Disabilities Education Act (IDEA) Amendments of 1997. *Council for Exceptional Children. (www.cec.sped.org)*

Turnbull, H. Rutherford III & Anne P. Turnbull. *Free Appropriate Public Education: The Law and Children with Disabilities.* 6th ed. Denver, CO: Love Publishing Company, 2000.

Wright, Peter W. D. & Pamela Darr Wright. *Wrightslaw: Special Education Law.* Harbor House Law Press, Hartfield, VA: 1999. (877-529-4332; *www.wrightslaw.com*)

Impact of IDEA on Students with ADD or ADHD

A brief summary of IDEA and its specific impact on students with ADD or ADHD is provided below. Obviously, this overview only touches on the highlights of the law and is not intended to serve as legal advice. The actual law itself is complex, totaling hundreds of pages in length. Of course, with a complicated law like IDEA, there will always be some exceptions to these general statements. A more careful review of the law and state regulations will be necessary if conflicts arise between the school and family.

Key IDEA Revisions

Major revisions to IDEA were enacted by Congress in 1997, and the final U.S. DOE regulations accompanying the law were released in March of 1999. For the first time, the revisions to IDEA **officially listed ADD and ADHD as eligible conditions** under Other Health Impairment, a special education eligibility category. Including students with attention deficit disorders is *not* a new requirement but simply a clarification of previous DOE policies.

Other IDEA revisions having a major impact on teachers and parents of these students include:

- Inclusion of *regular* education teachers in IEP meetings;
- Expansion of the parent's role in the IEP process;
- Expansion of parental access to records;
- Emphasis on earlier development of *positive* behavioral interventions, supplementary aids and services, and use of assistive technology;
- Modification of disciplinary policies allowing stricter consequences such as expulsion for drug, alcohol, or weapons offenses;
- Provision of frequent feedback to parents, at least as often as for students in regular education, regarding a student's progress on her IEP goals;
- Conducting Functional Behavioral Assessments to prevent repetition of misbehavior.

Highlights of IDEA-Part B

1. **Definition of a Child with a Disability.** Only children who have a disability are qualified for special education services under this federal education law. IDEA includes thirteen categories of disabilities under which children can qualify. The official definition of a "child with a disability" has been expanded under the "other health impairment" (OHI) category to include:

   - Attention Deficit Disorder (**ADD**), and

4

- Attention Deficit Hyperactivity Disorder (**ADHD**).

2. **Eligibility Categories for Students with ADD/ADHD.** Although three categories are often used to provide services to students with ADD or ADHD, the 1997 IDEA revisions make it clear that OHI, or Other Health Impairment, is one of the primary eligibility categories that should be considered for students with attention deficits. See Summary 42.

   Until recently, two other special education service categories were often used for these students:
   - Specific Learning Disability (**SLD**); see Summary 43.
   - Emotional and Behavioral Disorder (**EBD**) or Serious Emotional Disturbance (**SED**).

3. **Incorporation of 1991 U.S. DOE/OCR Policy Memo on ADD/ADHD.** In 1991, the U.S. Department of Education (Office of Special Education and Rehabilitation Services and Office of Elementary and Secondary Education) and the Office for Civil Rights jointly issued a major policy memo to clarify that ADD and ADHD were covered by existing law under OHI or Section 504. Key elements of the memo were incorporated into the revisions of IDEA. (See *Teenagers with ADD*, Appendix B, for a copy of the memo.)

4. **Reasonable Classroom Accommodations and Modifications.** Under IDEA, teachers must make a variety of changes in the classroom to help students with disabilities achieve some *"educational benefit."* For example, they might modify the way the student is taught or tested, adjust class scheduling, or modify homework. A list of suggested accommodations and modifications is included in Summaries 13-A to 13-E, 41, 44, and 45.

Individualized Education Program (IEP)

The purpose of developing an IEP is to identify each student's strengths and needs, develop a plan to meet those needs, and then deliver needed services. It is important to remember that ***the student's needs, not the disability category, must drive the educational plan!*** So, if a student with ADD/ADHD needs specific services, such as tutoring in math, they may attend a class where they can receive that service, even if it is labeled the "SLD classroom" or "Varying Exceptionalities Resource classroom."

1. **IEP Team Membership.** In general, IEP teams serve three or four major functions: 1) special education eligibility determination, 2) development of the IEP, 3) conducting Manifestation Determination Reviews, and 4) determining appropriate placement. In some states, one committee may serve all these functions. In other states, there may be two or three separate committees.

   Membership of the IEP team was expanded by the 1997 revisions. Each IEP team must now include:
   - Parents
   - At least one special education teacher, if any time is or may be spent in special education
   - At least one regular education teacher, if the student is or may be in regular class or other activities

- A least one team member who is knowledgeable about the child and the disability
- A local school representative qualified to supervise special education who has the authority to allocate resources
- A person to interpret evaluation results, typically the school psychologist
- Others at the parent's or school's discretion
- The student, when appropriate. Teenagers should be included as often as possible. Ultimately, parents should decide whether or not the teenager attends any of the eligibility, IEP development, transition planning, or placement committee meetings. Obviously, if the meeting may damage the student's self-esteem because negative comments may be made about her, it would not be in her best interests to attend. Sometimes students submit input in writing or through an earlier discussion with the parent or teacher. See Summary 64 for a discussion of self-advocacy.

2. IEP Content

Mandated Components

The six mandated components, discussed in greater detail in Summary 44, are:
1. present level of educational performance, including strengths,
2. goals and objectives, including expected achievement,
3. services to be provided and time to be spent in regular education,
4. dates of services,
5. evaluation procedures,
6. individualized transition goals and objectives, at age fourteen or earlier.

Other IEP Requirements

In addition to the mandatory IEP requirements, the following issues must also be addressed: *(New IDEA requirements or those with increased emphasis in the 1997 revisions are marked with an asterisk.)*

Academic Issues

- *Accommodations and/or modifications* in the classroom or school day
- *Measurable annual goals and objectives,* complete with objective criteria showing how they will be assessed.
- *Assistive technology* devices and services (laptop computer, "Alpha Smart," "Phonic Ear," "Spell Checker.") See Summary 13-E for more details. Obviously, students must be taught to use these devices efficiently.
- *Supplementary aids and services* (notetaker, speech therapy, counseling, occupational therapy). See Summary 13-E.
- If English proficiency is limited, services to address the student's *language needs.**

- *Extent to which (the amount of time) the child is not in regular class and extracurricular activities.**

  If a student's disability prevents her from participating in extracurricular events, these barriers must be identified and appropriate accommodations and/or modifications provided. For example, the basketball coaches may need to repeat directions or double check to see that these students understand their instructions.

- *An extended school year (ESY).* The need for an extended school year must be based upon the student's needs and her IEP. If needed services are currently not available, the school system will have to develop the services. See discussion in Summary 44.

Testing Issues

- *Modifications needed for state or district wide achievement tests** (extended time, use of a calculator, testing in a room with no distractions. See Summary 44.).

Progress Reports and Records

- *Regular updates* for parents.* Reports on progress in the general curriculum must be given at least as often as for students in regular education.

- *Parental access to "all" student school records** (not just "relevant" ones)

Behavioral Issues

- *Positive behavioral intervention strategies** for the student whose behavior impedes his or her learning or that of others (i.e., develop a Behavior Intervention Plan). For example, when a student cannot focus on completing school work, it impedes her ability to learn and positive behavioral strategies should be implemented. (See Summary 63.)

Vocational Issues

- *Transition service* needs. See Summary 48.
- By age 14 or earlier, the school will provide *guidance on the student's course of study.* The transition goals in the IEP regarding the student's course of study will be updated annually. For example, if the student plans to be a rock star, she should consider taking all the music courses that are offered.
- By age 16, direct transition services will be provided, including interagency responsibilities or linkages. For example, the regional technical school and vocational rehabilitation involvement may be spelled out.

Supports for Regular Classroom Teachers

- *Supports needed for teachers**: Teachers should be asked, "What do you need to make this IEP work?" For example, the teacher may need a classroom or teacher's aide.

Discipline under Part B

In general, the new IDEA revisions focus on helping students succeed by:

1. intervening early and using positive behavioral interventions,
2. determining what may have triggered a student's failure or misbehavior (the antecedent behavior),
3. reviewing and modifying the present IEP, if needed.

1. **A Behavior Intervention Plan (BI)**: When a student disrupts class, uses profanity with teachers, refuses to follow school rules, or misbehaves in other unacceptable ways, the school is required to focus on why the behavior occurred. After conducting a Functional Behavioral Assessment, the school will typically develop a *Behavior Intervention Plan*. Implementing the strategies in the Plan should prevent reoccurrence of these same problems. The school has a responsibility to develop a clear plan to teach the student positive behavioral skills to substitute for inappropriate behavior.

   Deficits in executive function may also be addressed in BI Plans to help the student cope or compensate for attention deficits. The new law emphasizes using behavior plans *earlier* to prevent more serious problems. See Summary 63 for guidance on conducting a Functional Behavioral Assessment and developing a Behavior Intervention Plan.

   - If a student's misbehavior cannot be handled by the classroom teacher, a *Functional Behavioral Assessment* will be conducted and then a *Behavior Intervention Plan* developed as part of the IEP.
     - Functional Behavioral Assessment (FBA): These assessments are intended to *identify the antecedent event* (the action that triggers misbehavior). When a student is referred for an evaluation or staffing at an IEP meeting, the school psychologist will identify problem behaviors by talking with the student and teachers involved. Based upon the assessment, the school may change antecedent behaviors or consequences of the student's misbehavior. See Summary 63 for more details.
     - Next, a Behavior Intervention Plan is developed and implemented.
     - If the present Behavior Intervention Plan isn't working, school personnel must revise and change it to address the behavior that resulted in the suspension.
   - A student who is suspended for more than *ten days* in a school year and whose behavior is a manifestation of the disability must have a *Functional Behavioral Assessment* and a *Behavior Intervention Plan.*

2. **Change of Placement:** Examples of changes of placement include school suspension beyond ten days, expulsion, placement in an *Interim Alternative Educational Setting (IAES)*, and high school graduation with the same diploma as any other student.

4

- Only an IEP Team or occasionally a hearing officer may make a change in placement. Anytime a change of placement occurs, an IEP Team meeting must be scheduled.

- The school may remove a student to an *Interim Alternative Placement Setting (IAES)* immediately if drugs or weapons are involved.

  - However, if a school system wishes to quickly remove a student from her present placement because of alleged violent behavior, an *expedited due process hearing* must be held first and a hearing officer must determine if the violent behavior is dangerous. Typically an immediate and substantial risk of injury or harm to self or others must be present before a student may be removed from her home school.

  - If the school schedules an expedited due process hearing, the new IEP and recommended placement may take effect within ten days unless the parents object.

3. **School Suspensions:** Most school suspensions beyond ten days are considered a **change in placement,** so state and federal review policies must be followed. For disciplinary purposes, school systems may:

   - *suspend a student for up to ten days* (for violations of school regulations, without an IEP meeting). Educational services are not required for the first 10 days of a suspension.

     - if a suspension **exceeds ten days during a school year**, the school must provide the educational services necessary for the student to appropriately progress in the general curriculum and advance toward achieving the goals in the IEP. The IEP Team will determine what services are needed.

   - *suspend a student for additional removals of up to ten days* as long as removals do not constitute a pattern

     - If a student is repeatedly suspended for the same behaviors, an IEP meeting and a special review known as a *Manifestation Determination Review* will be required before disciplinary action is taken.

   - **move** *the student to an IAES (Interim Alternative Education Setting)* for **up to 45 calendar** days, for possession of drugs or weapons or dangerous behavior, if students without disabilities are disciplined the same way for the same misbehavior.

4. **School Expulsions:** A school expulsion is different from a suspension. Typically, a student is suspended for less serious offenses for only two or three days, although it may be up to 45 days. When a student is expelled, it is for more serious offenses and often involves a removal from the home school for perhaps a year or sometimes permanently. However, even when a special education student is expelled, the school system is still responsible for providing a free appropriate education.

- When a student is expelled from school, it is considered a change of placement, so an IEP meeting and a Manifestation Determination Review must be held.
- Some systems have alternative schools where these students are educated. At a special program developed by the school system in Kenosha, Wisconsin, students receive a half-day of academic instruction. During the last half of the day, social services (child welfare, juvenile justice, and mental health staff) conduct groups or teach needed skills such as anger management, conflict resolution, and problem solving. A description of the Kenosha Program is provided in Summary 49.
- Other small school systems may provide educational services through contracts with large school districts.

5. **Interim Alternative Education Setting (IAES):** An IEP Team or hearing officer may place a student in an IAES (another school setting), but for no more than 45 days. The following conditions must be met:

   - The student is allowed to participate in the general curriculum (continue the same subject content).
   - The student will continue to receive special education services and modifications that enable her to meet the goals of her IEP.
   - School officials will provide services designed to teach alternatives to problem behavior that led to placement in the IAES.

6. **"Stay Put" Requirement:** In most cases, the student is allowed to **"stay put"** in her current placement, awaiting an IEP Team meeting or disciplinary hearing, pending determination of whether the misbehavior is related to her disability. If the parents and IEP Team cannot agree on a change of placement, parents may ask for an *impartial hearing.* In the interim, until the dispute is resolved, students must remain, or "stay put," in their present placement, except when:

   - a weapon is carried to school, or
   - drugs are possessed, used, or sold at school or a school function, or
   - a physical danger is created (poses an immediate and substantial risk of injury to self or others).

7. **Manifestation Determination Review:** Before a student is suspended, expelled, or placed in another setting, a Manifestation Determination Review must be conducted to determine whether the misbehavior is a manifestation of the student's disability.

   - If the behavior *is related* to the disability, the IEP Team must determine appropriate services and placement. In other words, special education students may be disciplined differently than the stated school discipline procedures. The school may impose a disciplinary action that is appropriate for the student's disability.
   - If the misbehavior *is not related* to the student's disability, then the school may use the same discipline procedures it uses with all other students. However, the school must continue to educate the student.

4

Timely notifications and reviews are required:

- If a student is placed in an IAES, school officials must notify parents of that action no later than the day they make the decision.
- As soon as possible, but within ten days after the change of placement decision is made, the IEP team must determine if the behavior is a manifestation of the child's disability.

Conducting a Manifestation Determination Review

A school must:
- consider the special education evaluation,
- observe the student,
- consider the IEP and the student's placement, and determine if the placement is appropriate.

In addition, the school must decide:
- if the IEP and placement were appropriate,
- if the IEP and placement were implemented,
- if supplementary aids and services were provided,
- if behavioral intervention strategies were provided,
- if the student understood the consequences of her behavior,
- if the student was able to control her behavior.

The key issue here is whether the student has a neurological disorder such as ADD or ADHD that may interfere with her ability to control her impulsive behavior.

8 Injury to Self or Others

- A due process hearing officer may also order placement in an IAES, even if the parents object, if the current placement is substantially likely to result in injury to the student or others.
- First, the school must show an effort to minimize the risk of harm in that setting by using supplemental aids and services.

9. Definition of a Weapon

IDEA defines a weapon as:
- "weapon, device, instrument, material, or substance, animate or inanimate, that is used for or is readily capable of, causing death or serious bodily injury,"
- except . . . "a pocket knife of less than 2½ inches long."

10. Students Not Yet Eligible for Services:
If a student has a disability that was never identified, and is facing major disciplinary action such as suspension or expulsion, she is eligible under the provisions of IDEA in certain circumstances:

- If the school had knowledge that the child had a disability;
- If the parents stated in writing that the child needed special education;
- If the child's behavior or performance demonstrated the need for special education;

- If the child's teacher expressed concern about the child's behavior or performance to other school personnel.

The school must set aside disciplinary actions until an evaluation has been completed.

Resources

National Resources

See the Resources listing in Summary 39 for publications and web sites that provide information on IDEA and Section 504, as well as copies of the complete law.

Regional Resources

The U.S. Department of Education provides funding for several regional education resource centers within each state. These centers operate independently of state and local school systems and have different names in each state. For example, in Georgia, they are known as Georgia Learning Resources Services (GLRS), and in Texas, Education Service Centers (ESC). These centers often provide training for teachers and parents on special topics including ADD/ADHD. Parent Training Information Centers (PTIC) are also available in each state. In Georgia, they are known as "Parents Educating Parents." If local officials do not know the phone number of your PTIC, contact your state department of education, special education division.

Local Resources

Several individuals in each local school system are very knowledgeable regarding IDEA and Section 504 guidelines.

- Administrators and special education teachers at individual schools are knowledgeable regarding federal laws.

- Each school system has a **Director of Special Education** and a **Section 504 Coordinator.** Teachers may contact them if they have any questions about these federal laws or reasonable accommodations.

- With the advent of "inclusion" of special education students in regular classes, **special education teachers** or **consultants** may be available to provide technical consultation regarding teaching strategies to regular classroom teachers.

- Some schools have an **ADD/ADHD Consultant** who is also knowledgeable about IDEA and Section 504.

- Check also with **local parent support groups** such as CHADD, ADDA, or LDA. They often have very up-to-date information.

Web Sites

- Arizona State Department of Education, Special Education Section: *www.ade.state.az.us/ssa/specialed.htm*

- GLRS: *www.glrs.org*—The Georgia Learning Resources System (GLRS) provides information regarding training, newsletters, books and videos to help special education students.

- NASDE: *www.nasdse.org*—The National Association of State Directors of Special Education has information on regulations and implementation of IDEA.

- NICHCY: *www.nichcy.org*—The National Information Center for Children and Youth with Disabilities offers excellent resources for educators, families, and other professionals. They have a wide variety of publications including fact sheets, bibliographies, issue papers, and information on IDEA that may be reprinted off the Internet.

- PACER Center: *www.pacer.org*—The Parent Advocacy Coalition for Educational Rights (PACER) helps parents and families of children with disabilities. PACER provides many excellent reader-friendly summaries on a range of topics: IDEA, Emotional and Behavioral Disorders, employment strategies for youth, workshops, articles, and publications. Their publication, *Honorable Intentions,* and their IDEA Summaries all contain excellent information on the new education law and regulations.

- USDOE/OSEP: *www.ed.gov/offices/OSERS*—The Office of Special Education and Rehabilitative Service, U.S. Department of Education web site also offers more information about IDEA.

- USDOE/OSEP: *www.pbis.org*—The OSEP website offers excellent information about positive behavioral strategies and functional behavior assessments from the Technical Assistance Center on Positive Behavioral Interventions and Supports (PBIS).

SUMMARY 41 — Reasonable Accommodations and Modifications*

1991 U.S. DOE/OCR ADD/ADHD Policy Memo

Prior to 1991, federal education guidelines regarding ADD/ADHD were nonexistent. As awareness grew about the impact of attention deficit disorders on school performance, the U.S. Department of Education and Office for Civil Rights jointly issued a key policy statement regarding the education of these students. The major elements of that policy memo were incorporated into the 1997 IDEA revisions. Policy memos are very important documents because they have the effect of law, and as such, affect court decisions.

This DOE/OCR memo contained specific suggestions regarding **reasonable accommodations and/or modifications** that teachers will find helpful. The memo, which applies to development of both IEPs and Section 504 plans, basically stated that if ADD or ADHD **"adversely affects a child's educational performance,"** then the student is entitled to extra supports and accommodations in the classroom. The accommodations provided below are listed almost verbatim from the US DOE/OCR memo. The accommodations listed on the next page are suggestions from several veteran educators and from my own experience as a teacher and school psychologist. Frequently, experienced teachers have been providing accommodations such as these for many years. They automatically make adjustments for any students who are struggling regardless of whether or not they are eligible for services under IDEA or Section 504. These accommodations are often listed in the student's IEP under educational services to be provided.

US DOE/OCR Memo (1991)

- structured learning environment
- repeat and simplify instructions
- provide visual aids
- use behavior management
- adjust class schedules
- modify test delivery
- use tape recorder
- computer-aided instruction
- audio-visual equipment
- modified textbooks or workbooks
- tailor homework assignments
- consultation
- reduce class size
- a notetaker
- one-on-one tutors
- special resources
- classroom aides
- services coordinator or case manager to monitor student progress and ensure implementation of the IEP
- modify nonacademic times (lunchroom, recess, PE)

Additional Suggestions

- pair with student who checks that assignments are in writing
- guided lecture notes (S-13-A)
- untimed tests
- weekly progress reports
- break assignments into segments; grade sections separately
- use overhead projector for teaching
- meet teacher at end of day; check homework & books
- modeling of desired skill by teacher
- extra set of books at home
- use of calculator
- reduce distractions (don't seat near door or pencil sharpener)
- multiple choice tests
- oral tests
- handwriting does not lower grade
- keep same teacher 2nd semester, if successful

- put month's assignments in writing
- Books on Tape
- teach skills: time & anger management
- study skills class
- use multisensory approach
- seat positive role models nearby
- use flash cards
- use mnemonics
- give chapter outlines
- use two desks that the student moves between
- allow the student to stand if she chooses
- use color to note and avoid errors; e.g., highlight changes of math signs

* *The terms "accommodations and modifications" are not defined in federal law and frequently are used interchangeably.*

What Is Other Health Impairment (OHI)?

Until recently, most teachers were unfamiliar with the term *Other Health Impairment (OHI)*. OHI was a seldom-used and relatively unknown special education category. Instead, most students with attention deficits received special education services under the Specific Learning Disabilities (SLD) or Emotional and Behavioral Disorders (EBD) categories of IDEA. However, in the 1997 revisions to IDEA, **ADD and ADHD were added to the list of eligible conditions under Other Health Impairment (OHI).** Technically, inclusion of ADD and ADHD under OHI is *not* a new provision, but, rather, clarification of existing DOE policy.

If a teacher is concerned about the academic progress of a student with an attention deficit, he or she should seek advice from other school personnel or make a referral to the IEP eligibility team. The team will decide whether or not to ask the school psychologist to conduct an evaluation and determine the proper special education eligibility category. In years past when OHI was still unknown, some teachers hesitated to refer a student for special education evaluation if they were pretty certain the student didn't meet the stringent criteria for SLD or EBD. Since some teachers may still not be familiar with OHI criteria, a brief review may be informative.

OHI Definition

> OHI *"means having limited strength, vitality, or alertness due to chronic or acute health problems that adversely affect a student's educational performance."*

In the 1997 IDEA revisions, an attempt was made to clarify the term "limited strength, vitality, or alertness" with regard to students with ADD or ADHD:

> *"a child's heightened alertness to environmental stimuli that results in limited alertness with respect to the educational environment."*

Determining OHI Eligibility

Keep in mind that each state has its own specific requirements for OHI, which you may determine by asking the local special education teacher, the school psychologist, or the special education director for the school system. Teachers should be aware that unlike eligibility for specific learning disabilities, no severe discrepancy in test scores is required for OHI eligibility.

Georgia's OHI Guidelines

Although the information required by your state for the OHI label may not be precisely the same as is required in Georgia, most likely the same general types of information (academic and medical) may be needed. In Georgia, two key steps are necessary for determining OHI eligibility; completion of:

1. the school eligibility report, and
2. a medical report from the student's physician.

However, some states no longer require a medical report. In Virginia, for instance, a report from the school psychologist may be used instead of a medical report.

School Eligibility Report: School personnel will gather relevant information and complete an eligibility report. Any required formal testing may be done by the school psychologist or an educational diagnostician, but the teacher may be asked:

1. to complete a behavior rating scale, and
2. to describe the student's academic performance and behavior with regard to alertness in class (paying attention, sleeping), class participation, independent work habits, homework, ability to complete tests within class time frames, grades received in class to date, potential underachievement, relationship with peers, and compliance with rules.

Typically, **failing a class is** considered an important indicator that the "student's learning is adversely affected by his or her ADD/ADHD." However, class failure is not the only determining factor for eligibility. Sometimes, students with ADD or ADHD may be passing their classes primarily because of the extraordinary efforts of parents and tutors. According to a policy memo from the Office of Special Education (OSEP) dated April 5, 1995, "the evaluation should consider information about outside or extra learning support provided to the child when determining whether a child who receives satisfactory grades is nevertheless not achieving at age-level. The child's current educational achievement may reflect the service augmentation, not what the child's achievement would be without such help."

Medical Evaluation: A physician may complete a medical report and include the information listed below. As part of the medical evaluation, a good social-medical history may be obtained. Sometimes, the doctor, psychologist, or school social worker may complete this interview. Regardless of who does the interview, they should look for any coexisting conditions that may affect a student's school performance, including: anxiety, depression, sleep disturbances, deficits in math computation, or problems with memorization. Examples of information that may be obtained in this interview are included below in parenthesis. A completed sample medical report is provided in my first book, *Teenagers with ADD.*

1. **Diagnosis and medical history** *(ADD, depression, anxiety, sleep disturbance)*
2. **Current medication/side effects** *(Ritalin and Zoloft; when medication wears off in 3 hours, problems with attention will return; even with medication, forgetfulness, disorganization, and an impaired sense of time may still be problematic)*

3. **Conditions that may interfere with regular attendance or functioning in school** *(difficulty paying attention, forgetful, disorganized; sleep disturbance, may be tardy; academic problems, math computation deficits & slow processing speed)*
4. **Medical Prognosis** *(excellent, if student continues to take medication and school provides needed accommodations and/or modifications)*
5. **Recommendations and Comments** *(schedule difficult classes at times when medication is at peak effectiveness, provide appropriate classroom accommodations and/or modifications)*
6. **Signature** *(doctor)*

Next, the IEP team will review all relevant materials and make a decision regarding OHI eligibility.

General Observations

The OHI category may actually be a better diagnostic match for ADD and ADHD than SLD or EBD. Most students with attention deficits never quite fit the criteria for a specific learning disability (SLD) or emotional and behavioral disorder (EBD). However, some schools have begun giving dual diagnoses—for example, when both ADD and SLD are present.

Students with ADD/ADHD often have serious learning problems, but they may not meet the strict eligibility criteria for a specific learning disability. (See the next summary.) In some school systems, even if a student qualifies for SLD, the school may suggest that she no longer meets the SLD eligibility criteria if her academic skills improve so that she is working on grade level.

That leaves only the EBD category. This category may not always be appropriate either, since the behavior problems of students with attention deficits may not be that severe. Furthermore, the key characteristics of ADD/ADHD, such as inattention and impulsivity, are very important diagnostic criteria for OHI. However, these same characteristics are not particularly significant in determining eligibility under the SLD or EBD categories.

Not only is OHI a better diagnostic match, but parents and teenagers themselves may prefer OHI (or SLD) since these labels are often less stigmatizing than EBD.

4

Section 4 | Federal Laws Governing ADD/ADHD

The ADD/SLD Connection: Specific Learning Disability (SLD)

Specific Learning Disability (SLD) is an IDEA eligibility category that may apply to some students with ADD or ADHD. In the past, researchers have found that approximately **25 to 30 percent of students with attention deficit qualify for SLD in math, reading, or spelling**. However, new research from Dr. Susan Mayes and Susan Calhoun has shown that nearly **65 percent of these students have a learning disability in written expression.** This study of children who were referred to a child diagnostic center is one of the first clinical studies to evaluate the written expression skills of students with attention deficits. Of course, children who are referred to clinics for evaluation often have more serious learning problems, so the rate of problems found in this study is probably higher than a teacher would find in her own classroom.

A student may qualify for special education under the SLD category if she has significant learning problems in one or more of the seven areas listed below.

- Oral Expression
- Listening Comprehension
- Written Expression
- Basic Reading Skills
- Reading Comprehension
- Mathematics Calculation
- Mathematical Reasoning

The ADHD/SLD Connection

1. Rates of Learning Disabilities found in children with ADHD:

   - 8-39 percent in reading
   - 12-30 percent in math
   - 12-27 percent in spelling
   - 65 percent in written expression

2. Rates of ADHD found in students with Learning Disabilities:

   - 82 percent

Determining SLD Eligibility

To qualify for SLD in many states, a student must show a **severe discrepancy** between intellectual ability (IQ test scores) and academic achievement (reading and math grade level test scores from a group test such as the IOWA). Sometimes scores on a test such as the IOWA may be used for preliminary screening to determine whether further evaluation is needed. A student is usually considered to have a severe discrepancy if:

1. She receives a standardized achievement score on an individual achievement test such as the Woodcock-Johnson Psychoeducational Battery that is a significant number of points lower than
2. her cognitive ability score (IQ) on a test such as the Weschler Intelligence Scale for Children (WISC).

The point spread may need to be 20 points or higher, but varies from state to state.

Currently, many states are relying less on point spreads and more on subtleties of the evaluation process. For example, the eligibility team may consider **processing strengths and weaknesses** identified during the evaluation. Some states have broadened their definition of what constitutes a learning disability to include problems with processing information that is read, written, or spoken.

As discussed in Summary 42, IEP eligibility teams also consider information about the **student's classroom performance** in making their judgments. School psychologists may look at samples of written work, take current class performance into consideration, and compare the student's ability with her present achievement levels. Failure of classes is also taken into consideration. Students with passing grades may also be considered for eligibility, especially if the student is passing primarily due to the extraordinary efforts of parents and/or tutors

A Federal Policy Memo Affecting SLD Eligibility

Unfortunately, in the past a student could have serious learning problems but not qualify for special education services. For example, a ninth grade student with ADD/ADHD who had an IQ of 140 and achievement test scores for math and language skills on grade level probably would not have been eligible for special education under SLD even if she was failing five of six classes. However, on April 5, 1995, the Office of Special Education (OSEP) issued a Policy Memo stating that **students with high IQs may not be automatically excluded from the SLD disability category."** Each child who is evaluated for a suspected learning disability must be measured against his own expected performance, and not against some arbitrary general standard."

Resources

Barkley, Russell A. *Attention–Deficit Hyperactivity Disorder.* 2nd ed. New York: The Guilford Press, 1998.

Mayes, Susan Dickerson & Susan L. Calhoun. "Prevalence and Degree of Attention and Learning Problems in ADHD and LD," *ADHD Reports*, V. 8, N. 2, April 2000.

SUMMARY 44

Writing an Individualized Education Program (IEP) for Students with ADD or ADHD

An IEP is a written plan that is mandated by federal education law (IDEA) for each student with a disability. (See IEP discussion in Summary 40.) The IEP describes the special education and related services that each student needs.

To ensure that parents are actively involved in the development of the IEP, federal regulations state that the finalized IEP should *not* be written before the eligibility meeting. In other words, parents should not be given completed IEPs at the meeting and asked to sign them without ever having any meaningful input. This doesn't mean that there is no preparation for IEP meetings. Rather, most people, including parents, come to the IEP meeting ready to discuss several ideas. In fact, some teachers ask the parents' permission to develop a draft IEP in advance. However, they make it clear that it is only a draft and additions may easily be made.

Classroom teachers and parents play a key role in developing and implementing a successful IEP! Both of them have significant responsibility for:

1. identifying problem areas and strengths,
2. contributing suggestions for innovative interventions, and then
3. implementing the plan.

When developing an IEP, it is important to keep in mind that some of the student's behavior problems may actually be caused by academic failure. So, be certain to address their academic problems in the IEP.

Typically, the school's role in implementing the IEP is the primary role that is written in the IEP. However, from a practical standpoint, the IEP reflects the teacher/parent partnership. So, I suggest spelling out in the IEP what teachers, parents, and the student will all do. The parent can be a more effective "equal participant" if actively involved in the IEP development and implementation.

Activities and responsibilities required by the IEP may be recorded in several different ways:

1. as an objective in the IEP,
2. as a program or service included in various sections, such as "special education program" "supplementary aides and services," "related services," or "assistive technology,"
3. checked off on a menu of services,
4. attached as a separate form such as an "Individualized Transition Plan,"
5. written in the minutes of the IEP meeting, or perhaps,
6. by verbal agreement, and not put in writing at all.

Mandatory Components of the IEP

IDEA requires that an IEP include these six components:

1. "A statement of the child's present levels of educational performance" (academics and behavior issues; strengths and needs).
2. A statement of "annual goals and short-term instructional objectives," plus expected achievement, for each area in which the student is experiencing difficulties.
3. "A statement of specific educational services to be provided to the child and the extent to which the child will participate in regular educational programs." Includes special education program, accommodations, and related services.
4. The "projected dates for initiation of services and the anticipated duration."
5. "Appropriate objective criteria and evaluation procedures and schedules for determining whether the short term instructional objectives are being achieved."
6. Individualized transition planning, by age 14 or earlier.

Teacher Involvement in Developing an IEP

Usually, teachers are more heavily involved in developing certain sections of the IEP than others. Below are the areas where teachers are most likely to be asked to provide information or suggestions.

Identifying Problems and Strengths

Teachers should review the student's performance in their class and come to the meeting prepared to discuss the student's *academic and behavioral strengths and problems.*

All too often, only behavior problems, such as emotional blow-ups, talking back and arguing, use of profanity, or other impulsive behaviors are addressed. Common academic problems and *executive function deficits* are frequently overlooked and should be considered. For example, problems with memorization, slow processing speed, written expression, disorganization, forgetfulness, or impaired sense of time are important to note. When academic issues are dealt with effectively, behavior problems are sometimes greatly reduced.

Writing Goals and Objectives

Teachers should think ahead about the important issues to be addressed and come prepared to make suggestions for innovative interventions. Several suggestions for goals and objectives are provided below as examples. Summaries in Section 2 (Academic Issues), Section 3 (Executive Function), and Section 6 (Classroom Management and Challenging Behaviors) should be especially helpful here.

4

Section 4 | Federal Laws Governing ADD/ADHD

Goals and objectives to address the important issues:

- **Goals:** Typically, goals are broader than objectives and cover a longer period of time such as a school year.

    1. The student will improve written language skills so that she is on grade level.
    2. The student will maintain passing grades, C or higher.
    3. The student will improve memory skills by learning compensatory strategies.
    4. Student will explore career interests and become more aware of possible career opportunities. *(Example of a goal for an individualized Transition Plan. See Summary 48 and objectives for goal 4 on the next page for more details on transition planning.)*

- **Short-term Objectives:** Short-term objectives state what the student will learn and must be measurable. That is, the teacher must know when the student is successful. Objectives usually cover a shorter period of time, such as a grading period or quarter. Writing meaningful objectives is often very difficult. Here are several objectives to help the student complete homework, maintain passing grades, and improve memory or writing skills. A system for reminding the student to use the skills listed in these objectives will have to be built into the process. Progress will be assessed at the end of the grading period.

Objectives for meeting Goal 1: Improve written language skills—

1. The student will improve written language skills from 6th grade level to an early 7th grade level (on grade level; based upon Language Arts teacher assessment compared with county writing standards; scores on the Woodcock-Johnson Achievement Test)
2. The student will use pre-writing strategies to organize her thoughts using webs and outlines (skills in 2-4 taught and assessed by teacher);
3. The student will organize her writing into paragraphs with a topic sentence, supporting and concluding sentences;
4. The student will use editing strategies when completing weekly essays that are to be graded: spell check, grammar check, dictionary, and thesaurus.

Objectives for meeting Goal 2: Maintain passing grades—

1. The student will maintain a daily assignment notebook, recording all assignments, improving from 50 percent completion to 90 percent of the time during this grading period (a reminder system will be established and monitored by the teacher).

    1.1 An alternative objective may be: The student will dictate assignments into a small tape recorder.

2. The student will know her homework assignments and take the right books home 90 percent of the time (improvement from 50 percent). (Special education teacher sets up a system; teacher or behavioral aide meets with the student the last period of each day; checks assignments and books needed.)

3. The teacher and parents will both sign and send the assignment book back and forth from school (monitored by teacher & parent).

4. The student will complete assigned work in class and homework 90 percent of the time (improve from 50 percent completion rate; monitored by the teacher).

Objective for meeting Goal 3: *Improve memory and compensatory skills—*

1. The student will use at least two memory strategies to compensate for memory deficits and to learn new information: mnemonics, visualization, sketching, chunking/associating, and application to familiar situations (skill taught to student and parents by special education teacher; skills jointly assessed by teacher and parent observations; discussed via phone conference).

Objectives for meeting Goal 4: *Explore career interests and become aware of career opportunities—*

(During the semester, the student will participate in several activities that will be monitored by the special education teacher)

1. The student will complete a career interest inventory and meet with her parents and teacher to review the results.
2. The student will learn more about five career options of interest.
3. The student will learn about job skills that are critical for maintaining employment.
4. The student will write a resume.
5. The student will participate in a job shadowing program.

Making Suggestions for Special Education and Related Services

Teachers may make suggestions about a student's ***special education program.*** For example, they might suggest:

- one hour of Algebra in a self-contained special education resource room;
- one hour during the last period of the day for organizational assistance and related services;
- remainder of time in regular education classrooms with classroom accommodations as needed.

Students are also entitled to any ***related services*** that are necessary for them to benefit from special education services. Related services include:

- **Education/counseling**—Provide educational counseling on a range of topics:
  - the impact of ADD/ADHD on the student,
  - problem solving,
  - getting along with peers,
  - anger control,
  - time management,
  - study skills.
  - Train older students with ADD or ADHD to act as mentors or coaches for younger incoming students with the same condition. See Summaries 64-69 for tips on teaching these skills.

- **Assistive technology**—items that the school may have to purchase for one student; for example the school may buy a relatively inexpensive laptop such as "AlphaSmart" that a student may type on but must later connect to a printer. The "Phonic Ear," which amplifies the teacher's voice to help the student pay attention, is another example of assistive technology. Some electronic items such as a calculator or hand-held "spell checker" may be purchased by the family.

- **health services** (medication monitoring)

- **speech therapy**

- **psychological services**

- **occupational therapy**

- **home-school liaison**—a school social worker or special education teacher may be designated to act as a liaison to ensure that regular communication occurs between the school and home.

- **parent training**—for example, on ADD/ADHD or effective parenting and homework strategies.

- **community resources**—information for the family on available resources in the community, such as local ADD/ADHD groups (CHADD, ADDA, Federation or Families for Children's Mental Health, National Mental Health Association, or Alliance for the Mentally Ill) or services from their local mental health center.

Teachers should also consider whether the student needs **extended educational services** (ESY). Sometimes when a student continues to do poorly in school, she can benefit from instruction beyond the traditional school day or year. The decision to provide an extended school year must be based upon the student's needs.

Although most students will not need **year round programming,** a few may benefit from a summer program to keep them from falling behind academically. However, for some students, school is such a negative experience, they really need the three-month break.

Other types of extended educational services to consider include:

- instruction before or after school
- a tutor after school
- instruction on the weekend
- summer school classes
- a tutor during the summer
- a packet of materials sent home to the family during the summer with telephone monitoring from an educator.

Recommending Accommodations and/or Modifications

Providing the right classroom accommodations and/or modifications is often the key to a student's success at school. There are therefore many suggestions on choosing and implementing accommodations throughout this book. Summary 41 contains a list of "reasonable" classroom accommodations and modifications. Summary 46 discusses specific learning problems and classroom accommodations for a student named Mark who has the inattentive form of ADD. Summaries 13-A-E and 14-20 also contain helpful suggestions regarding academic issues.

Many schools have a menu of accommodations/modifications for students. A sample menu from Walker County Schools in Georgia is contained in Appendix B3. One drawback to using menus, however, is that sometimes accommodations are limited to only those ideas on the list. Remember, these menus are only suggested lists and *any* needed accommodation may be added. In addition, the major reason for having all the summaries in this book is to give teachers, parents, and other educators a broad range of effective strategies to include in an IEP and use in the classroom!

Below are just a few examples of accommodations that may be appropriate for students with ADD/ADHD:

Accommodations for Related Academic Concerns:

- give untimed tests
- provide a notetaker
- give two sets of books
- give homework assignments in writing
- use a weekly report
- shorten tests in science and math
- shorten assignments in math
- supports for teacher to include weekly consultation between regular and special education teachers and consultation from the ADD consultant

Accommodations on Statewide Assessment Tests:

- give extended time
- allow use of a calculator
- repeat directions an unlimited number of times
- read parts of the test to the student in a small quiet group.

Suggesting Intervention Strategies to Address Behavioral Issues

Most IEPs do not, but should address behaviors related to **executive function deficits,** such as: disorganization, tardiness, forgetfulness, emotional blow-ups, sleep disturbances, talking back, and arguing. Examples of strategies that may be written in the IEP include:

- Help the student organize her locker, plan the best times to go by and pick up books, and review best routes from class to class to help the student avoid being late to class.
- Parents will be notified as soon as possible if the student is in danger of failing a class.
- In the event of a family or emotional crisis, parents will determine when enough homework has been completed.
- If the student suspects she is about to blow up, she has permission to go to the guidance office.
- Extra time, up to five days, will be given for completion of work. A plan will be developed to help the student turn in school work on time.
- See Summary 45 for a discussion of seven common ADD/ADHD related behaviors and suggested behavioral intervention strategies that may be incorporated into the IEP.

A **Behavior Intervention Plan** may be necessary if disruptive behaviors continue, especially if they in suspension from school. See Summaries 60-63 for examples of common behaviors and intervention strategies, as well as more information on developing Behavior Intervention Plans. See also Summary 45 for information on identifying the antecedent behavior—the event that triggers the problem.

Implementing and Monitoring the IEP

Once the IEP is approved, teachers must implement academic or behavioral accommodations/modifications in the classroom as soon as possible. The IEP will note who is responsible for implementing the objectives in the IEP.

To **evaluate** whether or not the student is achieving her objectives, teachers must follow what the IEP says. The IEP states what measures or tests will be used and how often—for example: "daily work samples, weekly reports, teacher records, or grades."

Teachers are also involved in **monitoring and revising** the IEP and the student's progress on an ongoing basis. When the Plan is not working effectively, teachers and parents must study and revise it. Parents or teachers may request a meeting at any time to revise the IEP.

IEP Attachments

IEP forms are often streamlined and do not tell the whole story with regard to the services the student will actually receive. Teachers and parents may attach a list of accommodations and/or modifications similar to Summary 41 to provide more detail regarding specific accommodations the student will receive.

The information parents gather in preparation for the IEP meeting, such as a summary of their teenager's strengths, their concerns, and the student's needs, may also be attached to the IEP. A few schools may even ask parents to write a vision statement regarding their hopes and dreams for their teenager.

The Written vs. Unwritten IEP

IDEA mandates that IEPs must be recorded in writing. However, IEPs and Section 504 Plans are usually written fairly quickly and may not contain all the details regarding specific classroom accommodations that are actually provided to the student. In reality, an *Informal Plan* often exists in addition to the IEP. This Informal Plan is fluid, changing over time as teachers and parents try different strategies to help the student succeed.

As long as the student meets IEP goals and objectives, and parents and teachers are both happy, then it may not cause any problems if all the details are not recorded in the IEP. However, putting everything in writing is clearly the best policy. Just as "good fences make good neighbors," ***putting IEP content in writing helps maintain the most positive relationship between teachers and parents.*** This helps avoid misunderstandings and hurt, angry feelings later. So, if changes will be made over time, write that as an added step in the IEP: "In addition to the accommodations listed in the IEP, the teacher and parent will communicate with each other immediately if the student begins to struggle. Adjustments to the IEP may be made and accommodations may be added as needed in between IEP meetings."

The key to an effective IEP is to maintain regular communication between home and school! As long as parents and teachers are talking to each other, accommodations may be added or deleted as needed. Communication may be done by telephone, fax, or e-mail. Teachers might informally call or e-mail the parent as needed, brainstorm solutions, and then make needed accommodations in class.

4

Accommodations and Strategies for Coping with ADD/ADHD Behaviors

As Section 3 discusses, several ADD/ADHD behaviors linked to deficits in executive function may cause major problems at school. They include:

- acting before thinking,
- disorganization, forgetfulness,
- emotionality, and
- an impaired sense of time.

These characteristics, often occurring in combination, have a profound impact on the student's school work and behavior. In addition, these characteristics often influence behavior in subtle ways that, on the surface, do not appear to be related to the student's condition. Frequently, these issues are not addressed in the IEP or Section 504 Plans.

When behaviors typically result in a disciplinary action being taken against a student, then these ***issues should be identified in the IEP or Behavior Intervention Plan (BIP).*** Specific objectives should also be included in the IEP or BIP to teach the necessary coping skills. Then teachers can work with the student to learn the deficit skills, provide supportive intervention strategies, or make accommodations to reduce the frequency of these problems. Remember, discipline should be *instructive,* not just punitive!

Several common ADD/ADHD-related behaviors and intervention strategies are discussed below. Since each student with this condition exhibits different problem behaviors at school, each IEP will be different and may not necessarily address all the issues raised in this summary. Statements in *italics* are examples of accommodations or intervention strategies that may help the student cope with or compensate for the ADD/ADHD behaviors. These strategies may be formally listed as part of the IEP, checked off on a menu of services, or simply discussed and written in the minutes.

Strategies for Addressing ADD/ADHD Behaviors

Organizational and Memory Problems

Below are suggestions for addressing organizational and memory problems. For more detail about these problems, see Summaries 22, 29, and 30.

Forgetting Homework Assignments and Not Turning in Work: Frequently, disorganization and forgetfulness are lifelong problems for people with attention deficits. Students often don't know their homework assignments or forget to turn them in. In addition, long-term projects may be completely forgotten or remembered the night before they are due. When students with ADD or ADHD get behind, they sometimes feel so overwhelmed they need help getting back on track. A Behavioral Intervention Plan should be developed to help the student correct or compensate for her organizational deficits and forgetfulness.

If the objectives for the IEP are for the student to: 1) know daily assignments and 2) turn in homework, intervention strategies such as the following may be needed. Obviously some students will not need all these accommodations to be successful.

- *Row captains will pick up homework from all students and check to see that assignments are written down.*
- *An organizational coach (teacher or another student) will meet the student at the end of the day to check that assignments are written down and proper books taken home.*
- *Extra time (up to 5 days) will be given for completion of work.*
- *The student may keep an extra book at home, especially for difficult subjects.*
- *Parents will be notified about long-term assignments and their due dates.*
- *Reduce homework if appropriate.* (See discussion in next paragraph, plus S-24.)

Not Completing Homework/Getting Zeros: Several factors may be contributing to the student getting zeros for not turning in homework: disorganization, forgetfulness, slow processing speed, lack of medication, or emotionality. Most of these issues are addressed and intervention strategies suggested in the previous paragraph and Summaries 23 and 24. However, one issue most teachers and parents don't fully consider is whether too much homework is being assigned. According to Drs. Sydney Zentall and Sam Goldstein, **teachers often underestimate the amount of time it will take students with special needs to complete homework.** (See Summary 24.) When homework is overwhelming because it takes more than a couple of hours to complete, the amount of homework must be reduced. To help a student consistently complete homework, several strategies from Summaries 23-26 may be used:

- *Identify learning problems and make modifications in the classroom. (See Summaries 11 and 13A-E.)*
- *Determine whether homework is taking too long. If necessary, reduce assignments accordingly.* (Generally, the total time spent on homework in all subjects should be no more than 1½ hours for a ninth grader and no more than 2 hours or so for a senior. See Summary 24.)
- *In periods of high stress, parents will determine how much homework should be done, even though it may be less than the teacher originally assigned. Parents will sign and return the homework paper indicating that it is completed.* (Summary 25)

Class Failure: When academic and executive function deficits are not addressed, the student may be in danger of failing a class. It is important for the teacher to work with the teenager and her family to prevent school failure. As explained in Summary 1, these students don't learn as easily from punishment and reward as other students. So, when a student with an attention deficit is failing, she is more likely to feel overwhelmed and give up rather than learn the intended lesson. Obviously, the most important thing to do is provide accommodations or modifications that will prevent class failure. The suggestions above will help. Including this statement in the IEP of minutes of the IEP meeting may also be helpful:

- *Parents will be notified in a timely manner if a student is failing so that steps may be taken to get her back on track academically.*

Impulsive Behaviors

Bad Language or Talking Back: It is not unusual for students with attention deficits to speak or act impulsively, especially when their medication has worn off. Often they regret the action but it cannot be taken back. Sometimes students talk back to a teacher or use bad language. Of course, these are not acceptable behaviors, nor is ADD or ADHD an excuse for misbehaving. But it may be helpful if teachers can determine whether characteristics of ADD/ADHD are contributing to the misbehavior. For example, talking back may occur when medication has worn off. Typically, teachers can handle these misbehaviors without imposing severe consequences.

- *Ignore minor comments, especially if the student is following teacher instructions.*
- *If bad language is used in front of a teacher, depending on the severity, loudness, and to whom the profanity is directed, the teacher has several options. See Summary 62 for suggestions.*
- *Determine whether the blow-up occurred during a time when medication has worn off. If so, parents may ask their doctor for help in adjusting the medication.*
- *Make certain that learning problems have been identified and the student is receiving appropriate accommodations in the classroom.*
- *If the problem continues, refer the student to the vice principal in charge of discipline, who will determine appropriate discipline.*
- *If suspension is unavoidable, send the student to in-school suspension instead of out-of-school suspension. As suggested in Summary 64, use time spent in suspension ("Organized Study" or "Time In") to teach pro-social skills as described in the Skillstreaming section.*

Misbehavior and Emotional Blow-ups: Students with attention deficits are more likely to misbehave at several specific times:

- during transitions—for example, lunch, recess breaks, after school, or on the bus ride home,
- when the schedule or class structure changes (a substitute is present),
- when there is a personal crisis (failing a class, breakup with a girl-friend), or
- when medication has worn off.

At these times, some students with ADD or ADHD may talk back to a teacher, refuse to obey a teacher request, yell, hit the wall or locker, cry, or fight. Teach the student to recognize when she is about to lose control and have a crisis plan to avoid potential blow-ups. As explained in Summary 69 on Anger Management, students can 1) learn which issues seem to trigger blow-ups, 2) learn to recognize internal feelings of anger and rage, and 3) learn to seek help when these events occur.

- **If the student suspects she is about to blow up,** *she has permission to go the counselor's office to talk with the counselor or just sit and cool off.* (Don't ask the student to find a written pass in the heat of an emotional blow-up. Give blanket permission to go to the counselor or place the permission card in a designated spot on the teacher's desk where she can always find it.)

- **If a student has an emotional blow-up,** *the regular procedures for handling disruptive behavior may be followed.*
    1. *For example, the vice principal for discipline may become involved if the student is fighting.*
    2. *However, the final consequence imposed may be different because the student is eligible for special education or Section 504. For example, the student may be referred to in-school suspension instead of a regular three-day suspension.*
    3. *Ideally, the vice principal will be familiar with this student's record and have a personal relationship with her. Disciplinary action is handled more easily if it is built upon a personal relationship. For example, the vice principal is more likely to know how to handle the student without further escalation of the problem.*

- **If blow-ups are serious and may result in suspension,** *as discussed in Summary 40, a Behavior Intervention Plan should be developed to help the student cope more effectively with conflict. Positive behavioral strategies should be used. Parents should ask their doctor for advice to determine if medication should be adjusted.*

- **When a substitute teacher is present,** *there are several things that could be done:*
    - *The substitute is given a note regarding this student's difficulty with change. A couple of suggestions along with the student's seat location are also provided.*
        - *For example, the substitute may introduce herself to a couple of students, including this student.*
        - *Ask the student to assist in various ways— pass out a written worksheet or assignment to the rest of the class.*
    - *In advance, the regular classroom teacher or counselor may discuss this difficulty with the student. Ask her how teachers can best help her cope with this challenge. The procedure for her to follow is discussed in advance.*
    - *Teach the student to help the substitute; have the student rehearse the proper behavior for when a substitute is present.*

- *Place a classroom aide in the room for that period to assist the substitute.*
- *If the substitute is in a regular class, send the student to her former special education teacher for this one period*

Impaired Sense of Time

Late to Class. Students with ADD/ADHD may frequently be late to class due to difficulty in accurately judging the passage of time or weak organizational skills. If a student is frequently late to class, analyze when and why the problem is occurring:

1. Identify the classes where the student is arriving late.
2. Determine why she is late. Does she go by her locker? go the long way? have trouble opening her combination lock? meet a friend to chat?
3. Correct the problem (e.g., organize the locker as described in Summary 29, assign a locker that is closer to the student's classes, practice opening the combination lock, or skip the meetings with the friend).

If necessary, include an objective in the IEP:

- *Tardies will be handled by the special education teacher or an administrator (rather than automatically punishing tardies, as some schools do, by prohibiting student participation in sports, attendance at a school dance, or other extracurricular activities, taking points off her grade, or requiring after school detention).*
- *Develop a plan to prevent tardies.*

See Summaries 31-35 for additional suggestions.

Impaired Sense of Time Plus Sleep Disturbance

Tardy to School: Students with attention deficits often have problems getting to school on time. Researchers tell us that 50 percent of these students have serious sleep disturbances (problems waking up, falling asleep, and getting restful sleep). If this is a major problem, suggest that parents talk with their physician. A detailed discussion of strategies for dealing with sleep disturbances is available in *TEENAGERS WITH ADD*. Share these suggestions with parents:

- *Buy an alarm clock for the student.*
- *Connect lights, the TV, and stereo to a timer that is set to come on at a designated time.*
- *Wake the teenager up earlier to allow more time.*
- *Some doctors recommend waking the student 30 minutes early, giving her medication, then letting her sleep until the regularly scheduled wake-up time. This makes it easier for the student to focus on getting ready for school.*
- *Get clothes and books ready the night before.*
- *Don't take Ritalin or Dexedrine too late in the day.*

- *Record a wake-up message from a close friend or herself.*
- *Get a physical examination to rule out other problems.*
- *If sleep disturbances are causing major problems, talk with the doctor about medication. Several medications commonly given for sleep problems include Benadryl or melatonin. In addition other medications such as Clonidine, Tofranil, or Trazadone serve a dual purpose, helping with sleep and also leveling off emotional mood swings or aggression.*

SUMMARY 46

Accommodations for One ADD/ADHD STUDENT*

(Attach to the IEP or Section 504 Plan)

NAME **Mark**   AGE **17**   GRADE **12**

STRENGTHS: High IQ (Intellectually gifted); Visual Analytic Skills; Higher Level Verbal Reasoning; Visual Spatial Ability

Learning Problem	Behavior Observed	Accommodations
Inattention	Difficulty paying attention in class	Ensure all day medication coverage
	Difficulty staying on-task	Use group response techniques
	Difficulty studying independently	Use more visual teaching materials
	Doesn't pay attention to detail	Have a partner double check
	Makes careless errors	Stand near the student to increase her attentiveness
Poor Memory	Can't memorize multiplication tables	Use a calculator for class work, homework, and tests
	Difficulty spelling words correctly	Use a spell checker
	Difficulty memorizing foreign words	Use a word bank for class work and tests
		Use multisensory approach; student writes words, history facts, etc. on 3x5 cards
		Use color to highlight facts, especially errors
		Use peer tutoring
		Put often-used facts such as punctuation rules or word lists on laminated cards for easy use
Slow Processing Speed and Slow Retrieval of Information	Writes very slowly; Takes class notes very slowly	Obtain guided lecture notes from teacher
	Doesn't double check answers	Get a copy of another student's notes
	Difficulty retrieving formulas and facts	Appoint a class notetaker; photocopy notes and distribute
	Takes twice as long to do homework and classwork	Modify class and homework assignments; e.g., every 3rd Algebra problem
		Give extended time for tests
	Takes twice as long to complete tests	Use calculator to do and check school work
	Slow recall of math facts; slow math computations	
Poor Language Expression (Oral and Written)	Difficulty organizing thoughts	Allow to use computer at home and school
	Difficulty writing essays, recognizing main topics	Modeling by teacher; use overhead to brainstorm essay ideas, develop outline, write a draft
Weak Verbal Fluency	Slower to answer questions	Give extended time on essays and tests
	Reluctant to answer in class	Ask question; give extra time to respond

Learning Problem	Behavior Observed	Accommodations
Poor Listening and Reading Comprehension and Poor Working Memory	Difficulty following multi-step verbal instructions	Keep instructions brief and simple
	Doesn't remember assignments	Provide written list of class and homework assignments (by teacher or another student)
	Weak reading comprehension	Write instructions/examples on the board
Poor Organizational Skills	Does not turn in homework or write down assignments	Appoint "row captains" to collect homework and check to see that assignments are written down
Weak Executive Function	Difficulty starting work	Provide prompts from parent or teacher
	Difficulty maintaining effort	Provide positive reinforcement when working
	Difficulty finishing assignments	Give written instructions; use Post-It notes
	Disorganized	Use another student as a coach; ask student to "read to the clip" --use a paperclip to divide reading assignments

Although learning problems, behaviors observed, and accommodations are listed in columns, in reality many of these issues may overlap and one accommodation may help with several problems.

These are just a few of my favorite accommodations and modifications. See Section 2 for a detailed discussion, plus many other suggestions.

SUMMARY 47

Federal Civil Rights Law: Section 504 and ADD/ADHD

For some students, their ADD or ADHD may not be considered enough of a disability to qualify them for special education services under IDEA. But they may still struggle in school if accommodations are not made for their executive function deficits, inattention, and other symptoms. Fortunately, their rights to accommodations are guaranteed by Section 504 of the Rehabilitation Act of 1973.

This civil rights law ***prohibits discrimination against people with disabilities*** by any agency that receives federal funding. Eligibility criteria for Section 504 are broader than IDEA, making it easier for children with emotional or biochemical disorders to receive services.

Section 504 states:

> *"No otherwise qualified individual with a disability in the United States ... shall solely by reason of his or her disability, be excluded from participation in, be denied the benefits of, or be subjected to discrimination under any program or activity receiving Federal financial assistance...."*

Under the law, a "qualified individual with a disability" is anyone who "has a physical or mental impairment which substantially limits one or more of such person's major life activities." Learning is typically considered to be a "major life activity." So, the question that the school must answer is whether or not the student's ability to learn is impaired by her ADD or ADHD. To help teachers and parents understand this law, each local school system has developed a policy statement on Section 504 and has a designated Section 504 coordinator.

Major Section 504 Provisions

Because Section 504 only applies to programs receiving federal funding, it generally covers students in public school, but not most private schools. The guidelines in Section 504 that apply to education are almost identical to IDEA, with a couple of exceptions:

- A Section 504 Plan is developed instead of an IEP.
- Adaptations are offered only in *regular* classrooms, not in special education classes.

There are also subtle differences in the level of services offered under IDEA vs. Section 504. Under Section 504, schools are only required to provide "commensurate opportunities" to students with disabilities. Under IDEA, schools must provide an education that provides some "educational benefit" to students with disabilities. Obviously, legal aspects of Section 504 are open to interpretation and vary widely, just as with IDEA. Generally, the intensity of services delivered under IDEA must be greater than under 504 to ensure that the student "benefits"—in other words, improves academically or behaviorally. However, most schools do their best to help all students regardless of IDEA or 504 eligibility.

Typically, the issue of educational benefit comes into play only if parents sue the school system because their child's academic achievement is below expected levels. For example, an eleventh-grade student with an above average IQ was provided half an hour reading instruction weekly but was still reading on a fourth-grade level. The school had met its obligations under Section 504 but *not* under IDEA. In 1993, the U.S. Supreme Court ruled in *South Carolina vs. Carter* that the student did not benefit from the educational program provided by the school and ordered that the parents be reimbursed for tuition in a private school.

Steps for Obtaining Services Under Section 504

The steps for obtaining services for students under Section 504 are similar to IDEA requirements. In general, a teacher would begin by talking with the person who chairs the IEP or Section 504 eligibility committee. (The school may have more than one committee that determines eligibility for services under IDEA and Section 504.) Although evaluation criteria vary from state to state, the evaluation for 504 eligibility is usually not as formal as IDEA evaluations. It may involve a review of existing group test results, the cumulative folder, past grades, teacher comments, and classroom observation. See Summary 50 for a discussion of what to look for when reviewing information.

Writing a Section 504 Plan

The information contained in Summaries 44-46 on developing an IEP will also help teachers develop a Section 504 Plan. Basically, a Section 504 Plan is like a stripped-down version of an IEP. Students with 504 Plans usually do not have as many needs as students with IEPs, so they may not receive as many accommodations/modifications. However, students served under Section 504 Plans have the right to access most of the same intervention strategies and classroom accommodations as students with IEPs. The major exception is that they are not placed in a special education classroom.

The Office for Civil Rights (OCR) has given no formal guidance regarding the content of the 504 Plan. However, some local school systems have developed their own guidelines. Although a uniform format is not mandated, following the basic content of the IEP may be helpful. In particular, it is important to identify strengths, learning or behavior problems, and necessary classroom adaptations. Although transition plans are not addressed in Section 504, it would be in the student's best interest to provide some transition services. A member of the staffing team will be designated to write up the plan and distribute copies to each involved teacher, administrator, the parents, and the student's records.

Once a student has a 504 Plan, her disability must generally be taken into account in disciplinary actions by the school. Although not mandated under civil rights law, some current legal rulings have held that a *Manifestation Determination Review* must be held prior to any change of placement. See Summary 40 for an explanation of Manifestation Determination Reviews.

Transition Planning: After High School, What Next?

Transition planning is one of the most important but neglected elements of educational planning for students who have ADD or ADHD. The Individuals with Disabilities Education Act mandates that all students 16 and older must have transition goals and objectives in their IEP to help with long-term career planning. And by age 14, students must have some transition planning done related to courses they should take in school. Ideally, career planning should begin in elementary school. (Transition planning is *not* mandated for students with 504 Plans, but ideally 504 Plans will include some transition services.)

IDEA states that the individualized Transition Plan (TP) should help the student make the transition from high school to:

"post secondary education, vocational training, integrated employment (including supported employment), continuing and adult education, adult services, independent living or community participation."

Several federal initiatives such as the "School-to-Work Opportunities Act of 1994" have placed great emphasis on career development planning for all students. In spite of this increased attention, the typical TP does not include very many helpful suggestions for career development. The limited development of the TP is probably because most teachers are unfamiliar with some of the exciting opportunities that could be offered. Some schools, however, have transition specialists, who are actively involved in developing each student's TP.

Federal law states that transition activities should be based upon:

"the individual student's needs taking into account the student's preferences and interests, and shall include instruction, community experiences, the development of employment and other post-school adult living objectives, and when appropriate, acquisition of daily living skills, and functional vocational evaluation."

An incredible wealth of information is available regarding transition planning. Several resources, including web sites, are listed at the end of this summary. A brief overview is provided here of components that are often included in a comprehensive career development program.

Comprehensive Career Development Programs

Here are examples of issues that may be addressed by writing a related objective to include in the IEP, TP, and/or Section 504 Plan.

Self-knowledge and Student Development:

- Self-determination training
- Self-advocacy

- Problem-solving skills
- Social skills
- Money management skills
- Medication awareness and management

Assessment:

- Interest inventories
- Vocational/Career Assessment

   A vocational/career assessment can help the student increase her self-awareness and identify potential career interest areas. Two commonly used tests to help students begin to identify career interests include the Career Occupational Preference System (COPS), and for older, college-bound students, the Strong Interest Inventory.

Work Skills:

- Filling out a job application
- Searching want ads
- Writing a resume and cover letter
- Preparing for an interview
- Role playing a job interview

Educational and Career Exploration

   Debbie Wilkes, who is a transition specialist in Richardson, Texas, wisely advises students and parents that ***"Education ... not just college is the key."*** It is important to make it clear that great jobs that don't require a college degree do exist. But students and parents also need to know that additional education is often needed to qualify for these technical and highly skilled jobs.

   Consider which, if any, vocational/career or technology classes the student should take. If a student doesn't plan to go to college upon graduation, write an objective related to deciding what job training will be appropriate. If the student plans to attend college and will need an untimed SAT or ACT, the "untimed tests" accommodation should be documented as part of her IEP or Section 504 Plan. Other objectives to consider:

- Researching career options
- Volunteering as a means of career exploration
- Career planning
- Job shadowing
- Visits to job sites
- Mentors from local industry
- Supervised employment
- Academic supports
    - Tutoring
    - Making up missed credits to graduate on time

Transportation:

- Learning to drive
- Studying for the driver's test
- Taking and passing the test

Collaboration with Other Agencies: Several community agencies may teach skills or provide supports that will help the student make a successful transition to the adult work world.

- Goodwill
- Vocational Rehabilitation
- Big Brother Big Sister, especially their mentoring program

Resources

Books

Brown, Dale S. *Learning a Living: A Guide to Planning Your Career and Finding a Job for People with Learning Disabilities, Attention Deficit Disorder, and Dyslexia.* Bethesda, MD: Woodbine House, 2000.

Feldman, Wilma. *Finding a Career that Works for You.* Plantation, FL: Specialty Press, 2000.

Field, Sharon, Jim Martin, Bob Miller, et al. *A Practical Guide for Teaching Self-Determination.* Reston, VA: The CEC and the CEC Division on Career Development and Transition, 1997.

West, Lynda L., Stephanie Corbey, Arden Boyer-Stephens, et al. *Integrating Transition Planning into the IEP Process.* 2nd ed. Reston, VA: CEC, 1999.

Tests

Career Occupational Preference System (COPS). Available from Edits, P.O. Box 7234, San Diego, CA 92167. (619-222-166; www.edits.net)

Strong Interest Inventory. Developed by Stanford University Press; available from Consulting Psychologists Press, Inc. (800-624-1765; www.cpp-db.com) This test may be more appropriate for students 15 years of age or older who plan to attend college.

Web Sites

- *Career Development and Transition*, a Division of the Council for Exceptional Children: www.cec.sped.org—The Council publishes a catalog and numerous documents that are helpful for students in special education.

- *Education World:* www.education-world.com—Several helpful articles are available at this site, including an article on job shadowing, an overview of several model school-to-work programs, and *Career Counseling Resources on the Internet*—which contains links with online resources related to: self-assessment and interest inventories; career information; writing resumes and cover letters; job interviews; job listings.

- *Division on Career Development and Transition*/University of Illinois at Urbana-Champaign: www.uiuc.edu/sped/dcdt—This website offers several interesting publications: training for transition specialists; integrating transition planning into the IEP; a student self-determination guide; and competencies for transition specialists.

- *School-to-Work*: www.stw.ed.gov—This helpful web site contains information about several school-to-work topics: state directors for activities in your area; legislation; model programs; a template for developing a program.

Publication Catalog

Oklahoma may be the only state that has a separate Department of Career and Technical Education. As a former lobbyist, I know that typically when a program is pulled out and elevated to a full department status that means the state legislature has given the issue a very high priority. A catalog is available of the materials they have developed:

- *Career Stuff: Counseling and Teaching Materials*: A catalog of counseling and teaching materials. (405-743-5163; www.okvotech.org/resrc/default.htm) Examples of some of the impressive range of materials available are listed below. Check with the department of education in your state and ask if they have similar career materials.
  - A job search guide that gives sample resumes, tips on completing an application, proper dress, and interview skills.
  - Handouts on career clusters, such as business, health and design, communication, and art, that include potential career options, degrees required, characteristics of people who work in this field, needed skills, and recommended high school courses.
  - A Job Shadowing Guide
  - Career Day Planning Guide
  - Career Development Activities for middle and junior high school
  - Career Development Activities for mid-high/high school
  - *The Career Connection, from Learning to Earning,* interesting magazines for all ages.
  - Basic Strategies: Meeting the Needs of Vocational Students

4

Continuum of Services for Students with ADD/ADHD in the Kenosha School District

Contributed by Kathy Hubbard Weeks, ADD Consultant/504 Coordinator

Kenosha Unified School District No. 1 in Kenosha, WI, provides a range of educational services for all students. Since 1990, the school system has expanded special services that have benefited students with ADD/ADHD. *This school system may be one of the only public school systems in the country that has made a concerted effort to identify all students with ADD or ADHD and develop an individualized educational plan for each one!* The school system has also collected important statistics about this population, such as prevalence and class failure rates. According to their records for the most recent school year, 6.7 percent of their middle and high school students have been diagnosed with ADD or ADHD.

Although the educational services listed in this summary are available to all students, a large percentage of the participants have ADD or ADHD. Most schools offer evaluation, IEPs, Section 504 Accommodation Plans, counseling, alternative schools, and vocational services, but Kenosha has enhanced these traditional services. For example, the school district provides:

1. ***intensive training*** on ADD/ADHD for their teachers;
2. ***counseling*** groups for students with attention deficits;
3. ***consultation*** to teachers from an ADD Consultant/504 Coordinator;
4. ***an IEP or 504 Plan that is more attuned to the special needs*** of these students;
5. ***Attention Deficit Education Plans,*** developed for all students with ADD or ADHD who don't have either an IEP or 504 Plan;
6. ***graduation make-up credits*** via a computer program;
7. ***a partnership with local business*** to offer a broader range of high tech career training.

Innovative Services Offered by Kenosha

Some school systems may be interested in adopting some elements of these services. A brief description of Kenosha's more innovative services is therefore provided below:

■ **ADD Consultant/504 Coordinator:** A full-time position was established to consult with teachers, parents, principals, and doctors regarding students with attention deficit disorder. Currently, this position is held by a clinical social worker who is very knowledgeable about ADD/ADHD. Consultation regarding teaching strategies and behavior management strategies is also provided. The consultant monitors services to ensure that the needs of students with attention deficits are being met.

- **Attention Deficit Education Plan (ADEP):** Students with ADD or ADHD who qualify will have either an IEP or Section 504 Plan; all others students diagnosed with attention deficits who are in regular classes will have an Attention Deficit Education Plan.

- **School Counseling Services:** Counseling groups are offered to help students understand how an attention deficit affects them. Topics include self-advocacy, coping skills, anger management, social skills, organizational and planning skills, and problem-solving skills.

- **In-service Training on ADD/ADHD:** A 16-hour in-service is available to all teachers. Although voluntary, roughly 90 percent of all teachers have attended the training. A yearlong 30-hour advanced study group is also available. In-service credits that affect a teacher's pay scale are awarded for participation in these training sessions.

- **Parent Education:** The district sponsors an annual "Sharing and Caring Conference" for both teachers and parents. This conference focuses on the special needs of students with disabilities. During the year, the ADD consultant is available to provide training for parents at various schools as requested.

- **Reading Recovery:** For all elementary age students who are behind academically, this intensive reading program helps students make a year's gain or more in reading ability.

- **The Bridges Programs:** Although these four programs are open to all students, a high percentage of them have ADD or ADHD.
  - *Comprehensive Bridges Programs* (middle school-academics): At the *middle school* level, students who are behind academically receive intensive instruction in smaller classes. This service is available in all middle schools.
  - *Integrated Bridges Program* (middle school – academics): Each middle school has developed their own unique program to meet student needs. One school hired extra teachers to provide instruction. Another has a "synergy period" when students may receive extra instruction in a specific deficit area or enrichment in a gifted area.
  - *Off Campus Bridges Program* (expelled middle and high school students): Students attend classes three hours a day, earn credit toward graduation, and are transitioned back to their "home school" when expulsion ends.
  - *Bridges Class* (high school-academics): Students who have failed English or Math may retake the course in a class with a teacher student ratio of 1:15.

- **Accelerated Independent Study:** Any student who lacks credits and wants to graduate with her class may make up credits by completing a computerized curriculum at her own pace.

■ **Reuther Central High School:** (traditional vocational/alternative high school) This alternative high school offers JROTC (military), School Aged Parents Program, Infant/Child Learning Lab, and a Work Experience Program. The Credit on Credit Program allows the student to earn dual credits that may be applied to high school or Gateway Technical College graduation requirements.

■ **Non-traditional High-Tech Training:** Local businessmen were concerned that high school graduates did not have the skills needed to work in their businesses. So they worked with their local school system to develop innovative educational programs. Many instructors for these programs have worked in these fields and later in life decided they wanted to teach. These classes are targeted for bright students who want to work in high tech fields. Many students with attention deficits do better in situations when: 1) the material is of *special interest* to them and 2) the opportunities for learning involve *hands-on experience*.

- *Lake View Academy:* courses related to careers in manufacturing and engineering are offered. The program offers youth apprenticeships and job shadowing for both students and teachers. For example, a student who wants to be a fireman may intern with the local fire department. Local businesses contributed the funds to build the high school.

- *Indian Trail Academy:* a non-traditional high school that is open to all students, especially those who may work better in a non-traditional atmosphere. The Academy prepares these students for college, hi-technical colleges, or other highly skilled jobs. Each of the three areas of study offers coursework beyond traditional vocational classes.

  1. *Biotechnology and Environmental Studies*: health-related fields such as health care, pharmaceuticals, research, medical and biological science, environmental science and impact, urban and regional planning, forensics, and diagnostic laboratory testing.

  2. *Business and International Studies:* finance, banking, foreign languages, world cultures, management, leadership, management analysis, marketing, and training to work in the global economy.

  3. *Communications*: printing, graphic arts, creative writing, visual and fine arts, radio/television production, design, electronic music, film/cinema, technical writing, journalism, advertising and public relations.

So the Student Is Failing: What Should the Teacher Do Now?

Researchers tell us that students with ADD/ADHD are at ***greater risk of school failure***; roughly 30 percent have failed a grade. So it should come as no surprise that students with attention deficit disorders are often on the verge of failing a class, especially in middle and high school. When teachers see a student struggling to successfully complete school work and pass tests, it is best to intervene early, within the first three to four weeks of school, or as soon as possible after problems arise. Hopefully, the material in this book will add to the teacher's repertoire of skills so that he or she can more effectively help students who are failing.

These students are vulnerable during the transition years, especially the first year of middle and high school. The increased demands for organizational skills and independent work that begin in middle school overwhelm many of these students. In fact, sometimes parents say, "My child hit a brick wall when she started middle school." Many parents keep hoping that this will be the year that their teenager will suddenly mature and academics will no longer be a problem. So, they may be reluctant to tell the teacher about the diagnosis of ADD or ADHD. Parents want to "give the teenager a chance to make it on her own." Here are some suggested intervention strategies:

Problem Solve First

1. **Contact the Parents.** Call and talk with the student's parent: Start with the positives first.

   > *"Sarah is a delightful student. I really enjoy teaching her. She has .... (extremely creative ideas for writing). But I'm concerned she's having trouble making the transition to high school. She is not turning in her homework on a regular basis."*

   Sometimes if the parent will simply monitor homework completion, the student's grades will improve significantly.

   By the time the student gets to middle and high school, most parents have been through at least five years of academic struggles. They already know the typical kinds of problems their teenager has experienced and can probably suggest effective intervention strategies. So, the teacher may ask, *"Has she had problems like this before? What seems to work best with her? What have other teachers done that has helped?"*

2. **Review Current Performance.** Look over the student's class and homework. ***Look for a pattern*** of underachievement, uneven performance, strengths, and learning problems that seem to interfere with her ability to complete school work. Try to pinpoint the specific learning problems that seem to be causing the greatest difficul-

4

4

ties. For students with attention deficits, it may well be organizational and memory problems related to deficits in executive function.

3. **Check for Prior ADD/ADHD Diagnosis.** If a student has previously been diagnosed, some parents may mention it to the teacher at the first PTA meeting or early in the semester. In addition, a letter from their physician may be on file in the office confirming the diagnosis of ADD or ADHD, documenting any problems, stating known learning problems, and making some recommendations.

4. **Provide Accommodations.** Identify learning problems and give accommodations. See Summaries 13-A-E, 41, 44, and 45 to help the student succeed in class.

Seek Help from Others

If these initial strategies aren't enough, then the next steps may include:

5. **Schedule a Parent Conference.** Set a time for a more in-depth discussion of the student's problems. Discuss possible accommodations, the level of supervision parents should give, a system for parents to know homework assignments, and a strategy to maintain regular home/school communication, such as through a weekly or daily report.
    ■ If the student has ADD or ADHD, ask the parents about *medication.* See Summary 54 for suggestions of questions to discuss with the parent, plus Summary 55 for a checklist to help determine medication effectiveness.

6. **Review Records.** Review the student's cumulative folder, such as grades, school records, achievement tests, and old psychological evaluations or IEPs. Look for 1) teacher comments regarding behavior or learning problems, 2) effective intervention strategies, and 3) higher achievement test scores with lower than expected grades—in other words, a pattern of a student who is underachieving.

7. **Ask for Advice.** If accommodations and/or modifications alone don't work, ask for advice from other educators, such as a veteran or district level master teacher, guidance counselor, school psychologist, the vice principal, or if the teacher is lucky, the ADD/ADHD consultant. Ask whether this student is an appropriate referral for a teacher committee staffing.

Refer the Student to a Teacher Committee Staffing

If nothing else seems to work, the next step may be to refer the student to a committee of teachers for help. Many schools have developed committees of veteran teachers, in addition to their IEP teams, to help brainstorm solutions to help students succeed in school. These groups may have different names in different states. In Georgia, these committees are called student support teams (SST).

8. **The Role of the SST.** The student support team (SST) may:
    ■ suggest additional accommodations or strategies to the teacher; or

■ decide whether to refer the student to the IEP team for a special education evaluation.

9. **The Role of the IEP Team.** The IEP team may request that an evaluator administer some preliminary screening instruments before the school psychologist is ever involved. For example, they may schedule a variety of tests such as: a vision and hearing examination, academic achievement tests, or visual motor tests. (See Summary 6 for a list of specific tests.) The evaluator may again review the records, looking for information that will help identify learning problems or executive function deficits. He or she may also look for test scores, teacher comments, or reports of student behaviors that are indicative of ADD/ADHD.

10. **Screen for ADD/ADHD.** If the IEP Team suspects ADD or ADHD, a behavioral checklist may be completed. The local school system may have a checklist such as the Conners available or may use the DSM-IV criteria in Summary 5. Teachers may wish to review Summary 6 on diagnosis of attention deficit disorder for some of the basic characteristics school psychologists are looking for in the diagnosis.

11. **Ask for a Letter from the Doctor.** If the student has already been diagnosed with ADD/ADHD, the SST or IEP team may ask for a letter from the doctor to confirm the diagnosis. See Summary 42 for suggested content. A sample medical letter is available in my first book, *Teenagers with ADD*.

12. **The Psychological Evaluation.** Based upon the accumulated information, the IEP Team may ask the school psychologist to conduct an in-depth evaluation: classroom observations, review of records, review of preliminary screening results, and intelligence testing. A Functional Behavioral Assessment may also be done to determine when behavioral problems occur and what tends to trigger them. Additional assessments may also be done regarding cognitive processing and social and emotional development. A behavior rating scale may also be completed. The results of this evaluation will be presented to the IEP eligibility committee to help guide their decision making and planning.

13. **Payment for Medical Treatment.** Some schools have been reluctant to identify attention deficit disorders for fear that they will be stuck with the cost of a medical evaluation and treatment. However, many families have the money or insurance to pay for a doctor's visit and medication to treat the condition. When families cannot afford medication, assistance may be available from Medicaid if the student is eligible, a local service group or charity, or in some situations, the local mental health system.

What to Expect at the IDEA Eligibility Meeting

Based upon the results of the preliminary screening process, the student may be staffed by the IEP Team to determine special education eligibility. Usually the IDEA eligibility committee is comprised of veteran teachers, school psychologists, or administrators, as listed in Summary 40.

14. **School Input.** At the eligibility staffing, each person will have the opportunity to provide input regarding the student's strengths, present performance, challenges, and needs.

4

Section 4 | Federal Laws Governing ADD/ADHD

15. Family Input. Make certain that parents and the teenager give their input. They will have insights from previous years and probably have suggestions regarding which intervention strategies *have* and *have not* worked in the past.

- **Inclusion of the Teenager:** Committee members and parents must decide whether to invite the teenager to all the meetings or simply the meeting where intervention strategies are planned. If the meeting is too negative and becomes a recitation of every bad behavior or learning deficit the teenager has, it is probably best if she is not present. Teachers and parents may let the student decide whether to attend the meeting. See Summary 64 for a discussion of self-advocacy.

- **Seek Student Input Regardless:** Talk with the student and ask for her input before the meeting. Consider asking her to identify her strengths and the areas in which she is struggling in school. *"Maria, can you tell us what is causing you the most difficulty in school? Do you have any suggestions about what would help you solve this problem? What have teachers done to help you in the past? What helped and what didn't?"*

- **Depersonalization:** Consider using *depersonalization* as a tool to raise important issues. For example, *"Many students with ADD or ADHD often have trouble remembering to write down their homework assignments and take home the right books. Sometimes that seems to be true for you."* (Or, *"Does that seem to be true for you sometimes?"*)

- **Respect the Student:** Avoid comments about the student's work that may seem accusatory or demeaning. Many students with attention deficits have already had a lifetime of marginal academic performance and negative feedback from teachers. Without proper medication and accommodations, their self-esteem will plummet.

The IDEA Staffing to Develop the IEP

Once the student has been declared eligible for services under IDEA, another meeting will be scheduled to develop the IEP. See "Writing the IEP," Summary 44.

For more information on the IEP and Section 504, refer to the resources listed at the end of Summary 39.

Medication Issues

According to research from the new NIMH study (Summary 10), **medication is the most effective intervention for treating** the vast majority of children with attention deficit disorder! Clearly, it stands to reason that medications can make or break a student's success in school. It should come as no surprise that often one of the key reasons students don't do well academically is because their medication regimen has not been adjusted to get maximum benefits at school.

If you stop and think about it, one of the main reasons students take medication is to help them focus and stay on task *at school.* That means **teachers are often in the best position to provide the doctor with objective data regarding medication effectiveness***.* So, the more teachers know about medications and their impact on the student's work, the more likely the student with an attention deficit will succeed in school. If a student is struggling in school, problems with medication effectiveness should be considered as a possible contributing factor. Obviously, teachers can't correct a problem with medication, but they can share information with parents and encourage them to talk to their physician.

Here are a few typical reasons medications may not work:

- Sometimes the **dose of medication is not correct or is not being timed properly.** Frequently, medications for attention deficits provide only a peak academic work period of approximately three hours. So, the positive effects of medication have often worn off by midmorning

5

and the student is attempting significant amounts of school work without the benefit of any medication.

- Even when medication doses are done properly, ***medication may wear off during a key transition time***, for example, during lunch or after school for the bus ride home.
- Occasionally, the student is ***not on the right medication*** to improve his attention. For example, a student may find that Adderall works great for him but the first medicine he tried, Ritalin, did not really help, or vice versa.

Some teachers worry about students taking medication, possibly fearing future drug addiction. However, one recent study offers some reassurance that drug addiction is not a major risk. Researchers found that students with attention deficit disorder who took medication were less likely to abuse drugs than students with the condition who did not take medication.

Common Medications for Treating ADD/ADHD

The primary medications used to treat ADD and ADHD are all central nervous system stimulants. However, another class of medications, antidepressants, are also frequently prescribed for problems such as anxiety or depression that often accompany attention deficit disorders. When teachers know which academic and behavioral changes should occur with each type of medication, they have a better idea as to whether medications are working properly.

Frequently, a teacher may not even know which medication a student is taking. However, if a student is doing poorly in school, it is important for the teacher to find out about the student's medications. Sometimes parents tell the teacher about medications at the start of the school year. The teacher may also ask parents about medications the student is currently taking if he is struggling. Teachers and parents may review Summaries 51-56 together to determine whether there are potential areas of concern that should be discussed with the doctor.

Central Nervous System Stimulants

Stimulant medications, so called because they *stimulate* the central nervous system, are the medications of first choice in treating attention deficits. According to results of Positron Emission Tomography (PET) Scans, these medications actually increase activity and blood flow in the front part of the brain. This area of the brain is known to control memory, speech, and thought.

Impact on Behavior: These medications are the most effective for:

1. increasing attention and concentration and
2. improving school work and behavior.

For a more detailed discussion of the impact of stimulant medication, see Summary 52. These medications affect the levels of the neurotransmitters dopamine and norepinephrine, which, in turn, improve the student's ability to pay attention.

Length of Effectiveness: Most stimulants last for only three to six hours, respectively, for regular and sustained release medications. However, there are a couple of exceptions: 1) Cylert lasts roughly eight hours and 2) two as yet unproven new medications promise to last eight hours or more. Ritalin, Dexedrine, and Adderall are discussed in more detail in Summary 53. Both the brand and generic medication names are given below.

Stimulant Medications

Traditionally Prescribed Stimulants

- Ritalin™ (methylphenidate)
- Dexedrine™ (dextroamphetamine)

- Adderall™ (dextroamphetamine & amphetamine)
- Cylert™ (magnesium pemoline)

New Stimulant Medications Released in 2000

- Metadate™ (methylphenidate – 8 hours)
- Concerta™ (methylphenidate – 10 hours – FDA approved August 2, 2000)

Unclassified Medication That Stimulates the Central Nervous System

- Provigil™ (modafinil) [This new medication improves wakefulness; helps people with ADD/ADHD maintain a proper level of alertness; used to treat narcolepsy.]

Secondary Medications

Several secondary medications are used to treat conditions that may coexist with ADD or ADHD such as depression, anxiety, irritability, or aggression. However, these medications do not significantly increase a student's ability to pay attention in class.

Antidepressants

Although medications may be known by one categorical name such as antidepressants, they are often used to treat a variety of other conditions. For example, antidepressants are sometimes prescribed to treat anxiety, which may coexist with an attention deficit. In fact, antidepressants are used more often in children to treat ADD- and ADHD- related behaviors than they are to treat depression. Increasing levels of the neurotransmitter, serotonin, is one of their most important functions. Higher levels of serotonin give us a sense of well being, reduce irritability and aggression, and often help ensure a good night's sleep.

Knowing this important information gives a teacher a better understanding of which behavior changes to expect when a teenager takes antidepressants. In addition, the teacher may help a student or his parents understand why he was prescribed an antidepressant. Otherwise, the student may refuse to take an antidepressant because he knows he is "not depressed."

Impact on Behavior: Each class of antidepressant works in a slightly different way to increase levels of serotonin in the brain. These medications are prescribed to help with several issues:

1. reducing moodiness,
2. leveling off emotional highs or lows,
3. improving frustration tolerance,
4. reducing irritability and aggression,
5. reducing impulsivity, and
6. treating depression.

When levels of serotonin drop, irritability and aggression increase. One group of antidepressants, the Tricyclics, also helps improve sleep. Anafranil™ is often prescribed for students with ADD/ADHD who may also have coexisting Tourette Syndrome and/or Obsessive Compulsive Disorder (OCD).

Length of Effectiveness: Unlike Ritalin and Dexedrine, which last only three to six hours, antidepressants build up in the bloodstream and are effective all day.

Common Antidepressant Medications

Tricyclics

- Tofranil™ (imipramine) [in addition, helpful with Tourette Syndrome]
- Norpramin™ (desipramine)
- Pamelor™ or Vivactyl™ (nortryptyline)

Selective Serotonin Re-uptake Inhibitors (SSRI's)

- Zoloft™ (sertraline)
- Paxil™ (paroxetine)
- Prozac™ (fluoxetine)

Miscellaneous Antidepressants

- Welbutrin™ (bupropion)
- Effexor™ (venlafaxine)
- Anafranil™ (clomipramine) [reduces compulsive activity, rigidity, anxiety, irritability related to Tourette Syndrome and Obsessive Compulsive Disorder]

Antianxiety Medication

- Buspar™ (buspirone) [reduces coexisting worrying, nervousness, and anxiety]

Other Medications

Several medications used to treat other conditions are also effective in treating certain aspects of ADD and ADHD.

Impact on Behavior: Generally speaking, these medications are often used to reduce impulsivity, oppositional behavior, anger, and aggression. They are often used in combination with Ritalin, Dexedrine, or Adderall.

Antihypertensives *(Typically prescribed to reduce blood pressure; may also reduce hyperactivity, impulsivity, aggression, sleep problems, and tics.)*

- Catapres™ (clonidine)
- Tenex™ (guanfacine)

Mood Stabilizers *(Typically prescribed to level off moods; may also reduce emotional-blow-ups, mood swings, hyperactivity, impulsivity, and aggression; some students feel these medications dull their ability to think clearly.)*

- Depakote™ (valproic acid) [also prescribed to treat seizures]
- Lithionate™ (lithium carbonate)

Resources

Barkley, Russell A. *Attention Deficit Hyperactivity Disorder.* New York: The Guilford Press, 1998.

Brown, Thomas E. *Attention Deficit Disorders and Comorbidities in Children, Adolescents, and Adults.* Washington, DC: American Psychiatric Press, 2000.

Elliot, Paul. "How I Treat ADD: Lessons You Won't See in the Books, Learned from 25 Years in the Trenches." ADDA Conference presentation, Atlanta, GA, 2000.

Helbing, Joan. "Beyond 'Did you take your meds?': Medication and Treatment at School." CHADD National Conference presentation, Washington, DC, 1999.

Prince, Jefferson B. "An Update on Recent Advances in the Pharmacotherapy of ADHD." ADDA Conference presentation, Atlanta, Georgia, 2000.

Wilens, Timothy E. *Straight Talk about Psychiatric Medications for Kids.* New York: The Guilford Press, 1999.

Impact of Stimulant Medication on School Performance

Researchers tell us that *when medication is working properly, certain changes in behavior will occur. If these changes are **not** observed, then the medication is not working properly.*

Dr. James Swanson and his colleagues at the University of California (Irvine) conducted a "review of the review" of the literature that included thousands of research articles on attention deficit disorders. These studies provide convincing evidence that the student's *school work improves significantly* when stimulant medication is taken.

Researchers have reported that stimulant medication is slightly less effective for students with ADD (55 to 65 percent) when compared to ADHD (70 to 90 percent). Medication response for students with ADHD alone often seems miraculous, with grades jumping from Ds and Fs to As and Bs. However, when coexisting conditions are present, the medication response is not as dramatic. Sometimes a second medication is needed to treat coexisting conditions. For students who have the inattentive form of ADD, the reduced medication effectiveness may perhaps be linked to the executive function deficits that plague many students. Hopefully, researchers will begin looking for new medications that will help improve executive functions.

Effect of Medication

When medication is working, teachers should see the following changes:

Increased:

- attention and concentration,
- compliance,
- effort on tasks,
- amount and accuracy of school work produced.

Decreased:

- activity levels,
- impulsivity,
- negative behaviors in social interactions,
- physical and verbal hostility.

Teachers should be aware that when *medication wears off* mid-morning or after lunch, problems with inattention, impulsivity, and irritability may reappear.

Even when medication is working properly, *some behaviors will **not** improve significantly* or will immediately become problems when the medication wears off:

- disorganization,
- forgetfulness,
- impaired sense of time.

So, most students with ADD or ADHD will continue to:

- lose books and papers,
- forget homework assignments, long-term projects, the weekly report, and to stay after school for a teacher conference or detention,
- have difficulty planning ahead,
- have difficulty knowing how to budget time necessary to complete a long-term project.

Numerous suggestions are provided in Section 3 to address these executive function deficits.

Collecting Information Regarding Medication Effectiveness

The checklists included as Appendices A7 and A8 are good resources for assessing medication effectiveness at school. Teacher input regarding medication effectiveness is especially critical!

Action of Stimulant Medications
Regular vs. Sustained-Release (SR) Forms

The three most commonly used stimulant medications are Ritalin, Dexedrine, and Adderall. Researchers tell us that all three medications are equally effective in treating ADD and ADHD. However, individual student response to each medication may vary. Ritalin and Dexedrine are available in a regular, a sustained-release, or a longer-acting form. Adderall comes only in a longer-acting sustained release form.

Regular Tablets (Ritalin or Dexedrine)

Ritalin is the most commonly prescribed medication for ADD and ADHD and is the medication with which most teachers are probably familiar. This does not mean it is always the most effective medication for any given student, however. Doctors have found that response to these medications varies from person to person. Some teenagers respond better to Ritalin; others to Dexedrine or Adderall. Effective medication *dosages* also vary from student to student. Generally, teenagers require higher doses of these medications than children. Occasionally, however, an older teenager may actually take less medication than an elementary school child. In addition, some teenagers may metabolize the medication more quickly so it doesn't last as long. As a result, medication must be taken more often.

As shown in the diagram below, regular tablets of both Ritalin and Dexedrine usually take 15-30 minutes to begin working. After the medication starts working, ***peak academic work time may last only 2½ to 3 hours*** before the effectiveness begins to fade. For example, a teenager who takes regular Ritalin at 7:00 will have medication working effectively from 7:30 to 10:00 or 10:30. If he doesn't take the next tablet until 12:00, medication will not be effective again until 12:30. Consequently, there is a one- to two-hour window with no medication. A student may be completing his work and behaving at 9:00 but by 11:30, as medication wears off, he may be failing and misbehaving. When medication wears off, emotional blow-ups or fights are more likely to occur. ***If this medication problem is corrected, typically the student's behavior and school work will improve.***

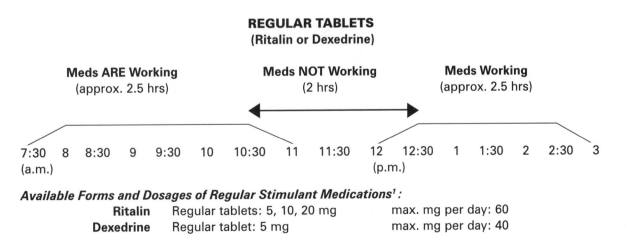

REGULAR TABLETS
(Ritalin or Dexedrine)

| **Meds ARE Working** | **Meds NOT Working** | **Meds Working** |
| (approx. 2.5 hrs) | (2 hrs) | (approx. 2.5 hrs) |

7:30   8   8:30   9   9:30   10   10:30   11   11:30   12   12:30   1   1:30   2   2:30   3
(a.m.)   (p.m.)

Available Forms and Dosages of Regular Stimulant Medications[1] :

| **Ritalin** | Regular tablets: 5, 10, 20 mg | max. mg per day: 60 |
| **Dexedrine** | Regular tablet: 5 mg | max. mg per day: 40 |

Side Effects

Of all the stimulant medications, Ritalin has been studied the most extensively over the past three or four decades. In general, stimulants are considered very "clean" medications because they are in and out of the body in four to six hours. **Side effects are minimal.** Reported side effects of both regular and sustained-release stimulant medications include *loss of appetite* plus problems with *sleep*. However, timing the medications so as not to interfere with meals or bedtime is usually effective in eliminating these problems. In most cases, the medication does not cause sleep problems. In reality, sleep disturbances are often present *before* the student ever begins taking stimulant medication. Furthermore, researchers tell us that stimulants **do not stunt student growth.**

Infrequently, if the teenager is taking too much medication, teachers may observe negative side effects that include depression, lethargy, or "losing his spark." Of course, depression and lethargy may also be caused by other problems. Teachers may share their impressions or results of the rating scale (Appendix A7) if asked by parents or during a staffing or planning conference.

Sustained-Release [SR] Medications (Ritalin, Dexedrine, Adderall)

Sustained-release medications typically last four to six hours, as opposed to regular tablets, which may last only two and a half to three hours. Researchers have recently found that one dose of Adderall is effective for a whole school day.

Longer-acting sustained-release medications have great appeal for middle and high school students. First, since they only need to take one dose in the morning, they can avoid the embarrassment of taking medication at school. Second, they typically will not have to remember to take an additional dose of medication at school.

Watch for the new stimulant medication, Concerta, which promises to last up to ten hours. According to anecdotal reports from the medication trials, Concerta should provide an additional option for students needing all-day dosing. Concerta's dosing level is slightly higher in the afternoon to compensate for the daily medication tolerance discussed in Summary 54. Obviously, the medication's impact on appetite will have to be monitored.

Ritalin SR: One note of caution: a Ritalin SR (20 mg) tablet does not provide the full 20-mg dose it promises. (Both Dexedrine SR and Adderall actually last longer than Ritalin SR.) Teachers have long observed that the Ritalin SR did not work as effectively as regular Ritalin. Researchers have confirmed this observation: a 20-mg Ritalin SR provides roughly 10 mg of medication instead of the expected 20 mg. Some students report that Ritalin SR works in waves of effectiveness, perhaps because it is a tablet instead of a capsule.

Ritalin SR
4-6 hrs

7:30   8   8:30   9   9:30   10   10:30   11   11:30   12   12:30   1   1:30   2   2:30   3
(a.m.)   (p.m.)

Dexedrine SR and Adderall: On the other hand, Dexedrine SR and Adderall are available in a variety of strengths and deliver the promised level of milligrams. They both appear to have a smoother, more even release of medication and last longer than Ritalin SR. Researchers should be able to tell us fairly soon whether or not the new medications, Metadate and Concerta, are also effective.

Dexedrine SR or Adderall
6-8 hrs

7:30 8 8:30 9 9:30 10 10:30 11 11:30 12 12:30 1 1:30 2 2:30 3
(a.m.)   (p.m.)

Available Forms and Dosages of Sustained-release (SR) or Extended-release (ER) Stimulants*:

Ritalin	SR tablet: 20 mg	max. mg per day: 60
Dexedrine	SR capsule: 5, 10, 15 mg	max. mg per day: 40
Adderall	SR tablet 5, 10, 20, 30 mg	max. mg per day: 40
Metadate	ER tablet 10, 20 mg	max. mg per day: 60
Concerta	SR capsule 18, 36, 54 mg	max. mg per day: 54

Drawbacks of Sustained-release (SR) Medications

Although a sustained-release medication is often the best option for middle and high school students who don't want to go to the office and take medication, a few problems have been reported with these medications:

- SR medications may ***take longer to begin acting,*** up to an hour or more, plus they ***do not raise medication levels to as high a peak*** as regular tablets. So, for some students, SR medications alone may not work. To solve this problem, some doctors combine a regular and sustained-release medication, for example, a 5 mg regular Dexedrine with a 20 mg SR Dexedrine.
- If a student takes an SR medication as he is walking out the door to school, it won't be effective for an hour, possibly halfway into first period.
- Erratic or uneven absorption of this medication may also be a problem.
- Over time, a student may build up a tolerance to Ritalin SR, thereby reducing its effectiveness. Increased tolerance to Dexedrine SR or Adderall may also be a problem, but has not been studied.

---

* *Please note that higher doses of these medications are often prescribed for teenagers than for children. The dosages listed here are the maximum total milligrams that a teenager may take over two, or perhaps three, doses in one day. Some teens, however, may get good results with less medication.*

SUMMARY 54: What Educators Need to Know about Medication

As explained in Section 4, students who are doing poorly in school may be referred to a Student Support Team (or similar group in your state) for a staffing to brainstorm about ways to help them succeed in school. *Since an inappropriate medication regimen may be an underlying problem, members of this team need to have a basic understanding about medication issues.* An awareness of the issues below will help team members make an educated guess about whether or not medication is a problem.

Potential Medication Problems

1. When teenagers reach puberty, **hormonal changes may affect medication** and adjustments may be needed.

2. The **dosage may be too low** to obtain maximum benefit at school. (A recent NIMH study identified this as a major problem.)

3. Parents and teenagers often **don't know when peak medication dosages have been achieved.** Getting medication "right" is not easy, especially in complex cases of ADD/ADHD.

4. It may simply be the **wrong medication** for the teenager. Even if one stimulant does not work, a different one may work quite well.

5. As discussed in the preceding summary, some students develop **a tolerance to medication,** especially the sustained-release form. Not only can students develop a tolerance over a period of months but they can also develop a tolerance during the course of the day. To solve this problem, Concerta has added a slight increase as the medication is released during the early afternoon to get uniform results all day.

6. The student may **metabolize medication quickly,** so the effects may wear off earlier than expected.

7. In addition, the **initial morning dose may wear off** well before the second dose becomes effective, leaving roughly a two-hour period without any medication.

8. The teenager may take medication early in the morning to help him be alert enough to get up at 6:30 or 7:00. As a result, the **medication may wear off by 9 or 10** in the morning.

9. Sometimes **Ritalin SR doesn't work as expected**. As explained in Summary 53, a 20-mg Ritalin SR tablet doesn't deliver the full 20 mg dosage.

10. The student may **forget** to take his medication or perhaps **refuse** to take it. Sometimes teens become embarrassed about taking medication or don't want to go to the office or clinic, and problems with "medication refusal" arise.

11. ***Coexisting problems may be present and untreated***. Two-thirds of teens with attention deficits have at least one coexisting problem. (See Summaries 1, 10, and 72) Another medication may be needed in addition to Ritalin, Dexedrine, or Adderall to effectively treat the student.

Getting Medication "Right"

School officials are often surprised to learn that finding the best medication for each teenager is not an exact science. In fact, a lot of trial and error is often involved. In reality, most doctors don't have the time or manpower to accurately assess medication effectiveness. Although some teenagers may luck out and get the right medication and dose on the very first visit to the doctor, this doesn't happen very often.

Typically, after a teenager takes medication, the doctor receives a general report from the family regarding their subjective impressions about the medication and its impact on the student's school work. Rarely is any objective measurement taken to determine whether the medication is working properly. So, if the student's school work improves a little even though he is still struggling, parents often think, "This must be as good as the medication gets." Parents then maintain the same ineffective medication dosages, when in reality, there is a good chance that school work could improve significantly with proper medication levels. (See Summary 10.) The fact is, when a student is struggling, it is almost impossible for a doctor to get medication right without input from teachers.

Questions to Determine Medication Effectiveness

To determine whether the student's medication is working effectively, several important questions must be answered. Teachers may tactfully lay the groundwork for discussing medication with the parent by saying something like this:

"We are trying to look at everything that may possibly interfere with your son's ability to succeed in school. Teachers have told us about his performance in class. The school psychologist has looked over his school records and will do an evaluation to look for learning problems. You have told us about his struggles with homework. One other area we should consider is his medication and how it is working while he is at school. By asking a few questions that you and his other teachers should be able to answer, we should have a pretty good idea if the medication is working properly. You may not know all the answers to these questions but you can call and tell us later."

By answering as many of the following questions as possible, teachers and parents will have a good idea if medication is a significant problem. If physician follow-up is necessary, this information will be extremely helpful to the doctor as he considers adjustments in the medication. Summaries 51-56 on medication will also be helpful in assessing the effectiveness of a teenager's medication.

Obviously, it is not the teacher's role to suggest specific medications to parents. However, as parents review the summaries in this section, they may decide to discuss possible alternatives with their doctor.

1. **What medication is the teenager taking?** *(See Summary 51 for a discussion on medications.)*

   - Is it a central nervous system stimulant like Ritalin, Dexedrine, or Adderall?
   - Is it an antidepressant like Tofranil, Zoloft, or Prozac?
   - Is it a regular or sustained-release (SR) medication?
   - Is the medication brand or generic? Many students have found that the generic methylphenidate doesn't work as well as Ritalin.

2. **How much medication is the teenager taking?**

   One of the most common reasons for school failure and misbehavior is that the student is not getting enough medication throughout the day for it to work effectively. In fact, as explained in Summary 10, researchers tell us that most students are taking doses that fall below the peak effectiveness levels identified in a recent NIMH study. Ask how much medication the teenager is taking in each dose. It is important to know the milligrams being taken per dose. Common forms and dosages are given in Summary 53. If parents don't know the answer immediately, they may have a prescription bottle at the school nurse's station or they may look on the bottle at home.

3. **How often does the teenager take medication?**

   A student may take medication one to three times a day. Some may take medication at home in the morning and not take it again all day. Unfortunately, the medication may wear off earlier than the teacher and parents expect. The diagrams in Summary 53 show the approximate time of day when both regular and sustained-release medications typically wear off.

4. **What time does the teenager take each dose of medication?**

   Timing of these doses is critical to give all-day coverage. Depending on the timing of the first morning dose, a dose at noon or one o'clock may come too late, leaving an hour or two without any medication coverage.

   Ask the teenager or parents what time the student takes his first dose of medication. Some parents have such terrible battles with their teenager each morning, they give the medication as early as 6:30 so the teen can get organized and get to school on time. As a result, the medication may wear off as early as 9:30 or 10:00. The second dose may not be taken until noon, and perhaps another smaller dose may be taken at 3:00 in the afternoon. As shown in Summary 53, when this pattern is followed, medication has worn off by midmorning and the teenager is attempting school work for approximately a two-hour period without the benefit of medication.

   The student may need to take medication earlier or more frequently during the day. Switching to a sustained-release may also be a viable option. Or, some doctors prescribe a combination of regular and sustained-release forms of the same medication to achieve peak medication effectiveness.

5. Is the medication working effectively?

Medication checklists usually contain medication symptoms only—for example, headaches, insomnia, and loss of appetite. Unfortunately, they do not measure whether or not the medication is helping the student do better in school—which is often one of the primary reasons for taking medication. Teachers may find the checklist in Summary 55 more useful. This checklist assesses the most critical school issues, such as whether the student is passing the class or completing his work. A regular medication symptom checklist may be used in conjunction with this one, if needed.

When stimulant medication is working effectively, teachers will see specific changes in behavior, such as better grades, completion of more school work, and increased compliance. A list of expected behavior changes is contained in Summary 52. Teachers may complete the rating scale in Appendix A7 to determine whether medication is working effectively. If the changes listed in this summary are not observed, then something may still be wrong with the medication. If a teenager has been doing well and then his school performance suddenly drops, several factors such as those listed earlier in this summary may be causing the problem—e.g., puberty, medication tolerance, generic medication.

Sometimes adults forget to ask the real experts, the teens themselves, how the medication works for them. Actually, some of them are quite good at articulating how medication is helping. Others have great difficulty judging its impact. But regardless, ask the teen to complete Appendix A8.

6. If medication is not working effectively, what changes are needed?

Fine-tuning medication is critical! It will take the teenager, parent, teacher, and doctor working together to find the best medication regimen. Encourage parents to meet with the doctor and share the information regarding the medication's effectiveness collected by the team.

Medication Effectiveness at School

Student's name: __Sam__   Date & class: __Algebra__

Completed by: __Mrs. Davis__   Time of day observed: __11:30a.m.__

To assess the impact medication is having on a student's school work, each teacher should answer several key questions. When medication is working properly and learning problems have been identified, the student should be doing much better in school. If the teacher cannot check the "Strongly agree" and "Agree" columns, then problems may still exist in several areas: 1) the proper accommodations are not being provided for the student's learning problems, 2) executive function deficits are not being addressed, or 3) the medication regimen may not be right for the student. Please circle the answer that best describes the student's behavior.

Academic Performance:

When the student is in my class, s/he:	Strongly Agree	Agree	Neutral	Disagree	Strongly Disagree
1. pays attention	1	2	③	4	5
2. completes class and homework	1	②	3	4	5
3. does work correctly	1	②	3	4	5
4. complies with requests	1	②	3	4	5
5. makes passing grades	1	②	3	4	5

ADD/ADHD-Related Behaviors, Including Executive Function

If the student is on medication and is not doing well in school, what else could be causing continuing problems? Are there any ADD/ADHD-related behaviors that are interfering with the student's ability to succeed in school?

ADD/ADHD-Related Behaviors:

The student:					
6. is organized	1	2	3	④	5
7. manages time well	1	2	③	4	5
8. remembers things easily	1	2	3	④	5
9. is on time to class	1	②	3	4	5
10. is on time to school	1	2	③	4	5
11. thinks carefully before acting or speaking	1	②	3	4	5
12. is awake and alert in class	1	2	3	④	5

Ask parents about any sleep problems. According to them, the student:

13. falls asleep easily	1	2	3	4	⑤
14. wakes up easily	1	2	3	4	⑤

Comments: __This student is still struggling with some ADHD behaviors. Additional accommodations or a medical consultation may be needed.__

Student Comments about Medication

The teenagers and young adults featured in my video, *Teen to Teen: the ADD Experience*, made some very insightful comments about stimulant medications. These candid comments may give teachers a better understanding of the impact medication has on students.

■ *"Medication calms me down and it helps me concentrate."* — Julie, seventh grader

■ *"If I don't take my medication, I forget the small details in Language Arts, like writing down the work. Because if I don't take it, I just sit there. The medicine also helps me stay awake. If I don't take it, that's one of my first signs, I'm practically falling asleep."*
— Jerry, high school sophomore

■ *"It helps me some. But if I'm not 'on' that day or if I'm really out of it or I don't want to study something, it's not going to make me study anything. But it does help a lot."*
— Maresa, high school senior

■ *"Well, it definitely helps me. I used to take classes that were back-to-back, long, three-hour classes. I would always notice that my notes would be almost perfect to begin with. But towards the end of my last class, I would end up having drawings and doodles and all kinds of stuff that would just kind of fade. You could just watch it as my medicine faded off. It definitely helps me with school work."*
— Alex, college student

■ *"I don't like the way medication makes me feel but I know I need to take it so I can do okay in school."*
— Lewis, high school graduate and irrigation contractor

■ *"It doesn't do me any good to study unless I've had my medication. Otherwise, I won't remember what I studied."*
— Alex

■ *"I used to take meds at school and I hated it. Because kids would ask, 'What are you doing at the office?' and that makes you feel bad."*
— Katie, sixth grader

■ *"It helps me to get my work done. It doesn't really affect my personality that much except maybe I don't yell out in class as much or get in trouble as much."*
— Jerry

■ *"It helps me with my work. It helps me focus on what needs to be done. If I don't take my medication, I get to my job and I forget what's going on. I have to sit and think and I don't know what I'm doing. I do this and I do that and I don't get anything done. With my medication I pull myself together and I complete the job and I complete it well."*
—Lewis

5

■ *"I've taken both Ritalin and Dexedrine. I think both cut down on impulsivity a lot."*

— Jerry

■ *"Medication cuts down on impulsivity but it only lasts while you're on it. So you can be impulsive afterwards."*

— Alex

■ *"In seventh grade I had to switch medications. I don't know if it's because I went through puberty or what. I was taking Ritalin and going along just fine. Then all of a sudden the Ritalin dropped off and really no matter how much I took, it didn't really help me that much. So I had to switch medications. We tried a couple of medications and decided Dexedrine worked best. Recently I switched to Adderall."*

— Jerry

■ *"Dexedrine sustained release lasts a lot longer for me than the Ritalin sustained release. It lasts about six to eight hours."*

— Lewis

■ *"It takes at least an hour for Adderall to kick in. I notice the effects fading somewhere around six to eight hours later."*

— Maresa

■ *"They say I have a sleep disturbance. I'd go to bed at 9 o'clock at night and couldn't fall asleep until 1 or 2 o'clock in the morning. I'd just lay there awake. Now I take imipramine (Tofranil) to help me go to sleep. Sometimes I'll be sitting there awake and I'll know I haven't taken my medicine because I can't fall asleep."*

— Jerry

■ *"On my medicine I'm real calm and straightforward and don't really care to laugh a lot. But off of it, I'm whew … my mind is really bouncing around. That's what's great about it. It's me."*

— Lewis

■ *"I think the medication does have an effect on creativity. When you're not on Dexedrine, your mind just races back and forth between so many things. You can start off on one topic and end up on some other topic way far away from there within seconds. I think that has a lot to do with creativity. When you're on Dexedrine, your mind doesn't race as much and you won't have as many ideas pop into your head."*

— Alex

■ *"I knew medication worked because one day I walked into class and I was making chicken noises. When the medication kicked in, I quit making noise and I knew it was working."*

— Lewis

■ *"My friends tell me not to take medication before I come to a party because I'm more fun without it."*

— Travis, high school senior

■ *"My main concern was that I would have side effects from the medication and that I personally wouldn't be able to detect them. I was afraid I'd have all of these horrible side effects and that I wouldn't know. That I'd be barking like a dog or something."*

—Maresa

■ *"I still have side effects. I can't eat lunch and I can't sleep if I take it too late. Sometimes I get moody when the medication wears off."*

— Lewis

Resources

Teen to Teen: the ADD Experience, produced and edited by Chris A. Zeigler Dendy, 1999. Information is available from *www.chrisdendy.com*

Classroom Management and Challenging Behaviors

Prevention is the best behavior management strategy! Some of the best ways for a teacher to head off behavior problems from students with attention deficits include:

1. **Ensure that the student with an attention deficit disorder is succeeding academically.** That means learning and medication problems associated with attention deficits must be addressed. Once these problems have been addressed, these students will typically have fewer behavior problems at school. Earlier sections of this book provide suggestions for dealing with academic issues.

2. **Provide a supportive, structured classroom.**

3. **Be aware of which teaching techniques and ways of speaking to students can either increase or decrease the likelihood of misbehavior.**

6

4. Be aware of ADD/ADHD behaviors and how they affect a student's performance in the classroom. For example, Dr. Sam Goldstein points out that sometimes it hard to tell the difference between inattention and noncompliance. If a student does not do as a teacher asks, is it because he was not paying attention, or intentionally refusing to do as the teacher requested?

The summaries that follow offer additional suggestions to help teachers avoid potential problems. In addition, there are strategies for coping more effectively with students with ADD/ADHD when they do have problems. Classroom management techniques and behavioral strategies are briefly reviewed. Other school-based intervention strategies such as peer mediation are also discussed.

Classroom Management

Good classroom management is critical and is often the best way to prevent potential discipline problems. To use a sports metaphor: the best defense is a good offense. In other words, teachers are more likely to avoid behavior problems by having a clearly defined classroom routine in place.

Problems Contributing to Misbehavior

First let's review some of the potential problems that researchers believe may contribute to misbehavior in the classroom. They include:

1. lack of a positive, personal relationship between the student and teacher,
2. class rules that are not clear,
3. vague expectations from the teacher,
4. too little structure or routine in the classroom,
5. transitions from one activity to another (entering & leaving class, riding the bus, changing tasks within a class, lunch, returning from active classes like PE),
6. work that is too difficult,
7. work that takes too long to complete,
8. too little feedback from the teacher,
9. work that is not high interest or novel (is repetitive, perceived as boring or not meaningful),
10. work that does not hook or maintain a student's attention,
11. seating that is too near distractions (the door, aquarium, pencil sharpener),
12. overcrowded classrooms.

Proactive Classroom Management Strategies

Keeping these potential problems in mind, teachers are encouraged to use ***proactive classroom management strategie***s such as those included in this summary to prevent misbehavior in class. The suggestions provided here come from many sources, including nationally known educators Robert Reid of the University of Nebraska, Clare Jones at Arizona State University, and Ann Welch at the University of Virginia; from veteran classroom teachers who are also parents of students with attention deficits; from school psychologists; and from my own personal experience in teaching, school psychology, and mental health.

6

Building Rapport

Students with attention deficits are often described as being difficult to motivate. Teachers who take the time to build a strong rapport with these teenagers will be able to work with them more effectively. For better or worse, *the academic performance of these students often depends on whether or not they like the teacher!* These students will pass a subject one semester and fail it the next because of personality conflicts with the new teacher. Students with attention deficits like teachers who like and respect them in return. Conflicts between teachers and students are more easily resolved when a strong rapport exists.

1. **Make an effort to get to know students personally.** Ann Welch gives an example of a teacher who did not like a particular student but went out of her way to get to know the student better. The teacher found time for one-on-one talks by sitting with the student at lunch or talking with him during a break. Eventually, she found something she liked about the student.

2. **Greet students at the door by name.**

3. **Make a class bulletin board of both academic and nonacademic interests or skills.** Ask students to bring pictures of themselves involved in various activities: hobbies, sports, or accomplishments. A different class could be featured each month. A separate board could be used to display some of the students' best work. This makes it easier to find common interests or topics for enriching school work. For example, the student could write an essay on topics of interest to him such as photography, cars, or a website design.

4. **Give a couple of students extra attention.** Select a couple of students who need extra attention each day for some personal and positive interaction. Some students like public praise; others are embarrassed by it and prefer a pat on the shoulder or a quiet comment.

5. **Ask the teenager and parents to complete Appendix A10.** This form suggests ways of looking at ADD/ADHD behaviors in a more positive manner. Sometimes the student's behavior can actually be an asset in the adult work world. For example, hyperactivity may be viewed as high energy, bossiness as leadership, and day dreaming as a sign of imaginative thinking. Advise parents in advance that the form will be sent home so they can be thinking of their teen's positive qualities. Sometimes when parents have had a lot of conflicts with their teen, they may have trouble thinking of anything positive to say about him. Help them learn to reframe their teenager's positive qualities. When it is completed and returned to school, teachers should take a moment to review it and add a couple of things to the list.

Classroom Structure

1. **Post a written schedule** for the day, perhaps on the board.

   - Write the activities on the board. *"Continue class reports on science experiments."*

- Include the homework assignment on the board. *"Read pp. 119-130. Answer questions 1-10."*

2. **Prompt with specific cues** about needed materials and actions. *"Get out your book and open it to page 109."*

3. **Cue when changes or transitions are about to occur.** *"You have three more minutes to finish reading this section and then we are going to discuss it."*

4. **Develop a homework routine.** See Summary 24.

   - **Designate "row captains"** to see that homework assignments are copied down and that homework is collected.
   - **Ask students to copy their assignments** from the board at the same time the teacher or another student writes the homework on the board. (This provides a visual cue to write plus gives adequate time to write the assignment. When the teacher also writes the assignment, it slows her down, giving the student adequate time to write it down.)
   - **Place completed work in a designated spot.** Ask students to turn in class or homework at the same time each day and put it in the same place. If work is completed, allow them to turn it in. Do not ask them to keep it until "tomorrow." If the work will not be discussed in class, consider collecting homework near the beginning of class.
   - **Place completed work in one folder.** Suggest that the student place completed work for all classes in one colored folder. He may have difficulty keeping up with several different folders. Ask the student to tell you what works best for him. Although certainly no ideal, one student found that it actually worked best for him if he put his math papers in his math book when he finished them.
   - **Maintain this daily structure and routine.** Consistent class routine is important. These students don't handle changes or transitions well and are more likely to misbehave then.

Classroom Rules

1. **Have a few good rules (3-5).**

2. **Keep rules short and simple.**

3. **State rules in positive terms.** Tell students what to do rather than what not to do. Instead of saying *"Stop talking when you enter class,"* say, *"When you come into class, check the assignment on the overhead and start working quietly."*

4. **Post rules prominently.**

5. **Teach the rules.**

6. **Reinforce compliance.** Class rules work best when students:

   - are praised by the teacher for obeying the rules and
   - ignored or mildly reprimanded for breaking rules.

Giving Reprimands

Little research has been done on the effectiveness of reprimands for teenagers with ADD or ADHD. However, guidance for reprimanding younger children has been provided by my colleague, Dr. Ann Abramowitz, Associate Professor and Director of the Center for Learning and Attention Deficit Disorders at Emory University. Reprimands should be used sparingly and when they are used they should be mild. Try these out and see what works best with teens.

1. **Point to the rule,** if standing nearby. If the student does not see you, say his name, point, and say nothing else.

2. **Reprimand privately** in a calm, unemotional manner.

3. **State the reprimand firmly.** A reprimand doesn't have to be a negative statement. Teachers may simply state what the student should be doing. *"Start your work now."*

4. **Be brief and to the point.**

5. **Reprimand immediately** after the rule is broken.

6. **Stand near the student** and make eye contact. If the teacher touches the student, make certain the touch is in a "safe zone" such as the shoulder or hand. Some students may be overly sensitive to touch and may withdraw from it. Sometimes simply touching his desk or standing nearby may draw his attention to you.

Transitions

Students with attention deficits may have problems with transition times such as entering and leaving class, changing activities within a class, returning from an active class such as P.E. to do seatwork, going to lunch or leaving school, and riding the bus to and from school.

1. **Allow time for transitions** such as putting away books and papers or sharpening pencils.

2. **Segue, or transition, into work:** Help students transition into work by having an activity for them to start as soon as they walk into class. Have a list of vocabulary words from an essay or questions on the overhead projector. As part of the class routine, students know to start on this assignment as soon as they sit down. Occasionally, add some variety by including a fun activity. For example, ask a trivia question or *"What would you do with a million dollars?"* Ask a couple of students to answer.

3. **Model moving quickly** from one activity to another. *"Watch John (the student with ADD) show you how to move quickly from math to science."*

4. **Reinforce compliance,** possibly through a group reward. *"Good, you all moved quickly to get out your books and notebook paper. I'll add 28 points to our total class points—one for each student who did as I asked."*

5. **Group rewards:** Sometimes teachers will set up a point system for the whole class to earn privileges such as extra time for free reading, time to talk quietly with

classmates, having the teacher read to the class from a favorite novel, or a class pizza party. When a certain number of points are earned, students earn a group reward. See Summary 60 for more information on this topic.

- If students move too slowly getting class started, say *"When it is time for class to start, I would like for you to quickly get ready to work. Today the class didn't do that very well. Tomorrow, please come into class ready to work. When you follow this rule for five days, I'll give the class ten minutes of free reading time (or another reward)."*
- Subtract time lost during transitions from group free time: *"You were too slow getting started today so I'm going to subtract late time from your free reading period."* However, try positive strategies before reluctantly turning to negatives.

Scheduling

1. **Schedule challenging work before enjoyable activities.** *"When you finish your vocabulary words, you may have the rest of the time (five to ten minutes) for free-reading."*

2. **Develop an individualized class schedule.** When classes are scheduled prior to each semester, many students with attention deficits will need individualized schedules rather than computer-assigned classes. Consideration should be given to:

   - pairing students with teachers who work well with these teens and
   - modifying class schedules and peak medication times.

3. **Schedule difficult classes during peak medication times.** Peak medication times may range from three up to six hours a day, depending on whether or not medication is in a regular or sustained-release form. (See Summaries 51-55.)

   - Work with school administrators to schedule a difficult class approximately one hour (regular) or one to three hours (sustained-release) after medication is taken. Usually this means **scheduling the class during morning hours** when students are fresh and medication is working. Typically their school work deteriorates later in the day. The IEP may contain recommendations regarding class scheduling. Otherwise, the guidance counselor (class scheduler) should review past grades and ask recent teachers which subjects are most difficult.
   - Schedule hands-on classes such as computers, PE, Art, or other classes the student enjoys later in the day.
   - If students are struggling, **schedule them with former teachers with whom they have been successful.**

4. **Schedule half or partial school days.** Occasionally, if a student is in crisis and can't seem to handle whole days at school without blowing up, schedule him for half days. After problems are resolved and medication is stabilized, phase the student back into full-day scheduling.

Classroom Set-up

Some teachers assign seats to students because they believe it helps maintain better class discipline, makes record keeping and memorizing names easier, meets the students' academic needs, and/or allows placing students near positive role models. If teachers typically assign seats, then they may want to consider the issues below. Try these seating assignments and decide which one works best for each student.

1. **Give the student a choice.** If you don't assign seats for other students and the student with an attention deficit is doing his work, let him select his own seat. Many students with ADD/ADHD don't want to be singled out and are easily embarrassed. Obviously, most don't want to sit in the front row.

2. **Assign a front row seat? Maybe, maybe not.** Sometimes these students are seated in the front row near the teacher's desk to help them pay attention. However, the teacher's desk is often at the center of activity and may provide too many distractions for the student. Instead you may want to try one of the following options.

3. **Seat student two to three rows from the front near one side of the classroom.** If he becomes restless, the student may stand unobtrusively or lean against the wall.

4. **Use other students to provide visual cues.** Clare Jones suggests that distractible students will benefit from watching and taking visual cues from others regarding the activity of the moment. For example, the student can see classmates who are: 1) working on class work, 2) getting ready to do problems on the board, 3) opening their books to page 27, or 4) raising their hands to answer questions.

5. **If these other assignments do not work, assign him a seat near where the teacher provides instruction.** Some students may stay focused if they are seated near the teacher's podium, the overhead projector, or the area where the teacher is most often standing and teaching.

6. **Make a second seat or work station available.** This allows restless students to get up and move to a different table or desk to work on class work or projects.

   - One of the extra workstations may be a stand-up desk. The legs on some desks will extend, allowing the student to stand up and work. Placing a desk on blocks will also accomplish the same purpose.
   - Discuss how the student should move to a different desk (carry everything with you, move quickly, keep your mouth closed). Ask him to model the right way to move.

7. **Seat away from major distractions.** Avoid seating near distractions such as an open door, pencil sharpener, a loud air conditioner, or, for some students, the teacher's desk.

8. **Seating in groups:**

   - Place the student with good role models.
   - If a student misbehaves when placed with friends, work with him so they can be together. Tell him what he must do to earn the privilege of being in the same group with friends. *"When you obey the rules,*

talk softly so I can't hear you, and talk about the required project, then you may all remain in the same group."

- In any group teaching sessions, especially a circle, try seating the student across from you, rather than beside you. It may be easier to maintain eye contact or send a private signal to pay attention. Consider a "U" shaped seating arrangement.

Resources

Abramowitz, A.J., & O'Leary, S. "Behavioral Interventions for the Classroom: Implications for Students with ADHD." *School Psychology Review*, 20 (1991), 220-234.

Dendy, Chris A. Zeigler. *Teenagers with ADD.* Bethesda, MD: Woodbine House, 1995.

Jones, Clare. "Strategies for School Success: Middle School through High School." CHADD Conference presentation, New York, NY, 1998.

Reid, Robert. "Attention Deficit Hyperactivity Disorder: Effective Methods for the Classroom. *Focus on Exceptional Children,* V.32, N.4, December 1999.

Welch, Ann. "Increasing Academic Engagement of Students with ADHD." *ADHD Report,* V.7, N.3, June 1999.

Teaching Strategies That Affect Behavior

How a teacher provides instruction and supervision can help the student:

1. pay attention better,
2. participate in class more,
3. complete more work,
4. minimize behavior problems.

Drawing students into active participation in class, as well as interactions with the teacher, will also reduce misbehavior. Most teachers are already familiar with these strategies, but a brief review with an added ADD/ADHD twist may be helpful. Several of these suggestions are found in Robert Reid's review of best practice for teaching students with attention deficits (Summary 57).

Help Students Learn What You Are Teaching

1. Give assignments that are not too difficult or too long.
2. State your goal or main point clearly.
3. Give step-by-step instructions.
4. Model and demonstrate new skills.
5. Relate information to something in their personal experience.
6. Link to previous lessons.
7. Monitor understanding.
8. Provide corrective feedback.

Get Students to Listen

1. Teach the lesson with enthusiasm.
2. Use a more focused style; be concise.
3. Avoid lengthy lectures.
4. Invite frequent active responses from students rather than just having them sit quietly. (Active response strategies such as *group response* or *response cards* are discussed in Summary 13-A.)
5. Give a cue to listen. For example, the teacher says, *"Give me five."* Then he counts backward so that by the time he reaches one, the class is listening and ready to work.

Let Students Move

Providing students with attention deficits opportunities for movement often gives them a legitimate outlet for their restless energy and helps them pay attention better. Try these ideas with students:

1. **Help the teacher.** Ask the student to pick up homework from students, hand out materials, or straighten up bookshelves.

2. **Deliver messages.** Ask the student to take messages to the office or other teachers. Ann Welch gives an example of the teacher who sent a sealed envelope with this message inside, *"This student needed a movement break. Please thank him, and send him back."*

3. **Take a brief exercise break.** Ask students to stand, hold on to their desks, and stretch or jump. Exercise breaks may work better in middle school or block class scheduling where students are in one class for more than 50 minutes.

Make Expectations Clear

1. **Get the student's attention** before giving directions.

2. **Keep directions short and simple.**

3. **Be specific about what you want students to do**. *Say "Get out your math book and start on the first problem"* rather than *"Your assignment is on the board. Go ahead and start."*

4. **Don't give multi-step directions all at once.** Give two steps, wait for compliance, and then give the last two steps.

5. **Give clear directions.** Use simple language, give examples, or model the behavior.

6. **Give directions three times.** 1) Say directions. 2) Paraphrase them. 3) Give an additional cue by writing it on the board or overhead.

7. **Check for understanding.** If listening to directions seems to be a problem, ask the student to say it back to you or show you he knows what to do. Sometimes knowing whether these students are listening is tricky. They may be doodling and appear not to be listening but when asked can repeat verbatim what the teacher just said.

Avoid Academic Frustration

Students with attention deficits may have difficulty completing class work on their own. Their ability to control their own behavior and direct it toward completing work is often somewhat limited. To reduce the likelihood of misbehavior, teachers should address these issues:

1. **Task Too Long:** When class or homework takes too long to finish, these students will become frustrated and may misbehave. One classroom teacher was surprised

to learn that the homework she assigned was taking students twice as long as she thought it would. To determine whether assignments are too long try the strategy suggested in Summary 24. Or ask the whole class to report how long it takes to complete their homework. Then:

- Shorten assignments. See Summary 13-B.
- Vary activities within the assignment. *("Write definitions for ten vocabulary words and then use each of them in a sentence.")*
- Provide breaks during the school day.

2. **Task Too Difficult:** When class work is too difficult, students become frustrated and are more likely to misbehave. Match the difficulty of assignments to the student's skills.

3. **Difficult Homework:** When homework is too difficult and too long, again, students are more likely to misbehave. See Summary 24.

4. **Multi-step Tasks:** Students with ADD/ADHD often lack the organizational skills to complete work on a multi-step assignment such as a book report or an essay. To help:

- Give the student a job card with directions broken down step-by-step. See Summary 13-B.
- See Summaries 16, 17, 23, and 29 for more suggestions on written expression and organization.

5. **Getting Stuck:** When these students get stuck and do not know what to do next or how to do it, they are usually very impatient and hate waiting.

- Give students assistance cards to display on their desks when they are stuck. Write on one side, "Please help me" and fold it into a triangle so it stands up. On the other side, where the student can see it, write, "Please keep working."
- Acknowledge that the student needs help and that help is coming ASAP. Ask him to skip that problem or question and move on to the next one.
- Designate a nearby student who may be able to help the student with questions.

6. **Needing Feedback:** Students with attention deficits respond better to immediate, frequent feedback. See Summary 60 for a more detailed discussion of effective use of behavioral strategies.

- Self-correcting materials such as answer sheets, folders containing answers, or answer tapes can be helpful. This type of feedback is provided immediately, confirms correct answers, reduces failure, and can increase attention to task.
- Allow students to work together in peer tutoring situations. They can give each other feedback about their performance. See Summary 13-A.
- These students may also tutor students who are at least a couple of years younger. Typically, the tutor learns more than the person receiving tutoring. Tutors will need training in several "how to" areas: giving clear directions, encouraging and praising their students, providing

feedback on correct answers, correcting errors without being negative, and not helping the student too much or too quickly. It may help to review the suggestions in the paragraphs below with the tutor.

My Favorite Teacher-Student Communication Strategies

There are a few strategies that I have found especially effective when teaching students with attention deficits. For these strategies to work, it is important to bear in mind that successful communication will only work if you treat the student with respect. Avoid public embarrassment, sarcasm, and negative put-downs.

1. **Be positive.** Researchers tell us that three to five positive statements should be given for every negative comment. Expect the best of students. An article in *Teaching Exceptional Children* recommends that teachers use words that help build self-esteem. To many students with attention deficit, a teacher's words paint a portrait of the student's soul. (If the teacher says I can do it or that I'm smart, then I must be.) Students will work hard to become what the teacher says they are. Here are some suggested comments:

   "You're working really hard."   "You have the skill it takes to do this."

   "You're doing a great job."   "I can tell you've really got a talent for this sort of thing."

   "You seem very smart to me."   "You've put a lot of effort into this activity."

   "Well done!"   "Now you've got it."

   "You're getting better at this."   "I knew you could do it."

   If a student gives an answer that is incorrect, the teacher might say:

   "Can you think of another way to do (say) this?"
   "Let's go over this again."
   "Let's talk this through." (Talk through the steps. Sometimes hearing themselves talk helps students recognize where the error is.)
   "Read it to me. Does it sound right to you?"
   "Do you think something is wrong here?"

2. **Give students choices, but only two or three.** Give students a limited number of choices for assignments when possible. "You may choose between these two topics for your essay: 1) one of the major characters and how they changed, or 2) what you consider the most important theme of the novel." Remember, too many choices will be confusing and students may spend excessive time simply trying to make a decision. See Summary 38. Researchers tell us that when students are given choices, several good things happen:

   - They produce more work.
   - They are more compliant.
   - They are less aggressive.

3. **Use depersonalization.** Eliminate criticism and blame. Teach the student to cope with his ADD/ADHD behaviors. Describe the problem as one common for many students with this condition. "A lot of teenagers with ADD (ADHD) have trouble . . . (remembering homework, copying summaries). There are a couple of things that might help you. . . (a friend could remind you, I can give your assignments in writing). What would be most helpful to you?"

4. **Give "I" messages.** State how you feel (in private). "I am surprised (disappointed) that you didn't turn in your work. That is not like you. Is there a problem? What is going on?" "You" messages, as opposed to "I" messages, are often negative and blaming and may put the student on the defensive. "You aren't trying. You could do this work if you would just try." These students have experienced so many failures in school that they are very sensitive to the least bit of negative feedback. When they receive negative messages, many will begin to withdraw and shut down emotionally. As a result, they do less school work.

5. **Ask, "Is that a good choice or a bad choice?"** When a student is misbehaving, the teacher may ask "Is that a good choice or a bad choice?" The student gets the message that his behavior is inappropriate without a formal reprimand from the teacher. The student is learning to label and correct his own behavior. See Summary 64 for more information on this strategy, plus additional pro-social strategies for teaching new skills.

Resources

Dendy, Chris A. Zeigler. *Teenagers with ADD.* Bethesda, MD: Woodbine House, 1995.

Dohrn, Elizabeth & Tanis, Bryan. "Attribution Retraining: A Model Program." *Teaching Exceptional Children*, V. 26, N. 4 (1994), 61-63.

Teacher Actions that Escalate or De-escalate Problem Situations

The way a teacher handles a problem situation often determines the outcome. Will a problem situation *escalate* into a full-blown crisis or will the situation *be diffused*? The teacher's behavior often has a *dramatic* effect on the student's behavior. Although not by choice, when a student with an attention deficit is experiencing a crisis, the classroom teacher is often called upon to be a "crisis counselor." Obviously, teachers need to know how their actions affect students.

Actions that Escalate Behavior Problems

A list of behaviors that tend to escalate problem situations is provided below. *Avoid these behaviors*:

- nagging
- lecturing
- arguing
- putting a student down
- assassinating a student's character
- sarcasm

- yelling
- punishing harshly
- getting in the student's face
- slipping into power struggles
- punishing ADD/ADHD behaviors

Parents are more likely than teachers to be driven by frustration and desperation to try to physically control their teenagers. For obvious reasons, physical confrontations between teachers and students are extremely rare at school. Teachers and parents alike should avoid these behaviors:

- physically restraining
- grabbing
- pushing
- hitting
- slapping

Actions that De-escalate or Avoid Potential Crisis Situations

1. **Avoid public embarrassment:** Deal with issues in private. Some of these students will do almost anything to avoid being embarrassed. They may create a scene or cause a confrontation to divert attention away from the fact that they do not know how to do the work or do not know an answer.

2. **Acknowledge the student's feelings:** Respect his feelings. *"I know you're upset. Want to talk about it?"* If time is not available then, consider referring the student to a guidance counselor or talk privately after school. If the crisis is highly emotional, the student may need to talk "now" and not be able to wait until after school.

3. **Use active listening:** When the student is upset, diffuse anger: listen, reflect feelings, be understanding. Don't be judgmental or take sides. One way to acknowledge the student's feelings is through active listening. *"So, why are you angry with Sam? Well, if he went out with your girlfriend, I can understand why you are so upset. My class is waiting on me and I can't talk right now. I can talk with you after school. Can you wait until then or do you need to see the counselor now? Why don't you go talk to Ms. Manis [guidance counselor]. She'll help you figure out what to do."*

4. **Offer sympathy and understanding:** "Something must be wrong. It is unlike you to be so angry."

5. **Lower your voice, stay calm:** When an adult raises his voice, researchers tell us that the student's anger also tends to escalate.

6. **Make statements matter-of-factly:** Keep strong emotions out of your voice but still make your point. *"It is not okay for you to talk back."*

7. **Redirect interests:** With less intense emotional situations, teachers may be able to distract and redirect the student. Rather than ask the student to stop (talking/arguing), suggest an alternative behavior. *"I need your help. Will you carry these books for me?"*

8. **Be non-threatening:** When a student is agitated, give him plenty of space. Don't get in his face, put your hands on him, or use force when discussing the problem.

9. **Ask the student to step out of the room or remove his classmates:** Sometimes, the teacher may ask the student to step out into the hall to talk. The student may calm down, return to class, or be sent to the guidance office. However, if a student is totally out of control and there are safety concerns, the teacher may take all her students out of the class, leaving the student behind. This action removes the student's audience and may help him calm down more quickly. The teacher may call the office or send a student to ask for assistance and take the students outside or to the library. Then the teacher or another administrator can go back into the classroom to talk more calmly with the student.

10. **Teach anger management:** Teach the student the skills he needs to cope with anger and frustration. See Summary 69. However, don't expect miracles overnight. A student with an attention deficit often knows what to do but in the emotion of the moment may explode. If accommodations are in place at school and anger is still a continuing problem for this student, parents should talk with their doctor to see if medication may help.

11. **Develop a prearranged crisis plan:** For example, if teachers know that the student has occasional crises, give him permission in advance to go to the guidance counselor's office anytime he feels he needs to go. No questions asked. One teacher places a laminated permission card on his desk that the student can get and imme-

diately go to the counselor's office. This action helps teach the student: 1) to recognize when he is about to blow-up emotionally and 2) to take steps to avoid the crisis. Discuss alternative actions that the student may take if he feel a crisis brewing. The student may also request a referral to "peer mediation." Identify the issues that trigger crises and develop a list of alternatives to avoid them.

12. **Offer peer mediation**: In this program, a group of students meet to problem-solve and come up with a solution. Because of concerns regarding escalating violence, many schools have established formal peer mediation programs. Students may ask for and attend a session within the same day. Teachers may also refer students. See Summary 67 for more information on peer mediation.

13. **Prevent reoccurrence:** After the crisis, the teacher and student will develop a plan to prevent reoccurrence of the problem. Identify antecedent or "trigger" behavior and intervention strategies.

The Explosive Student

Occasionally teachers encounter an explosive student, who may or may not have ADD or ADHD. In his book, *The Explosive Child*, Dr. Ross Green, a child psychologist, offers insights regarding explosive, inflexible students. These students may feel a flash of anger almost before they realize what has happened. During a crisis, they are often not in a coherent frame of mind and do not think or act rationally. They need time to cool down and return to a rational state. When an (inflexible) teacher has a direct confrontation with an (inflexible) teenager in this state, it is a formula for a major blow-up. Dr. Green explains these blow-ups with this formula:

$$\text{INFLEXIBLE STUDENT} + \text{INFLEXIBLE TEACHER} = \text{MELTDOWN}$$

Sherry Pruitt, M.Ed., author of *Taming the Tiger*, coined the term "Tourette storm" to describe this neurological loss of control when it happens to students who have ADHD plus Tourette syndrome. The student's ability to access abstract knowledge is impaired so he is unable to understand the impact of his actions or the probable consequences. Pruitt explains that trying to talk with the student or touch him during this storm may lead to an even more violent outburst. Sometimes, students awaken from this storm with no memory of what has just happened. The student may be as surprised and bewildered as everyone else, and be horribly embarrassed to have been totally out of control.

It is so important for teachers to "know" their students and which ones are likely to have this explosive element to their personalities. **Direct confrontation is _not_ the best strategy** to use with these students. The strategies discussed in Summaries 60 and 62 will be more effective. The old adage of "pick and choose" your battles is critical with these students. Dr. Green classifies the severity of behaviors into three categories or "baskets." The behaviors that qualify for "Basket A" are nonnegotiable and require immediate confrontation or negotiation. Behaviors related to safety or illegal activity would fall into this category.

Even treatment professionals in residential facilities for young people with serious emotional problems are taught to avoid using direct confrontation or force with explosive youngsters. In fact, the non-confrontational conflict resolution strategies suggested under "Threatening to Fight" (Summary 62) were recommended by staff at an inpatient hospital.

Resources

Dendy, Chris A. Zeigler. *Teenagers with ADD: A Parents' Guide.* Bethesda, MD: Woodbine House, 1995.

Dornbush, Marilyn & Sheryl K. Pruitt. *Teaching the Tiger.* Duarte, CA: Hope Press, 1996.

Green, Ross W. *The Explosive Child.* New York: HarperCollins, 1998.

Phelan, Thomas W. *Surviving Your Adolescents.* Glen Ellyn, IL: Child Management, Inc., 1991. Dr. Phelan offers practical suggestions for dealing with adolescents and guidance for picking and choosing your battles.

Behavioral strategies are extremely important in teaching academics and in helping maintain order in the classroom. Basically, these strategies involve common-sense use of psychology. Teachers know that there are certain ways of talking with students that are usually more effective in motivating them to comply with rules, complete homework, and reduce the likelihood of emotional blow-ups. To get maximum effort and compliance from challenging students with ADD/ADHD, teachers must be skilled in using behavioral strategies.

Teachers often discover what parents have known for years: *behavioral techniques do not work as effectively with students with ADD or ADHD.* Dr. Russell Barkley and other experts explain that it is much more difficult for students with attention deficit disorders to learn from the consequences of past misbehavior and change their behavior. Since these students don't always learn from punishment and rewards like other students, they may repeat the misbehavior even though they have been punished. As an educator, school psychologist, and parent I was often puzzled and frustrated by this problem with my own sons. Often, the teenagers themselves find their own behavior puzzling. To my surprise, my son once apologized for his misbehavior by saying, "I'm sorry, Mom, but when you punish me it just doesn't seem to work."

Tips on Using Behavioral Strategies

The rules for using behavioral strategies are somewhat different for students with attention deficits. Dr. Russell Barkley, one of the leading international researchers on attention deficit disorders, gives the following tips for guiding students:

1. **Provide feedback immediately.** Feedback must be clear, specific, and occur soon after the behavior occurs.

2. **Provide feedback more often.** To be effective, positive feedback must be given more often than for students who do not have ADD or ADHD.

3. **Use strong, meaningful rewards and consequences.** Stronger reinforcers work better than just a verbal "good job." Try giving the student a pat on the back, tokens, points, food, privileges, or coupons to drop a low grade or skip a homework assignment.

4. **Provide positive feedback before negatives.** Punishment alone is not effective with these students. "Catch the teenager being good." When trying to help a student change inappropriate behavior, watch for good behavior and praise it immediately. Avoid making negative comments in hopes of stopping misbehavior. In-

stead of saying, "Stop talking," catch him working and say "Mark, I noticed that you came into class and started working right away."

5. **Be as consistent as possible.**

6. **Teach skills.** Barkley suggests teaching a student the specific skills he needs in the setting, or at the *point of performance,* where he actually must use the skills. For example, work on remembering to take home the right books and assignments by meeting the student after school when he must decide which books to take home. Simply telling the student to remember assignments, sending him to an organizational class, or punishing him will be ineffective.

7. **Anticipate problem situations and transitions** such as the presence of a substitute teacher or going to lunch or PE. Develop a plan for coping with the teenager.

8. **Keep a disability perspective.** ADD or ADHD *may* be a disability for some teenagers. Sometimes it is difficult to remember that the behaviors that frustrate us as teachers and parents are often caused by the disability.

9. **Practice forgiveness.** It is important to forgive students for causing problems that are often beyond their ability to fully control. And also to forgive *ourselves*, because as Dr. Barkley points out, teenagers with attention deficit disorders have the misfortune of sometimes bringing out the worst in us as adults.

Of course, as I say throughout this book, having ADD or ADHD is *not* an excuse for misbehavior, but it does provide an explanation for why these teenagers sometimes act as they do. Teachers may find these students more responsive when ***consequences are instructive, not just punitive!*** Teach the student the desired skills! Don't just punish the student for his disability. See Summary 61 for general suggestions for teaching new skills.

A Few Miscellaneous Thoughts

Use Praise Carefully

Interestingly enough, praise doesn't seem to motivate some students with ADD/ADHD. Teenagers seem to recognize when praise seems forced, phony, or over-inflated. Or they may feel insulted for being praised for a skill that they believe they should have already mastered. Lyndon Waugh, M.D., psychiatrist and author of *Tired of Yelling*, makes a good point: the teenager may see praise as another tool that adults use to *judge him* and decide whether or not he measures up. Teenagers also may dislike the feeling that they are being manipulated by praise. ***Praise should be brief and sincere. "Nice job."*** Sometimes a smile, a pat on the back, or a "thumbs up" sign are the most effective strategies. Get to know your students and what works best for them.

Point Systems or Token Economies

On paper, point systems sound wonderful, but in the average classroom they are a bear to manage. These systems require a lot of time and consistency to run effectively.

A Review of Behavioral Strategies - *Related summaries are noted by (S-#)*

Ignore minor misbehavior	"Catch him being good": and reward good behavior.
Use positive reinforcement	It should be immediate, consistent, and given more frequently for students with an attention deficit.
Provide more positives than negatives	Balance each negative interaction with 3-5 positives. The positives may include a smile or nod, a pat on the shoulder, or walking by his desk and writing a comment or check on his paper. See S-58 for more examples.
Use stronger rewards and consequences	They don't respond well to weak rewards. Consider material rewards, such as a coupon to drop the lowest grade, a reward provided by a parent, or a class pizza party.
Praise the part of the job that is done well	If the student starts his work but is daydreaming and hasn't finished it, say," *You completed the first ten problems. That's great! Now let's look at problem eleven.*"
Make consequences instructive, not just punitive	Punishment alone is usually ineffective. Students with attention deficits don't learn from rewards and punishment as easily as other students. Consequently, they may repeat the same misbehavior. Don't just tell the student what he did wrong. Teach him the desired behvior. For example, if the student continually forgets assignments and books, have someone meet him at the locker to get the right materials. See Summaries 29 and 61.
Teach desired behavior: shape behavior; start at the student's present level	Inappropriate behavior cannot be changed overnight. Reinforce each small improvement in behavior; start where the student is, teach him desired behavior; praise improvement. (S-28 and 61)
Use consequences and punishment wisely	Should be immediate, consistent, brief, and reasonable; not too harsh, not too restrictive; comment on the behavior, not the teen; avoid character assassinations. When punishment is used, it should be reasonable and done in conjunction with an incentive program. Typically, incentive programs are set up to allow the student to earn a reward or privileges by doing the desired behavior or task.
Avoid harsh punishment	Conflict will escalate when punishment is too harsh. Students may focus on getting even rather than learning from consequence.
Repeat consequences	Avoid escalating to harsher consequences. Repeating the same consequences is okay. Students will learn eventually.
Try grandma's rule: "The Premack Principle"	First we work and then we play. "*When you finish your outline, you may draw your family coat of arms for the report cover.*"
Use logical consequences	Where possible, make consequences the natural result of misbehavior, not an unrelated punishment. "*You didn't finish your class work. Please finish it at home tonight (or come by after school and finish it) and turn it in tomorrow.*" Avoid punishment and power struggles. The use of logical consequences are often delayed too long to be effective. See discussion in Chapter 5, TEENAGERS WITH ADD.
Provide more supervision	Teens with an attention deficit require more supervision than other students at a time when most educators are reducing the amount of supervision given.
Two favorite strategies:	
If you can't change the teen's ADD/ADHD behavior, change the environment	Even with medication, some symptoms of ADD/ADHD (disorganization, forgetfulness, and an impaired sense of time) may not improve. If all else fails and the student continues to forget homework, send, fax, or e-mail assignments home in writing. Work on the most important goal first, passing his classes. Develop a plan to help the student remember assignments as described in S-61.
Identify antecedent "trigger" behavior: develop a plan	Play detective. What triggered the misbehavior? If a teen acts out when a substitute teacher is present, then teach the student to cope with this change, prepare the substitute, place him with a former special education teacher for that period, or have a classroom aide present in the room.

Rewards must be changed every couple of weeks since they quickly lose their effectiveness. In addition, researchers tell us that students with an attention deficit aren't as easily motivated by rewards and punishment as their peers. Many teenagers who have this condition are tired of "behavior modification" since they have been on behavioral charts much of their lives. In fact, in answering an open-ended sentence completion, one teenager said, "All my life . . . 'I've been on stars and charts . . . and it feels like 'kibbles and bits'."

In spite of their drawbacks, point systems can be very effective under certain conditions. For example, if teachers are fortunate enough to have adequate manpower from a university program or special grant, these programs can be incredibly effective. Dr. Bill Pelham, University of Pittsburgh, has a wonderful model summer program that includes an intensive behavior modification component. This program was expanded to a year-round day-treatment program by Dr. Jim Swanson, UCLA-Irvine, at their NIMH multi-site study of ADD/ADHD. However, when teachers use a point system in a classroom without added support, it will be easier to implement the program if they keep it simple and low maintenance. Some educators say these programs may be easier to implement in middle schools than in high schools.

Group Rewards

Group rewards involve a degree of peer pressure that may be helpful. Sometimes teachers will set up a point system for the whole class to earn privileges. When the class as a whole earns a certain number of points, all of the students earn a group reward. The teacher may place marbles in a jar when certain tasks are done well. For example, a class of twenty-four students may earn twenty-four marbles each time all students come into class and quietly start working, turn in homework, or talk quietly in the lunchroom or on the roundtrip to the cafeteria. The program may be varied by using an "all or nothing" rule. In other words, all the students have to complete their homework or no points are earned by the class.

Allow students to generate a list of ten to twenty possible rewards. For example, group rewards may include activities such as 15 minutes listening to a radio, a popcorn break, no homework for one night, 15 minutes for free reading, talking quietly with classmates, having the teacher read to the class from a favorite novel, 15 minutes in the library, add 5 points to a daily grade, or 15 minutes free time. Individual rewards might be 15 minutes on the computer, first in line to lunch, helping in the office, choosing a new seat for one day, being the errand runner for one day, raising or lowering the flag, making school announcements over the intercom, 15 minutes in the art center, or as a larger reward, a class pizza party. In *ADHD Project Facilitate: ADHD Interventions*, Raymond Elliot and Lou Ann Worthington suggest listing rewards on cards and letting students draw a "Take-A-Chance Card."

Depending on the behavior the teacher wants to improve, she might also motivate students by saying,

- "When all of you complete your assignment for today, you can have ten minutes to talk quietly."

- "If you complete tonight's math homework and make at least 90 percent on it, you will receive five bonus points on the test Friday."
- "If you make a 100 percent on three spelling tests in a row, you may skip the fourth test."
- "When the whole class goes all day with less than five check marks for inappropriate behavior, you may have ten minutes free time."

Contracts

An agreement may be written up between the teacher and student regarding problem behaviors. The contract should describe how the student will act differently and what he will earn in return. For example, the student might sign a contract indicating that he agrees to complete his homework, and that for each five days he does his work, he will earn a reward (points added to a final grade or points toward skipping a homework assignment). However, signing a contract to change ADD/ADHD behaviors is no guarantee that the problem will stop. Other prompting strategies to help with forgetfulness and disorganization may offer better solutions. See Appendix A9 for a sample contract.

Peer Mediated Reinforcement

As we all know, some students continue to misbehave because they receive positive reinforcement from their classmates, such as laughter at their antics. Although reinforcement from the teacher is important, many students value peer approval much more. So, one way to tackle this problem is to teach the other students how to respond to misbehavior so that no one is reinforced for misbehaving.

Dr. Ann Abramowitz of Emory University is a well-known researcher on the use of behavioral strategies for students with ADD/ADHD. She explains how peer mediated reinforcement can be used for a student who is a continual disruption in class. However, simpler strategies should be tried first. In addition, some thought should be given as to how to use the approach without humiliating the student. Remember to avoid sarcasm.

1. The teacher explains to the class that *"it is easier for some students to concentrate and do their work. Some students want to do well but it is much harder for them."*
2. *"Perhaps you've noticed that sometimes it is hard for Charles to keep working on his assignments and he may start talking to everyone around him or do something to make us all laugh. He wants to do his work and not disrupt class and we can help him."* (The teacher has already talked with Charles in advance before she has this conversation with the class.)
3. *"It is important for you to be responsible and continue your work. Let's try to ignore Charles when he talks at the wrong times and don't laugh at the things he does."*
4. *"Charles can earn a reward for doing his work and not disrupting class. In fact, the whole class can also earn a reward if you ignore him when he talks to you at the wrong time, tap your paper as a reminder for him to work, and avoid laughing at him."*

6

Avoid Humiliation

Clare Jones, author of *ADD: Strategies for School-Age Children*, is fond of saying, ***"Humiliation is not a behavior management strategy!"*** So, teachers should be sensitive to whether or not the point system or peer mediated reinforcement helps the student learn something positive. For example, if the work is too difficult and the student with ADD/ADHD can't complete it, he may prevent the whole class from getting a reward. Then many of the other students may direct their anger and frustration at this student, further adding to his feelings of failure and frustration.

Resources

Abramowitz, A.J., & O'Leary, S. "Behavioral Interventions for the Classroom: Implications for Students with ADHD." *School Psychology Review*, 20 (1991), 220-234.

Barkley, Russell A. Adapted from "Eight Principles to Guide ADHD Children." *ADHD Reports*, V. 1, N. 2, April, 1993.

Dendy, Chris A. Zeigler. *Teenagers with ADD*. Bethesda, MD: Woodbine House, 1995.

6

"Shaping" Behavior
(Successive Approximation)

Students with ADD/ADHD are more likely than their peers to arrive in middle or high school without the skills they need to succeed in school. Teachers can sometimes use an effective behavior management technique called successive approximation to "shape" the behavior they would like to see. This technique involves praising effort and completion of a job that comes close to meeting expectations.

Steps in Shaping Behavior

1. **Start at the student's present level of functioning** rather than the skill level where adults think he should be! In other words, start "where the student is."
2. **Break the skills down into small steps,** usually three to five segments, leading toward the desired skill.
3. **Begin teaching the new skills.** This will not be an easy task and will require frequent repetition and great patience.
4. **Learn to recognize improvement and acknowledge** the mastery of each small step and the student's overall progress toward the final goal.

Teachers have used this strategy for years as they teach their specific subject content. For example, a Language Arts teacher breaks the process of writing an essay into smaller steps and begins teaching the student to brainstorm ideas and finally to write the introductory, middle, and closing paragraphs.

Most of the time teachers apply this technique to academic content but they may also use it to help shape classroom behaviors, such as listening in class, completing homework, or remembering to take books home. Several intervention strategies are included in Summaries 13-A to 13-E and 23 that may help with common problems. If the behavior is not too complex, the teacher may simply pick one or several of these strategies to help change behavior.

Shaping a Relatively Simple Behavior

Here is an example of how a teacher might try to shape the behavior of a student who blurts out in class, talks to others, and doesn't listen to the teacher:

The teacher starts out by counting the number of times this problem behavior occurs during one class. It's important to know how many times the student is having this problem now, so the teacher will know when the student actually improves. Next the

6

teacher talks with the student privately about his problems listening to the teacher. He may say something like this:

> *"Many students with ADHD have trouble listening in class. Without meaning to, they may blurt out answers or talk with other students when they should be listening to the teacher. I know these students really want to listen but it is very hard for them. Sometimes this seems to be a problem for you too (or Does this seem to be a problem for you too?). Do you have any suggestions for how I can help you listen?* (Get input.) *Here are some things we can try. I think you can teach yourself to do this with something called self-monitoring. First, we can move you closer to where I stand when I teach (and away from your talking buddy, Mary Katherine). Then we can try these things to help remind you to listen."*

The teacher may state the behavior in terms of the positive (what I want you to do) and negative (what I want you to stop). Here are the expected steps for shaping the desired behavior of listening:

1. **Sits quietly** (without blurting out or talking to a friend; however, he may not even be listening).
2. **Sits quietly and looks at teacher** (no blurting or talking).
3. **Sits quietly, looks at the teacher, raises his hand** (waits to be called upon) (no blurting or talking).
4. **Sits quietly, looks at the teacher, listens, raises his hand, and answers a question** (no blurting or talking).

The teacher or an aide may mark when and how often these behaviors occur during a one-hour class. For every five minutes the student is not blurting or talking, he earns points. When the student earns a certain number of checks or points for each five minutes he goes without talking to a friend or blurting out, he can earn a privilege of his choice—for example, a visit to the library, a pass to skip one night's homework, or bonus points on his grade. Sometimes the simple process of counting the behavior and getting feedback is intriguing enough to a student that that is enough to motivate him. He may not really care about a reward.

The teacher reviews the report with the student at the end of class. To be effective, feedback must be immediate, as explained in Summary 60. As an alternative, the student may come back after school to look at his results today compared with preceding days. Graph his improvement.

"Okay, you've already mastered steps one and two, now let's move to step three. Let me show you how to rate your own behavior. Here is a chart and here is how you mark it." Eventually, the student should learn to monitor his own behavior. (See Summary 64 on self-monitoring.) And over time, the rating of behavior will be completely phased out.

Shaping a More Complex Behavior

Sometimes behaviors are more complex or involve key executive function skills such as organization and forgetfulness. These skills may show limited improvement on medication, but quickly decline when medication wears off. Students with attention deficits often need help learning to compensate and cope with these executive function deficits. These complex skills must be broken down into several steps before a student's behavior can be shaped. For example, completing homework is a fairly complex skill that, when lacking, often results in school failure for these students. An example of how to shape these critical behaviors is provided below.

Shaping Homework Completion:

Goal: To complete homework assignments independently including knowing correct assignments and having the right books.

Start at the student's present level, and move from Point A to Point B by mastering one step at a time. Try to figure out which step represents the student's current level of functioning. For example, if he says he wants to write down assignments (step 2) but often forgets, let him select one of two options. Perhaps he and the teacher can ask his friend David if he will check to see that the assignment is written down. The objective is to move the student toward accepting increased responsibility for completion of his school work. Avoid extensive monitoring and interventions unless he is struggling or in danger of failing a class. Possible strategies to help achieve the goal are bulleted below.

I. Knowing Assignments and Having Correct Books

A. Beginning Point: *Doesn't know assignments or bring books home.*

1. Forgets to write down homework assignments almost every day; when parents ask, he says no homework was given or that it was done at school.
2. Says he wants to write down assignments but doesn't remember to do it.
   - Teacher writes down assignments weekly.
   - Another student double checks or writes assignments.
   - Row captains check assignments for all students.
   - Student keeps extra book(s) at home.
3. Writes down assignments occasionally.
   - Parents review homework assignments.
   - When student forgets books or assignments, parents take or send him back to school.
   - Student calls classmates to get assignments or borrow a book.
4. Remembers assignments and books most of the time.
   - Calls a friend from home if needed.
5. Writes down assignments; brings home the right books.
   - Parents don't need to monitor.

B. Target Behavior Achieved: *Student knows assignments and brings books home.*

II. Completing Homework (Tips for Parents)

A. Beginning Point: *No homework done.*

1. Parents get the student started on homework by talking through the assignment; clarify what must be done; help select work to do first, and supervise him the whole time, perhaps by actually being in the room.
   - If assignments are difficult, consider asking the student to take medication at four or five in the afternoon to help him concentrate and complete his work. See medication discussion in Summaries 52-55.

2. Parents get him started, monitor, and check completed work.
   - Drop in his room frequently; if needed, prompt him to refocus on his work.
   - Parents reward the student when he begins completing homework more independently. *"Once I remind you to get started, if you can finish your work on your own, you can study in your room. However, if you don't finish it in a reasonable period of time, you will have to work in the kitchen."*

3. Parents remind student to start; drop in and prompt only once or twice; check completed work.

4. Parents set a timer; student starts by himself; parents check completed work.
   - If he doesn't start on his own, parents prompt him after 15 minutes.

5. Student sets a timer, starts and finishes homework by himself; parents check completed work.

6. No monitoring is needed from the parents.

B. Target Behavior Achieved: *The student completes homework independently!*

In summary, both **ADD and ADHD present a lifelong challenge.** So it is not unusual for these students to require limited "coaching" all their lives. In truth, some of these skills may never be mastered totally. Adults with attention deficits must learn to compensate or rely on a coach (spouse, administrative assistant, or supervisor) to help them cope with similar deficits in the adult work world. See Summary 65 on coaching.

6

Tips for Avoiding Confrontations

Because of the inattention, impulsivity, and low frustration tolerance often associated with attention deficit disorder, teachers may sometimes find themselves in conflict with these students. *Rehearsing alternative strategies in advance* may help teachers handle the situation effectively and perhaps avoid an unnecessary escalation of the problem. Additional suggestions are provided in Summaries 64-69 to teach students the skills they need to handle their anger and conflicts more appropriately.

Situations That May Trigger Emotional Blow-ups

1. The reappearance of inattention, impulsivity, and irritability when the medication wears off mid-morning or afternoon;
2. having an emotional blow-up at home with parents before coming to school;
3. failing a test or class;
4. breaking up with a girlfriend or boyfriend;
5. not getting restful sleep the night before school;
6. not being on the "right" medication.

Interventions for Common Classroom Behaviors

Several intervention strategies are suggested for common behaviors that can be difficult to deal with in the classroom. References to other summaries are noted by (S-#).

Teachers should be cautious, however, in trying to eliminate all ADD/ADHD behaviors. Some of these behaviors may actually serve a useful purpose. Researchers are beginning to take a second look at some of their seemingly purposeless behaviors. For example, Dr. Sydney Zentall believes that fidgeting or doodling may serve a purpose to help the student learn. This physical activity seems to help the student maintain a higher level of mental alertness so that he can listen to the teacher or work on an assignment. Daydreaming may also be a time for creative thinking.

If a student's anger escalates to the point that he is losing control, a major Behavioral Intervention Plan (BIP) should be developed. Functional Behavior Assessments and BIPs are discussed in Summary 63.

1. Learning problems must be identified.
2. Assignments should be adjusted so they are not too long or too hard.

3. Accommodations must be provided in the classroom.
4. In addition, parents should ask for a consultation from the teenager's counselor or physician. Since aggression often masks depression, additional medication to treat the depression and irritability may be needed.
5. According to federal IDEA guidelines: (See Summary 40)
   - Conduct a Functional Behavioral Assessment and identify antecedent or "trigger" events that cause the behaviors.
   - Develop a Behavioral Intervention Plan.

Several veteran Gwinnett County (Georgia) educators met with me to identify key problems areas and identify effective interventions for this summary: Dr. Claudia Dickerson, Claudia Jordan, Candy Steventon, Jane Moser, Richard Wetzel, and Dr. Dale Carter.

Behavior	Intervention
Irritating behavior (Fidgety behavior, tapping a pencil or foot; forgetful; inattentive; daydreams; wears a hat in class)	Discuss behavior in private. Teach quiet tapping. If behavior is bothersome, find an acceptable alternative. Allow student to play with paper clips or doodle if it helps him concentrate and he can still listen or complete the work. Develop a private signal to remind the student to pay attention or stop fidgeting. (Pull on your ear.) Allow the student to earn the right to daydream for 5-10 minutes by first completing his assignment. Ignore or use one-word cues. "Hats!" ["Gum!"], said with a smile. This one word is used as a reminder to remove hats/gum in class.
Late to class	Ignore it if only one or two minutes late and if it occurs rarely. A raised eyebrow or statement of expectations may be more effective than sending the student to the office. "This is the first time you've been late. I expect you to be on time from now on." Ask, "Why are you late?" There may be a good reason. Review the student's routine between classes. He may be going to the locker too often. Help the student develop a better routine between classes. (S-46)
Late to school (Sleep disturbances and an impaired sense of time may contribute to tardiness)	Suggesting changes in routine may help: e.g., shower the night before, put books by the door. Suggest that the family talk with their physician about the possibility of a sleep disturbance plus treatment options. (S-46)
Avoiding school work (not completing or turning in homework)	Sometimes unexpected sympathy or respect will evoke a positive response. "Maybe you can help me understand some things. I think you really would like to do well in school. Yet, you seem to be avoiding your school work. So I assume you must have a good reason. Tell me what you think the reason is. (Listen.) Here's what I think might be happening...."
	Involve the teenager in the problem-solving process. "How can we solve the problem of ....?" Identify any learning problems described in S-11. Make classroom accommodations, e.g., reduce the amount of work, allow use of a calculator, as described in S-13-16 and 44-45.

Behavior	Intervention
Forgetting detention (or to stay after school)	If the student is willing, remind him, e.g., send a note to the last teacher, have a friend remind him. Have him set his wrist alarm. If the student forgets, assign a make-up time for detention and implement a plan to prevent future problems.
Not telling the truth (speaking impulsively; fear of punishment or failure)	If the student doesn't tell the truth about homework or academic issues, the work may be too difficult or too long. Adjust the amount and type of homework. (S-24) Identify learning problems. Make classroom accommodations. (S-42, 44, 45) Don't ask a question if you know the answer. Make a statement: "You hit Robert first." If a question is asked, the student may not be able to resist impulsively "showing off" or making a smart comment.
Taking things (acts impulsively; acts on a dare; doesn't think of consequences; intrusive; fails to identify boundaries of possessions and space)	Teach the student to ask to borrow an object rather than take it without permission. Deal with the student privately rather than publicly. Identify the type of items being taken and give the student an opportunity to earn the object. Ask parents to provide reinforcers. Structure time and the environment so he has less opportunity to take things. Monitor the student; don't let him stand at the end of the line unsupervised. If he forgets something and must return to the class, send someone with him.
Irritability (snaps at teachers, sarcastic)	Ignore minor things. Check medication (timing). Teachers and parents may find that the irritability is a reaction to medication wearing off. (S-52) Ask parents to talk with the doctor about the timing of medication; may take it more frequently or switch to a sustained-release.
Arguing/talking back (impulsively talking back without thinking of consequences)	Ignore minor mutterings, especially if the student is complying with teacher request all the while he is stating his disagreement. Don't argue with the student. It takes two to argue. Seldom is a teenager argued into submission. Anticipate when a student may challenge authority (a substitute teacher is present) and change the environment (train him to help the substitute, send to a former special education teacher for one period, or add a classroom aide).
Name calling (calls a student or teacher a name)	Consider ignoring an isolated event or muttering under his breath. State expectations: "It is not acceptable to talk (to a teacher) that way." Use active listening. "You seem upset. Do you need to go talk with the guidance counselor?" Refer to peer mediation to resolve disputes such as arguments, name calling, or fights between two students. (S-67) If done in front of class, say, "Let's step out in the hall ." Then talk privately. "What is wrong? This is unlike you to act this way." Give the student the opportunity to apologize in writing or verbally.
Easily frustrated (blows up, hits locker or wall, cries)	Keep your voice low and stay calm. If your anger escalates, the student's will also. Use active listening skills. Acknowledge his feelings: "I know you're upset. Want to talk about it?" or "Looks like you've had a lousy day. Want to talk about it?" Identify the source of frustration and intervene to prevent future reoccurrence.

Section 6 | Classroom Management and Challenging Behaviors

Behavior	Intervention
Angry outbursts (yells, screams, curses, throws books)	Identify what crisis has triggered the anger: failing a test, breaking up with a girlfriend, someone calling him a name. Giving unexpected sympathy or respect may be effective. "Something must be wrong. This is unlike you to be so angry. Do you want to talk about it?" Isolate the student and give him time to cool off. "Let's step outside in the hall." Or, "Let's walk to the guidance office together." If this is common, have a prearranged crisis plan. Give the student a pass to go to the guidance office when in crisis. He may go there and talk until he has calmed down or simply sit and calm down. (S-59) Designate a place in advance where he can sit and let off steam, e.g., the office of the guidance counselor, assistant principal, special education teacher, or coach. Help the student learn to recognize and cope with his own potential blow-ups. Work with parents to develop a strategy to help the teen cope with his anger. Have the student participate in anger management and peer mediation training. (S-66, 67, 69)
Threatening to fight (Student is yelling at another student; problem is escalating; threatening to fight)	Be non-threatening. Give physical space. Don't touch or shake your finger at students. Talk matter-of-factly. Keep your voice and actions neutral, devoid of emotion. Move to a position that is actually below eye level with the student, so the student looks down at the teacher. This often helps de-escalate an angry situation. To both students, state the behavior and why it is inappropriate. "Fighting will not be tolerated. We cannot allow you to hurt yourself or anyone else." If possible, separate the students. "Let's step out in the hall for a minute." Privately urge him to stop and think. "Don't fight with him. He's not worth getting suspended from school." State a positive consequence: "If you break this up now, you can go back to class or talk with the guidance counselor. . . . and a negative consequence: "However, if this continues, I will have to send you to the office." Or in a more serious situation: "However, if you don't put down the knife, I will have to call the police." (Ultimately school policy will probably require suspension or expulsion.) Give the student time to make a decision and save face, for 30-60 seconds. If he complies, he goes back to class or the guidance office. Otherwise, enforce the consequence. Send the student to the office. Or if necessary, call the office for help. If a teacher has time, walking the student to the office sometimes help diffuse the crisis. Use peer mediation to prevent fights. Trained students help others resolve their differences and agree upon a compromise. "If you break it up now, we can help you resolve your differences through peer mediation."
Fighting	Make brief commands. Keep your voice calm. "Stop now!" Make a statement in private that helps "save face." "He really isn't worth a suspension, is he?" Send for help. At least two adults are needed to break up a fight. Keep others back until help arrives. If the student is suspended but agrees to participate in peer mediation, consider letting him return early from a school suspension.

6

SUMMARY 63

Functional Behavior Assessment and Behavior Intervention Plans

When a student has shown a pattern of several disruptive incidents at school, especially if they place the student at-risk of a school suspension, the Student Support Team (SST) or IEP Team should meet to discuss strategies to prevent future reoccurrence. Since the team needs good information to develop an effective intervention strategy, a Functional Behavior Assessment (FBA) is often done before a Behavior Intervention Plan (BIP) is developed. Now that IDEA mandates early intervention using positive behavioral strategies, some school systems have developed guidelines for this process.

Functional Behavior Assessment (FBA)

Typically a good FBA will address several key issues:

- behavior
- context
- antecedent or "trigger"
- contributing factors
- function of behavior

- teacher response
- student reaction
- continuation of behavior
- potential rewards
- previous interventions

Teachers may find it helpful for planning purposes to have a list of behaviors that commonly occur in several of these FBA categories. A list was complied from information developed by the Gwinnett County (Georgia) School System, Chicago Public Schools, Walker County (Georgia) School System, and Joan Helbing, ADD Consultant, Appleton Area Schools in Wisconsin. See Appendix B5.

One Student's Misbehavior

Let's look at the information that was collected and analyzed during the course of a FBA for Ryan, a ninth-grade student who got into trouble for talking back, arguing, and using profanity in class.

1. **Behavior:** What is the behavior of concern?

   - Talking back, arguing, and using profanity; not complying with the teacher's request to write a math problem on the board.

2. **Context:** Where and when (class and time) did the problem occur? Who was involved?

   - Math class; 3rd period; 11:30; Mrs. Jones.

3. **Antecedent or "trigger":** What happened just prior to the problem that may have triggered it? If teachers can figure out what triggered the problem, they may be able to develop an effective solution.

6

- The teacher asked Ryan to write a math word problem on the board that had been assigned for homework the night before.

4. **Contributing factors:** What is going on in the student's world that may affect his behavior? Medication issues are often a contributing factor in behavior problems.

   - Ryan took his medication (regular Ritalin) at 6:30 a.m. So, by 9:30 that morning all his medication had worn off. He was not due another tablet until 12:30. (Or perhaps he forgot his medicine this morning. Or his medication dose may be too low.)
   - He played a basketball game last night and did not complete his homework.
   - Ryan is a poor math student and has always struggled in math class.
   - He was upset when he came to school this morning. He had an argument with his mother before leaving for school because he did not clean up his room last night when she told him to do it. By confronting her son just as he was leaving for school, the mother inadvertently sent her son to school in an angry, agitated state with no safe way to resolve their conflict.

   In other words, a combination of factors contributed to Ryan's confrontation with his teacher.

5. **Function of behavior:** What seems to be the purpose or reason for the behavior? Inappropriate behavior usually serves one of two functions: 1) to obtain something or 2) to escape something. Sometimes, however, because these students may act impulsively, they do not always have a clear reason for their behavior. It may be as simple as; *"I thought it, so I did it."*

   - Ryan did not know how to do the math problem and did not want to be embarrassed. By creating a diversion, the arguing and talking back, he was able to avoid having everyone know he could not work the problem. (Teenagers with ADD or ADHD are especially sensitive and will do almost anything to avoid being embarrassed and "losing face" in front of classmates. So, a student who doesn't understand how to do a math problem may misbehave to avoid looking dumb in front of his peers.)

6. **Teacher response and student reaction:** What did the teacher do? Her response serves as a consequence that may either escalate or de-escalate the situation. What did the student do after the teacher responded?

   Ryan: Initially he tried to explain that he had forgotten to do his homework, plus had a basketball game last night.

   Teacher: The teacher inadvertently escalated the problem situation by forcing the issue and using sarcasm. *"Ryan, stop making excuses. I said go to the board now and do the problem. If you're too lazy to do your homework, that's your problem."*

   Ryan: After the teacher forced the issue and used sarcasm, Ryan talked back and argued more.

Teacher: The teacher put him down and embarrassed him even further in front of his peers by saying, *"I'm not going to pamper you. Your mother may be overprotective of you. But I'm not going to do it."* (Although most teachers avoid such comments, this is an actual quote a teacher made to a student in front of the whole class.)

Ryan: After he was put down and embarrassed, he used profanity.

Teacher: The teacher sent him to the office for use of profanity.

7. **Continuation of behavior:** Why is the behavior continuing to be a problem? What is maintaining it? The behavior may be repeated because of the "contributing factors" or because the behavior is still serving an important purpose (function of the behavior). See Appendix B5.

   - He is in danger of failing her class.
   - He doesn't understand math the way she teaches it.
   - Ryan has had several run-ins with Mrs. Jones. There appears to be a personality conflict.

8. **Rewards:** What does the student view as a reward or positive reinforcement? This information may help teachers set up a strategy that will help the student change his behavior. The student may or may not need a concrete reward. Removing the threat of a negative response may be an adequate incentive for the student to change his behavior.

   - Ryan likes playing Nintendo, having friends over, and going to the movies on the weekend. He likes working on the student newspaper and acting in plays the drama club presents. Look at the student's strengths listed in response to Appendix A10, "Reframing ADD/ADHD."
   - If a behavioral program is developed, determine what the student considers a reward that he is willing to work toward earning.
   - No longer being embarrassed in front of the whole class is a positive reinforcer.

9. **Previous interventions:** What interventions were tried previously? What worked best?

   - After school detention.
   - In-school suspension for three days.

Obviously, this punitive strategy has not worked very well. The punishment made it clear what the student should *not* do but did not teach him what to do—in other words, new coping skills to use if the situation reoccurs. Now with the new IDEA guidelines, positive interventions must be instituted.

Behavior Intervention Plan

The positive Behavior Intervention Plan (BIP) is ideally built around the data obtained during the Functional Behavior Assessment. Once the teacher has analyzed the information gathered from the Functional Behavior Assessment, then she must develop a theory of why the misbehavior occurred. Next she will use this theory and information to develop an effective Behavior Intervention Plan.

In Ryan's case, the teacher might develop a number of intervention strategies to target the issues of concern. These intervention strategies may help address future problem behaviors, as well as antecedent and contributing factors.

Sample Intervention Strategies

1. Ryan was asked to write a math problem on the board. He refused.

- Talk with Ryan about this issue. Ask him to explain his reason for refusing to write the problem.
- If he is too self-conscious, don't ask him to write the problem on the board.
- If he does not mind, have another student write his work on the board.
- Discuss the inappropriate nature of his response to the teacher. Clearly this is not acceptable behavior.
- Explain that while he is suspended, he will have the opportunity to learn alternatives to handle conflict more appropriately.

2. Medication had worn off.

- The family will talk with their doctor.
- They will share key information with the doctor: the time medication is taken, the time the class is scheduled, and the completed medication rating scales (Appendices A7 & A8) regarding his school performance.
- Discuss with the doctor the feasibility of taking sustained-release medication or a second dose of regular medication at 10:30.

3. Did not complete his homework.

- Work with the family to develop a homework schedule.
- Parents will monitor homework completion in math.

4. Is a poor math student.

- Daily completion of homework by itself may be enough to learn the material.
- Arrange for a tutor, if needed.
- Use a weekly report to confirm completion of class and homework.
- Assess student for possible learning disability.

5. Is having conflicts with adults.

- Teach him skills for coping with conflict: anger management, conflict resolution, and pro-social skills. See Summaries 64, 66, and 69 for suggestions.

- Use the time he will spend in suspension, renamed "Organized Study" or "Time In," to learn self-management skills to cope with potential conflicts with adults. See Summary 64.
- Teach the student about typical ADD/ADHD behaviors.
- Share educational summaries from this book.
- View videos such as *Teen to Teen: the ADD Experience!*, described in Summaries 73 and 74.
- Suggestions are provided for shaping desired behavior in Summary 61.

6. Is having conflicts with his parents.

- Make parents aware of parent support group meetings such as CHADD and ADDA and educational classes they may offer.
- If parents show an interest, provide them with reading materials on ADD/ADHD.

7. Is having conflicts with Mrs. Jones.

- Provide the student with training on how to deal with frustration and a teacher with whom he has conflicts.
- Suggest training for the teacher. This is a situation where the teacher would benefit from knowing how to de-escalate problem situations (Summary 59).
- Schedule with a different math teacher next semester.

8. Has had previous conflicts with teachers.

- Develop a crisis intervention plan in the event the problem reoccurs.
- Allow the student to go, no questions asked, to the guidance counselor or a trusted teacher if he feels himself losing control.

(This summary incorporates information from Functional Behavior Assessment and Behavior Intervention Plan forms from: Appleton Area (Wisconsin) Schools; developed by Joan Helbing, ADD Consultant; Chicago City Schools; Gwinnett County (Georgia) School System; Walker County (Georgia) Schools.)

Resources

USDOE/OSEP Website: *www.pbis.org*—Recent revisions to federal education law have placed greater emphasis on the use of positive behavioral problems at school. This Office of Special Education website offers excellent information about positive behavioral strategies and functional behavior assessments from the Technical Assistance Center on Positive Behavioral Interventions and Supports (PBIS).

Self-management Strategies and ADD/ADHD

Self-management strategies are taught so that students will take increased responsibility for their own learning and behavior. When students learn to take charge of their own lives, their self-esteem is strengthened while demands on the teacher's time are reduced.

Self-management embraces a broad range of skills for students:

- problem solving,
- anger management,
- conflict resolution,
- self advocacy, and
- monitoring their own school performance.

Teachers need to recognize that students with attention deficits are slower to learn these skills and require a great deal of practice to master them. In addition, a conscious effort must be made to teach them the skills.

The Teacher's Role

Particularly as students with attention deficits reach adolescence, teachers should consider expanding their behavioral strategies to **include the student as a partner in the planning and problem-solving process**. At this age, teachers need to go beyond simply manipulating and controlling the student's behavior.

Obviously, teachers want students to be independent and take charge of their own lives. Unfortunately, researchers tell us that students with attention deficits often experience a significant developmental delay and are *not ready* for the same level of independence and responsibility as their peers. However, with supervision and practice, they *can* learn to solve their own problems. What better time to practice problem solving than during the somewhat sheltered middle and high school years when teachers and parents can still provide needed support and supervision? It is important to remember to **provide developmentally appropriate supervision**, which often means giving more support and for a longer period than for their peers.

Executive Function Deficits and Skill Training

As discussed in Section 3, executive function deficits cause students with attention deficits to experience problems with forgetfulness, organizational skills, time management, emotional control, and problem solving. Most students need help coping with these so-called "ADD/ADHD behaviors." Of course, medication helps a lot, but students also must be taught several basic skills that most of us take for granted.

6

However, don't expect miracles from skills training classes. These teenagers often "know what to do," but because of their impulsivity and difficulty with self-control, "don't always do what they know." So, even if students attend these training classes, they will not always act on this knowledge! Research on younger children tells us that teaching social skills is not particularly effective. Young students do *not* use the skills learned in training sessions. However, the verdict is not yet in on adolescents. So, don't be afraid to teach skills. Participating in these training classes certainly can't be harmful.

Critical Skills to Teach

Study and Organizational Skills

These skills may be defined broadly to include all activities that a student does or all supports he uses to succeed in school, for example:

- keeping a daily planner so that he knows his assignments;
- meeting a coach after school to organize his thoughts and make sure he takes home all the right books;
- establishing a set time to do homework;
- using mnemonics to remember important things;
- learning time management strategies to complete projects by developing and implementing a plan;
- dividing a large task into manageable sections;
- learning how to take notes;
- typing on a computer to express himself more quickly and clearly;
- using tools such as mechanical pencils or clipboards to work more efficiently.

Study Strategies: Numerous study or test-taking tips are available for teachers to give teenagers. Here are a couple of examples that may be helpful.

1. **SQ3R:** **S**urvey, **Q**uestion, **R**ead, **R**ecite, and **R**eview, known as SQ3R, is a strategy for reading textbooks with better comprehension.

   - **Survey**: Look over the chapter.
     Read the title of the chapter.
     Read the first paragraph.
     Read the section headings.
     Look at the pictures and their captions.
     Read the last paragraph or the summary.
   - **Question:** From your survey of the chapter, write down some questions.
   - **Read**: Read the chapter, section by section.
   - **Recite**: At the end of each section, look away from the book and summarize what you have just read.
   - **Review**: After reading the whole chapter, look back over it as a review of how all the parts are related.

2. Answering Chapter Questions:

- Read the first question.
- Start at the beginning of the chapter and read until you find the answer to the question.
- Answer the question.
- Read the next question, and read until you find the next answer.
- Continue until all questions are answered.

Test-taking Tips: Some schools provide students with test-taking tips for several different types of tests, including multiple choice, fill-in-the blank, true-false, and matching test questions. The *ADHD Project Facilitate* published some that were developed by West Feliciana Parish in St. Francisville, LA. Generally the tips include the following basic advice:

- Read questions carefully.
- Answer easy questions first. Put a check by answers you don't know and go back to them later. (This may not work for some students with ADD or ADHD because they cannot remember to go back to finish missed questions.)
- Look for "clue words" such as name, outline, define, explain, describe, discuss, or compare.
- If there is not a penalty, always guess.
- If you don't know the exact answer, write down something. You may get partial credit.
- On multiple choice tests, mark an "X" on the choices you know are wrong.
- Do not go back and change answers. Your first choice is usually correct.

Self-Awareness and Self-Control

These behavioral skills are among the tools the student learns to use to control or compensate for the characteristics of ADD or ADHD, such as acting or speaking impulsively and executive function deficits such as forgetfulness and time impairment.

- understanding the impact of ADD or ADHD on his life;
- appreciating his own strengths and special skills;
- understanding his own learning style so he knows how he learns best;
- learning to compensate for deficits by using classroom accommodations such as extended time on tests or a notetaker;
- learning to use anger management skills to avoid emotional blow-ups;
- using peer mediation and conflict resolution to solve problems in relationships;
- working with teachers and parents to use problem-solving strategies to resolve academic problems such as forgetting homework or not completing homework and failing a class;

- letting teachers, coaches, or friends teach him to compensate and master skills;
- taking medication to increase his attention and focus.

Self-monitoring

Self-monitoring is also an effective self-management tool for teenagers. When a new skill is taught, the student monitors his progress and assumes more control and responsibility for his academic work. Sometimes teachers use self-monitoring techniques for individual students or for a whole class. A fairly elaborate behavioral program may be set up that involves having students check whether or not they are working "on-task" at various intervals. Descriptions of these programs are available from the Council for Exceptional Children, in *Attention Deficit Disorder: Strategies for School Children* by Dr. Clare Jones, and *ADHD Project Facilitate: ADHD Interventions*, but here is a brief overview of a **self-monitoring program for a whole class:**

- A cue such as a beep or tone is played on a tape recorder.
- Each student marks on a form whether or not he was working on-task at that particular moment. Simply knowing that a beep is coming and then being reinforced for working helps change the students' behavior so that they increase the amount of time they are on-task.
- Intervals between beeps are varied but should be fairly frequent as the skill is taught. Beeps are gradually spaced further apart and ultimately phased out over time as students become more aware of being on task.

A self-monitoring program for an individual follows these same principles and might work like this:

- The teacher and the student discuss the program and the student says he wants to try it.
- They identify the behavior the student will monitor.
- The student is given a self-monitoring check sheet.
- The teacher shows the student what to do and practices with him.
- The student may wear an earphone so that he alone can hear the beep. When he hears the beep he marks on his paper whether or not he was working on task.
- The student may use a similar system at school and home.

Dr. Harvey Parker, author of numerous books on ADD/ADHD and co-founder of national CHADD, has developed a self-monitoring program, complete with a continuously playing signaling tape, instruction manual, and forms for school or home use.

Dr. Edward Shapiro and Dr. George DuPaul of LeHigh University have developed a comprehensive training program to help teachers cope more effectively with students with attention deficits. In addition to in-service training and on-site consultation, the program also includes a behavioral program for training students to monitor their own behavior. This program is slightly different from those described previously in that several different behaviors are rated.

1. Initially, the teacher rates the student on four to five behaviors of concern by giving a score of 0 to 5 at the end of class. For example, the student may be rated on whether or not he completed his class and homework, follows instructions, or comes to class on time.
2. Then the teacher talks with the student about the behaviors and shows him how to rate his own behavior.
3. Next, the student practices so that his ratings of his behavior match that of his teacher.
4. Gradually, the teacher ratings are phased out and the student is the only one rating his behavior.

This program increases the student's awareness of his behavior and teaches him the desired behavior.

Pro-social Skills

In teaching pro-social skills, educators teach responsible decision making—which often means teaching skills students are lacking. The use of "self-talk," or internal language, is one of the key skills needed to learn pro-social behavior. As the student is learning to use self-talk, the teacher provides the student with the words or language to control his behavior and make good choices, such as the phrases listed below. Next, the student is taught to use these phrases by himself when he faces a difficult situation. It may also help to ask him to visualize himself as he would like to behave (calm and in control).

- **Stop and think.** The teacher says *"Stop and think"* to interrupt the student's misbehavior.
- **Good choice or bad choice.** After the teacher has the student's attention, the teacher then asks, *"Are you making a good choice or a bad choice?"*
- **Choices or steps.** If the student recognizes that he has made a bad choice but does not seem to know how to correct the problem, the teacher may have to suggest the proper way to behave.
- **Just do it.** Once the student says what he should be doing, the teacher responds briefly and simply by saying, *"Just do it"* to help move the student into action.
- **How did I do?** The student may use self-monitoring to look at how well he handled this situation. The teacher can give the student positive feedback for handling the situation well.

Self-Advocacy

Students need to learn as much as they can about attention deficit disorder, how it affects their lives, and ways to compensate or master necessary skills. Teaching self-advocacy is critical. Critical times for self-advocacy include when the student attends

IEP meetings, as well as during daily interactions with teachers. Encourage the student to ask for what he needs in both these situations. *"I need untimed tests." "There is too much activity and noise in this area. May I take my test somewhere else?"* NICHCY has published "A Student's Guide to the IEP," which should be helpful to students.

Finding Time to Teach Social Skills at School

Teaching social skills to *all* students can have enormous benefits. When one program, Project Achieve, was implemented school-wide in a Florida school, academic scores and student behavior improved significantly. In addition, the number of fights, suspensions, and referrals for special education all dropped substantially.

Unfortunately, most schools do not have formal programs for teaching social skills to their students. Instead, teachers and parents need to identify the individual students who most need training in social skills, and then figure out how to provide it. Some options include:

1. **Include an objective in the IEP.** If particular social skills are listed as objectives in a student's IEP, then the school has to provide services to help the student meet his annual goals. So, services might include a special education teacher who can work with the student on social skills. Or the guidance counselor might schedule a social skills group for several students who need the training.

2. **Use Skillstreaming.** There are formal programs for teaching social skills to adolescents. One such exemplary program is *Skillstreaming the Adolescent,* developed by Arnold Goldstein and Ellen McGinnis. Here are a few examples of topics addressed in *Skillstreaming:* apologizing, dealing with someone else's anger, dealing with fear, standing up for your rights, responding to teasing, avoiding trouble with others, keeping out of fights, and dealing with embarrassment.

3. **Work on social skills with suspended students.** According to an article in *Communique,* the newsletter for the National Association of School Psychologists, some schools have given their in-school suspension program a new name such as OS (Organized Study) or R&R (Respect and Responsibility). They take advantage of time in suspension to teach pro-social skills through discussion groups or videos. The guidance counselor or another designated teacher may teach the class.

4. **Send to "time-in" to learn new skills.** Dr. Mario Hernandez and staff at the Florida Mental Health Institute, USF, in Tampa, developed a concept called *"time in."* Using this innovative procedure, teachers refer students to a "time-in" counselor who teaches them new skills to substitute for the behaviors that have been getting them into trouble. The counselor works with the students to "SOLVE" the problem and role-play their response:

> S – State your problem
> O – Outline your response
> L – List your alternatives
> V – View the consequences
> E – Evaluate your results

Resources

Batsche, G.M. & Knoff, H.M. *The Use of Classroom Based Social Skills Training to Improve Student Behavior: A Project ACHIEVE Training Manual.* Tampa: University of South Florida, 1995.

Elliott, Raymond & Lou Anne Worthington. "Teaching Study Skills and Using Study Aids." Tusculoosa, AL: *ADHD Project Facilitate: ADHD Interventions*, 1995. (Information available from mastrmnds@aol.com; www.mastrmnds.com).

Goldstein, Arnold P. & Ellen McGinnis. *Skillstreaming the Adolescent: New Strategies and Perspectives for Teaching Prosocial Skills.* Champaign, IL: Research Press, 1997.

Hernandez, Mario & Jo Palmer. *Time-In Counseling.* Tampa, FL: Florida Mental Health Institute (Adolescent Project, Research and Training Center for Children's Mental Health, FMHI, 13301 Bruce B. Downs Blvd., Tampa, FL 33612. 813-974-4461).

McMullen, Jerry. "A Prosocial System for Improving Student Discipline and Responsibility." *Communiqué*, October 1996.

NICHCY (National Information Center for Children and Youth with Disabilities). "A Student's Guide to the IEP." Washington, DC. 800-695-0285; wwww.nichcy.org.

Shapiro, Edward & George DePaul. *LeHigh University Consulting Center for Adolescents with Attention Deficit Disorder: A Training Manual.* A 30-minute videotape that describes key components of a model program and how a school system might establish a similar program is available. 610-758-6384.

Training Material

Harvey C. Parker, Ph.D., *Listen, Look, and Think: A Self-Regulation Program for Children.* Available through ADD WareHouse. 800-232-9273; www.addwarehouse.com.

Coaching Students with ADD/ADHD

Teenagers with ADD/ADHD often need a *coach* to help them succeed at school. They may need academic coaching or tutoring, but especially need help with *executive function deficits* such as disorganization, forgetfulness, memorization problems, and poor time management.

Typically, someone must act as a coach both at school and home and provide help in two major areas:

1. as an **organizational coach** to help the student with an attention deficit be more organized, write down homework assignments, take home the necessary books, and return homework to school;
2. as an **academic coach for effective learning strategies** to help him remember important things he needs to do, improve memorization skills or learn to compensate, and improve time management skills.

Coaching serves as a tool for modeling these skills so that the student learns to do them for himself or learns to compensate. The ultimate goal is independence through self-management.

How Much Help Do Students with ADD/ADHD Really Need?

When considering whether to provide organizational support to a student, both parents and teachers often express ambivalent feelings about "doing too much for the student." However, because ADD/ADHD can cause a *two- to four-year developmental delay*, these students' maturity and readiness to accept responsibility lag behind their peers. In addition, their disorganization and forgetfulness contribute to difficulty with seemingly simple classroom demands—for example, writing down and remembering to do their homework. These problems may improve briefly while medication is working, but benefits quickly disappear when it wears off.

If a teacher has repeatedly tried to teach a skill and the student just can't get it, repeated nagging is not going to make the problem miraculously disappear. The bottom line is that **these students need more support and supervision from teachers than their peers**. Their skill deficits are real and are not due simply to laziness or lack of motivation.

Providing Developmentally Appropriate Supervision

To ensure completion of school work, teachers and parents may need to supervise students with ADD/ADHD even in middle and high school. The alternative may be school failure for the teenager and, ultimately, dropping out of school.

The student's executive function skill deficits place him and his family *in direct conflict* with traditional middle and high school expectations that teenagers will take more responsibility for completing their school work. Some educators are expecting more than the student is capable of producing. Many of these students seem to "hit a brick wall" when they enter middle or high school because of the increased demands placed on them. They must deal with more classes, more teachers, and increased expectations to be organized and to assume greater responsibility for their work.

This is not to say that teachers should not expect anything of students or help them improve their skills and knowledge. Rather, ***develop the fine art of setting reasonable expectations that the student can achieve.*** An additional goal is for the student to become a respected partner and master of his fate rather than just a passive victim of a disability.

Giving Parents Permission to Be Involved with Their Teenager

Teachers might consider these facts when deciding whether: 1) to provide more support to the teen, and 2) to accept and not discourage parents from being involved as coaches. Edward Hallowell, M.D., and John Ratey, M.D., coauthors of the popular book, *Driven to Distraction,* explain that ***even adults with ADD/ADHD need coaches*** to help them remember the more routine responsibilities of life. They point out that ***disorganization and forgetfulness are lifelong problems*** for many people with attention deficit disorder. In adulthood, several different people may serve as coaches, including the spouse, secretary, administrative assistant, or a friend.

Teaching Students How to Master Skills and Compensate

Teachers and parents do a tremendous service when they teach these students to master or compensate for skill deficits.

- First, ***help them recognize their skill deficits*** without feeling bad about them.
- Second, ***teach them to learn to compensate for the deficit.***
- Third, ***show parents how to shape desired behavior and teach the student new skills or compensatory skills.*** Explain the concepts behind shaping behavior: start at the teenager's present level, teach each progressive step until the skill is mastered. Discuss the examples in Summary 61.
- Next, ***help parents find an organizational coach*** to meet the student after school to get the right books and assignments.
- Last, ***share information from summaries relevant to the student's specific needs.*** For example, Summary 23 addresses five points of vulnerability for school failure and summaries in Section 3 provide suggestions for coping with executive function deficits.

Who Are the Coaches?

The most likely candidates to serve as the teenager's organizational or academic coach are first the parents, and later on, a girlfriend or boyfriend. The student may also try to be his own coach, or a professional coach may be hired.

Parents as Coaches

Coaching may be difficult for parents because of the emotions involved. Obviously, when a student has forgotten his assignments and books for the four thousandth time, most parents have trouble dealing with the situation calmly. Ideally, an outside person would be hired as a coach. In reality, though, most parents cannot afford to hire someone else and the responsibility always falls back on the family. So, help students make the best of the situation.

1. Suggest that parents swap out homework supervision when one becomes frazzled and angry.
2. Sometimes other relatives, friends, or a college student from the neighborhood might be willing to take on the job of coach.
3. Another parent of a student with attention deficit, who may be more patient with someone else's teenager, might be willing to trade responsibilities for teaching skills. Or the parents could let their teenagers study together and alternate nights of supervision.

The Student as Coach through Self-monitoring

Summary 64 presents a variety of strategies that teachers and parents can use to teach the student himself to recognize his deficits, master key skills, and compensate for others.

Professional ADHD Coaches

Professional coaches may meet face to face with students or may provide coaching services by phone and e-mail on a weekly basis. Some coaches who specialize in working with students will also contact teachers and talk with them. Fees for coaching vary but it would not be unusual for a half hour to cost $25.

To find a coach, parents might contact a local or national ADD/ADHD group, such as CHADD and ADDA. These groups may be aware of local coaching resources and some coaches advertise in their newsletters.

The American Coaching Association is a well-known national group. However, many coaches who receive their training through ACA specialize in helping *adults* with attention deficits cope with the work world and may not be familiar with school issues unique to students. The ACA website contains a state-by-state listing of coaches, some of whom list their target groups (www.americoach.com; 610-825-4505). Another group, International Coach Federation, also has lists of coaches (www.coachfederation.org; 888-423-3131). As parents would do with any potential counselor, they should screen coaches to find someone they trust who could work effectively with their family. It is also important to inquire about what kind of training and certification the coach has.

Professional Consultants, Trained Tutors, or College Students Paid to Tutor

Private and public counseling and educational centers are available all across the country. Psychologists, social workers, educational consultants, and tutors are available to help parents and teenagers cope with attention deficits and other learning problems. Sometimes universities are also an excellent source of help. However, their help may be limited to only one hour a week and may not provide the daily guidance that is often needed.

Tips for Coaching

The coaching tips below have been adapted from suggestions by Dee Doochin and Holly Hamilton, trained ADHD coaches. These suggestions may be helpful to coaches regardless of whether they are teachers, parents, or other students.

The Coach's Toolbox

1. **Listening** is the most important tool in the coach's toolbox. However, the coach needs to know what to listen for in order to coach effectively. The following is a list of things coaches always listen for:

   - **Strengths:** Teachers and parents can use strengths to teach academics and develop supportive strategies. For example, a student might have a great personality, have incredible computer skills, or be creative. See Summary 70 and Appendix A10.
   - **Dominant learning styles:** Learning styles, or the way students take in information, are discussed in Summary 12. Using the teen's dominant learning style along with his strengths greatly increases coaching successes. Sometimes the comments that students make during coaching sessions reveal their dominant learning style(s):
     - **Visual:** *"I see"* or *"I get the picture."*
     - **Auditory:** *"I hear what you are saying."* Or *"It sounds like . . . "*
     - **Verbal:** *"So what you are saying is. . ."*
     - **Kinesthetic:** *"It feels like . . . "*
     - **Tactile:** *"So this touches on . . . "* or *"I finally grasp what you are saying."*
     - **Cognitive:** *"I understand"* or *"I know it now."*
     - **Issues of concern:** Important issues may include the identified problem itself or other obstacles that are keeping the student from dealing with the issues at hand.
     - **Desires and motivators:** Coaches need to find out the student's important lifetime dreams so they can identify what

the student will work for, help define the teen's goals, and provide reminders of why he is bothering to "finish his stupid homework."

2. **Using language effectively** is the second most important skill in the box. The coach needs to know what words to use and how to use them appropriately. This will help the coach communicate effectively in a nonjudgmental manner. Asking key questions is one of the most important jobs a coach has. The coach is helping the student brainstorm and come up with solutions, not just giving answers. See Summary 59 on actions that escalate or de-escalate problems and 66 on problem solving.

3. **Timing** is also critical for successful coaching. Coaches must understand how long the student can pay attention and what time of day his attention is working well. Students cannot benefit from coaching if their brains are tired, shut down, or spaced out. See Summary 53 for a discussion of peak medication times.

The Coach's Attitude

Several attitudes are necessary for a successful coaching relationship:

1. **Do not be invested in how a goal is achieved.** Students can successfully achieve a goal many different ways.
2. **Always start from where the teenager is** not from where you think he should be. See Summary 61 for a discussion of shaping behavior.
3. **Do not take personally anything a teen says or does.** As part of growing up, all teens test limits. In addition, teens with ADD/ADHD are extremely impulsive. They may tell the coach they hate coming to coaching sessions. In this case, the coach might express concern by asking, *"How can we make it better so that you don't hate it?"*
4. **Respect who the teen is and honor him for that.** This ties in with the next statement. At the same time, coaches have to set boundaries and make them clear.
5. **Give support and unconditional acceptance.** The relationship will not work otherwise. Showing genuine acceptance may be most important. If the teenager believes that you really care about him, he will be more open to working with you. See Summary 70 for a discussion on valuing teenagers with ADD/ADHD.

One Model School Program

Creative Coaching: A Support Group for Children with ADHD is a model curriculum developed by two guidance counselors for coaching students with attention deficits who are in early middle and elementary school. The program relies heavily on the "coaching" metaphor to increase interest and teach concepts. For example, a "hand signal" (touching the index finger to thumb) may be used with a student who is rambling, telling him to shorten his explanation. The curriculum addresses several important areas:

- listening
- paying attention
- organization
- self-concept
- controlling impulsivity
- understanding ADD/ADHD

- goal setting
- handling feelings
- communication
- friendships
- learning to relax

Teachers or guidance counselors in high school may be able to adapt this curriculum for the older age group. One nice thing about the curriculum is that the authors also suggest ways to practice and reinforce the new skills in the classroom and at home, or as Dr. Russell Barkley says, at the "point of performance." ***Practice at the point of performance increases the likelihood that students will master the skill being taught!***

Involving Teachers in the Game

Using the *Creative Coaching* curriculum, the group being coached is known as the "All Stars." After they have learned a specific skill such as paying attention, each student takes a colored half-sheet of paper, called the "High 5," back to the teacher. The paper includes a preprinted list of all 11 lessons with the current one circled. The teacher is asked to comment when he notices the student using the skill. For example, privately or in front of class, he might say, *"Johnny, I noticed that you paid attention and wrote down the assignment. Good job!"* Or the teacher may "coach" the student during the week by saying, *"Samantha, this might be a good time to pay attention and focus on copying the assignments off the board."* At the end of the week, the teacher writes down one or two positive comments regarding the student's use of the skills (or a skill learned earlier) and the student brings the "High 5" back to the group the following week. The comments on the card are then discussed in the group and used to reinforce the skill and to earn points for rewards.

Involving Parents in "Home Play"

The *Creative Coaching* curriculum includes "Home play" activities that involve parents in reinforcing the skills that were learned that week. Take-home sheets have activities designed to stimulate conversation between the parent and student about individual skills. Younger teens may enjoy when the counselor explains that this is an opportunity to get their parents to do homework. The parents do the work of writing the assignments while the student dictates the answers. On the back of the activity sheet, the skills are discussed and directions are given for parents to "catch" the student applying these skills, or "coach" him to use the skills as needed. Parents then write a positive weekly comment, which the student also returns to the group. Points are given for the activity, and the parents' comments are discussed in the group. Students may earn individual awards or the group may combine points for a group reward.

Resources

McDougall, Nancy & Janet Roper. *Creative Coaching: a Support Group for Children with ADHD.* San Antonio, TX: Glory Publications, 1998. Available through www.youthlight.com. This helpful curriculum guide was written by two guidance counselors who are also parents of students with ADD/ADHD. Although this guide is written for elementary school and lower middle schoolers, the topics it addresses are relevant to older teens. High school guidance counselors may be able to adapt the material.

Conflict Resolution

Teaching conflict resolution skills to students with ADD/ADHD is very important, since these students may be impulsive and irritable, especially when their medication has worn off or they are under stress. Learning more about problem solving, peer mediation, and anger management will help these students cope successfully with potentially volatile situations.

Problem-Solving Skills

Students with an attention deficit must be taught problem-solving skills for coping with school or homework issues and sometimes with relationship or behavioral issues. Learning problem-solving skills may help students understand how to analyze and talk their way through a problem rather than resorting to verbal attacks or fighting.

Students as Partners in Problem Solving

Help students develop their own solutions for completing homework and turning it in to the teacher. Students are more likely to comply with solutions they helped develop. A subtle message of respect is also conveyed: *"I know you really want to do better. ADD (ADHD) can make remembering homework assignments [chores, being on time] difficult. What can I do to help you remember?"* This is preferable to giving the implied message, *"You don't really want to do well. The only way you will do your school work [be on time] is if I, the teacher, make you complete it."*

- Discuss the problem at hand.
- Ask for the student's input on how to solve it. Generate several options.
- Give the student adequate time to respond, especially when slow processing speed is a problem.
- Listen to his input.
- Offer options, if he has no suggestions.
- Weigh the pros and cons of the options. Discuss them or help him list them.
- Help him pick the best option.
- Write down what the action will be and when it will start.
- Monitor and evaluate results. (*"Check back with me tomorrow and let me know if it worked."* If the student forgets to check with the teacher, the teacher should contact the student.)
- Change the plan if it is not working.
- Until proven wrong, assume good intentions.
- Assume the student is doing his best!

Conflict Resolution and Problem-solving in Relationships

Lyndon D. Waugh, M.D., author of *Tired of Yelling,* suggests fifteen key steps in teaching children and teenagers to resolve conflicts. These steps may help students improve their relationships with other students, their teachers, or parents.

The Thinking Steps

1. Assess emotions; recognize anger, it is a sign to resolve a problem.
2. Accept anger: it's okay, but handle it and behave well.
3. Gauge the intensity of anger on a scale of 1-10.
4. Who and what are you angry about? Don't misdirect it at the wrong person.
5. Do a perspective check: are you overreacting?

The Talk/Listen Steps

6. Select a good time and place for resolution.
7. Avoid coalitions; keep the argument between the right two people.
8. Express anger appropriately.
9. Listen actively.
10. Admit fault.

The Solving Steps

11. Brainstorm solutions.
12. Discuss pros and cons of each.
13. Decide and plan.
14. Do it.
15. Review/revise.

Communication Skills in Conflict Resolution

Communication skills are an integral part of conflict resolution. Some of the important skills that need to be taught include:

- understanding body language;
- using "I" messages;
- using reflective listening—getting the facts and understanding the emotions involved (*"So, you seem angry. Tell me what's going on."*);
- checking and validating the accuracy of the information gathered.

One school that successfully teaches communication skills as an integral part of their peer mediation program is Meadowcreek High School in Norcross, Georgia. Jane Moser, the Assistant Principal at the school, provides roughly 16 to 20 hours of training in communication and conflict resolution skills to each peer mediator. Meadowcreek uses *Conflict Resolution: A High School Curriculum* to train their peer mediators. A more detailed description of a different peer mediation program is provided in the next summary. The primary difference is that one program is run out of the assistant principal's office, and the other, the guidance office.

Resources

Conflict Resolution: A High School Curriculum. Available from: The Community Board Program, 1540 Market St, # 490, San Francisco, CA 94102. 415-552-1250.

Waugh, Lyndon, M.D. & Letitia Sweitzer. *Tired of Yelling: Teaching Children to Resolve Conflicts,* Marietta, GA: Longstreet Press, 1999.

Peer Mediation

Peer mediation is one of the most popular programs schools use to help reduce conflicts among students and to avoid potential fights or other disruptions. During mediation, a student trained in mediation techniques meets with the students who are having a conflict and helps them try to agree upon a solution to their problem. Sometimes students are referred to mediation instead of being disciplined in traditional ways such as detention or suspension.

Basic Rules for Peer Mediation

1. Both students must agree to peer mediation and to abide by the decision that is made.

2. Mediators are neutral and don't take sides.

3. A mediation session follows these procedures:
   - Mediators introduce themselves and ask the names of the two students.
   - Mediators state the rules— i.e., students must:
     - remain with the mediator,
     - listen without interrupting,
     - tell the truth,
     - treat each other respectfully,
     - solve the problem,
     - abide by their agreement,
     - sign the agreement (indicating they believe it "resolves the issues between them").

4. Mediators ask student 1 to tell his story, then summarize it.

5. Mediators ask student 2 to tell his story, then summarize it.

6. Mediators ask for possible solutions, then summarize them.

7. Students review the pros and cons of each solution.

8. Students choose a solution and plan how and when to implement it.

9. Mediators ask if both students are satisfied with the decision.

10. Mediators write the agreement.

11. Students sign the agreement to indicate agreement with the solution.

12. Session ends.

Key Concepts Taught in Peer Mediation

The skills below are formally taught to peer mediators so they can facilitate mediation sessions:

- understanding conflict,
- effective communication,
- listening skills,
- understanding anger,
- handling anger,
- confidentiality,
- peer mediation strategies.

Students receiving mediation also benefit by learning new skills such as:

1. strategies for avoiding angry confrontations, and
2. new coping skills that will carry over into their home and adult lives.

The next summary provides more information on violence prevention.

A Typical Peer Mediation Program

A description of a typical peer mediation program may help administrators decide whether this type of program may be helpful in their school. At Ridgeland High School in Fort Oglethorpe, Georgia, the peer mediation program is directed by Ottie Manis, one of the guidance counselors. Here are some key facts about the program:

- The high school has a population of just over a thousand students and has fifteen trained student mediators available.
- Three or four students are available each period to handle conflicts.
- Students may ask for mediation or be referred by a teacher or an administrator.
- Peer mediators participate in a minimum of fifteen hours of training.
- On average, a mediation session lasts approximately one hour.
- A mediation session is usually scheduled within fifteen minutes or so of a conflict. Occasionally, if the problem occurs at the end of the day or the student is suspended, the session will be scheduled the next day. Most are handled the same day of their referral.
- The counselor meets with the peer mediators and provides supervision twice a month during school hours for about forty-five minutes. A discussion of previous mediation sessions helps these students improve their skills and expand the range of interventions they may suggest.
- On average, four or five students a week are referred to peer mediation.
- Ridgeland uses the curriculum developed by Fred Schrumpf and others that is published by Research Press (see Resources).

6

Ridgeland High School was recognized by the Florida Mental Health Institute at the University of South Florida in Tampa as an exemplary school that has implemented school reform to help all students be successful.

Students with ADD/ADHD as Peer Mediators

Some schools make a point of recruiting and training peer mediators who have personal difficulties with conflict. This training is often very helpful to these students, who may learn helpful new skills as they teach them to others. No doubt students with ADD or ADHD would benefit from training as peer mediators.

Resources

Cunningham, C.E. & L.J. Cunningham. "Student–Mediated Conflict Resolution Programs." In *Attention Deficit Hyperactivity Disorder.* Edited by Russell Barkley. New York: Guilford Press, 1998. (www.guildford.com)

Schrumpf, Fred, Donna Crawford & H. Chu Usadel. *Peer Mediation: Conflict Resolution in Schools.* Champaign, IL: Research Press Publishers, 1997. (800-519-2707; www.researchpress.com). Available materials: program guide, student manual, and a training video.

Violence Prevention Programs

There is no research to suggest that students with ADD/ADHD in general are more likely to be violent than other students. However, educators across the nation are greatly concerned about growing violence among *all* students. Violence prevention programs are therefore mentioned here to give an idea of the information available on this topic, as well as the work being done to develop model programs to prevent violence.

Risk Factors for Violence in Adolescents

Although it is very difficult to identify potentially violent teenagers, the American Academy of Child and Adolescent Psychiatry lists several known risk factors:

- early involvement with drugs and alcohol,
- easy access to weapons, especially handguns,
- association with antisocial groups,
- physical or sexual abuse victims,
- pervasive exposure to violence in the media,
- first arrest occurring prior to age ten,
- first arrest for a serious offense,
- three or more arrests by age twelve.

Warning signs for violent behavior in children include:

- intense anger,
- frequent loss of temper or blow-ups,
- extreme irritability,
- extreme impulsiveness,
- becoming easily frustrated.

Poor school performance is also known to contribute to both violence and delinquency!

Conduct Disorder and Violence: As mentioned above, there is usually no reason to assume that students with ADD or ADHD are more prone to violence than other students. The one exception is among students with attention deficits who have also been diagnosed with a *conduct disorder*—meaning they habitually violate the rights of others and refuse to comply with rules. Fewer than one-fourth of students with ADD/ADHD eventually receive the diagnosis of conduct disorder. It is important to note, too, that even when students with conduct disorder are aggressive, they may not necessarily be violent. Conduct Disorder is discussed in more detail in Summary 72.

6

Model Violence Prevention Programs

Ten model programs from around the country were identified in 1996 by the Center for the Study and Prevention of Violence. A series of "blueprints" were developed to describe these programs. For information on these programs, including a bullying prevention program, life skills training, mentoring, and multisystemic therapy, see the web site for the Center for the Study and Prevention of Violence listed in the Resources.

School-Based Mentoring: One of the original "blueprint programs"—a mentoring program—was expanded to a school-based setting by Janet Ardoyno of Big Brothers and Big Sisters of Abilene, Texas. Through this program, high school students are recruited and trained to provide support and encouragement to younger students. The curriculum, *Character Building Traits,* was based upon materials developed by the Search Institute. The Institute offers materials to help students develop 40 key assets that are essential for healthy development. (See www.search-institute.org for more information.) Research has shown that this school mentoring program resulted in improved behavior, better grades, fewer fights, and a reduced likelihood of drug or alcohol use.

Second Step Violence Prevention Curriculum (preschool-Grade 9): The Second Step violence prevention curriculum was given an "Exemplary" rating by a USDOE Expert Panel on Safe and Drug-Free Schools. This program has been used in over 15,000 schools to teach children to change the attitudes and behaviors that contribute to violence. Both school and family components were developed. Available from the Committee for Children, Seattle, Washington. (www.cfchildren.org; 800-634-449)

Resources

Publications

American Academy of Child and Adolescent Psychiatry. *Understanding Violent Behavior in Children and Adolescents,* Facts for Families series. Washington, DC, 1996.

Character Building Traits curriculum. Available from Janet Ardoyno, Big Brothers/Big Sisters Program, 1216 N. 5th, Abilene, TX 79603. 915-677-7839.

Walker, Hill & Frank M. Gresham. "Making Schools Safer and Violence Free," *Intervention in School and Clinic*, V. 32, N. 4, March 1997, pp. 199-204.

Walker, Hill and Robert Sylvester. "Where Is School Along the Path to Prison?" *Educational Leadership,* September, 1991.

Organizations

Center for the Study and Prevention of Violence, University of Colorado, IBS #10, Campus Box 439, Boulder, CO 80309. (www.colorado.edu/cspv/blueprints.htm) "Blueprints" of model programs are available.

National Center for Conflict Resolution Education, Illinois Bar Center, 424 South 2nd St., Springfield, IL 62701. (217-523-7056; www.nccre.org)

Anger Management
By Kathy Hubbard Weeks

Some teenagers with ADD/ADHD have difficulty controlling their emotions when they are frustrated or upset. As a result, they may have an occasional emotional blow-up at school. Typically, teachers know which students have major problems with self-control. Any student who is struggling with emotional control (for example, screaming, yelling at other students or the teacher, or getting into fights) could benefit from anger management training.

Teachers may select a few of the strategies below to suggest to any given student. For example, the teacher may give the student a copy of the section, "Offer Alternative Ways to Handle Anger" and discuss it with him. However, this process may require more time than the teacher has available. If so, ask the guidance counselor or social worker to conduct an anger management group. Or, after a blow-up occurs, find out whether training can be provided while the student is in detention or school suspension.

Six Key Points Teens Should Know about Anger

When working with a teenager to teach anger management, there are six key points that teachers or guidance counselors may want to make initially. Ask the teen to record these points in a notebook that he can use as a reference in the future (or give him a copy from this book).

1. **Anger is a feeling.** In and of itself, it is not good or bad, right or wrong. It's what you do with your anger or how you express it that is important.
2. **It's okay to be angry,** but it's never okay to hurt yourself or someone else or damage property. Verbal abuse and physical violence are not okay.
3. **We learn how to express our anger by observing how others express their anger.** This can include parents, teachers, relatives, and friends, or characters on television shows, movies, or video games.
4. **We are responsible for how we express our anger.** We cannot blame others for our behavior. Even though someone may do something that makes us feel angry, we still can choose how to respond to that person. We can respond in a way that makes things worse or we can respond in a way that makes things better.
5. **Our goal is to accept angry feelings and channel or direct them in constructive ways,** not to repress or destroy the feelings.
6. **Feeling angry is like having an elephant sitting in the living room:** You can't ignore it. It won't go away. You can't deal with

anything else in your life until you have dealt with it. You must learn to cope with the anger: talk about it, take action to resolve it, or, if unresolvable, at least diffuse it.

Increase Awareness of Events That Trigger Anger

Sometimes students lack self-awareness and are not in touch with their own feelings. So, they cannot talk easily about their anger. For these students, it's usually safer and less threatening to talk about someone else's behavior than their own. It may help to make up a few stories with at least one or two examples that are similar to this student's real life situation:

- A student failed a class, yelled at his teacher, and called her an ugly name.
- A student's girlfriend broke up with him and found a new boyfriend. The three students had a confrontation in the hall and the boys got into a fight.

After this *safe* discussion, talk about how the student handles anger in his own life. Help the teen become aware of the kind of things that can trigger his anger. You might begin by saying something like, *"A lot of things can make people angry. Many people, not just teenagers with attention deficits, get angry to protect themselves from painful feelings, such as frustration or rejection or feeling stupid."* Then, try discussing the answers to the questions in this section.

What makes you angry?

1. frustrating school work or an irritating situation?
2. being criticized?
3. anxiety or fear about a situation over which you have no control?
4. feeling as if you are being attacked or fear that you could be?
5. feelings of dependency, sadness, or depression?

How do you use anger?

1. Do you use anger to:
    - avoid the situation?
    - gain control over it?
    - ward off an attack?
    - manipulate or have power over others?
    - retaliate or get revenge?
2. Does anger protect you from *painful feelings*, such as feeling incompetent, unlovable, unworthy, inadequate, or lonely?
3. When you are under stress, do you get angry more easily? What things stress you out?

Teach Students to Be Aware of Their Body's Response to Anger

Discuss the *physiological response* the human body has when we become angry.

Pay Attention to Early Physical Cues: Explain that we need to pay attention to the physical cues that our body gives us, so we can recognize when we are becoming angry. For example, a student may become tense, hold his breath, clench his fists, feel hot, or have pain or pressure in his head, chest, or stomach. Mentally, he may feel agitated, be unable to concentrate on anything else other than the problem or injustice. Next, he may want to hit or kick something, cry, scream, or begin developing a plan of revenge. In the early stages of anger we can still make good choices about what to do and how to respond. We are still thinking rationally.

To help a student think about how he responds to angry feelings, you might say:

"Think of a time when you were angry. What made you angry? Where did you feel the anger in your body? Did your muscles become tense? Did you clench your fists? Did you have pain or pressure in your head, chest, or stomach? Did you hold your breath? Did you feel hot?"

Do Not Ignore Early Warning Signals: Take action to avoid anger. If we ignore early warning signals, we are more apt to express our anger in a hurtful, ineffective, damaging way, which may result in feelings of remorse, shame, and embarrassment, and damage our self-esteem and relationships with others. Tell the student:

"Now that you know the types of situations that can trigger anger and how your body feels physically when you start to become angry, pay attention to these signals. Then you can intervene early and handle your anger better."

Offer Alternative Ways to Handle Anger

Brainstorm with the teenager about the different ways to manage anger and express it in a positive and assertive way. Ask him to write down strategies for anger management in his notebook and tell you which ones might work for him. Some examples are:

1. Learn how to express yourself better when you are angry.

- Express your feelings.
- Use "I" statements.
- Be respectful while communicating.
- Share your feelings without hurting people.
- Tell others what is bothering you by being direct, specific, and polite.
- Be honest. Give the real reason you want what you want.
  "I'm feeling …(frustrated) because … (I had plans to go to my friend's house after school and no one told me I had to stay after school for a teacher conference.) I want/would like… (for you or my parents to let me know at least a day ahead of time when I have to do something after school.")

Ask for what you want or need:

- Be assertive by telling others what you want and need without blaming, manipulating, or attacking.
- Ask, don't demand.
- Speak in a calm, quiet voice.
- Avoid swearing.
- Listen, be tolerant of others, and be willing to compromise
- Listen to what the other person is saying without interrupting.
- Try to understand the other person's point of view.
- Accept differences.
- Agree to disagree.
- Stop trying to control others.
- Be willing to compromise.
- Negotiate a "win-win" solution. *"Can we both get what we want from this solution?"*

2. **Take a time-out to calm down.** Take a break from the situation. When your emotions have calmed down (at least 20 minutes) come back to discuss the situation or approach the task from a different perspective.

3. **Manage your stress** through regular exercise, muscle relaxation, good nutrition, adequate rest, planning ahead, or allowing adequate time to complete tasks.

4. **Take a deep breath and count to ten.**

5. **Tell yourself to relax** and don't forget to breathe deeply and slowly.

6. **Learn self-soothing behaviors** that can be called upon when you become aware of anger in your body; for example, take a hot bath, ask someone to give you a massage, or listen to soothing, calm music.

7. **Use self-talk.** *"Okay, I can remain calm. I can maintain control. I just have to take a deep breath, relax, and let it go."*

8. **Ask yourself, "How important is this to me?** *Do I really need to be angry? Is it worth getting suspended or expelled from school?"*

9. **Keep yourself safe.** *"We need to discuss this later when we are less emotional and thinking more clearly."*

10. **Reduce the amount of stimulation** in your environment; it helps to maintain calmness. Go to a quiet, calm place.

11. **Go talk to a good friend** who will listen and support you.

12. **Brainstorm solutions** for the problem at hand, after things have begun to calm down.

Role-Play Solutions

The last step is to practice managing anger with the teen by setting up role-play situations. First, the teacher demonstrates how to manage anger in a given scenario.

Ask the teen for feedback about what the teacher did that was good, and what he or she could have done differently to make it better. Then let the teen demonstrate how he would manage his anger. The teen evaluates what he did well and what he would like to change. The teacher provides positive reinforcement only for the desirable responses. Ignore inappropriate answers.

Look for "Triggers" for Anger

Of course, removing the antecedent behavior or "trigger" that is causing the anger or frustration is critically important. Teachers should make certain any learning problems are identified, school work is adjusted so that it is not too long or too difficult, and needed accommodations are provided. Ultimately, medication may be necessary to help the student control his anger and impulsivity. The family should talk with their doctor about this issue.

A Word of Caution

Remember, don't expect miracles from simply teaching these students anger management. It will take time, maturity, and practice to master this skill. The student may still have emotional blow-ups, but at least he has begun learning the skills to use when something makes him angry. He will mature with time.

About the Author of this Summary

Kathy Hubbard Weeks is the ADD Consultant and Section 504 Coordinator for the Kenosha, Wisconsin Unified School District. Kathy is one of the pioneers in the area of school reform for students with ADD/ADHD. She was among the first to suggest enlisting other students to help children and teenagers with ADD/ADHD. She began a model program in her Kenosha school district in 1990. She also has time for a busy part-time private practice in social work, where her specialty is students with ADD/ADHD and their families. She has a unique understanding of ADD/ADHD, since she is also the mother of a teenager with ADHD.

6

Going the Extra Mile for Students with ADD/ADHD

I recognize that there are several factors that make teaching an incredibly difficult job. For starters, teachers are expected to develop individualized teaching plans for so many students, not just those with attention deficits. Second, ADD/ADHD is challenging for parents who have only one teenager and even more so for teachers who sometimes have several students with the condition. Third, colleges don't typically offer teachers specific classes in dealing with students who are challenging. Last, because of the adverse impact an attention deficit has on learning, teachers must often teach students who think and learn differently than the teacher does. It is very hard to understand someone who thinks and acts so differently from us.

In spite of these challenges, many teachers are successful in teaching students with attention deficits. When teachers make a special effort to help these students, it is an extraordinary gift to parents and their teenagers. The teacher's caring attitude and positive support often make the critical difference in whether or not the student is successful in school. In this section, I will therefore talk about the importance of teacher attitudes, beliefs, and values with regard to these students. Several common questions I often receive when I present workshops for teachers are also included.

Valuing the Student with ADD/ADHD

For many teachers, it is only natural to place the most value on teenagers who are good students and make the best grades. Students who make good grades tend to have key learning skills such as the ability to pay attention, memorize, complete homework, and make good test grades, which are often lacking in many students with ADD/ADHD. So, students who have attention deficits or learning problems may not feel valued by a teacher. Their talents and abilities that shine often fall outside the arena of a regular classroom. *It takes a special teacher to find the time and energy to make each student feel valued!*

My son was lucky and had several dedicated teachers during his school years. When a teacher looked for and found the worthwhile qualities in my son, I was so deeply grateful that I was sometimes moved to tears. Students seem to have a sixth sense about which teachers really like them. For example, when my son was in first grade, he began crying when I asked to see his first report card. His plea, "Please don't read my report card; my teacher thinks I'm bad," was profoundly insightful.

These teenagers are often very sensitive to a teacher's approval or disapproval. *Students with attention deficits tend to do well in classes where the teacher likes them* and may fail the same subject with a teacher who doesn't like them. Sometimes even the slightest hint of disapproval or an embarrassing put-down in front of classmates will doom any future positive relationship with a teacher.

Sometimes *teachers intimidate students without ever intending to do so*. For instance, a teacher may roll her eyes and say, "I explained that already. Weren't you listening?" This inadvertently sends an unspoken message, "I am not approachable. Do not ask me questions when you don't understand something." These students know they can't always pay attention and they miss important information. They are sometimes afraid to ask questions when they don't understand something for fear the teacher has already explained the material. If a teacher gives an embarrassing negative response, these students will forever be afraid to approach and ask for help. If a teacher finds this situation frustrating, try taking a breath, don't change facial expressions, and explain the material again for the forty-seventh time.

Reframe ADD/ADHD Behaviors

Although having an attention deficit disorder is not easy, it should not be viewed as a terrible thing. Many of these teenagers grow up to be successful, happy adults. Frequently, these students will naturally gravitate toward active hands-on careers that maximize their skills and don't penalize them for their ADD/ADHD behaviors. Unfortunately, the school years, with requirements for organization and memorization, are often the most challenging times for people with this condition. It may help a teacher to look at troubling ADD/ADHD behaviors, reframe them, and look for the positive aspects of these same behaviors. ***ADD or ADHD may be a disability in school, but it does not have to be a disability in life!***

Qualities that may not be endearing in a classroom may well be highly valued in the adult business world. A list of behaviors that could be reframed positively is contained in Summary 71 and Appendix A10. A few examples are provided here:

- These teenagers often have a wonderful ***zest for living***. Sometimes they seem to have more ***fun in life*** and are more ***creative*** than those of us who don't have ADD/ADHD.
- The pesky, talkative "class clown" may grow up to be a wonderful ***salesperson*** or bring welcome humor into many lives. Although most teachers would not want to teach a comic genius like Robin Williams, most of us greatly enjoy his humor. These ***out-going, friendly*** types add much-needed humor to life, put us at ease, and make us feel welcome.
- Hyperactive students often have ***high energy*** as adults and work long hours once they find a career or job they like.

Teachers can help parents and the teens themselves reframe their perception of attention deficits and look for the positives. ***Ask parents and students to complete Appendix A10.***

Identify Strengths

So often the only assessment of students who are struggling in school is a negative one. What are their deficits, problems, and shortcomings? In other words, the cup is viewed as half empty rather than half full. When teenagers are viewed only in light of their deficits, a negative self-fulfilling prophecy may be set in motion. For example, students who are told that they are bad, dumb, or lazy are more likely to act that way. Furthermore, according to one researcher, we may actually be unintentionally rationalizing the failure of our teaching efforts by describing a teenager as "unmotivated or lazy."

Seldom are the strengths and outside interests of the student identified or an attempt made to incorporate them into school work. Yet IDEA mandates that the student's strengths must be identified in the IEP. Recently, strength-based assessments have increased in popularity. These evaluations may be done informally by simply asking the student and parent to describe her strengths and completing Appendix A10. Or a formal assessment can be done using an instrument such as the Behavioral and Emotional Rating Scale (BERS). Dr. Michael Epstein, special education professor at the University of Nebraska, developed this scale as a way to identify and focus attention on a child's strengths. The BERS evaluates five areas.

1. **Interpersonal Strengths**—the student's ability to control his or her emotions or behavior.
2. **Family Involvement**—the student's relationship with his or her family.

7

3. **Interpersonal Strengths**—a student's feelings of competence and accomplishment.
4. **School Functioning**—a student's competence in school.
5. **Affective Strengths**—a student's ability to accept affection and express feelings.

Questions are also asked about the student's favorite hobbies, activities, or sports; best school subjects, best friend, favorite teacher, job responsibilities, and closest adult relationship. The scale may be completed in ten minutes by teachers, parents, counselors, or others who are knowledgeable about the student. Then a school psychologist or other trained professional may score and interpret the results. Additional information on the BERS is available at the end of this summary.

Believe in Teenagers with ADD/ADHD

Researchers tell us that when adults with attention deficits were asked how they coped successfully, they often said, *"Someone believed in me."* That someone was most often their parents, but the next most often listed person was a *teacher*. So, the impact teachers have on the lives of students with attention deficits can be profound! *Teachers often make the difference in the success or failure of students with ADD/ADHD.*

Resources

Epstein, Michael H. "Assessing the Emotional and Behavioral Strengths of Children." *Reclaiming Children and Youth,* V. 6 , N. 4, Winter 1998.

Epstein, Michael & Jennifer Sharma. *The Behavioral and Emotional Rating Scale (BERS).* Austin, TX: PRO-ED, 1998. A strength-based rating scale. (800-897-3203; www.proedinc.com)

Reframe: Building on Strengths

Name **Steven**   Grade **11**   Date **9/26**

STRENGTHS—*Home/Community/School*
1. a strong leader; not afraid to take charge
2. high-energy; works long hours
3. tenacious; doesn't give up; persuasive
4. confident public speaker
5. entertaining; always upbeat; makes others laugh
6. friendly; never meets a stranger
7. laser focused when working on an interesting project
8. independent thinker; not afraid to disagree
9. skilled in mechanical areas; works on cars and stereos
10. active in church youth group; a leader

Examples of Reframing Common ADD/ADHD Behaviors

When students are struggling, it is easy to get caught up in focusing on their problem behaviors. It is extremely important to stop and take time to identify each student's strengths and special talents. Examples of ways to reframe negative behaviors may help teachers and parents develop a list of the teenager's strengths. Remember that the desirability of behaviors changes over time. Characteristics that are not valued in students in school may be valued in the adult work world. Discuss the teenager's strengths with her. Ask her if she has anything to add to the list.

Bossiness: "leadership" (albeit carried too far)

Strong-Willed: "tenacious"

Hyperactive: "energetic"
"high energy"
"does ten projects at one time"
"works long hours"

Day Dreamer: "creative"
"innovative"
"imaginative"

Daring: "risk taker"
"willing to try new things"

Lazy: "laid back"
"Type B personalities live longer"

Instigator: "initiator"
"innovative"

Manipulative: "delegates"
"gets others to do the job"

Aggressive: "assertive"
"doesn't let people take advantage of her"

Questions Authority: "independent"
"free thinker"
"makes own decisions"

Argumentative: "persuasive"
"may be attorney material"

Poor Handwriting: "maybe she'll be a doctor one day"

SUMMARY 72
When Teens Continue to Struggle in School . . .

Finding Problems Hidden Beneath the Surface!

If teenagers with ADD/ADHD continue to struggle even after receiving accommodations at school and starting medication, more complex problems may be "hidden beneath the surface." Three common reasons many students struggle are discussed in the following paragraphs. Work with parents and teens to identify which, if any, of these problems are interfering with school performance.

1. Medication is not right.

- **Medication is too low:** Concern is sometimes expressed about medication being too high. But, in reality, doses that are too low are a more frequent problem, according to the 2000 NIMH study on attention deficit disorders. As teenagers go through puberty and hormones change, they may need higher doses of stimulant medications such as Ritalin or Adderall.

- **Medication has worn off:** Some stimulant medications really don't last very long, perhaps three hours or so, and may wear off before lunch. For example, when a student takes a regular 10 mg. tablet of Ritalin at 6:30 a.m., the peak academic effectiveness of the medication has worn off by about 9:30 that morning. So, students may be doing most of their class work without the benefit of medicine.

Correct dosages and timing of medication are critical. Obviously, since teachers aren't doctors, you may feel uncomfortable talking with parents about medication. However, proper medication is critical for school success, so please don't avoid discussing it. One way to approach this issue is to review Summaries 51-56 with parents and ask whether they think this is an issue that should be *discussed with their doctor*. You may also complete the medication checklist, Summary 55, which will show whether medication helps improve academic performance.

2. Learning problems and executive functioning deficits are not addressed.

- **Specific Learning Disabilities (SLD):** Twenty-five to thirty percent of students with ADD/ADHD also meet criteria for SLD. According to new research, when written expression is also evaluated, the rate of SLD is closer to 65 percent. See Summary 43.

- **Other Serious Learning Problems:** Many students have serious learning problems that interfere with their ability to learn and do well in school. Although these learning problems may not meet SLD criteria, they still cause major problems and should be addressed through classroom accommodations.

- **Executive Functioning Deficits:** Practically speaking, students with attention deficits have trouble memorizing and remembering information, quickly retrieving and analyzing information, organizing their thoughts, and developing and following through on a plan of action to complete written school work. See Summary 28.

Identify each student's unique learning problems and make appropriate accommodations. Most students with ADD/ADHD will benefit from one or more of the classroom accommodations listed in Summaries 41, 44, or 45.

If a student is still struggling, ***refer to the SST*** or ***IEP Team*** to determine if further evaluation is needed.

3. Other coexisting conditions are not treated.

As explained in Summary 1, 67 percent of all students with ADD/ADHD have at least one other coexisting condition that complicates treatment. A brief overview of these coexisting conditions is provided below.

Neurological Disorders

This section covers the neurological disorders that are most likely to occur along with ADD/ADHD. A more detailed discussion of these disorders is contained in both the American Psychiatric Association's *Diagnostic and Statistical Manual of Mental Disorders (DSM-IV)* and *Teenagers with ADD*. Keep in mind that this is just a brief overview and that each of these broad diagnostic categories is complex and may have several subtypes.

Anxiety Disorders

Although outwardly acting indifferent, many teenagers with ADD/ADHD worry a lot and experience anxiety regarding their school work. About 25 percent of them have an anxiety disorder. They may feel ***Generalized Anxiety*** or may experience more severe anxiety disorders such as ***Panic Attacks*** or ***Obsessive Compulsive Disorder***.

Generalized Anxiety Disorder is marked by three or more of the following characteristics:

- edginess
- muscle tension
- mind going blank
- irritability
- fatigue
- sleep disturbance

Students with attention deficits are especially fearful of being embarrassed in school. Typically, they recognize that they have problems listening. They're afraid that if the teacher calls on them, they will not have heard the question. Even when listening, they may get so flustered they may not be able to answer the question correctly. If the student also has slow processing speed, she may be so fearful of speaking in front of the class that she would rather accept a failing grade than speak.

Panic Attacks involve a period of intense fear, which starts suddenly and reaches a peak in roughly ten minutes. The student may experience four or more of the following symptoms:

- pounding heart
- shortness of breath
- feelings of being outside oneself
- chest discomfort
- dizziness
- fear of going crazy or losing control
- trembling
- nausea
- tingling sensations

One positive aspect of having anxiety from the teacher's standpoint is that the student is less likely to act or speak impulsively and more likely to want to complete school work.

Obsessive Compulsive Disorder (OCD) is associated with both *obsessions*—recurrent thoughts or impulses—and *compulsions*—repetitive behaviors or mental acts that the person feels driven to do (ordering, checking, counting, recopying work). This disorder has a tremendous impact on school performance. The student may have trouble being satisfied with written work and may obsess over the content and neatness of her handwriting. Obsessing over thoughts makes writing an essay especially challenging.

Tourette Syndrome (TS)

Tourette Syndrome causes repeated involuntary vocal sounds and physical movements called *tics.* Vocal tics may include grunting, clearing the throat, humming, spitting, or coughing. Motor tics may include eye blinking, shoulder shrugs, mouth opening, lip licking, grimacing, sticking the tongue out, or stretching movements. Symptoms wax and wane, and stress may make them worse. Sometimes when students try to suppress their tics, an explosive build-up of tension occurs. Sherry Pruitt, author of *Taming the Tiger*, refers to these blow-ups and loss of control as "Tourette storms." After the storm subsides, the child calms down and sometimes will have no memory of the blow-up.

Fifty to seventy percent of students with Tourette syndrome (TS) also have ADD/ADHD. Tourette Syndrome is six times more common in males than in females. The average age of onset for TS is 6.5 years.

Sometimes stimulant medication for attention deficit will exacerbate the tic symptoms. Consequently, some doctors will stop medication immediately since they are fearful that the tics triggered by medication may be irreversible. However, David Comings, M.D., author of *Tourette Syndrome and Human Behavior*, indicates that many of these students *can* take stimulants, but medication doses should be reduced or a different medication prescribed. Sometimes a student may have ADD/ADHD, Tourette syndrome, *and* obsessive-compulsive disorder, which further complicates treatment.

Mood Disorders

Depression

The official diagnostic criteria for depression tend to describe adult behaviors better than those of young people. For example, depression doesn't always involve sadness in teenagers. Generally speaking, young people who are depressed may experience bad moods, lack of enjoyment in life, irritability, or aggression. So, when a teen with ADD/ADHD is often irritable or aggressive, this behavior may really be masking depression. In fact, about 25 percent of teens with attention deficits are depressed. Frequently, however, when the depression is treated, the irritability and aggression decrease significantly. Inattention may also be a symptom of depression. Occasionally, inattention related to depression may be mistaken for ADD/ADHD.

Dysthymic Disorder

A milder form of depression known as dysthymia may also occur. To meet diagnostic criteria for dysthymia, at least two of these symptoms must be present for the better part of a year:

- changes in eating habits
- changes in sleeping habits
- reduced mental energy
- reduced physical energy
- difficulty making decisions
- low self-esteem
- feelings of hopelessness

Bipolar Disorder

Bipolar disorder includes alternating periods of extreme high energy (mania) and low energy (depression). This disorder is extremely difficult to diagnose in young people. In fact, some mental health professionals believe that it cannot be accurately diagnosed until the mid- to late twenties. Still, researchers have recently found that approximately 12 percent of teenagers with attention deficits also have the disorder. Bipolar disorder has also been diagnosed in younger children.

Differentiating between ADD/ADHD and bipolar disorder is difficult, since they share several common characteristics:

- excessive activity
- poor judgment
- impulsive behavior
- denial of problems

Occasionally, people with bipolar disorder may have a psychotic episode where they lose touch with reality. In other words, they may have hallucinations or delusions (of grandeur; think they're rich or that they are God). In contrast, people with ADD/ADHD alone will not exhibit psychotic symptoms, unless something unusual happens. For example, psychotic symptoms can be brought on by a chemical interaction between medication (Tofranil-imipramine) and illegal drugs (marijuana). For adults to be diagnosed with bipolar disorder, they must exhibit several of the following characteristics:

- inflated self-esteem or grandiosity
- racing thoughts
- excessive involvement in pleasurable activities (sexual indiscretions, spending sprees, foolish business ventures)
- talking more than usual
- distractibility
- decreased need for sleep

As young children, they may have a history of horrendous, lengthy tantrums that continue even when no one is watching. **_Symptoms in teens_** may include:

- irritability
- loud giggling
- day dreamy, floating quality
- hostility
- rejection of other people
- aggression or destructiveness

Since bipolar disorder is often baffling to the experts, obviously teachers aren't expected to recognize this disorder. My point in writing about the condition is to remind teachers that we know that some teenagers with attention deficits have bipolar disorder, but it may not be diagnosed for ten years or more. If a student is extremely difficult to handle, perhaps there are hidden reasons for her school failure and misbehavior. Unfortunately, teachers may never have the benefit of knowing that the student has one of these conditions.

Substance-Related Disorders

Treatment professionals describe substance problems in a range from less to more severe: _substance use,_ then _substance abuse,_ and finally _addiction_.

The two substances that teenagers with ADD/ADHD use most often are cigarettes and alcohol. Over 50 percent of these teens smoke cigarettes, which is double the rate of students who don't have ADD/ADHD. Alcohol use is at about the 40 percent level and marijuana use at 17 percent. These percentages are somewhat inflated by two subgroups of ADHD. Teens whose attention deficit coexists with conduct disorder or bipo-lar disorder have the worst substance abuse problems and poorest prognosis. Surprisingly, many teenagers with uncomplicated ADD or ADHD are no more likely than their peers to smoke, drink, or abuse illegal drugs. It is interesting to note that the actual age of onset for substance abuse is around 19, after students have graduated from high school. So the post high school years are a high-risk time for substance abuse.

One recent study by Timothy E. Wilens, M.D., author of *Straight Talk about Psychiatric Medications for Kids*, has presented some very encouraging news: **students with ADD/ADHD who take medication are less likely to abuse drugs than students with ADD/ADHD who don't take medication!**

If we look at predictors of substance abuse, two or three facts are important for teachers to know. School failure, low grades, and low self-esteem are predictors of future substance abuse. Since aggression and hyperactivity are also predictors, some students with attention deficits are definitely at risk for substance abuse. Teachers can help prevent some of these problems by helping students succeed in school and building their self-esteem. Schools can also offer after-school activities and opportunities for community service, which are also thought to be good ways to prevent drug abuse.

Disruptive Behavior Disorders

Oppositional Defiant Disorder (ODD)

Unfortunately for teachers and parents, Oppositional Defiant Disorder (ODD) is the most common coexisting condition among students with attention deficits, affecting about 67 percent of them. Generally speaking, teens with ODD are negative, disobedient, and hostile toward authority figures. As adults, we find this behavior especially irritating and difficult to cope with.

Teenagers with ODD have four or more of the following behaviors:

- loses temper
- argues with adults
- refuses to comply with adult requests
- blames others
- easily annoyed
- vindictive
- angry
- deliberately annoys people

Perhaps deficits in executive functioning skills make students with ADD or ADHD more likely to exhibit behaviors on this list. For example, difficulty controlling emotions could lead to more frequent blow-ups; working memory deficits make it difficult to recall past experiences to avoid repeating misbehavior; and speaking or acting before they think of the consequences can lead to confrontations with adults or peers. Frustration regarding their poor school performance may also contribute to these behaviors.

Conduct Disorder (CD)

About 22 percent of students with ADD/ADHD have a Conduct Disorder (CD). Conduct Disorder is characterized by behavior that violates the basic rights of others or breaks the law. Although fifteen behaviors comprise the criteria for CD, they include four broad categories. To qualify for CD, students must exhibit only three of the fifteen behaviors.

1. Aggression to people or animals
- intimidates others
- fights
- uses a weapon
- cruel to people
- cruel to animals
- steals while confronting a victim (mugging, armed robbery)
- forces sex on others

2. Destruction of property
- fire setting
- destroys property

3. Deceitfulness or theft
- breaking & entering
- lies
- steals things

4. Serious violations of rules
- stays out at night
- runs away
- truant before age 13

A Closer Look at ODD and CD: ODD and CD are a little different from the other disorders described in this section. Attention deficits, anxiety, depression, and bipolar disorder are all clearly biochemical disorders. On the other hand, ODD and CD are often perceived as intentional misbehavior. However, some researchers have shown that many ODD and CD behaviors have an underlying biochemical cause. Other researchers have also found differences in the brains of people with these disorders. Dr. Joseph Biederman, one of the leading international researchers on attention deficits, found that students with ADD/ADHD and Conduct Disorder had an average of *four additional psychiatric disorders,* such as depression, bipolar disorder, anxiety, or substance abuse. On the surface, it may look as though these young people engage in these behaviors intentionally or simply to be mean. In reality, however, many may be suffering from ***multiple biochemical disorders*** that are being untreated.

Behaviors of students with ODD are aggravating, but those with CD are much more serious and thus deeply troubling to teachers. Students with ADD/ADHD and CD seem to have the most serious problems and the poorest prognosis. For example, students with ADD/ADHD and CD are much more likely to abuse drugs, be expelled from school, and get into trouble with the law. They also have a higher rate of school suspension and dropping out when compared to students with ADD or ADHD only. Students who have an attention deficit plus ODD, on the other hand, are not at greater risk for a poor outcome in adulthood.

Handling ODD or CD in the Classroom:

- Reduce classroom frustration. Identify learning problems and make accommodations in the classroom.
- Teach students conflict resolution skills. See Summaries 66-67 for tips on resolving conflicts and peer mediation.
- Learn skills to defuse anger. Teachers who develop skills to defuse anger and handle conflict are more effective with these students. See Summaries 59-62 on actions that escalate or de-escalate conflicts, behavioral strategies, and avoiding confrontations, plus Summary 69 on anger management.

Take Home Message

My reason for writing about coexisting conditions is not to make excuses for inappropriate behavior, but rather to point out that the behavior of students with an attention deficit is often much more complicated than it appears on the surface. Treatment of these coexisting conditions is critical and may be the pivotal factor in pulling some youngsters back from the edge of life-long frustration, unhappiness, underachievement, and, for some, brushes with the law.

Resources

Barkley, Russell A. *Attention-Deficit Hyperactivity Disorder*. New York: The Guilford Press, 1998.

Biederman, Joseph, Timothy Wilens, Eric Mick, Thomas Spencer, and Stephen Faraone. "Pharmacotherapy of Attention-deficit/Hyperactivity Disorder Reduces Risk for Substance Use Disorder." *Pediatrics,* v 104, n 2, August 1999.

Brown, Thomas E. *Attention-Deficit Disorders and Comorbidities in Children, Adolescents, and Adults.* Washington, DC: American Psychiatric Press, 2000.

Dornbush, Marilyn P. & Sheryl K. Pruitt. *Teaching the Tiger.* Duarte, CA: Hope Press, 1995. This book addresses ADD/ADHD, Obsessive Compulsive Disorder, and Tourette Syndrome. One of the authors, Sherry Pruitt, directs a private learning disabilities center and is the mother of two sons with ADHD, OCD, and Tourette syndrome.

Haerle, Tracy. *Children with Tourette Syndrome: A Parents' Guide.* Bethesda, MD: Woodbine House, 1992.

When Parents Don't Believe It's ADD/ADHD

Parental reactions to a diagnosis of ADD/ADHD vary considerably. Some are **relieved** to finally discover the root of their teenager's problems, and others are **upset** and may **deny** the possibility of an attention deficit disorder. Several factors may influence a parent's reaction to this diagnosis.

1. Unfortunately, **negative publicity about medications** such as Ritalin is often a major concern. My own hometown newspaper, the *Atlanta Journal Constitution*, ran a series of terribly insensitive cartoons on medication for ADD/ADHD in the spring of 2000.

2. The **age** of the student may influence a parent's reaction. When children are still in elementary school, parents may be reluctant to believe that their child has an attention deficit. For some teachers and parents, this reluctance continues into middle and high school. They mistakenly assume that it could not possibly be ADD or ADHD since the student is not hyperactive. However, other parents whose children have struggled through elementary or middle school may be relieved to finally have an answer for why school has always been so difficult for their teenager.

3. **Cultural expectations** may also influence a parent's reaction to ADD/ADHD. A researcher at the University of Florida has found that some families tend to see the behaviors associated with attention deficits as being willful misbehavior or just laziness. Other families see the same behaviors as a potential problem and refer the child or teenager for treatment. Families that rely on strict physical discipline may be less likely to accept ADD/ADHD as the underlying cause of their teenager's struggles.

4. Sometimes **parents are divided** on the issue. One parent believes it is an attention deficit and wants to try medication and the other parent is adamantly opposed.

5. Other times, an **anxious or reluctant teenager** may be the reason that the family has been unwilling to try medication.

After the school evaluation has been completed and if the school psychologist believes the student has ADD/ADHD, the next step is to refer the teenager to a physician to rule out other medical disorders. At this point, some parents may be unwilling to accept a diagnosis or be adamantly opposed to medication. Educators should be aware that **parents often must go through a grieving process before they can accept a diagnosis of ADD/ADHD.** Dr. Elizabeth Kubler-Ross describes the following stages of the grieving process*:* denial, anger, bargaining, depression, and, ultimately acceptance. Parents will need time to come to grips with the sometimes-frightening unknowns linked to this diagnosis. Later, parents may need help *reframing* their perceptions of attention deficits more positively. See Summary 71.

Given that any given parent *may* react negatively to the suggestion that their teenager might have an attention deficit, what is the best way for a teacher to approach this issue? Let's start with the typical procedure teachers follow when a student is struggling in class.

1. The student is barely passing the class. The teacher meets with the student's parents.

2. Accommodations are made in the classroom. Parents provide support at home, yet the student still struggles.

3. An SST meeting is held. Teachers suggest intervention strategies, but they are not successful.

4. Referral is made to an IEP Team. An evaluation is requested. The parent gives permission for the evaluation. The school psychologist completes the evaluation and indicates that the student meets the criteria for attention deficit disorder. One of the recommendations includes referral to a physician for a medical evaluation to confirm the diagnosis or to rule out other problems.

5. Parents may be reluctant to accept a possible diagnosis of ADD/ADHD and may be hesitant to see a physician or not know a physician who specializes in diagnosis and treatment of attention deficits.

6. Now what does the teacher do?

Working with Parents Who Are Apprehensive about the Diagnosis

Although there are no easy answers for working with parents who are apprehensive or are not open to accepting ADD or ADHD as a diagnosis, the following suggestions may be helpful:

1. Sometimes the only thing a teacher, school psychologist, or principal can do is **wait until the parents reach a level of readiness and receptiveness** to discuss ADD/ADHD. Express concern and willingness to help when parents are ready:

   "I am so concerned about your daughter and want her to succeed in school. I worry about her self-esteem being damaged. I feel like she is doing her best and she really wants to do well in school. Failing classes is a terrible thing to happen to any student."

2. **Give parents time to grieve.** Listen while they talk through their concerns and then share helpful information.

   "You really seem worried about the possibility that this might be ADD/ADHD. I also know how much you love Michelle. You are her parents and you will do what is best for her. You may want to talk with Michelle's doctor and share the evaluation results. You may want to talk to another parent of a teenager with an attention deficit. Let me give you a phone number for the local parent group. Either your physician or members of the parent group should be able to tell you which doctors specialize in treating attention deficits."

3. **Refer them to a local parent support group.** A list of national support groups is included in the resources at the end of this summary. Administrators at local schools

often have phone numbers for local groups. If not, contact the district office of special education or local mental health center for phone numbers. Parents may also contact a national office to find a phone number for a local chapter.

4. ***Help educate the parents about ADD/ADHD.*** If they have not already reviewed the official DSM-IV AD/HD Criteria in Summary 5, give them copies: You might say to them:

> *"One of the surveys you completed for the school psychologist had these criteria in it. For your daughter to be diagnosed as having an attention deficit, she must meet six of these nine criteria. Did any of these characteristics sound like your daughter? How many of these traits does Michelle have?"*

The teacher may then comment on the number and types of behaviors she observed in class. *"I've noticed some of the same things you have. She seems ... (mention the ones you see) but she does really well with...."*

Next:

- Provide brief educational materials to read. Use the summaries in this book to educate the parents about various topics regarding attention deficits. Gradually increase the amount of information.
- Suggest that the family watch an educational video. Several may be available through the school or local library. Dr. Russell Barkley and Dr. Thomas Phelan both have good videos. My video, *Father to Father: The ADD Experience!*, has also been well received by guidance counselors, teachers, and parents. The "father" video features fathers of teenagers with attention deficits talking about the challenges of parenting these youngsters. Sometimes when parents see that other parents have experienced many of the same frustrations, they feel somewhat relieved and not so alone.

5. ***Help educate an anxious or reluctant teenager about ADD/ADHD.***

- Suggest that parents provide brief educational materials for the teen to read. Use the summaries in this book to educate the student about various topics regarding attention deficits. Gradually increase the amount of information.
- Suggest that the student talk with another teenager who also has ADD/ADHD and is taking medication.
- Suggest that the teenager watch a video on ADD/ADHD. Several may be available through the school or local library. Many teenagers with attention deficits have enjoyed my video, *Teen to Teen: The ADD Experience,* which features teenagers and young adults talking about the challenges of coping with ADD/ADHD. Guidance counselors, teachers, and parents have also bought the video to show special education classes and teen groups. Sometimes when teenagers see successful, positive role models and realize that other teenagers have experienced many of the same frustrations, they feel somewhat relieved and realize that they are not alone.

6. ***Help parents reframe ADD/ADHD more positively.*** Discuss the positive aspects of attention deficits and explain that many teenagers with ADD or ADHD are very successful. See Appendix A10 for ideas to discuss with the parents. Show parents the video, *Teen to Teen: The ADD Experience!*

7. ***Ask the parents if they would like to talk to a parent of a teenager with ADD/ADHD*** who is coping successfully. A member of a local parent group may be willing to answer questions for the parent. These groups may have additional materials or videos that may be helpful.

8. ***Consider scheduling an educational program*** on teenagers with ADD/ADHD and other learning differences. This program may help parents and teens better understand ADD and ADHD, the related challenges, and learn to identify and maximize the student's strengths.

9. ***Implement appropriate accommodations and teaching strategies*** discussed in Summaries 13-20, 41, 44, and 45.

Resources

Organizations

ADDA: National Attention Deficit Disorder Association, 1788 Second St., Suite 200, Highland Park, IL 60035. (847-432-5874; www.adda.org)

ADDA-SR: Attention Deficit Disorder Association-Southern Region, 12345 Jones Rd., Suite 287, Houston, TX 77070. (281-955-3720; www.adda-sr.org)

CHADD: Children and Adults with Attention Deficit Disorders, 8181 Professional Place, Suite 201, Landover, MD 20785. (800-233-4050; www.chadd.org)

Federation of Families for Children's Mental Health, 1101 King St., Suite 420, Alexandria, VA 22314. (703-684-7710; www.ffcmh.org)

NAMI: National Alliance for the Mentally Ill, Colonial Place Three, 2107 Wilson Blvd., Suite 300, Arlington, VA 22201. (800-950-6264; www.nami.org)

NMHA: National Mental Health Association, 1021 Prince St., Alexandria, VA 22314. (703-684-7722; www.nmha.org)

Videos

These videos may be available through your local library. Most can be ordered from ADD WareHouse (800-233-9273; www.addwarehouse.com) or from Amazon at www.amazon.com.

ADDA-SR
Never a Dull Moment
This video features several parents talking about their experiences coping with ADHD, especially when their children were first diagnosed. A portion of the proceeds from the sale of the video will be donated to ADDA, Southern Region. Available only through Ma Writer Production, Michele Arnold, 4917 Elm Street, Bellaire TX 77401 (713-666-8562 or e-mail: mawriter@earthlink.net)

Barkley, Russell.
ADHD: What Do We Know?
ADHD: What Can We Do?

These videos provide an overview of ADHD and effective ways to manage it.

Dendy, Chris Zeigler
Teen to Teen: the ADD Experience
Father to Father: the ADD Experience!

In the Teen video, a panel of teens and young adults talk about their experiences coping with ADD plus the things they do well. In the Father video, four fathers talk about their experiences parenting teens with ADD. Also available from: www.chrisdendy.com or Chris A. Dendy, P.O. Box 189, Cedar Bluff, AL 35959

Phelan, Thomas
All About Attention Deficit Disorder

This two-part video provides basic information about ADHD and behavior management at home and at school. Dr. Phelan is also well known for "1-2-3 Magic," his popular discipline strategies for younger children.

SUMMARY 74 Working with a Teenager Who Doesn't Take Medication

Sometimes, for a variety of reasons, students do not take medication for their ADD/ADHD.

- Unfortunately, stimulant medications do not work for a small percentage of students.
- All too frequently, medication refusal is a problem with teenagers. Teenagers simply refuse to take medication because they don't want to be different from their peers or they don't like how the medication makes them feel.
- Sometimes, one or both parents may refuse to consider medication for a variety of reasons, including fear of medication, fear and guilt that they have been "bad" parents, fear of the long-term outcome for their teenager, or because they are in denial and grieving for their teenager's problems.

Regardless of the reason, the teacher is faced with the challenge of trying to teach a teenager who has great difficulty paying attention and may be unable to learn easily. When this happens, teachers must use strategies that are effective for students with learning problems.

All of the summaries in Sections 2, 3, and 4 contain information that will help these students be more successful in school, regardless of whether they are taking medication for an attention deficit. Some of the most important general strategies are outlined below.

1. Value the student: Summary 70.

2. Build on his or her strengths: Appendix A10.

3. Help the student understand attention deficit, its related challenges, and her own personal strengths, and involve her as a partner in problem solving: Summaries 73 and 74.

4. Use multisensory, high-interest teaching strategies: Section 2.

5. Modify teaching strategies: Summary 13.

- 13-A: Modify teaching methods and resources; use more visual cues and reminders; use active learning strategies; increase class participation; use peer tutoring.
- 13-B: Modify assignments; reduce the amount of written work; break work into smaller segments.
- 13-C: Modify testing and grading; give extended time; adjust test format.
- 13-D: Increase levels of supervision; get other students and parents to help.

- 13-E: Use technology.
- Summary 65: Provide a coach.

6. Provide accommodations for executive function deficits: Section 2 and 3.

- forgetfulness: Summary 30
- memorization problems: Summary 22
- disorganization: Summary 29
- written expression problems: Summaries 14-17
- mastering math: Summaries 18-21
- impaired sense of time: Summaries 32-37

7. Provide structure and use good classroom management strategies: Summaries 57-58.

8. Use behavioral strategies that de-escalate problem situations: Summaries 59-61.

9. Teach the student self-management skills, plus help her manage ADD/ADHD behavior.

Teach skills the student is lacking: Summaries 64-69.

- conflict resolution
- peer mediation
- problem solving
- anger management
- time management

10. Anticipate and avoid potential problem situations. Identify situations that students with attention deficits don't handle well—for example, transitions such as going to lunch or PE or having a substitute teacher. Develop an intervention strategy to prevent the problem. Read the section regarding use of a behavior intervention plan in an IEP, Summary 40.

Teaching strategies, common learning problems, classroom accommodations, reasons for school failure, and suggested intervention strategies are discussed in more detail in Section 2 and in Chapters 9 and 10 in *Teenagers with ADD* (Woodbine House, 1995).

SUMMARY 75 — Tough Questions and Comments from Teachers

As I have traveled across the country providing training on ADD/ADHD, teachers have asked me many excellent but often difficult questions. Some questions are from teachers who are eager to learn more about teaching these teenagers effectively. Other questions are most likely born of frustration. Perhaps a teacher has tried traditional teaching methods that work for most students, but they just don't work as well for these students. Consequently, he or she may think, *"Surely, this student must be lazy. She is obviously very bright. If she would only try, she could do his work."*

If an educator believes that ADD/ADHD is just an excuse for a lazy student, I realize that I cannot change his or her mind by arguing. All I can do is explain what I have learned about the powerful influence the brain's biochemistry has over behaviors related to an attention deficit. This knowledge comes from my thirty-plus years as an educator and mental health professional, my study of the latest scientific research, and, more importantly, the profound personal experience of living with two sons, one with ADD and the other with ADHD.

Having been a teacher and not personally having an attention deficit, I empathize with educators: *teaching teenagers with ADD or ADHD can be extremely challenging!* The behavior and learning problems that these students exhibit make a teacher's job very, very difficult. Unfortunately, ADD/ADHD is often so complex that answers to questions about the disorder are seldom easy. Personally, I must confess that I have been humbled by having children with this condition. Clearly, I don't have any magic answers, but neither does anyone else. So, I will share my best thinking on these very difficult issues.

Questions and Comments from Teachers

1. "This teenager is lazy. He really doesn't even try. ADD/ADHD is just an excuse."

To the casual observer, the behaviors of these teenagers may look like laziness or apathy. When ADD/ADHD is improperly treated or learning problems have not been identified, a student may appear lazy or disinterested. However, this "I don't care attitude" often covers up a lot of emotional pain, depression, serious learning problems, and a sense of being overwhelmed. This attitude often really means, "I've given up!" They have been so worn down over time by continual school failure. Eventually, some teenagers who have experienced constant failure may give up in despair. One student said, "I can't wait until I get out of school so I can be successful."

It has been my personal and professional experience that the vast majority of these teenagers want to do well in school. In fact, many of these students must try harder and actually spend more hours on their homework than their peers. Giving these students the necessary supports to succeed in school is like throwing a lifeline to a drowning person. Most of them will grab hold and try to save themselves.

Revise the educational and treatment plans to correct problems with medication or make appropriate classroom accommodations and these teenagers ***can*** succeed in school!

As explained in Summary 1, this is *not* to say that these teenagers should be given permission to misbehave or not complete school work. Rather, the point is that teenagers with ADD or ADHD *may* have a disability and desperately need the teacher's understanding, support, supervision, and appropriate classroom accommodations. Having an attention deficit is not an *excuse* but rather an *explanation* for sometimes puzzling behavior. Remember also, ADD/ADHD is no picnic for these teenagers. They did not ask to have the disorder. One younger student prayed, *"Dear God, please don't let me have ADD."* Another teenager cried, *"I feel like I am going to die of anxiety or go crazy."* As with any teenager with a disability, they may become weary, give up, and have less than perfect days at school. However, with the teacher's support and understanding, they will return another day to tackle this challenge known as attention deficit disorder!

2. "Students with ADD/ADHD don't really need medication to help them concentrate. They could do their school work if they would just buckle down and work harder."

As explained in Summary 10, researchers at the National Institute of Mental Health have shown that ***ADD/ADHD is first and foremost a neurobiological disorder for which medication is the most effective treatment.*** Medication helps the neurotransmitters in the brain work properly so the student can concentrate, participate in class, and complete school work.

My current thinking about medication is 180 degrees away from where I began when I started learning about attention deficits. As I have studied the available research on ADD and ADHD and other biochemical disorders, I have developed an increasing respect for the influence of the brain's biochemistry on the behavior of these teenagers.

As a young mother, I had very conservative views about medication. I avoided taking any medication or giving it to our sons. Initially, I didn't want my sons on any medication, but desperation led me to try it. One son was in middle school and in danger of failing most of his classes even though he was intellectually gifted. He wanted to do well in school but was unable to do so. When we finally put him on medication, his grades went from Ds and Fs to mostly Bs and Cs. With our older son, the change was even more dramatic. His grades climbed from mostly Ds to As and Bs.

See Section 5, especially Summary 52, for a discussion of medication and its impact on the student's school performance. As explained in Summaries 54-56, determine whether medication is helping the teenager be more successful in school.

7

3. "When is enough, enough?" or "What should I do now? I've tried to help her and she still won't do her work."

Last year, at an educator's conference in Illinois, a frustrated teacher asked me this question. "When is enough, enough?" The question was asked informally after the workshop was over. I really didn't have a very good answer and stumbled through a response. I can only guess that this teacher was referring to his attempts to give a student with an attention deficit extra supports that the student didn't fully utilize. Or the student may have worked well for a while and then stopped doing all her work. Obviously, this can be very frustrating for a teacher who is doing his best to help a student.

The better a teacher understands attention deficits, the easier it is to set realistic expectations. Remember this: **ADD/ADHD is a disability** for some students. Progress is not going to move along in a nice, smooth upward line. Uneven academic performance is one of the hallmarks of this disorder. The student may make good progress for a while and then begin to backslide. Expect periodic slumps in school work: it is a normal occurrence. These teenagers may go through cycles of feeling worn out and overwhelmed. Sometimes students with attention deficits become depressed, and then just "shut down." Often, no one is more frustrated than the student is. Some just get better at covering up the hurt and discouragement. When teachers offer help, the student may be too overwhelmed to accept it. The end of the school year is often especially difficult for the student, parents, and teachers. By May, these students are usually worn out and may be ready to give up.

Teachers and parents can help if they **give students enough support to get them through the end of the school year.** Teachers should consider being more flexible and allowing make-up work to be turned in late or extra credit assignments to be submitted, especially if the primary goal is being met—*the teenager has in fact learned the material being taught*!

Teachers may worry that they are doing the teenager a disservice if they do not "hold her accountable." However, considering the disability and developmental delay involved, these teenagers will eventually learn to handle their own affairs or will learn to compensate for their skill deficits. Holding a student back to repeat a grade will not resolve these problems. The deficits will still be present. And, most likely, giving the student a failing grade will not change her behavior, but it may make her discouraged and depressed. Researchers tell us that students who fail classes are more likely to drop out of school. Specifically, Dr. Barkley tells us that 36 percent of students with attention deficits drop out of school.

When the student struggles and experiences failure during the school year, the educational and treatment plans need to be reassessed and revised. There is a major problem somewhere! The challenge is for the teacher to play detective and find out what the problem is. Several potential culprits are discussed in this book:

- The student's learning problems and/or executive function deficits haven't been addressed. (See Sections 2 and 3.)

- Sleep problems have not been treated.
- Medication is wrong, medication is wearing off, hormonal changes make medication less effective, or tolerance to sustained-release medication has developed. (See Section 5.)

4. "It's not fair to other students to treat this teenager differently. I don't want to lower my standards for this student."

For teenagers with complex cases of ADD/ADHD, the disorder is often severe enough to qualify as a disability. These students need classroom accommodations to help them cope with their deficits in academics, executive function, and self-control. In this situation, *"being fair" is defined as "giving each teenager what he or she needs to succeed,"* not simply giving every student the same thing. Teenagers and parents may argue that "it isn't fair" that the teenager has ADD or ADHD.

Teachers *must* give students accommodations that are included in their IEPs. According to one court ruling in West Virginia, a teacher who refused to implement accommodations in an IEP was held personally liable and fined 15 thousand dollars.

Because many problems associated with attention deficits are invisible, it may be difficult for educators and parents alike to accept that this condition can be a disability. The complexities of ADD/ADHD and the *invisible nature* of some aspects of the disorder are displayed in the diagram of the iceberg, Summary 4.

Teenagers with attention deficits may **have a different learning style** than their classmates. In addition, they may need to be evaluated differently to determine what they have learned. For example, let's consider a student with slow processing speed who is eligible for special education services. She is mainstreamed for math but is failing the class. She can do all the math problems correctly but she can't write fast enough to complete all of them on her test. The teenager is being tested on her ability to "read and write quickly" rather than her knowledge of math skills. By making accommodations for this teenager, such as an untimed test or reduced written work, the teacher is not lowering her standards. The teenager has mastered the math concepts being taught. Sometimes traditional testing methods create a barrier to accurately assessing the teenager's knowledge and should be changed by giving appropriate accommodations.

Federal education and civil rights laws mandate that students with ADD/ADHD whose learning is adversely affected must receive appropriate supports and accommodations.

5. "She is old enough to take full responsibility for completing her homework. If she doesn't do her work, let her fail. Punish her. She'll learn."

Teenagers with ADD/ADHD will eventually learn to accept responsibility for their actions, but because of their two- to four-year developmental delay, they will do it later than their peers. In the interim, teachers can help by ***providing accommodations, occasionally being flexible about submitting assignments on time, and "shaping" the desired behavior.***

Educators sometimes forget, or perhaps they don't know, that students with ADD/ADHD don't learn from punishment and rewards like other students. In addition, Dr. Barkley has observed, and I have learned from first-hand experience, that ***"Punishment alone is ineffective."*** Even younger children with attention deficits often recognize that punishment doesn't always work. Our youngest son shocked me when he was only eight by saying with regret, "I'm sorry, Mom, but when you punish me it just doesn't seem to work." Even at his tender age, he recognized what it took Dr. Barkley and me twenty years to learn.

In some respects, ADD/ADHD is similar to diabetes, where the problem lies in an inability to regulate blood sugar levels. Teenagers with attention deficits cannot regulate the levels of neurotransmitters in their brain. As Mary Fowler points out in her book, *Maybe You Know My Child,* we often blame and punish these children because of their disability. Yet we would never dream of blaming and punishing children for their disability when they are blind, paralyzed, or diabetic. Just as punishing a child who has diabetes doesn't change glucose levels, punishing a student with ADD or ADHD doesn't change neurotransmitter levels in the brain. But educating the student and providing reminders can help change her behavior.

A typical consequence for a student who doesn't do homework is failing the class and having to attend summer school. Unfortunately, these consequences are often *not* effective in changing the behavior of these teenagers. The consequence occurs too distant in time from the behavior of concern. Typically, after attending summer school, these students will fall into the same pattern of getting zeros for not completing their school work. To be effective, consequences must occur quickly, plus be *instructive,* not just punitive!

Because of my graduate training at Florida State University, I thought behavioral intervention strategies, when used properly, could solve any behavior problem. Consequently, I had used behavioral strategies with my son since he was very young. However, Dr. Barkley recommends *first, get the medication right,* and then use behavioral interventions to shape the remaining problem behaviors. Findings from the 1999 NIMH study on ADD/ADHD have also confirmed that medication works more effectively than behavioral interventions. Based upon my personal experience, I agree 100 percent with these conclusions. As someone who is skilled in using these interventions, I have reluctantly come to the conclusion that behavioral strategies are helpful, but *limited in their effectiveness!* Teenagers with attention deficits do not respond in a typical manner to behavioral interventions. This means these strategies are much more difficult to implement with students with ADD/ADHD.

Teach the student the skill you want her to have. Using a weekly report to ensure homework completion and making weekly activities contingent upon completing the work are much more effective strategies than punishment.

7

If the ADD/ADHD behavior can't be changed, then change the environment. For example, if a student is late to class frequently, help her organize her locker better or change her routes between classes. (Summaries 29-32)

6. "She lies. She hides her homework and test grades from her parents."

Students with ADD/ADHD may not always tell the truth! This is a common complaint from parents and teachers alike. Usually, it does not reflect a deep moral defect in the teenager. Instead, it may be an inappropriate coping mechanism the student is using to avoid punishment or unpleasant work. And let's face it, homework is especially unpleasant for these teenagers.

Lying may occur more often during stressful periods (especially if learning problems and executive function deficits have not been identified), during transitions, or near the end of the school year. Often, impulsivity plays a major role in lying. The student says the first thing that pops into her head. Later she may regret the impulsivity, but it is done and can't be taken back. At other times, she may truly forget something due to her memory impairment.

Dr. Ross Green, author of *The Explosive Child*, has this to say about ADHD and lying.

> *"Imagine being a child who has a whole bunch of knowledge stored in your brain about appropriate ways of behaving. Also imagine being so impulsive that this store of knowledge seldom prevents you from behaving inappropriately. In other words, you're continuously behaving in ways you 'know' are inappropriate, but you aren't gaining access to the knowledge that your behavior is inappropriate rapidly enough to keep you out of trouble. It's like there are two of you—the 'you' who engages in inappropriate behavior and the 'you' who clearly knows better. The stage is now set for lying.*

> *"Here's how. You behave inappropriately. Then after a brief delay, your knowledge about appropriate behavior finally kicks in, and you find yourself in the position of having to explain why you just behaved in a way you already 'know' was inappropriate. Most children with ADHD don't have the presence of mind to say, 'I know I shouldn't have done that; I just didn't access the information in time.' What many do instead is fall back on one of the most primitive defense mechanisms: denial. So what comes out of the mouths is, 'I didn't do it.'"*

This is not to say that lying is okay. However, the best strategy is to ***identify problem areas and make accommodations at school.*** Teenagers who are happy, succeeding in school, and have strong self-esteem have less reason to lie. Drs. Sydney Zentall and Sam Goldstein, authors of *Seven Steps to Homework Success*, suggest that punishment may *not* be the best approach.

Correct the problem by removing the need to lie. Students who are successful in school don't need to lie. Identify any learning problems and executive function deficits and make appropriate accommodations.

Teachers should maintain close contact with parents during stressful periods. Fax or e-mail a note or call and leave a message for parents regarding missed assignments or homework. This also removes the temptation for the student to lie about whether or not homework is due.

7. "I have other students with ADD/ADHD and they don't have this problem."

It is important to remember that ***all teenagers with ADD or ADHD are not alike!*** A student may have an attention deficit that is mild, moderate, or severe, plus may have several coexisting problems, such as learning problems, executive function deficits, slow processing speed, memory problems, a sleep disturbance, depression, anxiety, or obsessive compulsive disorder. The more severe the ADD or ADHD and the more coexisting problems that are present, the more challenging it is to teach and treat the teenager.

Learn more about each of these students. Identify his or her unique strengths and challenges.

8. Sometimes parents become angry and make unreasonable demands. How am I supposed to deal with them?

Like teachers, parents get very weary of dealing with ADD/ADHD behavior day-in and day-out. They become very frustrated dealing with just one teenager with this condition. So, most of them understand the challenges a teacher faces in a classroom setting with 25 other students. When teachers encounter an angry parent, what they may really be seeing, but may not recognize, is *parental fear*: fear about the future and fear about whether or not their teenager will cope successfully with this challenging condition. In other words, ***the anger a parent expresses may actually be masking their deepest fears about their teenager's future***.

Many parents feel very much alone in this battle with ADD or ADHD, especially when it is complex. Often parents cannot find treatment professionals who seem to know how to help their teenager. Parents come to fear the worst: potential school failure, dropping out, substance abuse, or brushes with the law. They *desperately* want your help but their fear may drive them to be less than tactful as they ask for help. Perhaps teachers can reframe their perceptions of these parents: the good news is, *"These parents care a lot about their teenager. They want to be involved. They want her to succeed. I'll try to help them channel their concerns."*

Unfortunately, the teacher is called upon to be the "counselor" who diffuses the parent's anger and channels it positively. ***Try active listening:***

"I know you are deeply concerned about your daughter. I'm sorry school is so hard for her. Together, let's develop a plan to ensure that she suc-

ceeds in school. What do you think the problems are? ..... What do you think she needs?...."

The parents may or may not be on target with suggestions for what the student needs, but usually they *know* what the problems are. As the teacher, you may come up with creative options they haven't thought of that may better address the teenager's needs, plus require less time from you. If the problems are identified first, then together you may come up with a **compromise** to meet the teenager's needs.

Sometimes parents may make **unreasonable requests at an IEP meeting.** For example, one parent went to a conference, handed the teachers my Summary 41 of 50 classroom accommodations and said, "I want all this for my teenager!" What do you do then? Obviously, classroom accommodations must be tailor-made to address a teenager's needs. Most teenagers with ADD/ADHD will *not* need all these accommodations. Perhaps a teacher might say,

> *"This information you brought us looks really good. You're exactly right—teenagers with ADD/ADHD do often need accommodations in the classroom to help them succeed in school. Usually, however, they need some, but not all, of these accommodations. Let's identify the specific things that are really difficult for your teenager and decide which classroom accommodations she needs. Typically, it is best to keep a plan simple at first and successfully implement a few strategies. Then more can be added later if needed. "*

Action Step

If a parent's requests are unreasonable, state what you can offer and then what your limitations are. Perhaps you can come up with a creative compromise: "I can give her untimed tests and allow her to use a computer for written work. But I can't always . . . remind her to write her homework down, prompt her to start working, etc."

Seek a creative solution: "John and Mary sit near your daughter, perhaps they could remind her of her assignment or actually write it down for her."

Involve the student in problem solving. **Give her a choice.** "Gina, students with ADD often forget to write down their assignments. One thing we can do to help you remember is to ask another student to remind you. Would you like to have either John or Mary remind you?"

9. The Student's parents are too involved. They are overprotective.

Remember, most students with attention deficits are developmentally two to four years behind their peers and experience critical deficits in executive function. Teachers and parents of these students must provide greater supervision and supports than ordinarily would be expected for this age student. Another way to think of this issue is that adults are simply providing *"developmentally appropriate supervision."*

Please give parents permission to be involved with their teen's school-work when needed. Do not criticize them or make them feel guilty for their greater level of involvement. Teach them how to provide supervision and reduce supports as the student accepts more responsibility. Several helpful suggestions are provided regarding supervision (Summary 13-D) and coaching (Summary 65).

Blank Forms

APPENDIX
A

APPENDIX A1 — The ADD/ADHD Iceberg

The Tip of the Iceberg—the obvious ADD/ADHD behaviors:

HYPERACTIVITY	IMPULSIVITY	INATTENTION
_____	_____	_____
_____	_____	_____
_____	_____	_____
_____	_____	

**2-4 YEAR
DEVELOPMENTAL DELAY**
Less mature
Less responsible
14 year old acts like 10

"Hidden Beneath the Surface"—
the not-so-obvious behaviors:

**NEUROSTRANSMITTER
DEFICITS IMPACT BEHAVIOR**
Inefficient levels of neurotransmit-
ters (norepinephrine, dopamine,
and serotonin) result in reduced
brain activity on thinking tasks

COEXISTING CONDITIONS
(2/3 have at least one other condition)
_____
_____
_____
_____

WEAK EXECUTIVE FUNCTIONING
_____
_____
_____
_____

ADD/ADHD is often more complex than most people realize! Like icebergs, many problems related to ADD/ADHD are not visible. ADD/ADHD may be mild, moderate, or severe, is likely to coexist with other conditions, and may be a disability for some students.

SERIOUS LEARNING PROBLEMS (90%)
(Specific Learning Disability; 25-30%)
_____
_____
_____
_____
_____
_____
_____

SLEEP DISTURBANCE (50%)
_____
_____
_____
_____

IMPAIRED SENSE OF TIME
_____
_____
_____
_____

**NOT LEARNING EASILY FROM
REWARDS AND PUNISHMENT**
_____
_____
_____
_____

LOW FRUSTRATION TOLERANCE
(Difficulty Controlling Emotions)
_____
_____
_____
_____

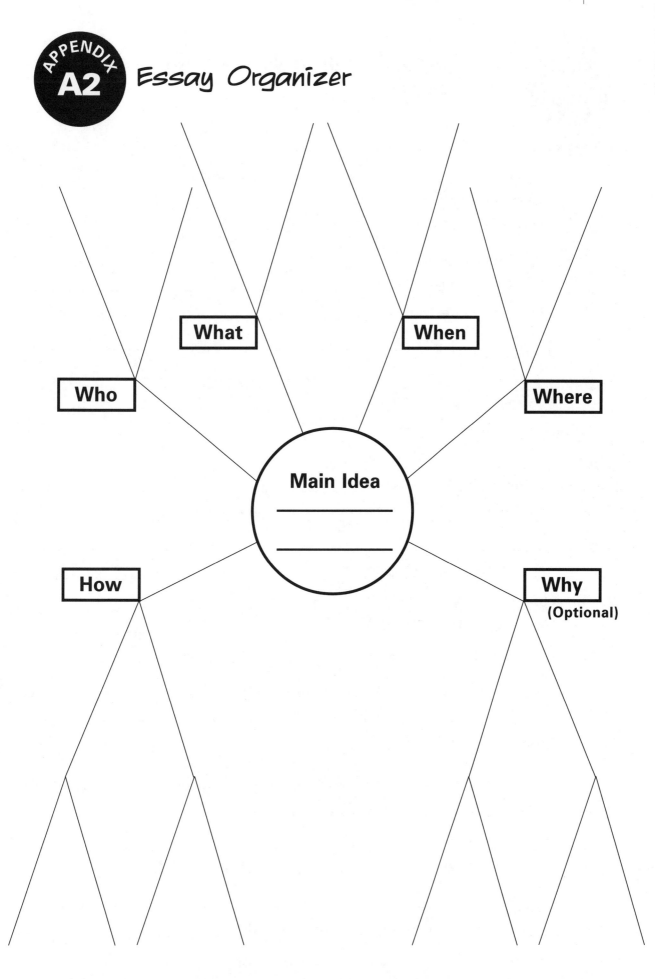

APPENDIX A2 Essay Organizer

What

When

Who

Where

Main Idea
_____
_____

How

Why
(Optional)

Student Outline for Writing an Essay

APPENDIX A3

I. Thesis Paragraph *(Topic—Mentors)*

    A. Definition _____

    B. Importance _____

    C. Three key traits _____   _____   _____

II. First Supporting Paragraph

    A. Topic sentence (1st trait) _____

    B. Supporting examples _____

    _____

    _____

    C. Transition to next paragraph _____

III. Second Supporting Paragraph

    A. Topic sentence (2nd trait) _____

    B. Supporting examples _____

    _____

    _____

    C. Transition to next paragraph _____

IV. Third Supporting Paragraph

    A. Topic Sentence (3rd trait)_____

    B. Supporting examples _____

    _____

    _____

V. Conclusion

    A. Restate the importance of having a mentor _____

    B. Restate the three key character traits

    _____   _____   _____

    C. Explain what difference a mentor would make in your life. _____

    _____

Developed by Marcy Winograd, English Department, Paul Revere Middle School, Los Angeles, CA.

Appendix A | Blank Forms

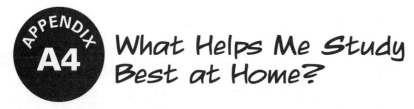

APPENDIX
A4

What Helps Me Study Best at Home?

A

Sometimes where, when, and how you study makes a big difference. Not every student likes to study the same way. What works best for you when you do your homework?

Put a ✔ next to the things that work best for you.

1. **When:** ____ right after school when I get home

     ____ after school, but after a break

     ____ how long a break do you need? _____

     ____ after dinner

     ____ in the morning

     ____ other _____

2. **With:** ____ myself only

     ____ someone in the room with me

     ____ a friend

     ____ parent

     ____ tutor

     ____ other _____

3. **Where:** ____ in my room   ____ in the kitchen

      ____ on the floor   ____ in the family room

      ____ on the bed   ____ in the dining room

      ____ at my desk   ____ other _____

4. **Conditions:** ____ sitting   ____ near a lamp

      ____ lying down   ____ in bright light

      ____ playing music   ____ walking around

      ____ in a quiet area   ____ other _____

5. **How long before a break?**

          ____ 15 minutes   ____ 1 hour

          ____ 30 minutes   ____ finish a certain part of the work

                    (one half, one third, or one section)

6. What helps me stay organized and complete my homework?

____ use an assignment book	____ plan what I do first
____ write down the assignments	____ estimate how long it will take
____ call a friend for assignments	____ put finished work in one place
____ keep an extra book at home	____ color code folders and book covers
____ dictate assignments on a recorder	

____ other _____

7. What helps me learn and remember information?

____ write things down
____ draw a picture
____ use a mind map
____ use flash cards
____ type it into a computer
____ listen to a tape recorder
____ read things out loud
____ talk about the information
____ make or build something
____ use associations; mnemonics
____ use songs or rhymes
____ other _____

Adapted from form developed by Joan Helbing, **Focus on ADD**, *the Wisconsin ADD Consortium Newsletter, February, 1998.*

Name: _____ **Class/Teacher:** _____

Project Title or Focus: _____ **Due Date:** _____

I. <u>Plan</u>: What do you have to do? What are all the project requirements?

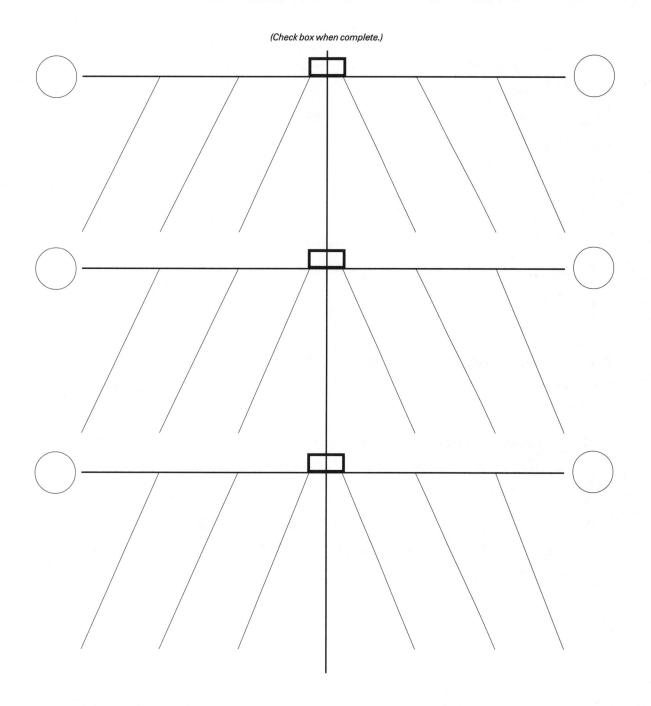

(Check box when complete.)

Project Graphic Organizer

Projects may be complex and involve multiple steps. Sometimes in the rush of completing the project some key information may be overlooked. Record all requirements on this page so that no steps will be forgotten. Good Luck!

I. Plan: What are all the project requirements? What do I need?

■ Complete the Project Graphic Organizer on the facing page.

Check resources needed:

____ library visit

____ books

____ magazine articles

____ Internet

____ interviews

_____

_____

Check products needed:

____ written report   ____ build a model

____ report cover   ____ maps

____ poster   _____

____ pictures   _____

____ bibliography   _____

____ timelines with dates

_____

II. Prioritize: Do I need to set priorities? _____yes _____ no

■ Which one do I need to do first? _____

■ Which one is most complicated and will take the most time? _____

■ Do I need to allow time to order a book from the library or schedule a visit for an interview? _____

■ Number the remaining parts of the project on the organizer in the order you will do them. _____

III. Schedule: How long will the project take? _____ (estimate)

■ Put steps on the Weekly Project Planner (see Appendix A6).

IV. Do it: Complete all the steps on the Weekly Project Planner.

■ Check each step off in color marker on the Project Graphic Organizer when it is completed.

Weekly Project Planner

Write in due date first. Then schedule each activity backward from there until all steps are written on the planner.

Activities may be scheduled at regular intervals to provide ballpark guidance. Of course, flexible scheduling is required for these students. Some nights the student may do four activities and the next night only one.

The student may decide to do all the research the first week and the written report the second. Or he may prefer to research half the topics, write the report and then work on the last half of the project.

Weekly Project Planner—Week 1 _____(month) _____						
	Monday	**Tuesday**	**Wednesday**	**Thursday**	**Friday**	**Saturday**
7:00						
7:30						
8:00						
8:30						
9:00						
9:30						
10:00						
10:30						
11:00						
11:30						
12:00						
12:30						
1:00						**Sunday**
1:30						
2:00						
2:30						
3:00						
3:30						
4:00						
4:30						
5:00						
5:30						
6:00						
Evening						

Photocopy needed research, plus the publisher's name, publication date, and city. Put it all in a folder.

Some work may be completed at school during class and visits to the school library; the rest may be done via the Internet at the local library and his computer at home.

Teachers will check student progress at regular intervals, answer questions, problem-solve, plan, advise if on track, and give encouragement.

Weekly Project Planner—Week 2 _____(month) _____

	Monday	Tuesday	Wednesday	Thursday	Friday	Saturday
7:00						
7:30						
8:00						
8:30						
9:00						
9:30						
10:00						
10:30						
11:00						
11:30						
12:00						
12:30						
1:00						Sunday
1:30						
2:00						
2:30						
3:00						
3:30						
4:00						
4:30						
5:00						
5:30						
6:00						
Evening						

Medication Effectiveness at School: Teacher Rating

Student's name: _____ **Date & class:** _____

Completed by: _____ **Time of day observed:** _____

To assess the impact medication is having on a student's school work, each teacher should answer several key questions. When medication is working properly and learning problems have been identified, the student should be doing much better in school. If the teacher cannot check the "Strongly Agree" and "Agree" columns, then problems may still exist in several areas: 1) the proper accommodations are not being provided for the student's learning problems, 2) executive function deficits are not being addressed, or 3) the medication regimen may not be right for the student. Please circle the answer that best describes the student's behavior.

Academic Performance:

	Strongly Agree	Agree	Neutral	Disagree	Strongly Disagree
When the student is in my class, s/he:					
1. pays attention	1	2	3	4	5
2. completes class and homework	1	2	3	4	5
3. does work correctly	1	2	3	4	5
4. complies with requests	1	2	3	4	5
5. makes passing grades	1	2	3	4	5

ADD/ADHD-Related Behaviors, Including Executive Function
If the student is on medication and is not doing well in school, what else could be causing continuing problems? Are there any ADD/ADHD-related behaviors that are interfering with the student's ability to succeed in school?

ADD/ADHD-Related Behaviors:

The student:					
6. is organized	1	2	3	4	5
7. manages time well	1	2	3	4	5
8. remembers things easily	1	2	3	4	5
9. is on time to class	1	2	3	4	5
10. is on time to school	1	2	3	4	5
11. thinks carefully before acting or speaking	1	2	3	4	5
12. is awake and alert in class	1	2	3	4	5

Ask parents about any sleep problems. According to them, the student:

13. falls asleep easily	1	2	3	4	5
14. wakes up easily	1	2	3	4	5

Comments: _____

_____

_____

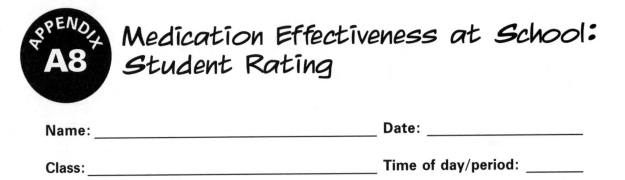

Name: _____ **Date:** _____

Class: _____ **Time of day/period:** _____

Sometimes students themselves are the best judges of how well medication is working. To assess the impact medication is having on your school work, please answer the questions below. When medication is working properly and learning problems have been identified, you should be doing much better in school. If you cannot check the "Strongly Agree" and "Agree" columns, then problems may still exist in several areas: 1) the proper accommodations are not being provided for your learning problems, 2) executive function deficits are not being addressed, or 3) the medication regimen may not be right for you. Please circle the answer that best describes your behavior.

Academic Performance:

	Strongly Agree	Agree	Neutral	Disagree	Strongly Disagree
When I am in class, I:					
1. listen and pay attention	1	2	3	4	5
2. complete my class work	1	2	3	4	5
3. complete my homework (at home)	1	2	3	4	5
4. do my work correctly	1	2	3	4	5
5. do what the teacher tells me to do	1	2	3	4	5
6. make passing grades	1	2	3	4	5

ADD/ADHD-Related Behaviors, Including Executive Function

If you are on medication and are not doing well in school, what else could be causing continuing problems? Are there any ADD/ADHD-related behaviors that are interfering with your ability to succeed in school?

ADD/ADHD-Related Behaviors:

These things describe me. I:					
7. am organized	1	2	3	4	5
8. manage time well	1	2	3	4	5
9. remember things easily	1	2	3	4	5
10. am on time to class	1	2	3	4	5
11. am on time to school	1	2	3	4	5
12. stop and think before I do or say anything	1	2	3	4	5
13. am awake and alert in class	1	2	3	4	5
Do you have any sleep problems? I:					
14. fall asleep easily	1	2	3	4	5
15. wake up easily	1	2	3	4	5

Comments: _____
_____

My main concern right now is: _____
Ways I am improving in this area: _____

Student Contract

Date: _____

I,_____ agree to do things listed below.
I will check each day I achieve my goal.

	M	T	W	T	F
1.					
2.					
3.					
4.					
5.					

I, _____ (teacher, parent, or other) agree
to provide assistance by

_____

We, _____ and _____, will meet
to discuss progress:
_____(when, how often, and where).

We have read and talked about this contract and are signing it to show that we agree to these terms.

Signatures:

_____

(student)

_____

(teacher)

Options:

- The following reward/privilege will be given to the student for successfully completing the contract. _____
  For example when the student earns 5 check marks, even if it takes more than a week, he gets reward/privilege provided by either the parents or teacher.

- The student will take this contract home to parents at the end of the week.

Reframe ADD/ADHD Behavior

APPENDIX A10

Name _____ Grade _____ Date _____

STRENGTHS
Home/Community/School

Examples of Reframing Common ADD/ADHD Behaviors

When students are struggling, it is easy to get caught up in focusing on their problem behaviors. It is extremely important to stop and take time to identify each student's strengths and special talents. Examples of ways to reframe negative behaviors may help teachers and parents develop a list of the teenager's strengths. A completed form is shown in Summary 71.

Remember that the desirability of behaviors changes over time. Characteristics that are not valued in students in school may be valued in the adult work world. Discuss the teenager's strengths with him. Ask him if he has anything to add to the list.

BOSSINESS: "leadership" (albeit carried too far)

HYPERACTIVE: "energetic" / "high energy" / "does ten projects at one time" / "works long hours"

STRONG-WILLED: "tenacious"

DAY DREAMER: "creative" / "innovative" / "imaginative"

DARING: "risk taker" / "willing to try new things"

LAZY: "laid back" / "Type B personalities live longer"

INSTIGATOR: "initiator" / "innovative"

MANIPULATIVE: "delegates" / "gets others to do the job"

AGGRESSIVE: "assertive" / "doesn't let people take advantage of him"

QUESTIONS AUTHORITY: "independent" / "free thinker" / "makes own decisions"

ARGUMENTATIVE: "persuasive" / "may be attorney material"

POOR HANDWRITING: "maybe he'll be a doctor one day"

Additional Information

APPENDIX B1 | Increased National Attention Focused on ADD/ADHD

In recognition of the profound impact ADD/ADHD may have on a student's life, attention deficit disorders have received significant national attention in the last couple of years.

NIMH ADD/ADHD Study

The National Institute of Mental Health has launched a new study involving almost 600 students with ADD/ADHD, ages 7-10, at six sites around the country. The fact that this study is the largest ever instituted by NIMH on any topic for any age group makes a strong statement regarding the profound impact of ADD/ADHD on the lives of children and their families. This study will have a significant impact on the way we teach and treat young people with ADD/ADHD. Preliminary results were released in December, 1999. Important findings so far include:

- ***Two-thirds of children with attention deficits had at least one other disorder*** such as depression, anxiety, or a learning disability.
- ***Medication alone was almost equally as effective*** in helping students as the combined treatment of medication plus behavioral interventions.
- ***Medication alone was much more effective*** than behavioral interventions alone.
- ***Many students may be receiving medication doses that are too low*** for maximum improvement in school work and behavior.

The implications for teachers to consider are:

- Students with ADD/ADHD who continue to struggle after receiving treatment and classroom accommodations may in fact have a ***coexisting condition that is not being treated.***
- ***Behavioral strategies alone will not significantly change*** the school work or behavior of students with ADD/ADHD.
- ***Medication is a critical part of treatment.***
- The ***teacher's report on how well medication is working,*** plus his or her ratings of medication effectiveness, are essential to help doctors know when medication doses should be adjusted. (See Appendix A7.)

American Academy of Pediatrics Clinical Guidelines on Assessment of ADHD

On May 1, 2000, the American Academy of Pediatrics (AAP) released new recommendations for primary care physicians, including pediatricians, to use when assessing school-age children for ADHD and ADD. Treatment guidelines are also currently being developed. A few of their key recommendations that may be of interest to teachers include:

- Evaluations should be done for children who show **signs of school difficulties, academic underachievement, troublesome relationships** with teachers or peers, and **other behavioral problems**.
- The diagnostic criteria contained in the DSM-IV as listed in Summary 5 should be used.
- **Information should be obtained** from the parents, classroom teachers, or other school professionals.
- **An assessment of coexisting conditions should also be done:** learning and language problems, aggression, disruptive behavior, depression or anxiety.

Surgeon General's Report on Mental Health

The first ever Surgeon General's Report on Mental Health was released in 1999. Attention deficit disorder was one of the few disorders that was discussed in some detail. Over the years, the Surgeon General's Reports have had a profound impact on shaping public policy and the health of the nation. The report offers these important findings:

1. Schools are often the major place where mental health problems are recognized.
2. Fewer than 2-3 percent of school-aged children with attention deficit disorders are being treated.
3. Some children who are taking medication did not fully meet diagnostic criteria for ADD/ADHD.
4. The American Academy of Child and Adolescent Psychiatry indicated that a critical part of effective treatment is to have the right educational accommodations and school placement.
5. Research has focused on the link between attention deficits and problems with two specific genes: a dopamine-receptor gene (DRD4) on chromosome 11 and a dopamine-transporter gene (DAT1) on chromosome 5.
6. Certain traumas or toxins in the environment, such as smoking during pregnancy, exposure to lead or excessive alcohol, or lack of oxygen during pregnancy may also result in development of ADD/ADHD.
7. The American Academy of Pediatrics issued a policy statement saying that medication alone is not adequate treatment for children with ADD/ADHD.

CDC/DOE-Sponsored Conference on ADHD

The Atlanta-based Center for Disease Control and Prevention and the U.S. Department of Education, Office of Special Education Programs, jointly sponsored a conference in September 1999 on *"ADHD: A Public Health Perspective."* The CDC and DOE are concerned about the public health implications of attention deficit disorders on the behavior of our young people, including their increased risk for school failure, dropping out of school, substance abuse, risk-taking behavior, and for some, involvement with the juvenile justice system. National researchers and experts on ADD/ADHD met to discuss:

1. the individual, social, and economic burden of attention deficits through the life span,
2. a definition of attention deficit disorder,
3. prevalence rates,
4. risk factors, and
5. effective intervention strategies. Many of the problems linked to ADD/ADHD are preventable when appropriate medical, behavioral, and academic interventions are provided!

NIH/NIMH Consensus Conference on ADHD

A consensus conference on ADHD was held in November 1998 by the National Institute of Health and the National Institute of Mental Health. National experts were invited to meet and reach consensus on the disorder, its diagnosis, assessment, and best treatment practices. Some of their conclusions were:

- **Attention deficit disorder does exist;** it is not a myth as some authors, media personalities, or newspaper articles have implied.
- **The prevalence of ADD/ADHD is between three to five percent.**
- **Attention deficit disorder is often inherited** and is relatively chronic over the life span.
- **ADD/ADHD can be accurately diagnosed by current criteria** in the DSM-IV.
- **Stimulant medications** such as Ritalin, Dexedrine, or Adderall are the most effective treatment.
- In spite of increased use of stimulant medication, **no detectable increase in stimulant abuse has occurred.**
- **ADD/ADHD can lead to significant impairments:** underachievement in school (retainment or subject failure), family conflicts, accidental injuries and driving risks, and coexisting disorders such as depression and anxiety.

See Summary 10 for a list of websites for these agencies.

Writing a Three-Part Essay

These basic tips may be helpful to parents who are working with their teenager as he or she writes an essay. The essay outline in Appendix A3 may also be helpful.

1. Introduction: "Tell what you are going to tell"

The introduction for a high school essay may include approximately three sentences, of perhaps 40 words total. The writer is like a fisherman who is trying to hook the reader.

- **Start with the hook.** Sometimes a question or quotation in the first sentence will hook the reader.
- **Include the thesis statement.** The main idea that is the basis for the whole paper is stated in this first paragraph. *"When I was five years old, I experienced something very unexpected when I went on a trip with my father."*
- **Model the desired behavior.** If the student is having trouble coming up with an introduction, the teacher or parent may write an example drawn from his or her own experience that addresses the assigned topic.
- **Include a planning statement.** Tell the reader what is coming in the essay, but don't let the cat out of the bag. *"This trip with my father is one I'll never forget for several reasons."* Also don't explicitly tell the reader what you are going to tell him. Don't say, for example, *"I am going to tell you about a situation I experienced...."*

Example of an Introductory Paragraph:

> *Have you ever known a girl who spent the night in a Young Men's Christian (YMCA) dormitory? When I was five years old, I went on an incredible trip with my dad. Several things happened on this trip that were very exciting."*

2. The Body: "Tell It."

The body of the essay may include from two to perhaps ten paragraphs of roughly 100 words each. It just depends on how much the writer has to say. There is nothing magic about a "five-paragraph essay."

- **Begin the first body paragraph with a transition sentence.** The transition sentence should link the first body paragraph with the introductory paragraph in some way. For example, *"My first experience was..."* or *"First we drove all the way to Atlanta. It was the first time I had ever been to such a big city."* This first sentence should be a concrete statement.

- **Write more information that is related to the opening sentence.** For example, the student may describe how he felt about the event, how he or someone else reacted, or give an example.
- **Use transition sentences to begin other paragraphs.** For example: *"Our next adventure took us to..."* or *"The following day we went to the Georgia Capitol building, where my dad was serving in the legislature."* Then add other related sentences.

3. The Closing Paragraph: "Tell You What I Told You"

The conclusion may also consist of about 40 words.

- **Begin the conclusion with a word signaling you are reaching the end.** For example, begin with *"Finally,"* *"In conclusion,"* *"In the end,"* or *"In summary."*
- **Summarize.** Writers don't have to repeat their thesis statement, but they may if they wish. However, don't use the same words that were in the introductory paragraph. You may also tell something you have learned.
- **Try to come up with a "zinger" for the last sentence.** Leave the reader thinking. The sentence may also be a personal one that describes the writer's feelings. *"I will never forget my exciting trip to Atlanta, the state capitol, and the YMCA."*

(Developed based on an interview with Claudia Jordan, a veteran high school Language Arts teacher in Swinnett County, Georgia.)

Menu of Classroom/Program Accommodations and Modifications

APPENDIX B3

Many school systems develop menus of possible classroom accommodations that may be helpful to students with ADD, ADHD, or other learning problems. This helpful menu was developed by the Walker County School System in LaFayette, Georgia. Do not be afraid to add other needed accommodations that may not be on the list. Numerous suggestions in this book can be effective and could be added to a student's IEP.

Name: _____

Date IEP Developed: _____/_____/_____
Duration: _____
Review Date: _____/_____/_____

Classroom/Program Modifications

Classroom/Program Modification Recommendations:
(To advance appropriately toward attaining goals; to be involved and progress in the general curriculum; to participate in extracurricular and non-academic activities; to be educated and participate with other non-disabled students)

A. Supplementary Aids and Services: (Access to/use of)

___Calculator
___Tape recorder (lectures and instruction)
___Reading marker
___Taped material/talking books
___Adapted furniture
___Note taker

___Visual aids to support instruction
___Modified/alternative textbooks and/or workbooks
___Feeding equipment
___Manipulative materials/study aids
___Times tables
___Augmentative/alternative communication

___Large print materials
___Computer/Word Processor
___Someone to read materials
___Preferential seating
___Study Carrel
___Other_____

B. Instructional Modifications or Supports for School Personnel:

___Secure attention before giving directions
___Have student repeat directions to check for understanding
___Material should be broken down into manageable parts
___Peer tutor/paired working arrangements

___Allow previewing of content, concepts and vocabulary
___Directions should be simplified as needed, oral, short, specific, repeated
___Oral directions should be supported with written backup
___Emphasis on major points

___Use techniques of repetition, review and summarization
___Provide frequent feedback and praise
___Check work frequently to determine level of understanding
___Other_____

Assignments:

___Written on board
___Substitute projects for written work
___Extra time for completion
___Given orally
___Provide peer assistance
___Provide printed copy of board work/notes

___Provide study guides/questions
___Provide extra review/drill and worksheets
___Assignment Notebook
___Presented and/or completed orally
___Reduce/shorten written assignments
___Reduce/shorten reading assignments
___Reduce number of spelling words
___Special projects in lieu of regular assignments

___Lower reading level of materials
___Opportunity to leave class for resource assistance
___Provide individual assistance
___Allow difficult assignments to be completed in resource room
___Other_____

C. Grading Modifications:

___Alternative/modified grading procedures (Specify)
_____
___Special education grades based on IEP mastery
___Course grades will be assigned by regular education teacher

___Course grades will be assigned by regular education and special education teacher
___Regular education grading will be used in the following classes/subjects:
_____
___Special education report card will be utilized
___Course grades will be assigned by special education teacher

___Interpretation of grades are designated on regular report cards
___Regular education grades based on effort, attitude and cooperation
___Grading modifications are designated on regular report cards
___Other_____

D. Testing Modifications: (Within the classroom)

___Extra time for completion of exams
___Lower readability
___Oral exam with oral response
___Short answer format
___Recognition format (multiple choice w/ two possible answers)

___Recall with cues format (fill in blank with word bank)
___Use of study sheets, notes, open book
___Include class participation in evaluation
___Fewer questions/problems on exams
___Alternative to tests (projects, reports, demonstrations, etc.)

___Individual/small group testing
___Oral exam w/written response
___Accept close approximations
___Allow tests to be taken in resource room
___Scheduling (Specify)_____
___Other_____

IEP Transition Services

This form serves as a reminder of key categories to address in a Transition Plan for teenagers. See Summary 48 for specific suggestions for possible services. This form was also developed by the Walker County, Georgia, School System.

Initial Transition Plan Date: _____   **Dates(s) Transition Plan Reviewed/Revised:** _____

Student Preferences, Needs, Interests: _____
_____
_____

Consideration of Course of Study (at age 14, or younger, if appropriate): _____
_____
_____

Needed Transition Services (at age 16, or younger, if appropriate):
(Include Interagency Responsibilities or Linkages, if any)

If needed, discuss the activities, person responsible, timelines, and anticipated outcomes of this activity.

*If the IEP Team determines that the student does not need services in one of more of these areas, include a statement to that effect and the basis upon which the determination was made.

*Instruction: _____
_____
_____

*Related Services: _____
_____
_____

*Community Experiences: _____
_____
_____

*Development of Employment and Other Post-School Adult Living Objectives: _____
_____
_____

If Appropriate, Acquisition of Daily Living Skills and Functional Vocational Evaluation: _____
_____
_____

Transfer of Rights (Required at age 17):
_____ was informed on _____ of his/her rights, if any, that will transfer at age 18.
        Student Name   *Date*

Functional Behavior Assessment: Common Behaviors

This partial list of behaviors may help teachers as they gather information and develop a Behavior Intervention Plan. The list was compiled from information developed by the Gwinnett County Georgia School System, Chicago Public Schools, Walker County Georgia School System, and Joan Helbing, ADD Consultant, Appleton Area Schools in Wisconsin. See Summary 63 for more information on Functional Behavior Assessment.

COMMON MISBEHAVIORS	CONTEXT	ANTECEDENT OR TRIGGER	CONTRIBUTING FACTORS
ignoring the teacher talking back and arguing yelling or cursing fighting destroying property disruptive behavior: talking to and laughing with other students inappropriately refusing to comply with teacher requests pushing or hitting a teacher smoking at school possession of a weapon or drugs at school bullying other students	class/subject: ■ gym/P.E., music, art, keyboarding, etc. ■ language arts, math, science, history, etc. location: ■ lunchroom ■ bathroom ■ hallway ■ outside, but on school grounds ■ at school function, but not on school grounds near school, but not on grounds time of day	transition: beginning or end of class, change from P.E., lunch, or between classes request by teacher verbal redirection by teacher verbal correction by teacher told "no" difficult task given teasing by other students confronted by teacher asked to speak in front of class having to wait for the teacher teacher attention to others close physical proximity; teacher is "in his face" visitor to class substitute teacher	medication has worn off failing a class learning problems in math or language arts ADD/ADHD behaviors: impulsivity, talking and acting without thinking; poor organizational skills; impaired sense of time breakup with girlfriend or boyfriend conflicting activities: ball game, school play, family or religious activities conflicts with parents rejection by a friend

FUNCTION OF THE BEHAVIOR	CONSEQUENCES	STUDENT REACTION	INTERVENTION STRATEGIES
to get attention escape or avoidance: ■ avoiding embarrassment ■ avoiding a difficult task result of skill or performance deficit: ■ cover up not knowing how to do the work ■ distract the teacher so she won't know he can't do the work justice or revenge acceptance and affiliation: "I'm one of the cool guys" power or control expression of self communication access to rewards symptoms of a disorder	response of teacher: ■ ignored ■ redirected ■ verbal warning ■ verbal reprimand ■ gave personal space ■ natural consequence ■ reflection ■ sent to office ■ removal of teacher's positive reinforcement ■ halted activity; waited for student to behave ■ physical restraint ■ parental contact ■ counseling ■ isolation in class ■ denied privileges ■ restitution ■ modified day (e.g., half day) ■ sent home ■ detention ■ in-school suspension ■ suspension ■ called police ■ administrative hearing ■ expulsion response of classmates: ■ reinforced behavior by laughing	stopped continued intensified; escalated was remorseful apologized cried displayed new behavior walked away from the teacher and out of class	modify antecedent teach alternative behavior praise special activities or privileges points or tokens tangible reinforcers teach self-control skills visit guidance counselor parent contact student selects reinforcing activity peer mentor self-management program written contract clarify rules & expected behavior change seating change schedule counseling reminders about expected behavior

Other Information to Gather

Continuation of Behavior: *If behavior is repeated, is it because of*

1. the "contributing factors," or
2. the behavior is still serving an important purpose ("function of the behavior")?

Rewards: *Talk with the student to find out what he or she thinks is a reward—what is important to him. The teacher can then give the student the opportunity to earn the reward by complying with school rules and behaving properly.*

Index

About the Author

Chris A. Zeigler Dendy, M.S., has over 30 years experience as a former teacher, school psychologist, mental health counselor and administrator, national consultant on ADD/ADHD and children's mental health, author, and advocate. She is the co-founder of the Gwinnett County CHADD chapter in Georgia. Her books draw upon her extensive professional experience, as well as her own personal experience of parenting two grown sons with ADD/ADHD.